THE SELF
Psychological and Philosophical Issues

THE SELF
Psychological and Philosophical Issues

Edited by

THEODORE MISCHEL

ROWMAN AND LITTLEFIELD
TOTOWA, NEW JERSEY

FIRST PUBLISHED IN THE UNITED STATES 1977
BY ROWMAN AND LITTLEFIELD, TOTOWA, N.J.

Library of Congress Cataloging in Publication Data
Main entry under title:

The Self.

1. Self. 2. Self (Philosophy) I. Mischel, Theodore, 1925–1976 II. Title.
BF697.S44 155.2 77–1508
ISBN 0–87471–969–0

PRINTED IN GREAT BRITAIN

To my wife Adele
and my sons,
Kenneth and Paul

Contents

Preface

This volume is part of a continuing attempt by a group of philosophers and psychologists to explore issues at the intersect of psychology and philosophy, particularly philosophy of mind and epistemology. Our first conference held in September 1967, was an initial attempt to test the usefulness of such cooperative theorizing and so focused on rather broad issues relating to the conceptual framework needed for the explanation of human actions (cf. T. Mischel, ed., *Human Action*, 1969). This was followed by conferences dealing with more sharply defined areas; the results of these were published, under my editorship, in *Cognitive Development and Epistemology* (1971) and *Understanding other Persons* (1974).

The present volume results from a closed working conference planned by the editor in consultation with some of the philosophers and psychologists who have been regularly involved in this enterprise, a conference designed to explore interrelations between philosophical analyses of the family of concepts relating to the self (e.g., self-knowledge, self-control, self-development) and empirical studies in psychology of the development and manifestations of self-control, self-knowledge, and the like. This conference was held December 19 through 21, 1975, at the Center for Psychosocial Studies in Chicago. In addition to those whose papers are published here, M. F. Basch, M.D., Associate Director of the Center, participated in the conference discussions. As in the past, first drafts of the conference papers were distributed to the participants prior to the conference, and the papers published here incorporate revisions which their authors made in light of our discussions.

The papers are arranged in this volume in terms of four topics which indicate the major theme they address. But the arrangement is, to some degree, arbitrary, since there are many inter-connections between these papers which are not brought out by this arrangement.

My introduction was written after the conference and points up some of these connections by focusing on issues which cut across the topics dealt with in these papers. These issues, and a good many others, were discussed by this group in Chicago, and my introduction has benefited from those discussions in obvious ways. But I have not provided a summary of those discussions. Instead, I have tried to develop a framework which connects these papers in terms of what I see as basic conceptual issues in the psychology of the self—issues which come up, in different ways, in all of these papers.

Support for this conference was provided by NIMH grant R03MH27160, and by the Center for Psychosocial Studies. We are grateful to Mr. B. Weissbourd, Vice-President of the Center, and to the National Institute of Mental Health for making possible the conference on which this volume was based.

On a personal level, I want at this point to express my abiding gratitude to my wife, Adele, whose love, empathy and understanding have been a constant source of support for me, and to my sons, Kenneth and Paul, whose development has been an enduring inspiration.

T.M.
December 1976

Publisher's Note:

Theodore Mischel died on 13 December, 1976 during the final stages of preparation of this book. We are grateful to Rom Harré for seeing the book through the press, and to John Greenwood for compiling the index.

January 1977

List of Contributors

WILLIAM P. ALSTON is Professor of Philosophy at the University of Illinois, Urbana, and editor of *Philosophy Research Archives.* Philosophy of psychology and philosophy of language are among his primary interests; his books include *Philosophy of Language* (1964) and *The Problems of Philosophy* (1971).

WILLARD F. DAY, Professor of Psychology at the University of Nevada, Reno, is the editor of *Behaviorism.* A leading spokesman for 'radical behaviorism', Day has contributed to many psychological journals as well as to *Philosophical Studies.*

KENNETH J. GERGEN, Professor of Psychology at Swarthmore College, has been engaged in socio-cognitive studies of self-processes. His books include *Personality and Social Behavior* (1970, with D. Marlowe), *The Psychology of Behavior Exchange* (1969), *The Self in Social Interaction* (1968, with C. Gordon), and *The Study of Policy Formation* (1968, with R. Bower).

DAVID W. HAMLYN is Professor of Philosophy at Birkbeck College, University of London, and the editor of *Mind. The Psychology of Perception* (1957), *Sensation and Perception* (1961), and *The Theory of Knowledge* (1971) are among his contributions to epistemology and philosophy of psychology.

ROM HARRÉ, University Lecturer in the Philosophy of Science, and Fellow of Linacre College, Oxford, and Visiting Professor in the History and Philosophy of the Social and Behavioral Sciences Program at the State University of New York at Binghamton, has been deeply involved in the critique and reformation of the methods of social and psychological research. His books include

Causal Powers (1975, with E. H. Madden), *The Explanation of Social Behaviour* (1972, with P. F. Secord), and he has recently edited a number of studies in the new style of social psychological research, under the title *Life Sentences* (1976).

George J. McCall, Professor of Sociology and Anthropology at the University of Missouri, St. Louis, is currently Visiting Scientist at the Center for the Study of Crime and Delinquency, National Institute of Mental Health, in Washington, D.C. His books include *Social Relationships* (1970), *Issues in Participant Observation* (1969), and *Identities and Interactions* (1966, with J. L. Simmons).

Theodore Mischel was Professor of Philosophy and Director of the Interdisciplinary Ph.D. Program in the History and Philosophy of the Social and Behavioral Sciences at the State University of New York at Binghamton. He edited and contributed to *Human Action* (1969), *Cognitive Development and Epistemology* (1971), and *Understanding Other Persons* (1974). He was editor (with P. Secord and R. Harré) of *The Journal for the Theory of Social Behaviour*.

Walter Mischel is Professor of Psychology at Stanford University. He has been primarily concerned with the study of personality in relation to cognitive social learning theory; his books include *Personality and Assessment* (1968) and *Introduction to Personality* (1971). Harriet Nerlove Mischel, Lecturer in Psychology at Stanford University, has contributed to many psychological journals and is co-author (with W. Mischel) of *Essentials of Psychology* (1977).

Paul F. Secord is Professor of Social Psychology and Chairman of the Department of Urban Studies at Queens College, City University of New York. He has been primarily interested in the study of self-processes and in the theoretical foundations of social psychology; his books include *Social Psychology* (1964, 1970, with C. Backman) and *The Explanation of Social Behavior*, (1972, with R. Harré). He is editor (with T. Mischel and R. Harré) of *The Journal for the Theory of Social Behaviour*.

CHARLES TAYLOR is Chichele Professor of Political and Social Thought at Oxford University. The conceptual foundations of psychology and the social sciences has been one of his primary concerns; his books include *The Explanation of Behavior* (1964) and *Hegel* (1975).

STEPHEN E. TOULMIN, Professor of Social Thought and Philosophy at the University of Chicago, has been concerned with the history and philosophy of the sciences and its implications for epistemology. His books include *The Philosophy of Science* (1958), *The Uses of Argument* (1958), *Foresight and Understanding* (1961), *Human Understanding* (vol. 1, 1972), and *Wittgenstein's Vienna* (1973, with A. Janik).

ERNEST S. WOLF, M.D., is Training and Supervising Analyst of the Chicago Institute of Psychoanalysis, Clinical Assistant Professor of Psychiatry at Northwestern University, and Associate Director of the Center for Psychosocial Studies, Chicago. His articles have appeared in many psychoanalytic journals.

PART I Introduction

1 Conceptual Issues in the Psychology of the Self: An Introduction

THEODORE MISCHEL

There is one point on which philosophers and psychologists, or at least those who contribute to this volume, can easily agree: the self is not some entity other than the person. Not too long ago, behavioral psychologists tended to ignore most issues involving the self—questions about the way a person integrates his beliefs, desires, and attitudes, as well as questions about processes of self-control, self-perception, self-evaluation and the like, in which a person becomes the object of his own activities—because they were afraid that any mention of 'self' involved the reification of a mysterious inner entity, a homunculus inside the person that is supposed to perform these activities. But while issues of this sort continue to engender some theoretical confusions (cf. Alston, this volume), the last decade or two has produced a great loosening of behavioristic restrictions and there is now a substantial body of behavioral research dealing with various aspects of the self. In addition, there is a tradition of research and theorizing about the self in social psychology that goes back to G. H. Mead, and there are, of course, psychoanalytic accounts of the self.

Such research and theorizing raises conceptual issues to whose resolution philosophers as well as psychologists can contribute. I will focus on three such issues, which cut across the topics discussed by the contributors to this volume, in order to bring out some of the connections between these papers and some of the ways in which psychological and philosophical approaches to the self bear on each other.

The Self as Agent

One important area of current psychological research, in the tradition that is broadly 'behavioral', deals with various dimensions of self-control; it covers such varied matters as delay of gratification, resistance to temptation, self-praise, guilt after transgression, control of visceral reactions, and moral reasoning. The paper by W. and H. N. Mischel reviews the results of such work on the determinants of various facets of self-control, and presents a conceptualization of the organization of self-control based on that research. What emerges, according to these authors, is a picture of the person as 'an active, self-aware problem-solver, capable of changing himself and achieving substantial self-control . . . to a much greater degree than has usually been supposed in psychology'.

Such empirical work can suggest that there is something wrong with the picture of man as a passive victim of unconscious impulses, or environmental contingencies, which used to dominate psychological theories, but the task of understanding what it is for a person to be an agent is a conceptual rather than empirical task. We need to understand how the notion that people are agents, a notion that was implicit in our ordinary conceptual scheme for talking about persons before being explicitly suggested by current research on various aspects of self-control, can be conceptualized without re-introducing the homunculi behaviorists rightly disdain.

One answer that has been proposed is, roughly, that in order for a system to be capable of action it must have some sort of internal model for representing its environment and its own states. For insofar as the behavior of a system is controlled, not just by external contingencies, but by its own, perhaps idiosyncratic, internal representations of its environment and needs, the system will not react passively to external stimuli but will behave more like an agent who is guided by his own beliefs and desires. This view has antecedents in 19th century writers like Dilthey, who distinguished between the idiographic and the nomothetic approach to the study of human behavior and stressed the importance of understanding people from 'inside', in terms of their own perspective on things. Recent variants of this approach have put the emphasis on the centrality of intentionalistic descriptions, i.e., descriptions given from the point of view of the agent in question. While the notion that behavior must be understood from the inside, in terms of the meanings things have for the person, has obvious links to the phenomenological tradition, it does not require the postulation of mysterious 'inner' entities or non-material substances. An intentionalistic approach to psychology is even compatible with doctrines of materialism and mechanism, since the behavior of sufficiently complex computers is appropriately characterized in intentionalistic terms (cf. Minsky, 1965; Boden, 1972; T. Mischel, 1976). Whether or not intentionalistic characterizations can be usefully applied to a system depends, not on what stuff the system is made of, but on whether its behavior is regulated by such 'control functions' as input classifications, problem-solving strategies, goal-states, etc., which can be represented in a material system of sufficient complexity.

But while the capacity for developing internal models of the environment may be a necessary condition for agency, it is not sufficient to distinguish human agency from that of lower animals. We can explain the behavior of a dog, or even the behavior of pigeons in a color discrimination task in a Skinner box (cf. Boneau & Cole, 1967; Boneau, 1974), in terms of the animal's 'beliefs' (internal representations of information) and 'desires' (hedonic expectancies, valences). But we think of people as responsible agents in a way animals are not. What more is there to the notion of self which we attribute to people, but not to lower animals? One difference becomes apparent when we notice that, though one might be tempted to say that a dog 'resists the temptation' offered by the meat on the table, one would not consider the dog's behavior an instance of *self*-control if it fails to go after the meat simply because its fear of being punished is greater than its desire for the meat.

Such behaviors, in which an organism does not do something it presumably wants to do because it has another want or aversion which is stronger, must be clearly distinguished from what Alston calls 'self-intervention'. Human beings, at least, have the capacity to engage in higher level activities which can affect the course of their own motivation. That is, a person may believe that his current motivations are such that he will soon be doing A, and his belief may be correct; but he may also be concerned to prevent himself from doing A, to do B instead, and so try to change his motivation in that direction. Alston's paper examines the complications that must be introduced in a want-belief model in order to account for such self-interventions. This model, which can be found in theorists like Lewin or Tolman and which is implicit in much current psychological research relating to the self, sees currently activated wants and beliefs as generating 'valences' for anticipated outcomes which, together with beliefs about the probability with which possible acts will produce various outcomes, give rise to action tendencies of different strengths. Since a case of self-intervention is one in which, ex hypothesis, the person's tendency to do A is greater than his tendency to do B, yet the person sets out to diminish the tendency to do A and to increase the tendency to do B, it seems as if the person is being split into two selves. Alston argues that we can explain self-intervention and preserve the unity of the person if we introduce two motivational systems in which different sorts of psychological states play the functional role of wants. His paper also explores the implications of this thesis for research on the acquisition of different sorts of wants and their role in the explanation and prediction of behavior.

Taylor's paper gets at a similar point in a rather different way. In line with the tradition which sees language as a man's distinctive feature, Taylor holds that the motivational life that is possible for us is profoundly affected by the fact that we can describe our own goals and desires. Because human desires can fall under a description for the agent, they become something about which he can have desires. Thus people have not only first-order desires but also second-order desires, desires about their own desires, which involves a ranking of first-order desires as themselves of a different level of desirability. It is not merely that language allows people to have far more sophisticated beliefs and wants, desires for fame or self-esteem as well as desires for food or sex; language also makes possible 'strong evaluations', qualitative evaluations of the worth of a desire as contrasted with mere preferences ('weak evaluations'). Though strong evaluation is contrastive and has as its object patterns of conduct that are themselves identified partly by the desires that motivate them, it is not necessarily moral evaluation or something that occurs only when some crisis forces deep reflection; 'cool' vs. 'hot and bothered' might be dimensions of strong evaluation that are importantly operative, perhaps quite unreflectively, in someone's life.

Taylor sees this language-based capacity for strong evaluation as definitive of the human agent, and his paper explores links between such an account of the self and concepts of choice, responsibility and identity. Since 'strong evaluation' has been construed, in different traditions, in terms of radical choice and responsibility, on the one hand, and in terms of the achievement of self-knowledge, on the other, Taylor's paper also bears on questions about the peculiar mix of decision and knowledge that may go into our self-knowledge. This is a point to which I will return.

On Taylor's view, the description of desires is essential to human motivation, so that we cannot hope to understand what motivates people without understanding the intentional descriptions which their desires have for them. But this does not imply that the description which a desire really has for an agent is the one of which he is conscious. Taylor can easily allow for the possibility that we may not be able to avow, or may resist avowing, some of the most important descriptions things have for us. For in talking about unconscious or repressed desires we are hypothesizing that the agent has a desire under some description which he will not, or cannot, avow; he is not conscious of the fact (if it is a fact) that what he desires really has that description for him. Desires may range from those which are consciously available to those which are repressed and unconscious, but the claim is that they can only be identified in terms of the description they have, or are hypothesized to have, for the person.

The notion that human motivation can only be understood from such an intentionalistic perspective seems to contrast with Alston's approach. For on the former view everything depends on the descriptions things have for the agent, so that one cannot have a reductive theory of human motivation which appeals to forces tending to produce various consummations, all of which can be characterized in external terms without reference to the agent's point of view. The want-belief model, on the other hand, does not differ essentially from explanatory models in the natural sciences; after all, concepts like 'valence' were introduced by Lewin on analogy to vector forces that can be summed in physics. It should, however, be noted that one can attempt to develop an idealized general theory of motivation with the help of Lewinian models and, at the same time, recognize that there may be an indefinite degree of qualitative diversity in the specific situations to which the model gets applied (i.e., differences in the 'meanings' things have for different persons, or for the same person on different occasions). No doubt, models of this sort are not without their dangers. They may mislead one into endowing wants or valences with dynamic character, as if an action were simply the resultant of this play of 'forces' or wants, rather than something done by the person who utilizes his wants, etc., to structure his conduct. But while it is, of course, the person who acts, any micro-analysis of motivation will have to be couched in different terms; the fine-grain analysis, whether it be a story about neurological processes, or about valences, or about intentionalistically characterized psychological processes, won't be a story about what the person does. To suppose that the person must reappear as a homunculus at the micro-level in order to preserve his agency would be as foolish as to suppose that agency inheres in wants, or valences, rather than persons. Thus while there are very important differences of detail between Alston and Taylor, they are analyzing the same sort of phenomenon; where there is 'higher level activity' of the sort Alston tries to explicate in terms of 'higher level motivation', what Taylor calls 'strong evaluation' will also be in the picture.

In different ways, Alston and Taylor are making explicit conceptual distinctions that are implicit in our ordinary understanding of what it is to be a self—a human agent as distinct from the sort of agent a dog can be said to be. Our commonsense notions that people differ from animals in having a will, that they can make decisions which are real because the course of their lives is changed by them, and the like, are important because they indicate conceptual distinctions that need to be made. Research programs which ignore such distinctions are not likely to ask the sort of questions that need to be asked in order to develop theories that can illuminate the behavior of persons.

But it is quite another matter to treat commonsense notions as quasi-empirical theories about how human agency, self-control, and the like, are in fact exercised—to suppose, e.g., that self-intervention is accomplished by an act of will, or by firmly concentrating on the principles one espouses. Questions about the strategies that can facilitate self-intervention, about the rules that can help someone who is eating himself to death to stop, or about the sort of cognitive restructuring that can enable someone to overcome a phobia, or to stand firm in the face of real dangers he fears, are empirical questions. To say that courage is the mastering or overcoming of fear is to make a conceptual point; one would not call someone 'courageous' if he rushes in unaware of the danger, or even if he is driven by a desire for revenge more overwhelming than his fear. But it by no means follows that the way to master one's fear is to dwell on it, or that the way to resist a temptation is to keep telling oneself that it would be wrong to give in. These are clearly matters for empirical investigation and the evidence indicates (cf. W. and H. N. Mischel, this volume) that effective self-intervention depends on the use of techniques which can neutralize the fear, or which cognitively restructure a tempting situation so that it becomes less tempting, and the like—in effect, techniques for making the difficult easy.

Can There Be a Science Dealing with the Self?

Another range of issues, relating to the nature of a scientific study of the self and the possibility of a science of persons, is raised both by research on the determinants of self-control and by research in social psychology that is cited in the papers by K. Gergen and G. McCall in this volume. According to W. and H. N. Mischel, empirical studies of self-control point up the idiosyncratic organization of persons, the lack of coherent linkages between trait-characterizations, which attempt to specify what people are like in terms of some reasonably small number of dimensions, and people's behavior. Attempts to predict what people will do, or what the same person will do in different situations, on the basis of trait-characterizations have had very limited success. Moreover, the empirical linkages between a person's behavior patterns and the stringency of his self-evaluations, or between a person's level of moral development and his self-control, or between such aspects of self-control as resistance to temptation, guilt after transgression, tendencies toward self-criticism, etc., appear to be very tenuous. While ratings of where someone stands with respect to, e.g., degree of self-control, tend to be fairly coherent when made by people who know the person and base their judgment on memory, that coherence tends to collapse when ratings are made by independent observers who watch what this person is actually doing in relevant situations. These authors therefore suggest that trait-characterizations—our judgments of what people, including ourselves, are like, whether they are self-controlled, friendly, aggressive, etc.—may be constructions which depend at least as much on what we bring to the situation as on what we actually observe. The point of this suggestion, which has been the focus of the recent 'trait controversy' in personality theory (cf. W.

Mischel, 1968; Argyle & Little, 1972; Bowers, 1973; Alston, 1975), is that we may construct trait-characterizations because we need to develop a reasonably coherent picture of what we and others are like, but the idiosyncratic organization of personality makes behavior largely situation-specific so that personality characteristics, which have been central to psycho-dynamic and other forms of personality theory, have very little scientific value for the prediction and explanation of behavior.

This emphasis on the situational determinants of behavior, with its rejection of theories of personality that appeal to traits or psychodynamic states, is, in some ways, consonant with views which have surfaced in the social psychology that has grown out of the work of G. H. Mead and C. H. Cooley. The 'social looking-glass' approach to the self, discussed in McCall's paper, sees the self as essentially a social construction; on this view, the institutional locus of the self is of overriding importance and our beliefs about ourselves are largely derived from others. Applying this to self-knowledge, Gergen's paper reviews recent work in social psychology which suggests that our self-conceptions, our emotional states, our self-esteem, etc., are all molded by communications we receive from others, by comparisons with others, by self-labeling which is itself socially learned and arbitrary, in the sense of being relative to a particular society at a particular time. We seem to rely on the behavior of others—or rather, our categorizations of that behavior—in order to interpret our own reactions to them; we use their reactions to us in order to understand our own behavior and feelings toward them. Even our understanding of what we, or others, do voluntarily, and so can be praised or blamed for, seems to depend on social rules. When the social context changes, when others come to regard us differently, we come to view ourselves differently, and memory cannot do much to correct this because memory-scanning is selective and can confirm virtually any self-concept. Gergen sees such research as implying that 'self-conceptualization is essentially an arbitrary process', and he therefore concludes that 'when considering self-knowledge it is unclear what there is to know'. Indeed, the very idea that there can be a science of persons—or, more generally, that social psychology can be a science (cf. Gergen, 1973)—is highly problematic. In Gergen's views, our 'internal states', i.e., wants, attitudes, beliefs, emotions, etc., may just not provide the sort of data which allow the development of a science of persons.

The task of understanding the implications of such research—be it findings about the lack of coherent linkages and stabilities in personality research, or findings in social psychology about the role which the social context plays in our characterizations of ourselves and others—is again a conceptual and, in that sense, philosophical task. For one thing, some standard philosophy of science points seem applicable. These findings may suggest, not that there are no stabilities, no objective materials for a science of persons, but that there is something wrong with the way these phenomena have been conceptualized. Questions like 'Am I (is he) submissive (aggressive, honest, conscientious, etc.)?'—always, no matter what—may have no answer, and people who suppose they can be answered are supposing that there is something to know about ourselves that isn't there to know. But if such conceptualizations were replaced by more specific, situation-related characterizations, then interesting stabilities might begin to appear. Lack of inter-observer agreement could also be due to the fact that the concepts in question have not been sufficiently well defined, much as there could easily be disagreement about whether some physical object is 'large'; with more precise definition there might be more agreement and so more of a sense that there is something objective there to be known. The selective character of self-descriptions, the fact that they single out one of a number of applicable characterizations, might also explain some of the variance in self-characterizations with changes in the social context.

Perhaps more important, it may be that the relation between behavior and the 'controlling variables' of which it is thought to be a function is being conceptualized in a way that is misleading. And that conceptualization may generate both scepticism about the possibility of a science of persons which tries to explain behavior in terms of what goes on 'inside', on the one hand, and the correlative suggestion, typical of the behavioristic tradition, that the determinants of behavior must be located 'outside', on the other. That is, psychologists often talk as if one had to decide between the following alternatives: Either (1) behavior is controlled by underlying (inner) mental structures—be they the traits of psychometrically oriented personality theory, or the ego, id, etc., of psycho-dynamic theory—structures which are relatively stable and exert a generalized, enduring effect on behavior across diverse situations; or (2) behavior is controlled by outer stimulus conditions and changes in response to environmental stimulus changes. On the first alternative, 'control' is supposed to reside in mental structures in a way that makes situations relatively unimportant; not the situation, but the different mental structure which different persons bring to it is supposed to be the 'controlling variable', and this is expected to manifest itself in consistently similar response patterns across a great diversity of situations. On the second alternative, the environment is supposed to exert control in a way that makes mental structures largely irrelevant; external stimuli are the 'controlling variables', and the fact that different people respond in different ways to what appears to be the same situation is to be explained in terms of the different conditions under which they encountered these environmental stimulus conditions in the past.

Now if these are the alternatives between which one has to decide, then a behavioristic approach, even the radical behaviorism defended by W. Day in this volume, may become attractive. For the alternative position has been formulated in a way that would allow it to get off the ground only if people did in fact behave consistently across diverse situations. But the counter-intuitive notion that people behave in pretty much the same way regardless of the situation confronting them is easily buried under massive empirical evidence for the situation-specific character of behavior. Further, the fact that the presumed mental structures are cast in the role of 'controlling variables' makes for trouble. For that suggests that behavior is controlled by 'inner' mental states which must be either conscious states discerned by introspection, or else unconscious ('theoretical') states postulated by the psychologist. On the latter alernative, the justification for positing these mental structures will have to be made out in terms of their 'utility,' their value for predicting and explaining behavior. But attempts to predict behavior on the basis of inferences about underlying traits, or psychodynamic states, have not met with much success; a person's direct self-reports and self-predictions turn out to be at least as accurate, if not more accurate (cf. W. Mischel, 1968, Ch. V). Explanations can, of course, be constructed, e.g., in psycho-dynamic terms, but this requires extensive interpretations which may treat what the person himself sees as important as really trivial, and what he sees as trivial (e.g., slips, dreams, etc.) as important. Given the lack of predictive success, one may wonder whether such 'explanations' are anything more than ad hoc constructions. If, on the other hand, one construes mental structures as conscious and so takes what the person himself says seriously, then one is confronted with evidence, of the sort cited by Gergen, for the dependence of self-characterizations on the social context. If one then tries to abstract the social context and to 'look inside' instead, one is not able to discriminate any palpable, hard data for a science. The search for 'controlling variables' that are 'inside' thus seem to get caught between introspection of amorphous 'internal states', on the one side, and speculation about unconscious mental states which lacks empirical justification, on the other. Finally, whether these inner structures be conscious or unconscious, the fact that they are supposed to be mental raises all the standard problems about how they could possibly be 'controlling variables' that determine (bodily) behavior.

Behavioristically oriented psychologists can then argue that all this justifies their 'opposition to mentalism' and that, unlike other approaches which direct attention away from behavior, they make it their business to look at behavior as it actually is. Now it seems eminently reasonable to suggest that we should observe what people do in specific situations, what consequences follow and how their behavior changes with changes in the situation and the consequences. But the trouble is that we won't see much that is of interest unless we look, not just at the subject's behavior in the present situation, but at the whole history of his commerce with 'similar' situations. Since this can be readily arranged only when one is studying animals in a laboratory, it has been difficult to extend behavioristic conceptualizations to human behavior as anything more than an 'in principle' extrapolation from the animal to laboratory. Behavior modification is the only area in which there has been a serious attempt to deal with people in terms of Skinnerian principles. But if the arguments developed by P. Secord in this volume are right, then the self-regulations and self-interventions which behavior modificationists are trying to develop in their clients cannot be consistently conceptualized within the operant paradigm which is supposed to be the theoretical background for behavior modification.

Analogous conceptual strains appear when, in order to fit self-deception into the Skinnerian framework, one has to interpret it as just the absence of self-knowledge, or when one has to construe what are normally called 'inner conflicts' as really conflicts that are in the environment (cf. Day, this volume). Nor can behaviorists make good the claim that by avoiding everything 'inner' they are giving us pure descriptions of what behavior is actually like. For behaviorists are not interested in just any description of behavior, whatever it may be; they want penetrating descriptions which will allow us to spot the controlling variables. But if descriptions of behavior which include claims about controlling variables can count as descriptions, then so can descriptions of behavior which include claims about 'inner' mental structures.

These unsatisfactory alternatives can be avoided by rejecting the conceptualization that requires us to decide between mental structures and environmental conditions as the locus of the 'controlling variables'. If we ask whether 'control' (agency) resides 'inside' or 'outside' the person, fear of homunculi may lead us to insist that all causes must be outside. But that question is badly put; agency resides neither in mental structures nor in stimulus conditions. It is the person who is the agent, and what we are trying to understand is how people come to discriminate various features of their environment as relevant to their conduct and how this gets incorporated into what they do. As Freud pointed out in connection with dreams (1916–17, Ch. V), a stimulus like the ringing of an alarm bell may be what occasions the occurrence of a dream, but it does not determine the structure or meaning of the dream. There is no point to trying to decide whether behavior is determined by the situation or by underlying mental structures in the person; both are relevant to what a person does, and what we are trying to understand is how they are relevant to what *he* does. This is not to repeat what has by now become a truism in psychology, namely that we cannot study persons in isolation but must study 'person-situation interactions' instead; it is rather to underline the need for an appropriate conceptualization of such interactions.

One suggestion can be found in Harré's ethogenic analysis of the genesis of social action. That analysis—deployed in this paper to provide a monodramatic account of justificatory talk about action, an account which can preserve the unity of the person in the face of the multiplicity of selves that appears in the accounts we give of our actions, as well as in psycho-dynamic accounts—sees the structure of action as determined by 'templates', plans, scripts, rules, scenarios and the like, which the person follows. But since templates of action are constructed for occasions, this account is compatible with, indeed requires, that some specific situation occasion the activation of one scenario rather than another. Self-intervention, the account of the self as agent developed by Taylor and Alston, can be construed as an account of what is involved in the reformulation or restructuring of templates for action; and the self, the agent and social actor, far from being a homunculus, can be seen as an organism whose functioning is made possible by physiological mechanisms of a sort envisaged in contemporary cybernetics (cf. Harré, this volume).

If mental structures are construed as templates of action, then they are not entities that can be characterized by trait names. Questions about whether a person is submissive or aggressive, etc.—i.e., whether such 'entities' inside the person 'control' the behavior patterns that appear across different situations—will be replaced by questions about the scenarios which a person constructs and follows, which raises correlative questions about the situation to which he is applying this scenario, about the occasion for which the template has been constructed. But it will be the situation as a social scene endowed with meaning that counts. And since the meaning of social situations is itself something negotiated between the interactors, it would not be surprising if there were significant differences between the meaning the situation has for some person and the meaning assigned to it by 'independent observers' who don't know him. Consequently, the lack of coherent linkages found in empirical studies of self-control may be a problem only for a certain kind of psychology. For its import may be that one cannot understand what people do when one attempts to by-pass completely any phenomenological analysis of what things mean to them. Ratings based on the memory of friends and acquaintances, who presumably don't avoid such analysis, are, after all, coherent—coherence only collapses when 'independent observers', who don't know the individual and watch his behavior, as it were from outside, provide the ratings.

An idiographic approach which makes such phenomenological and situational analyses central, is compatible with a search for nomothetic principles, in the sense of rules having some degree of generality. If such analysis reveals some if-then relationship, be it a rule about the consequences of some action—e.g., if a certain sort of tease occurs in a family at dinner time this will be retaliated by hitting—or a rule about the consequences of some form of mental representation—e.g., if a child represents a tempting object to himself in a certain way he will be better able to resist its temptation than if he encodes it in some other way—then one will, of course, expect the rule to be applicable not just to this child or this family.

While empirical investigation must determine the range of application for such if-then relationships, it seems likely that they will be both phase-specific (e.g., children between the ages of four and six and limited to some sub-culture (e.g., the tease is recognized as such in families of a certain sort). But this in turn raises questions about the ontogeny of such social behaviors as teases, about why they occur in certain phases and sub-cultures, and the like, and the investigation of such matters might lead to nomothetic rules of greater generality.

It is, however, crucial to note that the rules under discussion are rules which people can follow or violate, and this makes them very different from laws in the natural sciences. This point is obscured in discussions of behavior modification, when rules which have been found to be effective for changing behavior—e.g., if you want to stop smoking, then light up only when you are in the bathroom—are called 'contingencies' and that term is stretched to cover both rules, in the narrow sense, and natural laws (e.g., 'contingencies of survival'), on the ground that both state if-then relationships. On this view, rules and laws are two sides of the same thing: for the actor, the if-then relationship is a rule (if I want B, I should do A), while for the observer it is a contingency (if A happens, B will follow). But this way of looking at the matter obscures crucial differences. I can, of course, take advantage of if-then relations stated in natural laws in my actions; if I don't want the glass to break, then I will be careful not to drop it. But this is very different from taking advantage of a 'functional relation' discovered by behavior modifications, e.g., smoke only in the bathroom if you want to stop smoking. For in the former case my action is guided by a contingency that holds independent of me, while in the latter case the 'contingency' which guides my action is itself a rule which I would violate; that 'contingency' is there only if I conform to the rule. If I do, there will, of course, be a regularity for the observer, but that regularity is constructed by me, ultimately in terms of my perceptions of what is relevant to my conduct.

To assimilate this 'functional relation' to a regularity that holds in the world independent of me is not only to assimilate different things, it also misleadingly suggests that this 'contingency', like other natural contingencies that hold in the world, can be discovered by the observer without taking into account the meanings things have for the person, the way *he* discriminates what is relevant to his conduct. It suggests that, e.g., a tease is an item in the world which the observer can identify in much the same way he can identify a cumulus cloud, neglecting the fact that behavior which counts as a tease in one family may not count as a tease in another. In other words, it makes it sound as if the environment can be separated off from persons so that the 'controlling variables' that determine their behavior can be located in the environment. But these 'controlling variables' are able to control only to the extent that persons see them as relevant, and when persons are factored out the *relevant* environment—the scene which has social meaning—simply disappears.

This is not to deny that external observers may have an essential role in identifying the rules to which people are conforming; it is not to claim that whatever people say about their behavior, about what rules they follow and what meanings things have for them, goes. Since people are not always aware of such things—since they may even be defensively motivated to avoid such awareness—observers who carefully watch what goes on in such interactions, e.g., when there is teasing at dinner time, and who are not without some understanding of what such families are like, may be essential if we are to uncover the rules, or scripts, that generate such interactions.

Can there be a science that studies persons and their social behavior along such lines? Those who are familiar with Wittgensteinian arguments pertaining to the necessity of supplying outer criteria for inner states, are not likely to suggest that such a science could be developed if we turn away from the social context and attempt instead to discriminate our 'internal states' by introspection. But there are criteria, of varying degrees of tightness, which often make it possible for us to arrive at agreement about whether or not someone has a certain belief, intention, desire, attitude, or the like. My opinion about the other person's intentions or desires can, of course, be mistaken; it is not a fact about him, but then neither is the meteorologist's opinion that this is a cumulus cloud a fact about that cloud. No doubt, natural scientists have succeeded in developing more explicit and effective rules for correcting each other's opinions and so achieving the objectivity on which truth depends. But concepts like belief, intention and the rest, which we ordinarily deploy with far less inter-observer agreement than concepts in the natural sciences, are also part of a conceptual system—the one we normally use to make our own behavior and that of others intelligible. The business of tidying and tightening the complex interrelations between theses concepts and the criteria for their deployment, of developing and checking out the analyses which this conceptual system suggests, of determining the boundaries of its application, and the like, could be a properly scientific task for a social science.

As for the variable and culture-relative character of human conduct, evidence about the social dependence of the way people characterize themselves and others, about the cultural relativity of the rules they follow, and the like, does not show that objectivity, which is a necessary condition for any science, cannot be achieved with respect to persons. Perhaps a person would not be what he is, perhaps he would not hold the beliefs about himself and others that he holds, perhaps he would not conform to the rules to which he conforms, if he were not in a certain social context. It does not follow that there are no objective facts about that person in that social context; indeed, the evidence cited, if it is evidence, states such facts. It may well be that many of the features that are of interest for a science of persons are such that they hold true of people only when they find themselves in certain situations, or only when they stand in certain sorts of relations to other people. But these are facts about the person, relational properties which are just as objective and testable as any other facts, even if they are true only if the person stands in the specified relations. Again, there is little reason to suppose that rules which can be effectively used by contemporary Western girls to control over-eating could be effectively used by the Azande; but that, if true, is another objective fact. Considerations of this sort argue against an idea that a science of persons could be a Newtonian science which discovers principles applicable to all people, no matter when or where, much as the laws of motion apply to all matter, no matter when or where. But they are simply irrelevant to the attempt to discover and systematize objectively valid and general rules that are applicable to people, even if the individual's understanding of himself and his situation—which in turn may depend on the way he is situated in a particular socio-cultural setting at a particular time—serves as an 'antecedent condition' for such rules. It is hard to see why such rules could not provide an objective 'data base' for a science of persons.

That these are important differences between the form which a science of persons can take and the natural sciences, particularly if one takes Newtonian physics to be the paradigm of science, should be clear from what has already been said. Some very crucial differences between our knowledge of ourselves, our knowledge of other persons, and our knowledge of 'natural phenomena' whose occurrence is in no way responsive to us, are brought out in the analysis of self-knowledge which Hamlyn and Toulmin develop in this volume. Hamlyn stresses the idea that self-knowledge cannot be understood as just knowledge about ourselves; if such knowledge has no practical bearing on the way we lead our lives, it is not self-knowledge proper. A conceptually necessary condition for self-knowledge, so Hamlyn argues, is an attitude toward oneself which involves a kind of commitment to oneself; failures of self-knowledge can be analyzed as failures of self-commitment that prevent a person from leading a life that has a single and unitary sense. On this view, self-knowledge can, in an important sense, be mediated by decision. That is, if a person makes a significant decision about his future, that decision may change his understanding of what he is, his view of himself in relation to his past, his self-knowledge. One implication of this analysis can be put by saying that 'a central fact about self-knowledge is that there is no *thing* to know' (Hamlyn, this volume). But this point must be carefully distinguished from the one made by Gergen when he concludes that 'when considering self-knowledge it is unclear what there is to know'.

Hamlyn's analysis of self-knowledge clearly has connections with Taylor's account of 'strong evaluation', of how in coming to accept, either consciously or unconsciously, a new description of my desires I, at the same time, undergo an important change and become, in an important sense, a different person. A somewhat similar emphasis can be found in Toulmin's rejection of the notion that self-knowledge can be understood as just a matter of cognitive 'expectations about' oneself. Instead, Toulmin's analysis stresses expectations we may have *of* ourselves and others, which embraces hope and trust which may be disappointed or which may be unrealistic, rather than just predictive beliefs which may be falsified. Self-knowledge and knowledge of persons more generally is, so Toulmin argues, as much practical as it is theoretical; self-understanding and self-command are interconnected aspects of self-knowledge, and we cannot provide an adequate account of such knowledge if we treat it as a purely 'cognitive' matter that can be divorced from the 'affective', 'volitional', or 'practical' aspects of human interactions.

Now if one begins with a conception of knowledge that is derived largely from epistemological analyses of knowledge claims in the physical sciences, then one may wonder whether such accounts of 'self-knowledge' are really talking about 'knowledge'. Given standard accounts of knowledge as either propositional 'knowing that' or skills that can be analyzed as 'knowing how', one may ask what more there is to self-knowledge, what must be added to such garden varieties of knowing in order to get self-knowledge and whether what is being added can properly be called 'knowledge'. But it seems to be a centrally important fact about people, that they are related to the temporal dimension of their lives in a way that allows decisions about their future to affect their whole conception of themselves, including things that happened in their past. And while there is obviously an asymmetry between myself and others in this respect, other persons are also creatures with a past and a future and I may not be able to understand certain things about them unless I am able to view myself in a certain way. If this is true, it must inevitably affect what can count as self-knowledge as distinct from knowledge of other persons, on one side, and knowledge of other kinds of things, on the other. Perhaps then, as Toulmin's arguments suggest, we have things upside down if we ask what must be added to ordinary conceptual knowledge in order to get self-knowledge and practical knowledge of other persons; perhaps we should ask instead what must be taken away from personal knowledge in order to get conceptual, scientific knowledge. In other words, scientific knowledge may depend on what Toulmin calls a 'systematic abstraction of the cognitive', successfully developed over the last three centuries to organize and account for our experience with non-responsive 'things', but of limited relevance for understanding ourselves and other human beings—not only at the everyday level of commonsense, but also for the purpose of clinical and social psychology.

Descriptions of physical things also generate a contrast between 'objective' and 'subjective' which may lead one to doubt that self-knowledge, as well as 'practical' personal knowledge that it is not purely conceptual, can be 'objective'. Whether the stove is square is ordinarily regarded as an objective question whose answer depends on the stove, while whether it is warm is regarded as a subjective matter that depends on us more than on the stove; if 'warm' is to be an objective property that can be attributed to the stove, it would have to be specified as, e.g., some range of temperature which can be determined independent of us. Looked at in this way, objectivity is possible only if what is being described is some *thing* that is independent of us, so that we can produce descriptions that can be matched against characteristics of that thing which remain what they are independent of us and the descriptions we produce. But if the sort of arguments developed by Taylor and Hamlyn are right, then our descriptions of our experience are, in part, constitutive of what we experience, so that the clean separation of description and thing described is not possible when we are describing human experiences. If people raised in different cultures or sub-cultures come to internalize different ways of describing their experience, this may make what they experience different. For example, our experience of what mental illness is like, may well be different from that of people who conceptualize it as a form of demonic possession; the descriptions they internalized in growing up in their culture may have made their experience different, so that the language of demonic possession fits what they experienced when they fell apart. Nor can there be a question of matching a description against an independent object in the case of self-knowledge, if such knowledge can be mediated by decision, if putting forward and accepting a new description of what one desires can itself be a self-intervention that changes what one is.

If one thinks of objectivity as requiring that description and thing described be independent so that they can be matched against each other, then one may think that there can be no objectivity in such cases. But even if what we experience in mental illness is different from what was experienced by people in other cultures or periods who internalized different conceptualizations, it does not follow that there is nothing to choose between our account of what mental illness involves and the account of people who experienced mental illness as demonic possession, that it's all just a matter of what different groups happen to believe at different times. Granted that people who described what happens when they fall apart and lose self-control in terms of possession by a witch really experienced the loss of self-control in a way that differs from what we experience, there can still be good reasons for preferring our account of what is involved in the loss of self-control. It would be unfortunate if we tie the concept of objectivity to the description of external things and processes in a way that excludes on *a priori* grounds the possibility of objectivity in accounts of human experience (see also Taylor, this volume).

The Ontogenesis of the Self and Its Relation to Others

Psychological accounts which stress the social genesis of the self and the dramaturgical, role-playing aspects of self-presentation—an approach exemplified, in different ways, in the papers by Gergen, Harré, and McCall—also raise important issues about the way in which we are to conceptualize the relation of the self to others. How are we to understand the relation between the personal and the social? Does an account of persons which details the roles they come to adopt and the style in which they come to perform these roles, the way in which these roles come to be organized and integrated, and the like, exhaust what there is to know about the self? If we factor out everything social, are we still left with a self whose ontogenesis needs to be explained, perhaps in psycho-dynamic rather than social terms?

One point can be conceded to the 'social looking-glass' approach straight away: there is something very wrong with the suggestion, common in classical empiricism, that the self can be understood in isolation from others, as an independent center of consciousness that somehow constructs a world out of impressions received through the senses and in that way comes to discover that there are other persons in the world. There can be no 'problem of other minds' from an ontogenetic point of view because there is little reason to think that the child's consciousness of himself as a separate 'I' is an initial given; it seems rather to be something that grows out of a relationship with someone else, typically the mother, a relationship in which there is initially a consciousness of 'we' rather than 'I', a shared world in which there are meanings 'for us' rather than meanings 'for me'. Both empirical and conceptual considerations suggest that the question is not how inter-subjectivity can be created by primordially solitary selves, but how the individual self is constituted and detached from the primordial 'we' (cf. Harré and Wolf, this volume). My sense of myself as an individual who can take a personal stand—who can engage in 'strong evaluation' and decide, in opposition to the social surround, what is really significant for me—is thus a developmental achievement. Perhaps we develop this consciousness of being an individual self by coming into situations which force a choice between social groups, as when the adolescent rebels against his parents; and perhaps the adolescent could not sustain his new identity against the parents without the support of a peer group with which he comes to identify. This would suggest that the extent to which such individual consciousness is achieved may depend on one's culture; our emphasis on individuality is clearly not characteristic of many other cultures, and our culture may make possible choices and stands that are not possible in other cultures.

But even if we suppose that, e.g., Luther could not have taken the stand he did if he had been brought up in a different culture, there is an enormous difference between Luther and another person who may have been raised in the same culture but decided not to decide and to swim with the tide instead, and who hardly knows what to believe except in relation to some social group of which he is a part. Of course, I can only express the meanings things have for me in the language I get from my culture, and that may limit the range of possibilities that are open to me; but it does not prevent me from defining what is really significant for me—the stand I take—in opposition to the social groups of which I am a part. Clearly, the capacity for such self-definition does not develop in a vacuum. There must have been all kinds of preconditions that made it possible for Luther to take his stand, whether or not they be conditions of the sort explored by Erikson (1958). One need not think of Luther's stand before the Diet as a spontaneous act of 'free will', since that act, no matter what its special historical significance, was not an isolated act but an instance of a way of acting characteristic of Luther. But no matter how we may explain why Luther took the stand he did, we cannot explain away the difference between Luther and another person who does not take such stands.

But just this sort of difference tends to be minimized or distorted when the 'social looking-glass' tradition in psychology seeks to absorb the personal into the social. If personal identity is equated with the hierarchical organization of social roles (cf. McCall, this volume) then it becomes indistinguishable from social identity and it becomes hard to see what conceptual resources are available for distinguishing between a Luther and others who, though they occupy the same roles, do not take a significant stand. To take a less extreme example, a judge may be compassionate or he may be the opposite; but it would be very odd to suggest that to be a compassionate person is to have a certain sort of social identity. Being a compassionate person is not a social role, though compassion can express itself only in relation to others and so may be something that manifests itself in one's social roles, i.e., in being a compassionate judge, a compassionate father, and the like. There is no point to stretching the concept of 'social identity' to cover not only tinker and tailor but also 'compassionate person', because the distinction between the judge who is compassionate and the one who is not, is not a distinction that can be explicated in terms of social roles—at least not without emptying that concept of anything distinctively social and turning it into a rubric that covers any feature of the relations between persons, whatever it may be.

Normally we contrast relations which are personal with those which are social; the intimate 'personal' relations in which one stands to one's family are one thing, formal 'social' relations at official functions, or talking to the Provost of the University in his capacity as Provost, and the like, are quite another thing. Purely personal relations may be something of an ideal, since one usually relates to others, even one's wife or son, at least partly in one's capacity as husband or father. But that should not obscure the difference between highly stylized relations involving social status and personal relations, which can be called 'intimate' precisely because they are not locked into stylized social patterns but are relatively free of the constraints imposed by treating the other person as the occupant of some social role. Yet this, once again, is just what seems to get lost when social psychologists construe husband, wife, lover, etc., as roles and analyze intimate personal relations in terms of such roles. There may, of course, be marriages which can be adequately understood in terms of the roles played by husband and wife, e.g., he is playing the role of bread-winner and patriarch, she is playing the role of housekeeper and baby-doll. But precisely to the extent that we can understand their marriage in terms of such role playing, we can also say that their relation lacks personal intimacy.

It may be objected that 'role' is being used in an unduly narrow sense, that social psychologists define roles in terms of the shared expectations of some group, and that the group need not be some culture or sub-culture but can be limited to two persons, since the dyad is the smallest unit of interest to social psychology. This will, of course, allow one to construe not only tinker and tailor but also husband and wife, and not only husband and wife as social types but the behavior of this particular husband and this particular wife, as roles. But while stretching the concept of role in this way will enable us to explain the personal relation of husband and wife by talking about roles, it does so just because the concept of role has been emptied of its social meaning and made to cover the personal relations that are ordinarily contrasted with social relations. Normally, we speak of roles in connection with situations in which people treat each other as occupants of social positions; there are different socially defined patterns of expectations for London bobbies and New York cops. In this sense, there may be socially defined patterns of expectations for Victorian husbands and wives. But while any given husband and wife will have some patterns of expectations of each other, that pattern need not be role-structured and socially defined; indeed, one would normally say that the more personal their relation is, the less role-structured their expectations will be. All human relations, no matter what their specific character may be, depend on patterns of expectations people have of each other; but that is no reason to obliterate the distinction between relations that are social and those which are not social but personal.

We thus need to insist on a distinction, often slurred over in social psychology, between the social and the interpersonal or intersubjective. The self cannot be understood in isolation but only in relation to other persons; the very language of the self—the language of intentions, desires, motives and the like—can only be an intersubjective language. The issues on which one can take a personal stand typically involve others (as in Luther's case) and so cannot even be stated without reference to them. Self-control, self-reliance, and the like, are interpersonal competences which prepare one to deal with future situations involving others, much as compassion and the like are qualities of persons that can only be manifested in interpersonal relations. But not all relations between persons are social relations, in the sense of relations structured by social status or by socially defined role expectations.

Similar considerations apply to style, to the expressive and dramaturgical aspects of the relations between persons. There is a style appropriate to the way in which, e.g., English bank clerks perform their social role, a style which expresses social attitudes about the significance of money, the dignity of important institutions, and the like. Since we can say of someone that his personality at work is very different from what it is at home, there is a sense of 'self' in which the style in which a social role is performed can be called a 'presentation of self'. But there is another and quite different sense of 'self' in which we say that someone's personality shines through, or is expressed in, everything he does—in the different roles he performs and the way he performs them, as well as in the way he engages in those interpersonal relations that are not social roles. Personality in this more underlying and enduring sense may also be a matter of style, but a style that is personal rather than social: we can recognize the same personality at work in a variety of social and personal engagements because we can discern stylistic unities, characteristic of that person, in all of his interpersonal engagements. Whether he is doing his job as bank manager in the appropriate bank-managerial style, or whether he is relating to family or intimate friends, he is acting *in* character. But this sense of character, or self, cannot be just another socially stylized role performance.

The ontogenesis and vicissitudes of the self, in this intersubjective rather than social sense, are addressed by recent work in the psychoanalytic psychology of the self. This approach, discussed by E. Wolf in this volume, has grown out of the analysis of contemporary patients whose neurotic conflicts are primarily rooted, not in unresolved Oedipal fixations and the like, but in their sense of self—in the relative 'cohesion' or 'fragmentation' of the self. Unlike classical psychoanalysis, the Kohut-Wolf approach to the 'analysis of the self' is not concerned with hypotheses about underlying mental mechanisms; it focuses instead on the person's subjective experience, his sense of self, and attempts to analyze the ups and downs of self-esteem in relation to the person's largely unconscious ambitions, on the one hand, and his largely unconscious ideals, on the other. These in turn are seen as rooted in a sense of self that develops out of relations to others, beginning with the infant's relation to the nurturing mother, a development whose vicissitudes may lead to a self that is relatively cohesive—so that diverse aspects of the self, including sexual drives, are integrated in a matrix of personal relations—or a self that tends toward fragmentation, so that parts are easily wrenched out of the normal matrix of a cohesive self to become independent organizing centers—as in hypochondria, or the experience of being driven to unusual sexual goals, or other behaviors which the person himself may experience as irrational.

This psychoanalytic psychology of the self is clearly in the 'diagnostic-descriptive' rather than 'hypothetico-explanatory' mode; it speaks of various aspects of the self in clinical contexts 'not to speculate about concealed mechanisms, but rather to elucidate confused motivations' (Toulmin, this volume). Moreover, such an analysis of the conditions and stages that lead to the development of a cohesive, integrated self, or its opposite, links up directly, as Toulmin points out, with questions of autonomy, freedom and responsibility that have concerned philosophers.

Like other psychoanalytic approaches, this 'analysis of the self' is a reconstruction based on what transpires in the psychoanalytic situation, and this raises problems about evidence and empirical validation. But psychoanalysts in this tradition are addressing important issues that tend to be neglected in both the behavioral and the 'social looking-glass' traditions. We need empirical research to substantiate, or modify, the 'analysis of the self' offered by Kohut and Wolf. But we cannot neglect issues raised in the context of this sort of 'psycho-dynamic' analysis of the self if we are to understand how people can develop into autonomous, rational agents, in a practical and moral sense which requires a proper appreciation of one's own standing in relation to other autonomous agents. Neither the analysis of social roles and of the 'presentation of self' in society, nor the study of the determinants of self-control and the like, seem to address this range of issues about the self, about the formation and deformation of what may be called a person's 'character'. Empirical research that tests the developmental formulations suggested by Kohut and Wolf on the basis of psycho-analytic experience could add an important dimension to our knowledge of the self.

REFERENCES

ALSTON, W. P. Traits, Consistency and Conceptual Alternatives for Personality Theory, *Journal for the Theory of Social Behaviour*, 5, no. 1, April, 1975.

ARGYLE, M., and LITTLE, B. R. Do Personality Traits Apply to Social Behavior? *Journal for the Theory of Social Behavior*, 2, no. 1, April 1972.

BODEN, M. *Purposive Explanation in Psychology*, Cambridge: Harvard University Press, 1972.

BONEAU, C. A. Paradigm Regained? Cognitive Behaviorism Restated, *American Psychologist*, 29, May, 1974.

Boneau, C. A., and Cole, J. L. Decision Theory, the Pigeon and the Psychophysical Function, *Psychological Review*, 74, 1967.

Bowers, K. Situationism in Psychology: An analysis and a critique, *Psychological Review*, 80, 1973.

Erikson, E. H., *Young Man Luther*, New York: Norton, 1958.

Freud, S. *Introductory Lectures on Psychoanalysis* (1916–17). Standard Edition, vol. XV, London: Hogarth Press, 1953.

Gergen, K. J. Social Psychology as History, *Journal of Personality and Social Psychology*, 26, 1973.

Minsky, M. Matter, Mind and Models, *Proc. of Int. Federation of Information Processing Congress*, 1, Washington: Spartan Books, McMillan & Co., Ltd., 1965.

Mischel, T. *Psychological Explanations and their Vicissitudes*, in W. J. Arnold, ed. *Nebraska Symposium on Motivation*, 23, Lincoln: University of Nevada Press, 1976.

Mischel, W. *Personality and Assessment*, New York: John Wiley & Sons, 1968.

PART II Self-Control and the Concept of Agency

2 Self-Control and the Self

WALTER MISCHEL AND HARRIET N. MISCHEL

We will start with an overview of some of the main types of self-control that psychologists have researched. We will then examine the patterning or organization of self-control behavior and consider some of the most important variables that influence the individual's ability to exert control over the environment and himself. Finally, we will discuss some of the broader implications of research findings on self-control for the nature of the self that does the controlling.

I. The Varieties of Self-Control

Psychologists investigating self-control have used a variety of paradigms and have defined it in many somewhat different ways, guided by such diverse concepts as 'will power', 'ego strength', 'mastery', 'competence', and 'internal control'. All of these concepts involve the idea of volition ('will') and deal with the ability of the individual to affect his own outcomes and to influence his personal environment. Regardless of whether this influence is judged to be good (prosocial or 'moral') or whether it is judged negatively, it always entails the individual's efforts to modify conditions and/or his behavior in the light of particular goals. Let us briefly consider major examples of empirical investigations of the many varieties of self-control.

A. DELAY OF GRATIFICATION

An especially striking characteristic of self-control is that people frequently impose barriers on themselves, interrupting their own behavior and delaying available gratification. When a delay of gratification is imposed on an individual by external conditions we talk about 'frustration'; when the delay is self-imposed we call it 'voluntary delay'.

The ability to voluntarily refuse immediate gratification, to tolerate self-imposed delays of reward, is at the core of most everyday concepts of 'will power' and the parallel psychological concept of 'ego strength'. It would be difficult to imagine socialization, or indeed civilization, without such self-imposed delays. Learning to wait for desired outcomes and to behave in the light of expected future consequences is essential for the successful achievement of long-term, distant goals. Even the simplest, most primitive steps in socialization require learning to defer one's impulses and to express them only under special conditions of time and place, as seen in toilet training. Similarly, enormously complex chains of deferred gratification are required for people to achieve the delayed rewards provided by our culture's social system and institutions.

The importance of self-control patterns that require delay of gratification has been widely recognized by theorists from Freud to the present. The concept of voluntary postponement of gratifications for the sake of more distant, long-term gains is fundamental for many conceptualizations of complex human behavior and has been studied extensively.

To explore the variables controlling self-imposed delay of reward, one research program has studied delay of reward and self-control with direct behavioral measures (Mischel, 1966, 1974). In this research subjects usually have to choose among actual alternatives that vary in delay time and value (e.g., immediate smaller versus delayed larger rewards) in realistic situations. For example, preschool children are given a choice between getting a less valuable but immediate reward or a more attractive reward for which they must wait. Choices of this type, involving age-appropriate outcomes, have been presented to older children and adults by means of questionnaires that describe the choices verbally, as well as by creating real choice situations.

To a considerable degree a person's willingness to defer gratification depends on the outcomes that he expects from his choice (Mischel, 1966, 1968). Of particular importance are the individual's expectations that future (delayed) rewards for which he would have to work and wait would actually materialize, and their relative value for him. Such expectations or feelings of trust depend, in turn, on the person's history of prior promise-keeping and on past success with waiting behavior and other forms of planful, goal-directed self-control. When the attainment of delayed gratification requires the person to reach particular achievement levels, then his willingness to work and wait or these future outcomes also hinges on his expectations that he can adequately fulfil the necessary contingencies (Mischel & Staub, 1965). These expectations depend not only on his direct personal experiences, but also on his observation of the behavior of social models, such as peers, parents, and teachers (e.g., Bandura & Mischel, 1965; Stumphauzer, 1972).

B. EVALUATIVE SELF-REACTIONS AND SELF-REGULATION

Another aspect of self-control is the way that people judge and evaluate their own behavior and reward and punish themselves. In the typical animal laboratory the organism performs, and the experimenter or his apparatus reinforces him at predetermined points. Unlike the animals in the researcher's laboratory, people exert considerable control over the rewarding and punishing resources available to them. They congratulate themselves for their own characteristics and actions; they praise or abuse their own achievements; and they self-administer social and material rewards and punishments from the enormous array freely available to them.

A critical aspect of self-regulation thus stems from the fact that people assess and monitor themselves. Self-praise and censure, self-imposed treats and punishments, self-indulgence and self-laceration are manifestations of this pervasive human tendency to congratulate and condemn oneself. Traditionally, learning research with animals generally has focused on the effects of environmentally or externally administered reinforcers. More recent work has begun to clarify the processes through which persons learn to set their own performance standards and to make their own self-reward contingent upon their achieving these self-prescribed criteria. To adequately understand human social behavior, we must know how the person self-administers and regulates rewards and punishments that are in his own control.

Whether or not an individual rewards or condemns his own behavior hinges not only on what he does, but also on the exact context and circumstances of his performance. The standards that a person has been rewarded for using (e.g., Kanfer & Marston, 1963a, b) and those he observes other people using (Bandura & Kupers, 1964; Masters & Mokros, 1974; Mischel & Liebert, 1966) all affect how he will self-reward his own behavior.

Self-regulatory processes are not limited to the individual's self-administration of such outcomes as the tokens, 'prizes', or verbal approval and disapproval that have been favored in most previous studies of self-reinforcement (e.g., Bandura, 1969; Kanfer & Marston, 1963; Kanfer & Phillips, 1970; Mahoney 1974; Masters & Mokros, 1974; Mischel, Coates, & Raskoff, 1968). An especially pervasive but relatively neglected feature of self-regulation is the person's selective exposure to different types of positive and negative information about himself.

Almost limitless 'good' and 'bad' information about the self is potentially available (for example, in the form of memories), depending on where one looks and how one searches. An individual can seek, and usually find, information to support his positive or negative attributes, his successes or failures, almost boundlessly. He can focus cognitively, for example, on his past, present, and expected assets or liabilities, and attend either to his strengths or to his weaknesses by ideating about selective aspects of his perceived personality and behavior. Affective self-reactions, as in the enhancement of one's own self-esteem, hinge on selective attentional processes through which the individual exposes himself only to particular types of information from the enormous array potentially available to him. By means of such selective attention the individual can make himself feel either good or bad, can privately congratulate or condemn himself and, in the extreme, can generate emotions from euphoria to depression. Given that every person perceives himself as having *both* some positive and some negative qualities, what determines his attention to one or the other type of attribute? To answer such questions, one program of research has been studying the interactions between situational and dispositional variables that guide the process of selective attention to (and memory for) information about oneself of different affective value (Mischel, Ebbesen, & Zeiss, 1973, 1976).

Related research has shown the importance of the person's momentary emotional state both for his self-reactions and for his reactions to others. Whether one feels good or bad, happy or sad, influences such diverse actions as generosity and charitability to other people as well as to oneself. Specifically, positive feelings tend to encourage greater generosity (e.g., Isen, Horn, & Rosenhan, 1973) and altruism (e.g., Rosenhan, Moore, & Underwood, 1976) as well as greater noncontingent self-gratification (e.g., Mischel, Coates, & Raskoff, 1968; Moore, Underwood, & Rosenhan, 1973), and lead to more selective attention to one's personal assets rather than to one's weaknesses (Mischel, Ebbesen, & Zeiss, 1973, 1976).

C. CONTROL OF VISCERAL AND GLANDULAR RESPONSES

Most work on personality and self-control has focused on the control of motoric and verbal behaviors, e.g., voluntary actions and choices. Through the application of social learning principles it also may be possible to achieve substantial control of autonomic responses, such as the 'involuntary' glandular and visceral responses involved in emotion (Miller, 1969) and of the electrical waves that accompany brain activity (Kamiya, 1967; Stoyva & Kamiya, 1968).

Indeed, laboratory explorations with animals indicate that such supposedly involuntary bodily responses as salivation, kidney functions, stomach contractions, blood volume in the periphery of the body, heart rate, and brain waves all can be significantly affected by making reinforcement contingent upon increases or decreases in those responses. Some representative findings with animals show that rewards contingent on specific body changes affected those changes predictably, e.g., intestinal contractions can be increased or decreased through rewards. The effects were highly specific, so that reward for intestinal contraction or relaxation did not affect heart rate and vice versa. The implications of these findings are exciting for future form of therapy for all sorts of emotional and psychosomatic problems, though it is too early to promise any cures (cf. Miller, 1969).

In some human investigations, the individual is made aware of his own bodily responses (for example, by observing an ongoing recording of his brain waves). If he gets appropriate immediate feedback about changes in these responses he may learn to control them voluntarily (Kamiya, 1967), perhaps in a manner similar to that employed by Zen masters and mystics. Studies of this type suggest the possibility that people may be able to achieve far greater control over themselves and their own bodily states than usually has been believed. If individuals can learn and apply appropriate social learning and feedback principles to themselves they may be able to achieve mastery over many aspects of their being, including their physiological state.

D. MORAL REASONING

In addition to learning diverse forms of overt self-control, people also differ in their ideas and attitudes about justice, right and wrong, and the nature of conscience. Kohlberg (1969) has studied these individual differences, focusing on the child as a 'moral philosopher' who constructs theories about morality. Influenced by Piaget's cognitive developmental stages, Kohlberg has hypothesized three levels of moral thinking (preconventional, conventional, and postconventional), each containing two related stages. Kohlberg believes that these six moral stages follow a developmental progression that is a function of increasing cognitive maturation. While social experience may affect the rate of progress across stages, he believes that the nature of the sequence is fundamentally the same even in such widely different cultures as the U.S., Taiwan, Mexico, Turkey, and Yucatan. A person's stage position is inferred from the kind of reasoning displayed on a Moral Judgment Scale that presents a number of moral dilemmas. At present, there is substantial disagreement about the existence of distinct moral stages and about the utility of inferring a person's moral stage in efforts to predict his relevant moral behavior (e.g., Kurtines & Grief, 1974; Mischel & Mischel, 1976).

These selected examples must suffice, though there are many other studies of various aspects of self-reactions and self-control, including experiments on the determinants of self-criticism (e.g., Aronfreed, 1968; Grusec, 1966), resistance to temptation (e.g., Burton, Maccoby, & Allinsmith, 1961; Mischel & Gilligan, 1964), and conscience and guilt after transgression (e.g., Grinder, 1964).

II. The Organization of Self-Control

How can one find underlying unities and extract generalizations from these many forms of control? Many personality psychologists have searched for individual differences in stable, cross-situationally consistent aspects of self-control. For this purpose, measures of individual differences on dimensions of ego strength, impulsivity, self-regulation, moral thought and conduct were constructed and then explored by empirical studies. The basic intention of this approach was to find consistent cross-situational individual differences in self-control.

A. THE SEARCH FOR SELF-CONTROL DISPOSITIONS

Representative both of the approach and the findings in this vein is work on voluntary delay of gratification as a personality dimension. Based on studies of choice preferences for immediate, smaller versus delayed but more valuable outcomes, two contrasting patterns of delay and impulsivity have been conceptualized as extreme poles (e.g., Mischel, 1966).

At one extreme is the person who predominantly chooses larger, delayed rewards or goals for which he must either wait or work. This person is more likely to be oriented toward the future (Klineberg, 1968) and to plan carefully for distant goals. He (or she) also is apt to have high scores on 'ego-control' measures, to have high achievement motivation, to be more trusting and socially responsible, to be brighter and more mature, to have a high level of aspiration, and to show less uncontrolled impulsivity (e.g., Mischel, 1966, 1976). This extreme pattern resembles what has been called the 'Puritan character structure'. Socioculturally, this pattern tends to be found most often in middle and upper socioeconomic classes, and in highly achievement-oriented ('Protestant ethic') cultures. This pattern of high ego strength is also related to a relatively high level of competence, as revealed by higher intelligence, more mature cognitive development, and a greater capacity for sustained attention (Grim, Kohlberg, & White, 1968).

At the opposite extreme is the individual who predominantly prefers immediate gratification and rejects the alternative of waiting or working for larger, delayed goals. Correlated with this is a greater concern with the immediate present than with the future, and greater impulsivity. Socioculturally, this pattern is correlated with membership in the lower socioeconomic classes, with membership in cultures in which achievement orientation is low, and with indices of lesser social and cognitive competence.

In their extreme forms both these patterns might be 'maladaptive': the excessively 'high delay' pattern might characterize an emotionally constricted person whose gratifications are perpetually postponed, and the extremely 'immediate' pattern an impulsive person who does not behave in accord with long-term goals and who is not congnizant of the ultimate consequences of his present actions. Clinically, persons diagnosed as 'delinquents' and 'psychopaths' are often characterized by an immediate reward choice pattern.

B. THE DISCRIMINATIVENESS OF SELF-CONTROL

A polarity of gratification patterns has descriptive value. But note that self-control patterns also tend to be highly discriminative and idiosyncratically organized within individuals (Mischel, 1973). In fact, the extensive network of correlations found with measures of delay behavior has supplied evidence not only for some consistency, but also for equally impressive discriminativeness. For example, Trinidadian lower-class Blacks often preferred immediately available, albeit smaller, gratifications in choice offered by a White promise-maker (Mischel, 1958, 1961a). In their past experiences promises of future rewards from Whites had often been broken, and they had participated in a culture in which immediate gratification often was modeled and rewarded extensively (Mischel, 1961b, c). Nevertheless, the same people saved money, planned elaborately, and were willing to give up competing immediate gratifications in order to plan ahead for many future outcomes (such as annual feasts, religious events, and carnival celebrations) whose preparation and realization were under their own control, making it plain that any generalizations about their cross-situational 'impulsivity' are not justified.

The relatively great discriminativeness that characterized delay of gratification is echoed in results from many studies of self-control conducted by other investigators. Empirical research on self-control and moral behavior has concentrated on three areas: moral judgment and verbal standards of right and wrong (e.g., Kohlberg, 1963); resistance to temptation in the absence of external constraint (e.g., Aronfreed & Reber, 1965; Grinder, 1962; MacKinnon, 1938; Mischel & Gilligan, 1964); and post-transgression indices of remorse and guilt (e.g., Alinsmith, 1960; Aronfreed, 1964; Seers, Maccoby,

& Levin, 1957). These three areas of moral behavior turn out to be either completely independent or at best only minimally interrelated (Becker, 1964; Hoffman, 1963; Kohlberg, 1963).

Specificity also tends to be the rule within each area. For example, an extensive survey of all types of reactions to transgression revealed no predictable relationship among specific types of reaction (Aronfreed, 1961). Likewise, Sears (1965) and his co-workers did not find consistent associations among various reactions to transgression. Again, in a study with teenage boys, Allinsmith (1960) inferred moral feelings from the youngsters' projective story completions in response to descriptions of various kinds of immoral actions. The results led Allinsmith to conclude that a person with a truly generalized conscience is a statistical rarity. In the same vein, Johnson (1962) found that moral judgments across situations tend to be highly specific and even discrepant in many cases.

The findings on the discriminativeness of self-control and moral behavior thus give little support for the belief in a unitary intrapsychic moral agency like the superego, nor for a unitary trait entity of conscience or honesty (Mischel, 1968, 1971). Rather than acquiring a homogeneous conscience that determines uniformly all aspects of their self-control, people develop subtler discriminations that depend on many moderating variables and involve complex interactions (Mischel, 1973). For example, to predict an individual's voluntary delay of gratification accurately one may have to know his age, his sex, the experimenter's sex, the objects for which he is waiting, the consequences of not waiting, the models to whom he was exposed recently, his immediate prior experience, and a host of other variables. The discovery that self-control, like other important qualities of human behavior (Mischel, 1968), tends to be discriminatively organized, encouraged a more process-oriented approach that focused on the analysis of the many variables involved in self-control, as discussed next.

III. Some Determinants of Self-Control

A psychological analysis of self-control must distinguish two components: the person's *competence* (capacity) to engage in self-control behaviors, and the motivational (incentive) variables that influence *performance* of those behaviors in particular situations. This distinction between competence and performance reflects the basic difference between acquisition (learning) and performance (e.g., Bandura, 1969; Mischel, 1973). *Acquisition* or learning depends on cognitive-sensory processes. The products of acquisition are a person's competencies, that is, the total repertoire of what the individual knows and *can* do. Such competencies are the result of the person's total genetic and psychosocial history. They include what the person knows, and the skills, rules, and cognitive capacities which he has acquired and which enable him to generate (construct) behaviors (Mischel, 1973). *Performance*, in contrast, depends on motivational variables as will be discussed shortly.

A. THE ABILITY (COMPETENCE) TO EXERT SELF-CONTROL

Though cognitive maturation and social learning throughout life one acquires an increasingly large set of competencies for generating organized behavior. These competencies include knowledge of the structure of the physical world (e.g., Piaget, 1954), the social rules, conventions and principles that guide conduct (e.g., Aronfreed, 1968; Kohlberg, 1969) and the personal constructs generated about self and others (e.g., G. Kelly, 1955). Some psychologists have discussed these acquisitions in terms of information processing and information integration (e.g., Anderson, 1972; Bandura, 1971; Rumelhart, Lindsey, & Norman, 1971); others refer to schemata and cognitive templates (e.g., Aronfreed, 1968; Piaget, 1970).

We use the concept of *cognitive and behavioral construction competencies* to encompass the whole range of man's psychological acquisitions and to refer to the diverse cognitions and behaviors that a person is capable of constructing. We speak of 'constructions' to emphasize the *constructive* fashion in which information seems to be retrieved and processed (e.g., Neisser, 1967) and the active organization through which it is categorized and transformed (e.g., Anderson & Bower, 1973). The concept of construction competencies also emphasizes the person's *cognitive activities* (i.e., the operations and transformations that he performs on information) in contrast to a residue of finite cognitions and responses that he passively 'has'. Everyone acquires the ability to construct a wide range of potential behaviors that can be used for self-control, although there obviously are great differences between people in the range and quality of the potential self-control patterns they are able to generate.

B. FROM COMPETENCE TO CONDUCT: PRACTICING SELF-CONTROL

Whether or not the person who knows how to exert self-control does so at any given time (or chooses, instead, other courses of action) hinges on motivational considerations in the particular psychological situation. Till now we have considered what the individual is capable of doing, i.e., his competencies and abilities. But the same person who is capable of the most rigorous self-control also may be capable of impulsive and 'uncontrolled' action. To go from competence and potential self-control to actual performance, from construction capacity to the construction of behavior in specific situations, requires attention to the determinants of performance. Here the variables of greatest importance are the person's expectancies and subjective values.

1. EXPECTED RESPONSE CONSEQUENCES To predict specific behavior in a particular situation one must consider the person's specific expectancies about the consequences of different behavioral options in that situation (e.g., Mischel & Staub, 1965). The individual's behavior-outcome expectancies guide his selection of behaviors from among the many which he is capable of constructing within any situation. In part, expectancies about behavior-outcome relationships may be based on direct experience (e.g., Rotter, 1954, 1972). But such expectations depend not only on the outcomes one has received for similar behavior in similar situations, but also on the consequences one has observed happening to others. Information about the outcomes that other people get may provide valuable information about the probable consequences to oneself for trying similar behavior. For example, after observing appropriate other people ('models') get positive consequences for a response pattern, one tends to act more readily in similar ways (e.g., Bandura, 1971).

There is considerable support for the significant role of cognition and observational processes in the development and alteration of self-control patterns, relatively independent of any direct reinforcement. The evidence for this comes from studies on the transmission of delay behavior through modelling without any direct reinforcement. In a typical experiment (Bandura, & Mischel, 1965), it was found that self-imposed delay of reward was determined in part by the delay choice patterns displayed by social models. Presumably information about the choice patterns displayed by prestigeful models led observers to expect more positive consequences for choosing in a similar manner and hence led them to adopt the modeled pattern. Changes in delay-of-reward behavior were also found to be a function of exposure to symbolic (written) medeling cues, as well as real-life models.

2. SUBJECTIVE VALUES What people choose to do also depends on the *subjective values* of the outcomes which they expect (Mischel, 1973; Rotter, 1954). For example, given that all children expect that approval from teachers depends on practicing self-discipline in the classroom, there may be differences in the frequency of such self-control due to differences among the children in the perceived value of obtaining the teachers' approval. Similarly, while for one individual approval from peers in a particular situation may be more important than parental approval for a particular behavior pattern, these values may be reversed for a second person and irrelevant for a third.

The subjective (perceived) value for the person of particular classes of events (that is, his stimulus preferences and aversions) is an important determinant of all behavioral choices, including those involved in self-control. As a result of social learning, many stimuli acquire the power to induce positive or negative emotional states in the person and to function as incentives or reinforcers for his behavior. The subjective value of any stimulus pattern may be acquired and modified through instructions and observational experiences as well as through direct experiences and obviously may change substantially in the course of development.

The affective value (valence) of any stimulus depends on the exact conditions—in the person and in the situation—in which it occurs. The many variables known to affect the emotional meeting and valence of a stimulus include its context, sequencing and patterning (e.g., Helson, 1964), social comparison processes (e.g., Festinger, 1954), and the cognitive labels the person assigns to his own emotional arousal state (Schachter & Singer, 1962).

3. SELF-REGULATORY SYSTEMS Self-control often involves more than

appropriate decision making; it requires the individual to regulate his own behavior even in the face of strong temptations and situational pressures for long time periods and without the help of any obvious external supports. Each person partly regulates his own behavior by self-imposed goals (standards) and self-produced consequences. Even when there are no external constraints and social monitors, people set standards for themselves and criticize or commend their own behavior depending on how well it fits their expectations and goals (Bandura, 1971; Kanfer, 1971; Kanfer & Marston, 1963; Mischel, 1974).

A basic quality of self-regulatory systems is the person's adoption of *contingency rules* that guide his behavior in the absence, and sometimes in spite of, immediate external situational pressures. Such rules specify the kinds of behavior appropriate (expected) under particular conditions, the performance criteria (standards, goals) which the behavior must achieve, and the consequences of achieving or failing to reach those standards. Different individuals may differ of course, in each of these components of self-regulation, depending on their unique earlier histories or on more recent experiences (e.g., situational information).

Some of the components in self-regulation have been studied in research on goal-setting and self-reinforcement (e.g., Bandura & Whalen, 1966; Bandura & Perloff, 1967; Mischel & Liebert, 1966). The findings indicated that even young children will not indulge themselves with freely available immediate gratifications; instead, they follow rules that regulate conditions under which they may gratify themselves. Far from being simply hedonistic, children, like adults, make demands of themselves and impose complex and often stringent contingencies upon their own behavior. These self-imposed criteria are grounded in the observed standards displayed by salient models as well as in the individual's direct socialization history (e.g., Bandura & Walters, 1963; Mischel & Liebert, 1966).

If modeling cues and direct tuition for a pattern of standards are congruent they tend to facilitate each other; if they conflict (as they so often do in life) the observer's behavior is affected jointly by both sources e.g., Mischel & Liebert, 1966; Rosenhan & White, 1967). Thus modeled standards for behavior are most likely to be adopted when they are consistent with the standards used by the model for himself as well as in his direct training. When there is a discrepancy between what is practiced and what is preached, observers are more likely to adopt for themselves the least stringent available standards for behavior. Mischel and Liebert (1966), for example, found that when models imposed stringent standards for behavior upon children and displayed similarly rigorous standards in their own self-evaluation, all children subsequently adopted those high standards without exception. But when the adults permitted and encouraged lenient standards in the children, the youngsters subsequently were uniformly lenient with themselves, even when the models had been stringent in their own standards.

After the person has set his standards (terminal goals) for conduct in a particular situation, the path toward their realization may be long and difficult. If so, progress may be mediated importantly by symbolic activities, such as praise and self-instructions, as the person achieves sub-goals en route. When reinforcing and noxious stimuli are imagined, their behavioral consequences may be the same as when such stimuli are presented externally (e.g., Cautela, 1971). Such covert activities help maintain goal-directed work until the performance reaches or exceeds the person's terminal standards (e.g., Meichenbaum, 1971). Progress toward goal attainment also may be aided by self-generated distractions and cognitive operations through which the person can transform the aversive 'self-control' situation into one which he can master effectively (e.g., Mischel, Ebbesen, & Zeiss, 1972; Mischel & Moore, 1973; Mischel, Moore, & Zeiss, 1976). When important goals are attained, positive self-appraisal and self-reinforcement tend to occur, whereas the individual may indulge in psychological self-lacerations and self-condemnation if he fails to reach significant self-imposed standards.

People can readily perform *cognitive transformations* on stimuli (Mischel, 1974), focusing on selected aspects of the objective stimulus; such selective attention, interpretation and categorization may substantially influence how any stimulus effects their behavior. The significant role of cognitive transformations in self-regulation is demonstrated in research on the determinants of how long preschool children will actually sit still alone in a chair, waiting for a preferred but delayed outcome, before they signal with a bell to terminate the waiting period and settle for a less preferred but immediately available gratification (e.g., Mischel, Ebbesen, & Zeiss, 1972; Mischel, 1974). The findings showed that the same child who on one occasion terminates his waiting in less than half a minute, may be capable of waiting by himself for long periods, on another occasion a few weeks earlier or later, if cognitive and attentional conditions are conducive to delay.

Research on cognitive transformations during delay also helps to clarify the role of *attention in self-control.* Almost a century ago William James noted a relationship between attention and self-control, and contended that attentional processes are the crux of the self-control phenomena usually subsumed under the label 'will' (or, since James' time, under the concept 'ego strength'). In James' words, 'Attention with effort is all that any case of volition implies. The essential achievement of will is to attend to a difficult object...' (1890, p. 549). Beginning with the research of Hartshorne and May (1928) some correlations have been found between indices of moral behavior and measures of attention or resistance to distraction on mental tests (e.g., Grim, Kohlberg, & White, 1968). Such correlations have led to the suggestion that a person's ability to resist temptation may be facilitated by how well he attends to a task. 'Yielding to temptation' (e.g., cheating) in most experimental paradigms hinges on the subject's becoming distracted from the main task to which he is supposed to be attending. In such paradigms a subject's ability to focus attention on the task and to resist distraction automatically may make it easier for him to resist such temptations as cheating.

Investigations of the role of attention during delay of gratification, however, revealed another relationship: *not* attending to the goal (potential reward) was what facilitated self-control most dramatically (e.g., Mischel, Ebbesen, & Zeiss, 1972). More detailed analyses of attentional mechanisms during delay of gratification showed that the crucial variable is not whether or not the subject attends to the goal objects while delaying but, rather, *how* he focuses on them (Mischel, 1974). It was found that through instructions the child can cognitively transform the reward objects that face him during the delay period in ways that either permit or prevent effective delay of gratification. For example, if the child is left during the waiting period with the actual reward objects (e.g., pretzels or marshmallows) in front of him, it becomes difficult for him to wait for more than a few moments. But through instructions he can cognitively transform the reward objects in ways that permit him to wait for long time periods (e.g., Mischel & Baker, 1975). If he cognitively transforms the stimulus to focus on its nonarousing qualities, for example, by thinking about the pretzel sticks at little brown logs, or by thinking about the marshmallows as round white clouds or as cotton balls, he may be able to wait for long time periods. Conversely, if the child has been instructed to focus cognitively on the consummatory (arousing, motivating) qualities of the reward objects, such as the pretzel's crunchy, salty taste or the chewy, sweet soft taste of the marshmallows, he tends to be able to wait only a short time (Mischel, 1974).

Likewise, through instruction the children can easily transform the real objects (present in front of them) into a 'color picture in your head', or they can transform the picture of the objects (presented on a slide projected on a screen in front of them) into the 'real' objects by pretending in imagination that they are actually there on a plate in front of them (Moore, Mischel, & Zeiss, 1976). And it is what is in the children's heads—not what is physically in front of them—that determines their ability to delay. Regardless of the stimulus in their visual field, if they imagine the real objects as present they cannot wait long for them. But if they imagine pictures (abstract representations) of the objects they can wait for long time periods (and even longer than when they are simply distracting themselves with abstract representations of objects that are comparable but not relevant to the rewards for which they are waiting). Through instructions about what to imagine during the delay period, it is possible to completely alter (even to reverse) the effects of the physically present reward stimuli in the situation, and to cognitively control delay behavior. But while in experiments the experimenter provides instructions (which the subject often obligingly follows) about how to construe the stimulus situation, in life the 'subject' supplies his own instructions and may transform the situation in many alternative ways. By knowig the relevant rules of cognitive transformation, and utilizing them during self-control efforts, individuals may be able to attain considerable mastery in pursuit of their goals even in the face of strong countervailing situational pressures.

Self-regulatory behaviors also may involve 'priority rules' for determining the *sequencing* of behavior and 'stop rules' for the *termination* of a particular sequence of behavior. Self-control behaviors, like other complex human actions, depend on execution of lengthy, interlocking sequences of thought and action. The concept of 'plans' as hierarchical processes which control the order in which an organism performs a sequence of operations (Miller, Galanter, &

Pribram, 1960) seems applicable. Introspectively, we do seem to generate plans. And once a plan is formed and adopted (to give a paper, to take a vacation, to join a political protest movement) a whole series of sub-routines follows. While the concept of plans is intuitively plausible, it has not yet led to the necessary personality-oriented cognitive research. Helpful first steps toward the study of plans are the concepts of behavioral intentions (Dulany, 1962), intention statements and contracts (e.g., Kanfer et al., 1974), and 'scripts' (Abelson, 1976). Self-instructions and intention statements are likely to be important aspects of the individual's plans and the hierarchical organization of his self-regulatory behavior. Recent research suggests that even young children are capable of using plans to greatly facilitate self-control, for example in efforts to sustain goal-directed work in the face of competing distractions and temptations (e.g., Patterson & Mischel, 1975, 1976).

In sum, the exercise of self-control depends on the individual's self-regulatory systems, which include: the rules that specify goals or performance standards in particular situations; the expected consequences of achieving or failing to achieve those criteria; self-instructions and cognitive stimulus transformations to achieve the self-control necessary for goal attainment; and organizing rules (plans) for the sequencing and termination of complex behavioral patterns in the absence of external supports and, indeed, in the face of external obstacles.

C. INCREASING SELF-CONTROL

In recent years psychologists have recognized increasingly that effective therapy programs often depend on enhancing the client's self-control directly. Most behavior change programs now attempt to increase the individual's independence and competence as rapidly as possible so that external control of his behavior by the therapeutic regime can be reduced quickly and ultimately terminated. Many techniques can help to achieve that objective (e.g., Bandura, 1969). For example, although carefully dispensed external reinforcement (like tokens or praise) may be necessary at first to help a disturbed child learn to speak, read, and write, the satisfactions deriving from these new activities, once they begin to be mastered, should help him to maintain and develop them further, even when the therapist's help is gradually withdrawn. Similarly, while a hospitalized psychiatric patient may require tokens to initiate more adaptive new behavior, such as rehabilitative work, ultimately the new behaviors themselves, if properly selected, should provide him with enough gratifying consequences so that he can maintain his new gains on his own. In other words, the new, more advantageous behaviors, which the person first practices to get 'external' reinforcement, should be chosen to have reinforcing properties that gradually make them rewarding in their own right.

These examples also mirror the gradual shift from external to internal control in the acquisition of new but difficult skills outside the therapeutic situation under the conditions of daily life. The young child who is learning to play the piano may at first be highly dependent on praise, attention, threats, and parental guidance to induce him to practice. However, to the extent that his learning program is structured effectively (by design or accident), his piano practice will be increasingly supported by the pleasure of the activity (e.g., the sounds he produces, and the satisfactions and 'sense of competence' he starts to derive from playing). If the learning experience is successful, then in time the child 'wants to play' and 'loves the piano'. This transition, subjectively, seems to involve a shift from performing to please others to performing to please oneself, a transition from behavior for the sake of the 'extrinsic' rewards it yields to behavior or 'its own sake'—that is, for 'intrinsic rewards'. Depending on social learning conditions, the behavior that offers the intrinsic rewards for which people strive may range from painting miniatures to racing sports cars, from playing the flute to wrestling, from climbing rocks to yoga exercises, from lifting weights to writing papers about the self. Thus whether or not an activity becomes intrinsically rewarding may have less to do with the activity than with the manner in which it was learned and the conditions influencing its performance. Often in the course of socialization the conditions of learning inadvertently are poorly arranged. We see that fact in the frequency with which activities like piano practice or schoolwork become occasions for family quarrels rather than for pleasure.

Therapeutic efforts to improve self-management and self-regulation directly, especially in excessively impulsive individuals, are providing many different promising methods. These techniques, based mainly on learning concepts, make it possible for people to achieve much more self-directed behavior. Some good results have been found in areas that range from studying to the control of weight, smoking, and crippling fears (Watson & Tharp, 1972). A favorite technique provides the person with 'controlling responses' that help him to resist the pressures of the situation and to pursue, instead, his more difficult but desired objectives. Controlling responses include various self-instructions designed to sustain the individual's continued work and effort even under difficult conditions (e.g., Kanfer & Zich, 1974; Meichenbaum & Goodman, 1971). For example, young children are helped to resist transgression if they are first given a verbalization (such as 'I must not turn around and look at the toy') to repeat to themselves later when they are alone and faced by the temptation (Hartig & Kanfer, 1973). Likewise, anxious individuals may be helped to cope by learning and practicing calming, problem-solving self-instructions which they can verbalize to themselves when faced with stressful situations (e.g., Meichenbaum & Cameron, 1974).

IV. The 'Self' in Self-Control

We have surveyed examples of self-control, the organization of self-control, and some of the variables that influence its genesis. Now let us consider, at least briefly, the nature of the 'self' that is exerting control, in light of the empirical research sketched earlier.

A. THE SELF AS THE PERSON

The concept of 'self' makes most psychologists highly ambivalent. On the positive side, they appreciate the subjective reality of the experienced 'self'. Beyond infancy, each of us seems 'aware of himself', at least some of the time, and each mature person discriminates between the self, perceived as a distinct entity, and the rest of the world. This perceived identity, this self-consciousness, seems to be a basic human experience whose loss may be seen as no less than a loss of 'reality' itself.

But on the negative side, many psychologists (ourselves included) are reluctant to create a self as an extra causal agent that dwells in the person and somehow generates or causes behavior in ways that are separable from the organism in which 'it' resides. They are troubled, for example, by a self like this one hypothesized by Carl Rogers:

> ... when the self is free from any threat of attack or likelihood of attack, then it is possible for the self to consider these hitherto rejected perceptions, to make new differentiations, and to reintegrate the self in such a way as to include them (Rogers, 1947, p. 365).

It seems that for Rogers the self does not merely equal the 'me' or 'I' or 'ego'; it is rather a self distinct from the whole person and from what he or she does—it is even a self that can 'reintegrate the self'.

Many psychologists are not willing to give the self such extraordinary causal powers. As Gordon Allport noted years ago:

> To say that the self does this or that, wants this or that, wills this or that, is to beg a series of difficult questions. The psychologist does not like to pass the buck to a self-agent.... It is unwise to assign our problems to an inner agent who pulls the strings (Allport, 1961, pp. 129–30).

How can one avoid the traps of pseudo-explanations (into which the concept of a self as causal agent quickly leads) without throwing out the subjective reality of self-experience (self-awareness) and without neglecting the person who does the experiencing? A first step might be to fully equate such terms as the 'self', the 'I', and the 'ego', and to treat each as a synonym for the total individual. This equivalence should at least reduce the chance of being beguiled by 'explanatons' in which the 'self' is used to account for the individual's behavior, or in which a person's problems are seen as due to his 'weak ego'. Behavior is generated by the person, not by a self, ego, or other agent distinct from the individual. And 'self-control' refers to the powers of the person to regulate or control his own actions, thus overcoming the power of 'stimulus (situational) control'.

It is hardly unique to suggest equating the self and the person. Such diverse theorists as Skinner (1974) and Royce (1973) seem to agree on that point. As Royce put it:

The 'self' here is not a mental construct, but a living organism, a person. When I say that I cut myself shaving this morning, I do not mean that I cut a mental construct. Likewise, if you hit *me*, that 'I' who got hit is not some 'ego' of Freudian theory. We are talking here not about one's self-concept or self-image but about the existing reality. And this reality is the same referent when we say, 'I understand', or 'I choose' or 'I run' . . . The person or self, then, *is* the behaving organism (Royce, 1973, p. 885).

B. SELF-AWARENESS

Freud's impact has led to a widespread belief that some of the most basic aspects of oneself are likely to be unconscious and beyond the reach of awareness. In fact, little empirical research supports this belief and much contradicts it (e.g., Holmes, 1974; Mischel, 1976). Many psychologists are beginning to realize that if we do not stop our 'subjects' by asking the wrong questions, and if we provide appropriate structure, they often can tell us much about themselves directly. Of course what someone can tell us about himself will always be constrained by the limits of the individual's own awareness. Too often, however, psychologists have assumed that people were unaware when in fact they were simply being asked the wrong questions.

In the context of 'verbal conditioning', for example, careful inquiries suggest that subjects may be far more aware than was originally thought (e.g., Spielberger & DeNike, 1966). Similarly, while a belief in the prevalence of distortions from unconscious defenses such as repression is the foundation of psychodynamic assessment, the experimental evidence for the potency—and even the existence—of such mechanisms remains remarkably tenuous (e.g., Mischel, 1976). With regard to 'subception' and 'discrimination without awareness', for example, Eriksen (1960) argues, on the basis of much research, that 'a verbal report is as sensitive an indicator of perception as any other response that has been studied [p. 298]'—people have not been shown to be more sensitive in their autonomic reactions than in their verbal reports. Thus in laboratory research into unconscious responding, just as in the context of personality testing, what the person tells us directly turns out to be as valuable an index as any indirect signs (e.g., his galvanic skin responses). And in clinical contexts, the self-report competes well with (or excels) the clinical expert's best judgments (Mischel, 1968; Peterson, 1968) and the most sophisticated tests.

Even young children may have extensive awareness not only of themselves but of basic psychological principles. To explore such awareness, in some pilot work we have started to ask young children what they know about psychological principles about how plans can be made and followed most effectively, how long-term work problems can be organized, how delay of gratification can be mastered. We also ask them to tell us about what helps them to learn and (stimulated by Flavell) to remember. Although our results are still very tentative, we are most impressed by how much even young children know about functioning. To illustrate, our interviews suggest that even at age eight youngsters may be able to discuss 'plans' articulately and give good examples of when and how they use them to structure and organize their behavior (e.g., 'Tomorrow I'll clean up my room . . . next week I'm going to have a birthday party—if Mommy helps me . . .).

Children at ages nine and ten seem able to elaborate fairly complex self-instructional plans that they report using to control such problematic behaviors as their own aggression and reactions to frustration. For example: 'To control myself to not get so angry and mad and not hit so much I can just say (before I get into a fight) Now, Joanie, do you want to get hurt? No! Do you want to get hit? No! Do you want to get in trouble? No! So then, I don't hit as much 'cause I don't want to get hurt and everyone else is stronger than me'.

Another child says: 'I just think of Dad hitting me'. And another one comments: 'Sometimes when I'm real mad (but don't want to hurt someone else) I just hit myself instead. Or bang my head. Or slam a door. Or maybe ignore them. Or call a friend up. Or go on a walk. Or make a muscle big. And you kind of think, "I'm gonna get in trouble—this guy is not exactly a weakling".' In the same vein, another child notes: 'Instead of getting mad at the teacher you think—if I don't control myself next thing I'll be in the principal's office!'

By age ten, some children in our interviews seem to have well-developed ideas about the nature, organization, and function of plans in their own lives. They may distinguish, for instance, between the intentional aspect of a plan ('I'm planning to clean up my room tomorrow because I'm planning to have a friend over'), its informative function ('a plan tells you what to do and when and where and how to do it'), and its execution ('you have to make yourself do it when the time comes: planning is the part you do beforehand but then doing it is the actual right there part'.). At older ages, children seem aware of many strategies for forming and implementing effective plans (e.g., elaborate mental rehearsal, public commitment, externalizing the plan by sharing it with others, re-arranging and 'marking' the environment, using mnemonics, etc.).

Wth greater age, there also may be increasing reliance on a kind of cognitive 'short-hand' in which the formation and implementation of many complex plans may become more automatic, abbreviated, and rapid, without requiring extensive or explicit self-instructions for each step in an increasingly complex organizational hierarchy. As one eleven-year-old put it: 'If I had to teach a plan to someone who grew up in a jungle—like a plan to work on a project at 10 a.m. tomorrow—I'd tell him what to say to himself to make it easier at the start for him. Like "If I do this *plan* (emphasized word) on time I'll get a reward, and the teacher will like me and I'll be proud". But for myself, I know all that already so I don't have to say it to myself—besides it would take too long to say and my mind doesn't have the time for all that—so I just remember that stuff about why I should do it real quick without saying it—it's like a method that I know already in math; once you have the method you don't have to say every little step'.

Comments of this type suggest that even young children may be remarkably aware of some of their own information processing strategies, the 'space' limitations in activated memory, and other features of cognition. Note also that, unsurprisingly but reassuringly, the gist of natural plans to increase control generally seem congruent with findings from behavior modification efforts. Those findings show, for example, the value of giving clients controlling responses that are incompatible with the to-be-avoided behavior, and of providing a focus on the negative consequences of transgressions plus the positive consequences of self-control (e.g., Mahoney, 1974). The nature, development, and behavioral consequences of the individual's activity and control strategies certainly merit systematic attention, as the related explorations of Flavell and his associates on 'metamemory' attest (e.g., Kreutzer et al., 1975). At this point our pilot work is still at an early stage. Nevertheless, it already seems to lend some support to the view that even relatively young children may organize their behavior in terms of intentions and rules that they can at least partly verbalize and use to exert better control over their environment and themselves.

C. PERCEIVED CONSISTENCY AND BEHAVIORAL SPECIFICITY

It is widely assumed that the self—no matter how one defines it—is characterized by consistency and continuity. Indeed, the experience of subjective continuity in ourselves—of basic oneness and durability in the self—is perhaps the most compelling and fundamental feature of personality. Conversely, the loss of a sense of felt consistency may be a chief characteristic of personality disorganization.

Generally each person manages to reconcile his seemingly diverse behaviors into one self-consistent whole. People are skilled at transforming their seemingly discrepant behavior into a constructed continuity, making unified wholes out of almost anything. But how can one reconcile the widely shared perception of continuity in personality with the equally impressive evidence that behavior is highly discriminative and shows substantial changes when measured objectively even across seemingly similar settings? The voluminous evidence available on this topic of consistency and specificity (Mischel 1968), based on many sources (clinical, experimental, developmental, correlational), suggests that the mind functions like a remarkably effective reducing valve that creates and maintains the perception of continuity even in the face of perpetual observed changes in actual behavior. While this cognitive construction of continuity is not arbitrary, often it is only very tenuously and complexly related to the events that are construed.

Much evidence documents that our cognitive constructions about ourselves and the world—our personal theories about ourselves and those around us—tend to be extremely stable and resistant to change. Studies of the self-concept, of impression-formation in person perception and in clinical judgment, of cognitive sets guiding selective attention—all these phenomena and many more document the consistency and tenacious continuity of many human construction systems (e.g., Chapman & Chapman, 1969; Mischel, 1968; Shweder, 1975). These construction systems often are built quickly and on the basis of little information (e.g., Kahneman & Tversky,

1973); but after they are established, they may become exceedingly difficult to disconfirm and discard even in the face of contradictory evidence.

When we go beyond cognitive and intellective dimensions to the domain of personality and interpersonal behavior, and when we observe behavior as it unfolds *in vivo* rather than as raters judge it from longterm memory, consistency evidence has proved surprisingly hard to find. On the basis of past research on this topic, one should no longer be surprised when the cross-situational consistency of behavior patterns turns out to be quite low. We cannot even start to cite here the extensive evidence indicating that noncognitive global personality dispositions are much less global than traditional personality theorists and commonsense have assumed them to be (Mischel, 1968). We already noted the relative specificity of various indices of self-control. That is hardly unique. A great deal of behavioral specificity also has been found regularly for such character traits as rigidity, social conformity, aggression, dependency, and on virtually any other non-intellective personality dimension (Vernon, 1964; Mischel, 1968; Peterson, 1968).

In sum, recognition of the existence of sharp discriminativeness in behavior must be coupled with the realization that consistent impressions are constructed easily about generalized characteristics. People invoke stable dispositions as ways of summarizing, describing, and explaining behavior and tend to go easily beyond the analysis of specific actions to the attribution of generalized dispositions in the actors. In the process of categorizing information about the self and others, one tends to jump quickly from the observation of discrete acts to the inference of global internalized dispositions (Heider, 1958). Thus while behavior often may be highly situation specific, it also appears that in daily life people tend to construe each other as if they were highly consistent, constructing consistent selves even on the basis of relatively inconsistent behavioral fragments, readily perceiving unity in the face of behavioral specificity and discriminativeness.

D. WHERE IS THE LOCUS OF CAUSATION? PERSON-ENVIRONMENT INTERACTION

B. F. Skinner (1974) and other radical behaviorists make a point of avoiding 'pseudo-explanations' by refusing to invoke either the self or the person as a causal agent. Instead, they attribute the 'control' (cause) of behavior, including the behaviors in 'self-control', to the individual's environmental and genetic history. Such an extreme emphasis on the environment successfully avoids animism and 'ghosts', but it does so at considerable cost. It ignores the ways in which the individual *transforms* the environment psychologically, processing information about events selectively and constructively in light of his or her own psychological state, monitoring his own behavior, and intervening actively between the impinging stimulus and the response that is ultimately generated. It also ignores the fact that behavior reflects a continuous *interaction* between person and conditions rather than a one-way influence process in which the environment molds the person (Mischel, 1973).

Skinner argues passionately for the significance of the environment, and specifically the 'contingencies of reinforcement' as determinants of human behavior. But the credibility of his position seems undermined by his extreme neglect of the interaction between person and environment, revealed in glaring oversimplifications like this:

> Whatever we do, and hence however we perceive it, the fact remains that it is the environment which acts upon the perceiving person, not the perceiving person who acts upon the environment (Skinner, 1971, p. 188).

These curious assertions bolster the stereotype that behaviorally-oriented psychologists lose the person in a one-sided focus on the environment. In Skinner's case the stereotype may fit: the charge of 'situationism in psychology' (Bowers, 1973) seems justified when the environment is depicted as molding man without recognition that man acts on the environment; indeed, much of the effective human environment consists of people, not of things or of a contingency-generating apparatus. Skinner's occasional claim for the one-way impact of the environment on the person creates a bizarre schism in which the individual's capacity to change the environment (which, curiously, seems a fundamental feature of his original concept of 'operant' behavior) is somehow denied.

Such environmental extremism encourages critics to charge that in recent years psychology has been overemphasizing the importance of the environment and the situation while underemphasizing—or even, 'losing'—the person (e.g., Bowers, 1973; Carlson, 1971). Bowers (1973, p. 307) attacks a 'situationism' that emphasizes situations as the causes of behavior while 'being inattentive to the importance of the person'. Situationism is defined as an explanatory bias that tends 'either to ignore organismic factors or to regard them as... subsidiary to the primary impact of the external stimulus' (Harré & Secord, 1972, p. 27).

Closely paralleling the charge of 'situationism' is the humanistic protest against the behavioral (experimental?) approach in general. The essence of the humanistic protest is that behaviorally-oriented psychologists (i.e., 'situationists') treat and manipulate man as if he were externally controlled rather than a free, self-determining being responsible for his own actions and growth. Some of these criticisms and charges seem justified objections against a simplistic environmentalism (e.g., B. F. Skinner, 1974). The characteristics of the environment interact with the people in it, and it would be hazardous to ignore either side of this interaction.

While psychologists must recognize the importance of environmental determinants, it would be unreasonable to make the environment *the* determinant; similarly, it is essential to recognize each individual as an active determinant of behavior, but unreasonably pre-emptive to make the individual *the* determinant. To look for *the* locus of control in either person *or* environment risks obscuring their continuous dynamic interaction. To present causal powers either for the person or for the environment exclusively also seems to guarantee incomplete explanations and assures an exercise in futility.

E. SOME ATTRIBUTES OF THE SELF

To try to summarize the basic gist and implications of psychological research about self-control is to attempt the impossible. The research is too diverse, the range of alternative interpretations too large, to achieve a fair summary. But we can comment on one or two of the themes that strike us as especially important.

One of these themes probably holds little surprise for philosophers but still is controversial among many psychologists. This theme is that the human being is an active, self-aware problem-solver, capable of changing himself and achieving substantial self-control through the application of rational principles to a much greater degree than has usually been supposed in psychology. This theme conflicts with the image of man as the passive victim of his own unconscious impulses, trapped by biography and circumstances, capable only of superficial change (except through long-term therapy) that has been dominant in our field. In our view, research on the self and self-control also leads to an image of the person as multiply influenced by a host of internal and external determinants and as idiosyncratically organized on the basis of past experience and future expectancies, defying efforts to classify him on any single or simple common dimensions, including a dimension of self-control.

REFERENCES

ABELSON, R. P. Script processing in attitude formation and decision making. In J. S. Carroll and J. W. Payne (eds.), *Cognition and social behavior*. Erlbaum, 1976.

ALLINSMITH, W. The learning of moral standards. In D. R. Miller and G. E. Swanson (eds.), *Inner conflict and defense*. New York: Holt, Rinehart & Winston, 1960, pp. 141–76.

ALLPORT, G. W. *Pattern and growth in personality*. New York: Holt, Rinehart and Winston, 1961.

ANDERSON, J. R. & BOWER, G. H. *Human associative memory*. New York: Wiley, 1973.

ANDERSON, N. H. Information integration theory: A brief survey. *Center for Human Information Processing* (technical report no. 24), University of California, San Diego, 1972.

ARONFREED, J. The nature, variety, and social patterning of moral responses to transgression. *Journal of Abnormal and Social Psychology*, 1961, **63**, 223–40.

ARONFREED, J. The origin of self-criticism. *Psychological Review*, 1964, **71**, 193–218.

ARONFREED, J. *Conduct and conscience: The socialization of internalized control over behavior*. New York: Academic Press, 1968.

ARONFREED, J., & REBER, A. Internalized behavioral suppression and the timing of social punishment. *Journal of Personality and Social Psychology*, 1965, **1**, 3–16.

BANDURA, A. *Principles of behavior modification*. New York: Holt, Rinehart and Winston, 1969.

BANDURA, A. Analysis of modeling processes. In A. Bandura (ed.),

Psychological modeling: Conflicting theories. Chicago: Aldine-Atherton, 1971.

Bandura, A., & Kupers, C. J. Transmission of patterns of self-reinforcement through modeling. *Journal of Abnormal and Social Psychology*, 1964, **69**, 1–9.

Bandura, A., & Mischel, W. Modification of self-imposed delay of reward through exposure to live and symbolic models. *Journal of Personality and Social Psychology*, 1965, **2**, 698–705.

Bandura, A., & Perloff, B. Relative efficacy of self-monitored and externally imposed reinforcement systems. *Journal of Personality and Social Psychology*, 1967, **7**, 111–16.

Bandura, A. & Whalen, C. K. The influence of antecedent reinforcement and divergent modeling cues on patterns of self-reward. *Journal of Personality and Social Psychology*, 1966, **3**, 373–82.

Becker, W. C. Consequences of different kinds of parental discipline. In M. L. Hoffman and L. W. Hoffman (eds.), *Review of Child Development Research*, **1**, New York: Russell Sage Foundation, 1964, 169–208.

Bowers, K. Situationism in psychology: An analysis and a critique. *Psychological Review*, 1973, **80**, 307–36.

Burton, R. V., Maccoby, E. E., & Allinsmith, W. Antecedents of resistance to temptation in four-year-old children. *Child Development*, 1961, **32**, 689–710.

Carlson, R. Where is the person in personality research? *Psychological Bulletin*, 1971, **75**, 203–19.

Cautela, J. R. Covert conditioning. In A. Jacoby & L. B. Sachs (eds.), *The psychology of private events*. New York: Academic Press, 1971, 112–30.

Chapman, L. J. & Chapman, J. P. Illusory correlations as an obstacle to the use of valid psychodiagnostic signs. *Journal of Abnormal Psychology*, 1969, **74**, 271–80.

Dulany, D. E., Jr. The place of hypotheses and intentions: An analysis of verbal control in verbal conditioning. In C. W. Eriksen (ed.), *Behavior and awareness*. Durham, N.C.: Duke University Press, 1962, 102–29.

Eriksen, C. W. Discrimination and learning without awareness: A methodological survey and evaluation. *Psychological Review*, 1960, **67**, 279–300.

Festinger, L. A theory of social comparison processes. *Human Relations*, 1954, **7**, 117–40.

Grim, P. F., Kohlberg, L., & White, S. H. Some relationships between conscience and attentional processes. *Journal of Personality and Social Psychology*, 1968, **8**, 239–52.

Grinder, R. E. Parental childrearing practices, conscience, and resistance to temptation of sixth-grade children. *Child Development*, 1962, **33**, 803–20.

Grinder, R. E. Relations between behavioral and cognitive dimensions of conscience in middle childhood. *Child Development*, 1964, **35**, 881–91.

Grusec, J. Some antecedents of self-criticism. *Journal of Personality and Social Psychology*, 1966, **4**, 244–52.

Harré, R., & Secord, P. F. *The explanation of social behavior. Oxford*: Basil Blackwell, 1972.

Hartig, M., & Kanfer, F. H. The role of verbal self-instructions in children's resistance to temptation. *Journal of Personality and Social Psychology*, 1973, **25**, 259–67.

Hartshorne, H., & May, M. A. *Studies in deceit.* New York: MacMillan, 1928.

Heider, F. *The psychology of interpersonal relations.* New York: Wiley, 1958.

Helson, H. *Adaptation-level theory.* New York: Harper & Row, 1964.

Hoffman, M. L. Child rearing practices and moral development: Generalizations from empirical research. *Child Development.* 1963, **34**, 295–318.

Holmes, D. S. Investigations of repression: Differential recall of material experimentally or naturally associated with ego threat. *Psychological Bulletin*, 1974, **81**, 632–53.

Isen, A., Horn, & Rosenhan, D. L. Effects of success and failure on children's generosity. *Journal of Personality and Social Psychology*, 1973, **27**, 239–47.

James, W. *Principles of psychology.* New York: Holt, Rinehart and Winston, 1890.

Johnson, R. C. A study of children's moral judgments. *Child Development*, 1962, **33**, 327–54.

Kahneman, D., & Tversky, A. On the psychology of prediction. *Psychological Review*, 1973, **80**, 237–51.

Kamiya, J. Conditioned introspection. Paper read at the Institute of Personality Assessment and Research, University of California, Berkeley, 1967.

Kanfer, F. H. The maintenance of behavior by self-generated stimuli and reinforcement. In A. Jacobs & L. B. Sachs (eds.), *Psychology of private events.* New York: Academic Press, 1971.

Kanfer, F. H., Cox, L. E., Greiner, J. M., & Karoly, P. Contracts, demand characteristics and self-control. *Journal of Personality and Social Psychology*, 1974, **30**, 605–19.

KANFER, F. H., & MARSTON, A. R. Determinants of self-reinforcement in human learning. *Journal of Experimental Psychology*, 1963, **66**, 245–54. (a)

KANFER, F. H., & MARSTON, A. R. Conditioning of self-reinforcing responses: An analogue to self-confidence training. *Psychological Reports*, 1963, **13**, 63–70. (b)

KANFER, F. H., & PHILLIPS, J. S. *Learning foundations of behavior therapy*. New York: Wiley, 1970.

KANFER, F. H., & ZICH, J. Self-control training: The effects of external control on children's resistance to temptation. *Developmental Psychology*, 1974, **10**, 108–15.

KELLY, G. A. *The psychology of personal constructs*, Vols. 1 & 2. New York: Norton, 1955.

KLINEBERG, S. L. Future time perspective and the preference for delayed reward. *Journal of Personality and Social Psychology*, 1968, **8**, 253–57.

KOHLBERG, L. The development of children's orientations toward a moral order: I. Sequence in the development of moral thought. *Vita Humana*, 1963, **6**, 11–33.

KOHLBERG, L. Stage and sequence: The cognitive-developmental approach to socialization. In D. A. Goslen (ed.), *Handbook of socialization theory and research*. Chicago: Rand McNally, 1969, 347–480.

KREUTZER, M. A., LEONARD, C., & FLAVELL, J. H. An interview study of children's knowledge about memory. *Monographs of the Society for Research in Child Development*, 1975, **40** (serial no. 159).

KURTINES, W., & GREIF, E. G. The development of moral thought: Review and evaluation of Kohlberg's approach. *Psychological Bulletin*, 1974, **81**, 453–70.

MACKINNON, D. W. Violation of prohibitions. In H. A. Murray et al., (eds.), *Explorations in personality*. New York: Oxford University Press, 1938, pp. 491–501.

MAHONEY, M. J. *Cognition and behavior modification*. Cambridge, Mass.: Ballinger, 1974.

MASTERS, J. C., & MOKROS, J. R. Self-reinforcement processes in children. In H. Reese (ed.), *Advances in child development and behavior*, 9, New York: Academic Press, 1974.

MEICHENBAUM, D. H. Cognitive factors in behavior modification: Modifying what clients say to themselves. Research Report No. 25, University of Waterloo, Canada, July 23, 1971.

MEICHENBAUM, D., & CAMERON, R. The clinical potential of modifying what clients say to themselves. In M. J. Mahoney & C. E. Thoresen (eds.), *Self-control: Power to the person*. Monterey, Calif.: Brooks-Cole, 1974.

MEICHENBAUM, D. H., & GOODMAN, J. Training impulsive children to talk to themselves: A means of developing self-control. *Journal of Abnormal Psychology*, 1971, **77**, 115–26.

MILLER, N. E. Learning of visceral and glandular responses. *Science*, 1969, **163**, 434–45.

MILLER, G. A., GALANTER, E., & PRIBRAM, K. H. *Plans and structure of behavior*. New York: Holt, Rinehart and Winston, 1960.

MISCHEL, W. Preference for delayed and immediate reinforcement: An experimental study of a cultural observation. *Journal of Abnormal and Social Psychology*, 1958, **56**, 57–61.

MISCHEL, W. Delay of gratification, need for achievement and acquiescence in another culture. *Journal of Abnormal and Social Psychology*, 1961, **62**, 543–52. (a)

MISCHEL, W. Preference for delayed reinforcement and social responsibility. *Journal of Abnormal and Social Psychology*, 1961, **62**, 1–7. (b)

MISCHEL, W. Father absence and delay of gratification: Cross-cultural comparisons. *Journal of Abnormal and Social Psychology*, 1961, **63**, 116–124. (c)

MISCHEL, W. Theory and research on the antecedents of self-imposed delay of reward. In B. A. Maher (ed.), *Progress in experimental personality research*, **3**. New York: Academic Press, 1966, 85–132.

MISCHEL, W. *Personality and assessment*. New York: Wiley, 1968.

MISCHEL, W. Specificity theory and the construction of personality. APA Address of the Chairman, Section III, Development of Clinical Psychology as an Experimental-Behavioral Science, Washington, D.C., September, 1971.

MISCHEL, W. Toward a cognitive social learning reconceptualization of personality. *Psychological Review*, 1973, **80**, 252–83.

MISCHEL, W. Processes in delay of gratification. In L. Berkowitz (ed.), *Advances in experimental social psychology*, vol. **7**. New York: Academic Press, 1974.

MISCHEL, W. *Introduction to personality* (2nd ed.). New York: Holt, Rinehart and Winston, 1976.

MISCHEL, W., & BAKER, N. Cognitive appraisals and transformations in delay behavior. *Journal of Personality and Social Psychology*, 1975, **31**, 254–61.

MISCHEL, W., COATES, B., & RASKOFF, A. Effects of success and failure on self-gratification. *Journal of Personality and Social Psychology*, 1968, **10**, 381–90.

MISCHEL, W., EBBESEN, E. B., & ZEISS, A. R. Cognitive and attentional mechanisms in delay of gratification. *Journal of Personality and Social Psychology*, 1972, **21**, 204–18.

Mischel, W., Ebbesen, E. G., & Zeiss, A. R. Selective attention to the self: Situational and dispositional determinants. *Journal of Personality and Social Psychology*, 1973, **27**, 129–42.

Mischel, W., Ebbesen, E. B., & Zeiss, A. M. Determinants of selective memory about the self. *Journal of Consulting and Clinical Psychology*, 1976, **44**, 92–103.

Mischel, W., & Gilligan, C. Delay of gratification, motivation for the prohibited gratification, and resistance to temptation. *Journal of Abnormal and Social Psychology*, 1964, **69**, 411–17.

Mischel, W., & Liebert, R. M. Effects of discrepancies between observed and imposed reward criteria on their acquisition and transmission. *Journal of Personality and Social Psychology*, 1966, **3**, 45–53.

Mischel, W., & Mischel, H. N. A cognitive social learning approach to morality and self-regulation. In T. Lickona (ed.), *Morality: A handbook of moral behavior*. New York: Holt, Rinehart and Winston, 1976.

Mischel, W., & Moore, B. Effects of attention to symbolically-presented rewards on self-control. *Journal of Personality and Social Psychology*, 1973, **28**, 172–79.

Mischel, W., & Staub, E. Effects of expectancy on working and waiting for larger rewards. *Journal of Personality and Social Psychology*, 1965, **2**, 625–33.

Moore, B., Mischel, W., & Zeiss, A. Comparative effects of the reward stimulus and its cognitive representation in voluntary delay. *Journal of Personality and Social Psychology*, 1976, in press.

Moore, B., Underwood, B., & Rosenhan, D. L. Affect and altruism. *Developmental Psychology*, 1973, **27**, 129–42.

Neisser, U. *Cognitive psychology*. New York: Appleton-Century-Crofts, 1967.

Patterson, C. J., & Mischel, W. Plans to resist distraction. *Developmental Psychology*, 1975, **11**, 369–78.

Patterson, C. J., & Mischel, W. Effects of temptation-inhibiting and task-facilitating plans on self-control. *Journal of Personality and Social Psychology*, 1976, **33**, 209–17.

Peterson, D. R. *The clinical study of social behavior*. New York: Appleton, 1968.

Piaget, J. *The construction of reality in the child*. New York: Basic Books, 1954.

Piaget, J. Piaget's theory. In P. H. Mussen (ed.), *Carmichael's manual of child psychology*. New York: Wiley, 1970.

Rogers, C. R. Some observations on the organization of personality. *American Psychologist*, 1947, **2**, 358–68.

Rosenhan, D. L., Moore, B., & Underwood, B. The social psychology of moral behavior. In T. Lickona (ed.), *Morality: A handbook of moral behavior*. New York: Holt, Rinehart and Winston, 1976.

ROSENHAN, D. L., & WHITE, G. M. Observation and rehearsal as determinants of prosocial behavior. *Journal of Personality and Social Psychology*, 1967, **5**, 424–31.

ROTTER, J. B. *Social learning and clinical psychology*. Englewood Cliffs, N. J.: Prentice Hall, 1954.

ROTTER, J. B. Beliefs, social attitudes, and behavior: A social learning analysis. In J. B. Rotter, J. E. Change, and E. J. Phares (eds.), *Applications of a social learning theory of personality*. New York: Holt, Rinehart and Winston, 1972.

ROYCE, J. E. Does person or self imply dualism? *American Psychologist*, 1973, **28**, 833–66.

RUMELHART, D. E., LINDSAY, P. H., & NORMAN, D. A. process model for long-term memory. *Center for Human Information Processing* (technical report no. 17), University of California, San Diego, 1971.

SCHACHTER, S., & SINGER, J. E. Cognitive, social, and physiological determinants of emotional state. *Psychological Review*, 1962, **69**, 379–99.

SEARS, R. R., MACCOBY, E. E., & LEVIN, H. *Patterns of child rearing*. New York: Harper, 1957.

SEARS, R. R., RAU, L., & ALPERT, R. *Identification and child rearing*. Stanford, Calif.: Stanford University Press, 1965.

SHWEDER. R. A. How relevant is an individual difference theory of personality? *Journal of Personality*, 1975, **43**, 455–84.

SKINNER, B. F. *Beyond freedom and dignity*. New York: Knopf, 1971.

SKINNER, B. F. *About behaviorism*. New York: Knopf, 1974.

SPIELBERGER, D. C., & DENIKE, L. D. Descriptive behaviorism versus cognitive theory in verbal operant conditioning. *Psychological Review*, 1966, **73**, 306–26.

STOYVA, J., & KAMIYA, J. Electro-physiological studies of dreaming as the prototype of a new strategy in the study of consciousness. *Psychological Review*, 1968, **75**, 192–205.

STUMPHAUZER, J. S. Increased delay of gratification in young prison inmates through imitation of high delay peer models. *Journal of Personality and Social Psychology*, 1972, **21**, 10–17.

VERNON, P. E. *Personality assessment: A critical survey*. New York: Wiley, 1964.

WATSON, D. L., & THARP, R. G. *Self-directed behavior: Self-modification for personal adjustment*. Belmont, Calif.: Wadsworth, 1972.

3 Self-Intervention and the Structure of Motivation

WILLIAM P. ALSTON

A number of years ago a philosopher named B. A. G. Fuller wrote an article with the memorable title 'The Messes Animals Make in Metaphysics'. My topic in this paper will be the messes the self makes in motivation—how an otherwise neat model of motivation is rendered untidy by the necessity to take account of the ways in which the self enters into the picture.

I

First, though, I must clear the air a bit. The terms 'self', 'ego' and the like have figured in much loose talk in American psychology in the past few decades. The talk radiates from two main concerns: (1) the ways in which a person integrates his varied cognitions, desires, aversions, standards, attitudes, etc., into a more or less unified whole; (2) the ways in which a person becomes an object of his own perceptions, conceptions, beliefs, evaluations, judgments, desires and attitudes. These are important aspects of human life and will be recognized by any adequate psychology. But their discussion has been bedeviled by terminological and conceptual confusions that are easily avoided by the exercise of what Bertrand Russell called a 'robust sense of reality'.

Perhaps the main source of confusion has been an exaggerated fear of homunculi. It is all too easy to postulate a little man inside who does the integration and the self-observing. Freudian theory, among others, has come dangerously close to succumbing to this temptation. But in overreaction to such excesses, self-theorists have tended to deny, or at least ignore, the fact that there *is* an agent that does the integrating as well as the perceiving, the thinking, the desiring, the fearing, and so on—viz., the *person*, the *human being* whose behavior, thought, and feeling is being studied. To be sure, there is no ego or self that acts as an entity distinct from the remainder of the personality (Allport, 1955), but there is a self that *is* the person. That is who my-self is—me, W. P. Alston, the man writing these lines. If you know who he is, if you can identify him, pick him out from his surroundings, you have identified the agent of his perceivings, strivings, and fearings, *and* of his 'integrations' and other 'ego-activities'.

I would not waste your time with such platitudes were it not that their neglect has seriously confused discussion of the important phenomena mentioned above. In particular, the homunculus-taboo has led may theorists to *identify* the 'self' with a person's cognitions or evaluations of himself, or attitudes to himself. The self is 'an organized, fluid, but consistent conceptual pattern of perceptions of characteristics and relationships of the 'I' or the 'me', together with values attached to these concepts'. (Rogers, 1951, p. 498. See also Symonds, 1951, Syngg and Combs, 1949, Sherif and Cantril, 1947, Hilgard, 1949, Chein, 1944, Murphy, 1947). It may be said that this is merely a terminological matter, that these thinkers are merely exercising their rightful perogative in using the word 'self' for what we may, and they do, otherwise call the self-concept and self-evaluation. Even that would be bad enough. Surely it can only breed confusion to identify *my self* with my conception of *myself*. As if separating the morphemes could make the difference between subject and object! But behind the confusing terminology is the fact that fearing the inner agent, yet feeling a need for a 'self', these theorists have seized on the person's self-concept as a substitute, not noting that in order to explain their concept of a self-concept they are forced to employ the very concept of the (real, unitary) agent they are misguidedly seeking to avoid. Thus Rogers, as we have seen, explains his 'self' as a pattern of perceptions of the 'I' or 'me', whereas Murphy (1947, p. 996) speaks of the 'individual as known to the individual', and Hilgard of 'ones image of himself'. By putting 'I' and 'me' in shudder quotes Rogers does not alter the fact that the object of the perceptions with which he is concerned is nothing more or less than our old friend—the person, the human being—whose behavior we are engaged in studying. And the same can be said of the 'individual' that is the object of self-conception and the 'himself' that plays a similar role for Hilgard. Self-perception, -conception, and -evaluation is a very important aspect of human life, but we only darken counsel by confusing the conception with the conceived.

Sometimes the implicit denial that it is I that am my self is made explicit, as when Sherif and Cantril (1947, p. 4) say: 'apart from the constellation of these ego-attitudes there is no such entity as the ego'. But more often there is some recognition that cognitions and attitudes do not float in a void. However, this recognition is often expressed in ways that lead to further confusions. Thus a distinction is drawn between 'self-as-object' and 'self-as-doer'. (Hall & Lindzey, 1957) But this terminology misleadingly suggests that these are two different entities. Whereas the self (person) I perceive, when I perceive myself (!) is, obviously, the same as the self (person) that is doing the perceiving. This is not to deny that my perceptions or conceptions of myself may be inaccurate. But when they are inaccurate cognitions *of* myself, it is the same self that is doing the cognizing.[1]

Again, the 'self-as-doer' is sometimes conceptualized as a 'group of processes', like perceiving, thinking, remembering, and planning (Symonds, 1951) or a 'motivational-cognitive structure' (Chein, 1944). Here, again, in overreaction to the *inner* agent, one has shied away from any agent and left the thoughts without a thinker.

By contrast with these confusions I would like to suggest that our commonsense conceptual scheme provides a sound, unconfused way of talking about these matters. In our ordinary thought we make no distinction between the self, the person, the man/woman, the human being, etc. In fact, we have an indefinitely large repertoire of devices for referring to what we regard as one and the same entity—Wolfgang Amadeus Mozart, the composer of Don Giovanni, the son of Leopold Mozart of Salzburg, my favorite composer, and so on. Furthermore each of these phrases picks out the man, Mozart, the person Mozart, the human being Mozart. It would, of course, be unnatural to speak of the 'self Mozart'. But if Mozart were to catch himself loafing on the job, compliment himself on a good

[1] To be sure, there is a sense of object in which the object of self-perception may differ from the subject of that perception. If I see a wall in the distance, taking it to be a road, in one sense the object of my perception is the wall, in another sense the object is the way the wall appears to me (as a road). It is in the first sense that subject and object are always the same in self-perception.

piece of work, upbraid himself for letting an opportunity slip by, or take himself to be a competent musician, the entity to which he has directed these catchings, upbraidings, etc., is just the same as the one to whom we were referring with the above phrases. Surely when Mozart upbraids *himself*, the object of his reproaches is the same as it would be if I were upbraiding the composer of Don Giovanni. If not, one of us is under a serious misapprehension. The term 'self' (usually in compounds) is used for a person when *that person* is being spoken of as the object of a self-directed cognition, action, or attitude. The 'self' of whom we speak in everyday discourse is in no way to be distinguished from the individual man, and is no more problematical. If we know who (what) we are talking about when we use a proper name or other designation of a human being, we are in possession of all we need to talk about a self.

So my point is that there is no need to postulate any mysterious inner agent in order to attribute the various inner and outer doings, functions, and characteristics of a person to *something*. We simply attribute them to the same familiar agent we are accustomed to attribute them to in daily life. Nor is this orientation alien to psychology. Psychologists have as firm a grasp of this conceptual scheme, and use it as unhesitatingly, as anyone else. When they are investigating a certain person's perceptions, repressions, ego-strength, self-judgments, fantasies, thought processes, delay of gratification, or whatever, they find it unproblematic to attribute all these to one and the same entity, the same one they can ostensively locate in a certain chair in a certain room. They are far from feeling that the experiment must be held up until they make sure that a certain choice should be attributed to the same subject as a certain belief. It is only when they come to theorize about self-judgment, self-control, or the integration of behavior, that psychologists lose their grip on these matters and begin to talk nonsense of the above sort. By maintaining our hold on the everyday conceptual scheme, we will avoid conceptual quagmires and get on to the real problems—what functions are involved in, e.g., self-control, what determines, or influences their exercise, what are the antecedents and consequences of positive and negative self-esteem, and so on.

II

To return to my central topic. I want to determine in what ways the self, construed in the way I have just explained, has to be taken into account in the psychology of motivation; and I want further to determine what implications these have for the shape of a theory of motivation. But the topic of motivation is variously conceived; and for any one way of construing the topic, there will be alternative theoretical orientations for dealing with that set of problems. So I had better explain how I understand the problem of motivation I will be considering.

I construe the topic of motivation in a broad way, as concerned with the determination of behavior; it is the study of the way in which the immediate determinants of behavior combine to do so. It is an attempt to formulate what Tolman called 'principles of performance' (Tolman, 1955). And although 'behavior' in contemporary lingo is quite a mixed bag, I shall restrict myself to a consideration of the determination of intentional action, doing something one meant to do. To further focus the discussion I shall restrict attention to the determination of *what* action is performed, rather than, e.g., its magnitude or latency.

The theory of motivation I shall be considering is what is often called 'expectancy-value theory', but which I shall term 'Want-Belief (W-B) Theory'. Influential expositions can be found in Lewin, 1938, Tolman, 1932, 1938, 1951, 1955, 1959, Edwards, 1954, Rotter, 1954, and Atkinson, 1964. Stated most generally, it holds that a person's tendency to perform a given action is a function of the consequences the person believes that action to have, and the 'value' (positive or negative) those consequences have for that person. I shall develop my own version of the theory, but only so far as to provide a background for the specific concerns of this paper.

We may approach W-B theory by noting that S's expectations obviously have something to do with whether he performs a given action. Convince him that it is not the case, as he had supposed, that this road leads to Nether Walop, and, unless he has some other reason for taking it, he will not make this turn. But of course not all envisaged consequences will have this kind of impact. Convince him that the road in question goes through Wootton Basset, and his tendency to turn or not turn will remain unaffected. He didn't care whether he went to Wootton Basset. Thus expectations of consequences influence action only in connection with something that marks out consequences as attractive, aversive, or indifferent; this something is, at least in part, something within the individual. When we begin to say what sort of something that is, we leave the safe ground of the truistic.

Initially I shall give only a minimal characterization of this something, to be called a 'want', in purely functional terms. As a first shot, to say that S at time, *t*, has a want (W) for a goal state of type G is to say that S is in such a state at *t* that if he came to believe at *t* that doing action, A, would have some considerable chance of bringing about a G, his tendency (T) to do A would be thereby increased.[2] A W, whatever else it is, is a state that stands in the specified functional relation with beliefs (B's) and action tendencies (T's).

However this formulation does not suffice to isolate the non-belief component of the system. For one may be related in this way to a G by virtue of one's beliefs as to what that G will lead to. Thus suppose I have a W, in the above sense, for Samantha to feel grateful toward me, but *only* because I believe that in that case she will act affectionately toward me. If I were to lose that B, then expecting action, A, to lead to Samantha's feeling grateful would no longer increase my tendency to do A. Such a W is simply a resultant of another W (for Samantha's affection) *plus* a certain belief (B). To focus down on W's that constitute a separate influence on behavior we shall have to restrict the category to those that do not depend on B's about their objects, what we may call 'intrinsic' W's. Thus if I would want Samantha's affection, whatever I expected it to lead to, this would be a W in the restricted sense in which I will be using the term. This is not to say, of course, that beliefs about the consequence of G might not also increase or decrease its attractiveness; it is only to say that apart from all that it would still have some; and it is *that* component of its total attractiveness that is due to the W in question.

It will be convenient to speak of the total attractiveness or aversiveness of a particular envisaged state of affairs, whether this be due to its being the object of a W, its being believed to lead an object

[2] This formulation applies specifically to positive wants. Aversions could be explained along the same lines, but to simplify the discussion I shall confine myself to positive W's.

of a W, or both. For this we shall, following Lewin and Tolman, use the term 'valence' (V).

There is another, and thornier, relation between W's and V's I had better just mention, so as to avoid misunderstanding. Both the 'objects' of W's and the envisaged consequences (C's) of actions are general in nature; they are *types* of states of affairs, rather than particular objects or events, though they can 'involve' particulars. What I want at the moment is to eat *some* food, or, more specifically but still generally, to eat a *turbot au beurre blanc*; to receive affection, or, more specifically but still generally, to receive affection from Samantha. Many distinguishable concrete transactions could satisfy the description, 'eating a *turbot au beurre blanc*', or 'receiving affection from Samantha'. Thus what one wants is always that something or other should instantiate the *type* G; and we shall understand the 'objects' of W's in this way. Now envisaged consequences (C's), the bearers of V's, are also general; no matter how specifically we anticipate the consequences of my asking Samantha to have dinner with me—her eyes light up, she turns to me with a warm smile, and in a tremulous voice says . . .—still many distinguishable concrete occurrences could satisfy that description. Nevertheless C's are generally anticipated in much more detail than is packed into a W-object that is exemplified by that C. Thus suppose that I have a W for Samantha's showing affection to me, and suppose that I regard the C mentioned above as being a case of that. Nevertheless the C involves other features as well (she could still be regarded as showing affection even if her eyes did not light up). (And of course it may involve G's that are objects of other W's.) Furthermore it may require interpretation for me to see that C as a case of a certain wanted G. Thus even where a C does not owe its V, even in part, to what it is believed to *lead to*, but solely to the fact that it is taken to exemplify a wanted G, still (1) it will typically involve also a number of W-irrelevant features and so not be, so to say, wanted as a whole, and (2) its V may still depend on a B—not a B as to what it will lead to, but a belief as to what it *is*, what it counts as.

It is crucial that the W's and B's of which we are speaking are those that are currently 'activated'. Clearly there is a sense in which I 'have' many W's and B's that are not now influencing my behavior. I want very much to be president of my local Red Cross chapter, but I am wholly preoccupied with other matters at the moment, and that goal is not figuring in my current motivation. Again, at a certain point I was looking for a way to express appreciation to my co-worker; and although I knew perfectly well he has a special fondness for string quartet recordings, I just didn't think of it at the moment. In these cases the W and the B were not 'activated' and so, at that *t*, were not W's and B's in our sense. Call them 'latent' W's and B's, and think of them as higher level dispositions to form the corresponding activated W's and B's, given appropriate arousal conditions. To say that I want to be president of the Red Cross chapter (even though B's as to A's leading to that will not increase action tendencies at the moment) is to say that there are (realizable) conditions under which a W with that object will be formed (and perhaps that this happens significantly often). And similarly for B's. W-B psychologists are, properly, quite concerned with conditions of activation; and it is at this point that much research in other orientations impinges on W-B theory. I shall wholly neglect this important topic, except to say that it seems clear that W-arousal can be due either to intra-organic factors (drive-arousal, and ongoing trains of thought or fantasy), or the perception of goal-objects. I should also make it explicit that I do not make 'being conscious' a necessary condition for being activated.

W's and B's are, of course, to be construed as varying in strength. In a thorough treatment it would have to be considered whether there are multiple dimensions of strength for each, or, alternatively, multiple determinants of strength. With B's, e.g., there seems to be an important distinction between how firmly the belief is held and the subjective probability (if any) that is involved in its propositional content. However all that is sorted out, I shall assume that the distinguishable sources and/or dimensions can be combined according to some function into an overall degree of strength.

So the general picture is this. The currently aroused W's determine certain features of situations as desirable (attractive) in themselves; and various B's (as to what possible C's exemplify these features, and as to what C's are associated with, and may lead to, what others) will, together with the W's, determine positive and negative V's for various C's. (The B's in question include both general beliefs, e.g., that people generally respond positively to interest shown in them, and perceptual beliefs about the current environment and the state of the agent.) Then insofar as one believes that an action A (which one believes to be a live possibility at the moment) will lead to a C with a positive or negative V, this will augment or diminish the tendency to perform A (T_A).[3] Typically there will be more than one envisaged C of a given A, and so more than one source of the strength of T_A. Where, as is often the case, one sees two or more incompatible actions as live options, there will be some sort of interaction between the T's to the various contenders, with the actual behavior determined by the relative strength of the T's, and perhaps other factors as well. Exact principles await the further development of measurement of the crucial variables.

No doubt the situation is much more complicated than I have been presenting it.[4] For example, both B's and W's are constantly waxing and waning, coming into an activated state and becoming deactivated, as well as increasing and decreasing in strength. And these processes will undoubtedly influence each other. For example, the formation of perceptual beliefs will not only provide new possibilities for paths to the goals of current W's, but also (through the display of new goal objects) serve to arouse or strengthen various W's. Again, it seems that even if some 'behavior' is motivated along the lines of the W-B model, other behavior results simply from the activation of S-R bonds, or in some other way; and it may be difficult to dissect the stream of behavior into these components. But sufficient unto the day is the complexity thereof. I take it that this exposition will serve as a basis for discussion of the ways in which the 'self' introduces complications into the picture.

III

I shall organize my discussion by progressing through various 'grades' of what I shall jocularly call '"ego-"-involvement' or '"self"-involvement'. More soberly, I shall be discussing various ways in which reference to the self would come into an adequate account of motivation. In detailing these ways I shall begin with those that require the least modification of the above account and end with the one that requires the most.

[3] A T may be thought of a special case of a V, that case in which the bearer of the V is an action that S believes himself capable of performing contemporaneously.

[4] Atkinson and Birch, 1970 present a sophisticated discussion of some of the complexities that are not treated here.

The first way simply makes explicit something that is already implicit in any formulation of W-B theory, including mine. The principles tacitly presuppose that the W's and B's that combine to form T's, and the T's that interact to determine action, all belong to the same person (self). No one supposes that *your* currently activated W's are going to enter (directly) into the formation of *my* current T's. There is, so to say, a purely formal involvement of the concept of the self, as that 'within' which the motivational processes take place. The boundaries of the person are the boundaries of that particular motivational system. Thus the first grade of 'self'-involvement is:

I. A given motivational process, its constituents and its outcome, is attributable to one and only one person/self.

This principle is recognized by any theory of the determinants of action-selection. A Hullian S-R account is firmly committed to the view that only the drive state and habit-family of the subject under study affects his current reaction-potential.

At the next level we come to the phenomena that bring in the distinctive employment of the word 'self', viz., the ways in which a person takes that person as an object of cognitions and evaluations. We can see several ways in which this reflexive turn makes itself felt in W-B motivation, and we can order these in terms of increasing complexity. First, when a person comes to be aware of himself in distinction from other persons, he comes to have W's and B's that involve the concept of himself, that have some state, characteristic, or activity of *himself* as object. Before the formation of a self-concept the child will conceive the state of affairs he finds attractive as *the candy bar*, *the rattle*, *mama here*. But when he comes to distinguish between himself and other persons, he will distinguish between *his* having the candy bar and someone else's having it; and the attractive state of affairs is then conceived in terms of the former. Second, and more strikingly, self-awareness makes possible goals of a sort that one cannot have without it—dominance (*my* controlling *others*), prestige (*others* respecting *me*), security (*my* being free from danger). Thus our second grade of 'self'-involvement is:

II. Among the objects of a given person's W's and B's are states of that person (himself).

The second stage is restricted to goals involving some particular state, or status of the self. A higher level of sophistication is involved in taking holistic properties of the self to be attractive or unattractive —e.g., consistency or integrity. Thus our third stage:

III. Among the objects of a given person's W's and B's are holistic properties of that person (himself).

A still higher degree of cognitive sophistication is involved where the self-concept or one's evaluations of oneself figure in the objects of one's W's and B's; as when one has a desire for one's own self-esteem, or self-approval, and an aversion to one's own self-rejection or self-disapproval. Here we go up another level in the reflexive series; not only is S an object for S's cognition and evaluation, but now that second-level cognition or evaluation is itself an object for S. (I cannot have a desire for my own self-approval unless I can form the conception of my approving or disapproving myself.) A desire to preserve the integrity of the self-concept or to act in accordance with my self-concept would also be on this level. Thus our fourth stage:

IV. Among the objects of a given person's W's and B's are certain states of his own cognitions and evaluations of that person (himself) and relations of other things thereto.

Grades 2–4, though they require additional cognitive sophistication, do not, so far as I can see, require any complication of the basic concepts and principles of W-B theory. They provide new and more complicated filling for the theory—W's and B's of a sort that would not otherwise be available. But there is no reason to think that these W's and B's combine with each other and with other W's and B's to form T's in any fashion other than that in which simpler W's and B's do. If one is motivated not only by desires for food and drink, but also for fame, self-consistency, and self-esteem, it will still be true that stronger W's and stronger expectations will produce stronger T's. And although the measurement of all these things is still in a very rough stage, I see no reason for supposing that these more sophisticated W's can't be put on the same scale with less sophisticated ones, at least to the same extent that the latter can be put on the same scale with each other.

IV

However there is still another, and more radical, way in which the self comes into the motivational picture, and this *will* force a basic revision in the W-B model. One may intervene, 'throw oneself' into one's own motivational processes, seek to influence the outcome by one or another manipulation. Thus one may try to get oneself to write a letter one is reluctant to write, or try to make oneself act friendly toward someone; one may seek to resist the temptation to watch a tennis match, so that one can finish a paper. In these cases one does not just 'sit back' and let T-formation proceed as it may; one *does something* to affect the outcome; one interferes in the process. Or so it seems. Let's call this phenomenon 'self-intervention' (SI).[5]

Thus the fifth grade of self-involvement is:

V. One may do something to change one's own motivational processes from what they would otherwise have been.

It is easy to suppose that when SI is successfully carried out one's behavior is *not* determined by W-B interaction. One intervenes in order to bring about a result other than what would result from the current tendency field. Hence the W-B belief model is applicable only when one does not intervene. The intervention must be understood in quite different terms, as an exercise of *the will*, a faculty the doings of which are not causally determined and so not susceptible to scientific prediction. Philosophers have often taken this line. (See, e.g., Campbell, 1950.) However we can resist these conclusions and render the model applicable to cases involving SI, provided we are entitled to the following assumptions. (1) SI itself consists of actions that are motivated in the same way as any others, that are determined by the relative strength of tendencies formed in accordance with the W-B model. (2) SI, when well-advised, seeks to affect behavior by introducing, deleting, or altering just those factors that the W-B model singles out as affecting behavior. Granted those assumptions, the phenomenon of SI will leave unaffected the point that action-selection is always determined as the W-B model specifies. SI

[5] Paradoxically enough, SI has been almost completely ignored by those psychologists who make much of the self. It is, e.g., conspicuous by its absence from the list of conceptions of the self in Allport (1943).

will simply introduce some complications, the exact nature of which remains to be seen.

Surely these assumptions are quite plausible. (1) SI would appear to be goal-directed in just the same way as lower-level behavior. In fact the natural way to report it (as exemplified by my initial examples) is as an attempt to reach a certain *goal*, *viz*., oneself doing, or refraining from doing, something. Hence there would be the same antecedent reasons for regarding it as determined by whatever singles out certain goals as to be striven for, and singles out promising ways of reaching them.[6]

Assumption (2) is strongly supported by common experience. How does one resist the temptation to watch a tennis match when a job has to be finished, or resist a temptation to make an unkind remark to someone? By reminding oneself of the aversive consequences of yielding to the temptation. One depicts, in greater or less detail, the disapproval from oneself and others that will result from failure to complete the work. Or by reminding oneself of the attractive consequences of resisting the temptation, e.g. the approval, from self and others, that will result from finishing the work. Or one simply seeks to shut out the awareness of the attractiveness of the temptation; i.e., one seeks to deactivate the B's or W's that give the tempting activity its valence. Thus one may try to distract one's attention from these matters by a change of scene or activity. Again, one may try to provide new V's by offering oneself rewards for resisting, or threatening punishments for succumbing. All these devices are designed to alter the V's affecting the strength of competing T's, by altering the W's and B's that affect them.

To be sure, it sometimes seems that no such devices are used. Sometimes, it seems, I make myself do something just by an 'effort of will', just by exercising my capacity to will anything I choose, whatever the strength of the inducements to the contrary. It is these cases that have nourished the 'libertarian' position that the will stands outside the causal network. But a closer analysis will reveal more subtle devices of the sort already considered. When I pull

[6] We may also note, that if SI were not motivated in this way there would be no clear basis for regarding it is *activity*, as something the person *does*, rather than as something that is just *happening* in the motivational processes by which V's and T's are formed. At least this is the case if, as I believe, there is no way of distinguishing between what an agent *does* and what just *happens* to him, except by considering whether the occurrence in question was determined in accordance with the W-B model.

myself out of the slough of idleness and force myself to get to work, I may not engage in elaborate reflections on the consequences of doing or not doing so; but at least I tell myself in a stern (inner) tone of voice to get going; and that tone of voice will carry the threat of self-punishment for non-compliance. And even if we cannot introspectively find any such specific devices it would not be surprising if their deployment were sometimes unconscious, or so telescoped as not to be introspectively discriminable.

It is important for the further course of the argument to distinguish between SI and other phenomena that are frequently lumped indiscriminately with SI under such headings as 'self-control', 'impulse-control', 'resistance to temptation', and 'ego-activity'. As I have explained the term, SI always involves S's doing something in order to influence his own motivation. It necessarily involves higher level activity directed onto one's own motivation. Now studies on 'self-control' or 'resistance to temptation' often use as a sufficient criterion for these phenomena the subject's not doing A or not seeking G, where doing A or having G is something that is presumed to be attractive to him.[7] But of course that completely leaves open the question whether SI has occurred. Quite often one fails to choose an attractive alternative, *X*, just because some other alternative, *Y*, is more attractive, or because aversive consequences of *X* outweigh its attractiveness. And all this may happen 'automatically' without any need for S to do anything to *manipulate* valencies or expectancies. This will be the case if, e.g., aversive consequences have become strongly associated with *X* through punishment. Here the concept of SI does not apply.

Again we can have 'ego-activity' in many of its guises—impulse control, reality-testing, long-range planning, or scheduling, without SI. It is all a matter of whether *self-directed activity* is involved. Consider 'reality-testing'. Stated most generally, this is simply the use of information about means-end relationships in action-selection. It is a matter of doing what the best available information indicates has the best chance of attaining the goal, rather than just thrashing about wildly. Obviously this can, and normally does, take place without any SI. Expectancies are formed and influence behavior without my being motivated to influence this process. Again, the organization of long-range activities may or may not involve SI. If I have to bend my efforts to resist tempting distractions or to keep

[7] For references see page 93.

before my mind what it is I am trying to accomplish, that is SI. But if it is a fairly well-rehearsed routine that runs into no serious interferences, no SI is needed.

V

What complications does SI force in the W-B model? In discussing this question, the following terminology will prove useful. An action that is *not* designed to influence the current motivation of the agent (get him to do, or to refrain from doing some specific A now or in the near future) I term 'lower-level action' (LLA). Whereas an action that is so designed (an action involved in SI) we may term a 'higher level action' (HLA).[8] Processes that lead to LLA we may term lower-level motivation (LLM) and those leading to HLA may be termed higher-level motivation (HLM). Using this terminology we may say that HLA is action designed to influence LLM.

Now let's recur to the two assumptions we had to make in order to save the W-B model in the face of SI, the first having to do with the motivation of HLA and the second with its *modus operandi*. What complication do they entail for the model? As for the second, it requires only complications of detail. The basic principles governing the course of LLM remain the same. It will still be the case that it is the strongest T that issues in action at any given moment, and that T-strength is some function of the V of envisaged C's and the activated subjective probability of reaching them via that action; while the V of a C is determined by the strength of the contemporaneously aroused W's of the agent as they engage the way in which that C is cognized. The only difference SI makes to this picture is that it provides a new source of the activation, deactivation, strengthening or weakening of W's and B's. But the motivational processes *strictu sensu*, the formation of T's and their interaction, proceeds just as it would without SI.

The first assumption, however, is a different story. When we think through the phenomenon of HLM we will see that fundamental

[8] This formulation is designed to exclude action designed to modify the agent's wants, beliefs, traits, fears, likings, etc., with an eye to long range modification of his behavior but without any immediate application in mind. I am excluding this from my category of HLA simply because it does not raise the problem with which I shall be dealing.

revisions are required. Let's go back to our resistance-of-temptation situation.

When I try to make myself finish the paper instead of watch a tennis match, my HLA could be described in the most general terms as seeking to bring about an outcome of LLM different from what it would be apart from my effort. That is, I suppose that if matters were left to take their course the strongest action tendency would be T_a; and I make various moves that are designed to bring it about that the strongest T is T_b. A moment's reflection will assure us that this description applies to all HLA. If I did not suppose that LLM, apart from my SI, would (most probably) lead to an action other than the one my SI is designed to produce, my activity would be pointless.

Now let's make the very plausible assumption that people are sometimes correct in this presupposition, that in at least some of the cases in which S sets out to make himself do b, it is true that in the absence of SI what he would do is *a*. And let's think about the implications of this for HLM and LLM. As for HLM, at the moment of initiation of SI the strongest T is for some HLA, R, which is done to bring it about that in LLM T_b is the strongest tendency. Now the question is as to what gives T_R its strength. On the W-B model, it is a superior valence of its supposed consequences. We have already specified the most salient envisaged consequence—T_b being the strongest tendency in one's current LLM, and, more specifically, T_b being stronger than T_a. But why should one be interested in that? Obviously in order that one actually do *b* rather than *a*. Except for highly atypical cases[9] one would not aim at T_b's being stronger than T_a for any reason other than to get oneself to *do b* rather than *a*. And if T_R owes its strength to the probability of R's leading to S's doing *b* rather than *a*, it must be that doing *b* has a higher V than doing *a* in S's current HLM. For it is the V of anticipated C's that give a T its strength.

But now what about LLM at the moment the HLA, R, is performed? Does *a* or *b* have the stronger V there? If it is *a*, we are faced with the apparent contradiction that for S the V of *a* is both stronger and weaker than *b*. At the moment at which I begin to try to make myself finish the paper it would be true of me both that I want to watch the tennis match more than I want to finish the paper,

[9] For example, I might conceivably seek to strengthen T_b in order to prove that I could, or in order to win a bet. We may safely neglect such possibilities.

and that I want to finish the paper more than I want to watch the tennis match. But do our assumptions about SI force us to that conclusion? To answer that question we must make some distinctions within the general field of SI.

One sort of SI is that in which S is confronted with a choice between doing *a* and doing *b* in the near future, and where he is doing neither at the moment. He believes that, apart from SI, the course of LLM would lead to the superiority of T_a over T_b *when the moment of choice arrives.* Our tennis watching/paper finishing case most naturally fits into this category. Here it is certainly not *necessary* that T_a be stronger than T_b in LLM at the moment of initiation of SI. One's LLM may be in an instable condition, oscillating between dominance of T_a and of T_b. Even though one believes that T_a will be dominant by the time the moment of truth arrives, one may 'take advantage' of the temporary dominance of T_b to launch ones SI on the side of *b*. In that case there would be no paradox.[10]

However with other kinds of SI it is a different story. Consider the case in which I am actually engaged in doing *a* at the time I initiate SI on the side of *b*. I am actually watching the tennis match and am thoroughly enjoying it at the moment at which I start trying to tear myself away and get onto writing the paper. Here the assumption behind the SI is that T_a is *now* stronger than T_b in LLM, and will continue to be so unless I do something about it. Thus unless we are always mistaken about this, it is sometimes true that T_a *is* stronger in LLM at the moment of initiation of SI. All cases of making myself do something right away belong in this category. For even where I am 'doing nothing' at the moment (as when I try to make myself get out of bed in the morning), that 'doing nothing' will have the strongest valence at the moment in LLM.

A third type is that in which I try to stop myself from doing something I am just on the verge of doing, e.g., making an unkind remark to someone. Here too one ordinarily assumes that *at that moment* the balance of forces in LLM are such as to lead to doing *a* right away unless one intervenes.

It may be argued that in these cases one does not have to assume

[10] I am indebted to Richard Brandt for calling my attention to this possibility Brandt, indeed, holds (private communication) that all cases of SI can be construed in these terms, a view I now go on to dispute.

that T_a is stronger than T_b in LLM at the moment of intervention in order that SI have a point. All that is necessary is that one assume that T_a will be stronger than T_b in LLM over some appropriate stretch of time in the future. This leaves one free to suppose that it is during a temporary dominance of T_b that I start trying to continue its dominance in the immediate future. And if cases of the second and third types were always like that, again there would be no paradox. Now I think it must be conceded that this is a logical possibility. The minimum requirement for SI's having a point is only that T_a would (probably) be dominant, apart from T_b, during the period in the future within which the SI is aiming to influence the balance of forces. Nevertheless in many cases of the second and third types, our experience seems to indicate clearly that T_a is dominant in LLM at the moment we begin to try to combat it. At the moment my prickings of conscience become strong enough to lead me to try to drag myself away from the tennis match, I am very much absorbed in it; and it does not seem to me that my inclination to watch it has yet even temporarily diminished. And where I have that unkind remark on the tip of my tongue but try to inhibit it, there certainly appears to me to be a clear and *present* danger of my speaking it. I cannot discern any temporary remission that gives me time to strengthen the forces of inhibition. In fact in both these cases the only reason I have to suppose that T_a *will* be dominant in the relevant future is that I feel it to be dominant *now;* if I did not, I would (in these cases) have no reason to expect continued dominance. I would not argue that these deliverances of experience are infallible. Under strong enough theoretical demands they could be overriden, and we could suppose that there are remissions so fleeting or so masked as to be unnoticed by ordinary reflection. But if it is possible to construe the situation in an otherwise acceptable manner so as to preserve the clear testimony of first-person experience it would be preferable to take that course. To that task I now turn.

We are confronted with an apparent contradiction in the V-field. For S the V of *a* is both stronger and weaker than that of *b*. How can this be? One tack, of course, is to split S into two agents. SI involves the struggle of the 'lower' and 'higher' selves, of 'reason' against 'passion', of the 'soul' against the 'body', and so on. Each of these protagonists is then endowed with a more or less complete W-B system of motivation, depending on how thoroughly the two-agent theorist thinks through his position. This has been a popular move in the history of philosophy, and it has taken many forms. But although it may be that a plurality of agents under the same skin has to be postulated for certain pathological cases, it is highly counter-intuitive as an account of normal cases of SI. The difficulties into which we are led by such an account have been repeatedly catalogued, and I shall not take time to go into them here. Suffice it to say that there are many sources of the conviction that it is one and the same person who is both strongly inclined to keep watching the tennis match and is trying to get himself to work on the paper instead. We should hold to this conviction if at all possible.

Fortunately there is a way in which we can do so while still according full recognition to SI. We can think of one and the same agent as possessing two different motivational systems, two different systems of T-formation, one for LLM and one for HLM. We can then remove our apparent contradiction by assigning the superiority of V_a over V_b to the LL system (LLS), and the superiority of V_b over V_a to the HL system (HLS). There only appeared to be a contradiction because we were ignoring the fact that there are two V-fields involved in the single agent, not just one. This leaves room for one V to be stronger in one field and another V to be stronger in the other.

One may feel that there is only a verbal difference between posutulating two motivational systems and postulating two agents. And so there would if we were postulating two 'complete' systems. But, and this is the crucial point, our two systems are hierarchically ordered; one is higher level vis-a-vis the other; the HLS has as its sole function to generate T's to actions aimed at affecting the LLS. Thus an *agent* could not have only a HLS; that would be an explicit contradiction since a HLS is, by definition, a system for generating tendencies to affect *one's own* LLM. (Though there can be an agent with only a LLS; presumably the lower animals (or most of them) are of that sort.) LLM has a monopoly on the control of first-level action; and higher-level motivational systems can influence first-level action only by influencing *it*. The uniqueness of the LLS is, therefore, the guarantee of the unity of the agent. Hence there is no possibility of our two systems determining two different agents. To be a single human agent is to have two motivational systems related in this way.

Indeed, a more complete analysis of the situation would require us to recognize further levels of the hierarchy. Just as I can intervene to alter the current relative strength of first-level T's, so I can intervene in the processes of HLM. This is what happens when I come to feel that in inhibiting all my putatively aggressive impulses I have lost all spontaneity; and so I intervene to try to prevent myself from inhibiting a certain impulse. But two levels will keep us more than occupied in this paper.

Thus far we have distinguished our two systems, as to content, only by supposing that sometimes the relative strength of V's will be opposite in the two systems at the same time. What more basic difference in the systems do we have to postulate in order to yield this difference in V's? According to the model with which we are working, the V of C can be affected by (1) S's having an activated want or aversion for a G, where C is conceptualized by S as a G, and by (2) S's believing that C will lead (or will have some chance of leading) to something else that is positively or negatively valenced. So at the moment in question the HL system and the LL system must differ in one or more of these respects.

The second possibility divides into two. That difference might involve (a) *what* further states C is believed to lead to (difference in B's), or (b) the V's of those further states, or both. Now a difference of the (a) sort does not seem to be present in the everyday cases of SI we are considering. Whatever might be the case where one or the other system is suffering marked repression, or where other kinds of psycho-pathology are involved, it does not seem that in the ordinary cases of SI my 'higher self' has information lacking to my 'lower self' or vice versa. In our chief illustration it is not that my tendency to get myself to work on the paper is based on information that is unavailable to me *qua* tennis match watcher. If it were, the job of SI would be much easier; I should merely have to remind myself of that information to render the paper finishing tendency dominant in LLM. So we shall have to look elsewhere for our crucial difference.

As for (2b), a difference in the V's of the envisaged C's, even if that is involved it cannot be the final answer. For this answer invites the question: 'What determines the difference in *those* valences?' And if that difference in turn is due to differences in still further V's the same question arises again. And on pain of an infinite regress we must eventually come to some V-differences that are due to the first main determinant, the presence or strength of one or more W's. Thus at some point one of the systems must contain a W that is lacking in the other, or a given W must differ in strength in the two systems. In the ensuing discussion let's assume that the differences in our examples comes from the fact that whereas the HL system contains a want for a G (with *b* perceived as being a G), the LL system contains no such want, and that whatever positive valence *b* possesses in LLM is derived from B's that it will lead to other positively valenced states.

Now consider where this is leading us. There is a W in HLS that is absent in LLS. But in admitting this have we not, after all, fallen back into the two agents view? In saying 'there is a W for G *in system S*' we obscure the fact that in order for there to *be* a W some person must want something; otherwise the talk makes no sense. W's do not float out in some 'general systems theory' void. So how can we avoid the contradiction that S both does and does not want G at the same moment without splitting S into two agents? Well, we can turn this trick provided the structure of W's is different in the two systems, i.e., provided that the way S has to be related to G in order to want it differs for the two systems. In that case S could be related to G in one of these ways and not in the other, and the dilemma would be resolved.

But how can this be, seeing that we have laid it down that both HLM and LLM conform to the W-B model? If that is the case, don't the W's operative in both systems have to conform to the explanation of W's we gave in setting out the model? Yes, they do. But, and this is the crucial point, that specification was in purely functional terms. As we explained the term, S has a *W* for a G at t_1 *iff* the activation in S at t_1 of a B that doing A will have some chance of leading to a G, will increase S's T to do A. Anything that has that role vis-a-vis B's and T's is a W in the relevant sense of that term. *And psychological states of quite different sorts might conceivably play this role*. The functional characterization leaves completely open the question of what sort of state has this function. This is obvious if we think in terms of psychological descriptions. No one really knows how to give a physiological characterization of a desire to hear some music; and it is quite conceivable that different kinds of neuro-physiological structures or processes might meet the functional requirement. Even in physiological terms alternative possibilities are open at this stage of the art. A lowered cognitive threshold for musical stimuli, or an expectation that hearing music would be enjoyable might either, or both, fit the bill.

VI

With this step we have arrived at the basic claim of the paper. To understand the full range of cases of SI, we must recognize at least two motivational systems (systems for the formation of T's), one of which has as its function the formation of T's to act vis-a-vis the other. These systems must differ at least in the character of (at least some of)[11] the W's involved, i.e., they must differ in what kind of psychological state plays the W-role (for at least some of their constituent W's). And an adequate W-B theory of motivation will have to incorporate this complexity in its structure.

This is the conclusion that has emerged from the argument to date. And I might just leave it at that. However if my argument has been sound up to this point, it would be tantalizing at best to break off here without addressing the question of what sorts of psychological states play the W-role in the two systems? Thus before coming to draw implications of my central point for the psychology of motivation I shall make some suggestions along this line. However I accompany these suggestions with the warning that I feel less confidence in them than in what I have called the basic claim of the paper. Nor will I be able to give them the support they need and deserve.

Can we find plausible candidates for the W-role in our two systems? I believe we can. I propose that we approach the task via the ancient idea that SI involves a conflict between desire and duty, or between inclination and principle, between a lower, sensual nature and a higher, rational nature. Without subscribing to all the theological, moral, metaphysical, and psychological ideas that have grown up around this line of thought, we may extract from it the following suggestion.

HLW's consist in S's *having* certain principles or standards for the evaluations of persons. More specifically, for S to have a HLW

[11] Strictly speaking, the preceding argument shows only that a W for G must differ in character in the HLS and LLS only in those cases in which we have contrary V's in the two systems at the same moment. It is a further question, one into which I shall have no time to enter, whether all W's in a given system are of the same type. For simplicity of exposition I shall assume that this is the case, though the further developments in the paper only require the weaker conclusion.

at t_1 for, say, fulfilling his commitments, is for his 'belief in' (his *acceptance of*) the principle that one should fulfil his commitments to be activated at t_1. (When S 'accepts' a principle that positively or negatively evaluates G, I shall speak of S as having an 'evaluative stance' (ES) toward G.) The activation of this ES will provide a positive V for anything perceived by S as a carrying out of some commitment, e.g., finishing a paper. The concept of activation here is essentially the same as for other motivational factors; the ES is activated when he 'has it in mind' (not necessarily consciously) *and* is prepared thereby to act on it (or at least tend to do so). The principles that are involved in HLW's need not be moral principles, though they often are. Any principle that lays down what a person ought to do or be, what it would be desirable for a person to do or be, or the conditions under which someone is a good, admirable, respectable, or praiseworthy person, will qualify. (And of course the reverse side of the coin—principles that lay down what a person ought not to do or be, the conditions under which a person is despicable, blameworthy . . .) Any principle that furnishes a basis for judging a person, for reacting to him or to his doings with approval, praise, admiration . . . or the reverse, will be a principle of the sort we have in mind.

There are various indications that this way of looking at HLW's is correct. There seems to be a coincidence between the goals of SI and what is approved or disapproved by principles the person is prepared to espouse. Thus the person who frequently tries to resist carping is typically the person who strongly disapproves, on principle, of carping; and one who feels strongly that one should make strangers feel welcome will frequently try to get himself to do that when LLM does not suffice.[12] By contrast, we do not get the same correlation between the goals of LLA and the objects of ES's. It may be that succorance by a mother figure is powerfully attractive to a person, so that much of his effort is devoted to securing and maintaining this, while he does not regard this state with approval—quite the contrary. In this case we would not expect him to intervene on the side of succorance seeking, but, if anything, to intervene on

[12] Do not conclude from these examples that in SI the kind of action that is resisted or supported is always approved, or disapproved, *as such*. I may resist carping because I feel that it will prevent my 'getting ahead'. In that case the principle involved is a prudential one, and my ES is directed to the carping *qua* block to getting ahead.

the other side. This is an excessively familiar phenomenon—to be drawn to something of which one disapproves. I am not saying that the objects of ES's and of LLW's are perfectly, or even largely, negatively correlated. One may well *both* approve of social status and find it attractive. The point rather is that while HLW's are invariably mirrored in internalized principles, LLW's need not be and frequently are not.[13]

The ancient line of thought we are following does not speak with so unequivocal a voice on LLW's. Not only is it badly divided on the subject, but none of the accounts are as satisfactory or illuminating as the above suggestion concerning HLW's. The main split is between hedonists and their opponents. It is generally agreed that the satisfaction of a LLW is pleasant and its frustration unpleasant, but this fact receives different interpretations. To a hedonist (Mill, 1863) this indicates that to have a LLW for C is just to expect C to be pleasant; while his opponent (Hobbes, 1651) holds that C is pleasant only because one wants it, so that the nature of the want will have to be explained in other terms, e.g., as an impulse toward C, perhaps with an instinctual basis. One can find this opposition in twentieth century psychology, with McClelland (1953) a forthright hedonist and Tolman (1951), who puts more emphasis on drives, on the other side. It is more common, however, to straddle the fence.[14]

But beneath all these divergencies we can find some common ground. LLW's are conceived by all parties as distinctively different from their HL cousins in *not* being principle-based and in having a simpler cognitive structure. Even though LLW's may have *objects* of any degree of conceptual complexity, still the structure of the want, i.e., how the person has to be related to that object to want it, is simple enough to be shared by rats and dogs. Furthermore it is common ground that there are distinctive affective consequences of satisfaction or frustrations of W's, though many psychologists and philosophers are sceptical about the general notion of hedonic tone, or about our capacity to measure it objectively. For purposes of this paper I am going to adopt a hedonic conception of LLW's because I believe it is the most definite and promising general conception

[13] This conception of HLW's has some affinities with Charles Taylor's (1977, this volume) interesting conception of 'strong evaluation', though there are also differences, both of which the reader is invited to explore.

[14] Needless to say, this is all grossly oversimplified.

available at present. However all the points I will be making could equally well be made for any other conception that represents LLW's as not based on principles, and that takes account both of the generic character of W's and of the facts of motivation gleaned from experiment and common experience.

I suggest, then, that we think of a LLW for a G as an activated anticipation that a G if present now would involve an increase in hedonic tone (balance of pleasantness over unpleasantness), whereas a LL aversion to G may be construed as an activated anticipation that G if present now would involve a decrease in hedonic tone. We must stress the qualifier 'activated'. Of course I can have latent beliefs of this sort without the corresponding W. I may latently believe that drinking a gin and tonic would be most pleasant; but, being wholly occupied with the ongoing activity of writing a paper, I am far from thinking of a gin-and-tonic (even unconsciously). Since this belief is unactivated no such W need be attributed to me at this moment. Again it is crucial that the anticipation be for the affective consequence to follow *now*. At the moment I believe (actively) that if I were just coming off the ski slopes, a bowl of hot soup would be most pleasant, but having just finished a game of tennis in the broiling sun, I do not anticipate that it would be pleasant *now*.[15] Let's call LLW's, 'D's' (for *desire*).

I think no one would doubt that it is possible, and often actual, for a person to expect pleasure from C while not approving of his pursuing or having C; and contrariwise it is possible, and often actual, that a person should feel that he ought to do A but expect no (or little) pleasure from doing so. Thus ES's and affective expectations can be out of harmony; and so if each of them can play the W-role in V determination, this provides an answer to how it is that one and the same agent can possess two different motivational systems embodying opposed V's at the same time. Furthermore, as I have been suggesting, common experiences renders it overwhelmingly plausible that HLA is in line with evaluative principles accepted by the agent, while LLA is by no means always so. This encourages us to assign our two W-types to the two systems as we have done it here. The only doubt remaining is whether both of our candidates *can* play the W-role. Doubts may be expressed in both

15 Note that on this interpretation of LLW's, beliefs are doing the whole job in the LLM—the W's being a special kind of B. This is then, in a sense, a purely cognitive theory of LLM.

cases, but since they are more generally and strongly felt with respect to ES's I shall just briefly indicate my position on that issue.

To show that ES's are capable of functioning in HLM, we do not need to show that to have a positive ES vis-a-vis doing *a* is to have some T to do *a*. For what HLM motivates directly in this case would not be doing *a* itself, but rather doing something designed to increase the LLM for doing *a* (or decrease the LLM for doing something incompatible with doing *a*). And it does seem that by virtue of believing that I ought to finish this paper I thereby *at least* have *some* tendency to try to do what is required to get myself to work at finishing it. If we did not include that much bearing on conduct in our concept of an ES, how could we distinguish expressing a real ES (a real acceptance of a normative judgment) by saying 'I ought to finish the paper', from just mouthing the words, or using them to record a recognition that conventional standards have a certain application to this case. No doubt there are action tendencies more obviously involved in an ES, e.g., tendencies to react favorably or infavorably to cases of conforming or failing to conform to the principle involved. Nevertheless, I feel that it is quite plausible to hold that the tendency to encourage oneself to conform to the principle is also essentially involved. Indeed I believe that we could see how this latter tendency stems from the former, but that is too long a story for this occasion.[16]

VII

The upshot of the last two sections is that SI forces us to complicate the W-B model by distinguishing at least two motivational systems in the human being, one for LLA and one for HLA. Though in general the same set of activated beliefs is available to both systems, different kinds of W's are involved, thereby engendering the possibility of contrary V's in the two systems.[17]

[16] Thus we are taking a position intermediate between those who hold that accepting the principle that one should do A, can itself have no motivating power, and those who hold that it necessarily involves a tendency to do A.

[17] Note that this complication is quite independent of any distinction of systems that may be required to accommodate the operation of repressed W's. The considerations I am presenting would hold even if motivation were exclusively conscious and totally free from the operation of repression and other defenses.

No existing version of W-B theory recognizes this complication; they all envisage a single field of V's, determining a set of T's that engage in a single interaction for control of behavior. Even those versions that recognize something like SI try to accommodate it within a single system of T-formation, usually by stressing some particular W-object, like self-approval. Thus in Tolman's 1951 W-B model he assumes that a 'need' for one's own approval generalizes from a prior need for approval from others, once one comes to apply standards to oneself. These W's are not thought to differ in basic structure from the 'viscerogenic' ones, and they are thought to be competing with them in the same system. I take the last section to have shown that although LLW's for one's own approval can bring about conformity to principles when that simply 'happens' without the need for HLA, it cannot account for true SI.

W. Mischel's research into delay of gratification is also instructive in this regard. His theoretical framework is of the W-B sort; and although he does not elaborate the theory, he does apply it explicitly to a phenomenon that can involve SI, viz., the choice of a larger delayed reward over a smaller immediate reward. (1966, pp. 87–8; 1977, this volume). Even though he is well aware that S's typically engage in various kinds of self-directed behavior to maintain their resistance to choosing the immediate reward when it is available during all or part of the delay period, and although he has investigated this behavior in a series of studies (W. Mischel, 1973), he has not complicated his account of the motivation of delay behavior to take account of this. On the contrary he gives a one-level picture of the determinants of the phenomenon. 'Thus, whether an individual chooses an immediate, smaller reward or a delayed, larger reward in a given situation is a function of the relative strengths of the expectancies and reward values associated with each choice'. (1966, p. 87.)

VIII

If there are two quite different sorts of psychological states that play the W-role, this has important implications for the acquisition and measurement of W's, as well as for their functions in motivation; and approaches that ignore this distinction will have to be rethought. In the brief space at my disposal I shall just indicate how this works out for acquisition.

First I should make clear that I will be talking about the acquisition of what I earlier called 'latent' W's. This is what is under discussion in e.g., the literature on the origins of n_{ach} or of conscience, and it is latent W's that 'behavior therapists' try to alter in their 'counterconditioning' techniques. This problem is to be distinguished from the question of the conditions that lead to the activation of a certain W at a certain moment; I shall have nothing to say about the latter.

With a few exceptions, like the work on achievement motivation, most of the research that is relevant to the acquisition of LLW's and HLW's is carried on within a framework quite different from W-B theory. This includes the research on 'acquired drives' and 'secondary rewards', as well as much of the research on 'socialization', 'social learning', and the acquisition of 'self-control'. If we are to point up implications of our distinction for this research we shall have to translate it into the W-B framework.

My central point about acquisition is that the *structural* differences between LLW's and HLW's are inevitably reflected in differences in mode of acquisition. On our interpretation of LLW's as affective anticipations, how would we expect them to be acquired? Presumably the most basic way in which one comes to expect that a G will involve hedonic tone of a certain quality is by repeatedly experiencing that hedonic tone when a G is realized. Of course there are also derivative modes of expectation-acquisition. One may acquire such an expectation from being assured by someone else that it is so, or by seeing someone else being pleased or displeased by a G. And no doubt there are less reliable ways in which persons acquire expectations. But in this brief discussion I shall concentrate on the most basic way.

This means that the basic question of acquisition becomes: how does it come about that S experiences a G with a certain hedonic tone? If we may assume that certain associations of this sort are innate, affective arousal can be attached to new G's by classical conditioning, by both direct and cognitively mediated generalization, and by perceived means-ends relationships between new and old G's (if this is different from classical conditioning). Suggestions along these lines are excessively familiar in the literature. (Mowrer, 1950, 1960; McClelland, 1951; McClelland et al, 1953; Rotter, 1954;

W. Mischel, 1968.) There are other possibilities as well, e.g., 'vicarious' classical conditioning through witnessing the classical conditioning of another (Berger, 1962, Bandura and Rosenthal, 1967).

Now my basic point is that HLW's cannot be acquired in these ways. For whatever is so acquired *is* an affective anticipation, and so does not differ in character from LLW's in the way required for playing a role in HLM.[18] I shall now look at the literature on the acquisition of HLW's in the light of this point. But my earlier caution about the necessity for translation out of alien tongues applies doubly here. Not only is much of the relevant literature not within the W-B framework, but even the part that is does not explicitly draw the distinction between HLW's and LLW's. Hence we shall be considering research on what *we* would construe as the acquisition of HLW's, i.e., viz, the adoption of principles or standards.

In looking at what we may loosely call the S-R literature on these topics, the most striking thing, from the present point of view, is the persistent confusion of HLM and LLM. The literature surveyed in Bandura and Walters (1963), and in W. Mischel (1977, this volume) on 'self-control' is eloquent testimony to this. In study after study where 'self-control' or 'resistance to temptation' is the dependent variable, the actual criterion employed for this is simply the non-performance of an action (cheating, or violating rules concerning which toy may be taken or when) for which it is supposed the subject has some considerable motivation. (For a few examples out of a large crowd, see Hartshorne and May, 1928, MacKinnon, 1938, Sears, Rau & Alpert, 1963, Parke & Walters, 1967, W. Mischel, 1966, Walters, Leat & Nezei, 1963.) Once we make the distinction between LLM and SI we see that while the non-occurrence of a strongly motivated action might be due to SI, it *could* simply reflect the fact that within LLM its negative valence was stronger than its positive valence (or the fact that within LLM the valence of some incompatible action was even greater). In these

[18] A parallel conclusion holds for other interpretations of LLW's (assuming that there are other plausible interpretations). Thus if a LLW for a G is an anticipation of drive reduction on attaining G (where drive reduction is not construed as necessarily involving positively toned affect), then whatever process is responsible for the acquisition of these anticipations cannot produce HLW's.

latter cases there would be no need for SI to inhibit the performance. Very different motivational processes are involved in the two sorts of cases; and the acquisition of the resources for those processes will be correspondingly different. By lumping them indiscriminately under such headings as 'self-control' and 'resistance to temptation', terms properly applicable only to SI, one creates the unwarranted presumption that SI can be handled in just the same way as LLM. Even so discriminating a treatment as Justin Aronfreed's book, *Conduct and Conscience* (1964), is not wholly free of this blemish. The most general concept in his discussion is that of 'internalized control of behavior'. 'We might consider an act to be internalized to the extent that its maintenance has become independent of external outcomes, that is to the extent that its reinforcing consequences are internally mediated, without the support of external events like reward and punishment'. (p. 18) Unlike the authors cited above, he does make and even emphasize a distinction between the internal control of behavior by 'evaluative cognition' (conscience) and by more rudimentary means that do not involve self-cognition. Nevertheless, as we shall see below, he tends, perhaps encouraged by his coverall term, 'internalized control', to treat SI in terms appropriate to LLM.

Because of these assimilations we find a strong tendency in the S-R tradition to treat the acquisition of standards, conscience, and dispositions to self-control and resistance to temptation, in terms appropriate to the acquisition of LLW's. Thus the inhibition of sexual and aggressive responses through a sense of guilt is viewed as based on the classical conditioning of negative affect to sexual and aggressive responses, or the incipient beginnings thereof. (Dollard and Miller, 1950, Mowrer, 1950, Bandura and Walters, 1963) In Bandura and Walters (1963, pp. 178–9) the only reservation to the view that 'resistance to deviation results from the association of noxious stimuli with the commission of prohibited responses' is to allow vicarious associations. The following statement will give a good idea of this position.

> ... two sets of factors can play an important role in the acquisition and maintenance of self-control. While fear of punishment has undoubtedly an important deterrent effect, anticipation of punishment, with little accompanying fear may on many occasions guarantee social compliance. In other words, behavior that is

> interpretable as resistance to deviation may be instigated by a contemporary set of stimulus components, some of which are emotional ('fear', 'anticipatory guilt'), and others that are cognitive (Walters and Parke (1967))

And here is Aronfreed's (1964) basic statement of the role of punishment in 'internalized behavioral suppression'.

> ...one effect of punishment is to condition anxiety directly to the discriminative behavioral cues and cognitive representations which are intrinsically correlated with the transgression (e.g., to the child's cognitive representation of an actual performance of the transgression). The subsequent elicitation of anxiety by the intrinsic correlates of the transgression is then the motivation for suppression and the appearance of alternatives. (p. 169)

Both these accounts see the key to the matter in the formation of anticipations that the action in question will lead to negative affect and/or the elicitation of negative affect by the action itself (or the thought of it or intention to perform it). This may be the correct account of inhibition insofar as it occurs within LLM. But it tells us nothing about how an individual can form tendencies to influence his own LLM in opposition to what is there the currently strongest tendency.

Aronfreed, as we have seen, does separate out the 'internalized control' that comes about through the subject's evaluative cognition of his own behavior, and this is presumably roughly equivalent to our SI. Nevertheless, here too, the motivation to inhibit is said to stem from affective associations.

> ...an evaluative structure is not merely a cognitive scheme for the economical coding of information. It is the quality and magnitude of the affectivity that becomes associated with particular classifications which permit the structure to enter into the operations of value and to exercise some control over behavior. (p. 278)

In other words, the only way in which the adoption of a principle forbidding adultery can enter into the control of behavior is that negative affect has been associated with such acts. Internalized control by conscience differs from the more rudimentary sort only by inserting into the picture the cognitive content of self-judgment. But so long as it is affective anticipations that are crucial, we get no explanation of how in SI one can oppose the dominant trend of LLM.

How, then, can one understand the origins of HLW's? On our view of their nature the problem is that of understanding what is involved in the adoption of ES's toward persons. More specifically, we have to find a mechanism that will result in the adoption of a positive ES toward A, otherwise than by attaching positive affect to A; for the latter will not produce an ES that can go against a LLW for not-A. This requirement seems to be satisfied by some of the more prominent positions in the field, for example the identification position of Freud and others.[19]

Identification will be taken here in a broad sense to encompass any view according to which one gets at least one's earliest principles by taking them over from significant others. (Freud, 1923, 1933, Baldwin, 1906, Mead, 1934) This process will meet our requirement provided the acquisition of an ES is not conceived (as in Aronfreed) as the acquisition of an association requiring the attachment of affect to the *object* of the ES. The most prominent views satisfy this requirement. Thus on the Freudian concept of 'anaclitic' identification (Freud, 1917, Sears, 1957, Sears et al., 1965) the behavior and attitudes of the other are adopted because, since the presence of the other is rewarding to S, an imitation of the other acquires a rewarding quality by familiar generalization principles. This account clearly does not require that the *objects* of the positive or negative ES's thus adopted have antecedently aroused positive or negative affect. (Though, as we have seen, they can be expected to do so subsequently, as a result of the association they thereby come to have with the affectively toned experience of self-approval or self-disapproval.) Similar remarks can be made about the Freudian concept of identification with the aggressor. (A. Freud, 1946) There are other explanations of identification that derive rather from learning theory. Those most relevant to our present concerns have to do with the origin of such self-directed behavior as self-

[19] It also seems to be satisfied by the cognitive-developmental view of Piaget (1932) and Kohlberg (1969, a; 1959, b). I am not concerned here with what may otherwise be said for or against these positions, but only with whether they could explain the acquisition of ES's that can be in opposition to LLM.

criticism and self-administration of rewards. Investigations into these matters are highly relevant because in learning to criticize himself or to differentially reward himself on the basis of certain standards, the child is learning to take up certain ES's toward himself. Recent investigations (Bandura and Walters, 1963, W. Mischel, 1966) present evidence that one can acquire various sorts of behaviors, including these, simply by observing them in others without any reinforcement whatever. However the evidence also suggests that the child will not continue to behave in this way without reinforcement. Bandura and Walters (1963) suggest that self-critical behavior may be reinforced through its forestalling parental punishment, or by its securing reinstatement of the parents' affection or approval. (pp. 186–7) Aronfreed (1964) holds that the self-criticism acquires rewarding properties if the position of its analogue in the punishment behavior of the parents is such that it serves as a signal for the imminent cessation of aversive stimulation; by serving as such a signal it acquires a reinforcing value which generalizes to the child's imitation of it. W. Mischel (1966, p. 118) in explaining the influence of models on the tendency to such self-directed reactions, suggests that 'in our culture social learning experiences generate expectancies that emulating the behaviors of individuals who control and dispense valuable resources, and who have power, is likely to lead to positive consequences for the imitator'. These explanations, like the Freudian ones, are independent of any assumption that the contents of the principles involved have any attractiveness or aversiveness to the child *prior to* and as a condition of, his acquisition of the ES in question.

Thus identification provides a mechanism by which a person *could* acquire ES's with the required functional characteristic. It is worthy of note that one can adopt this position without saddling oneself with the following corrolaries, often supposed to be inseparable from it.

1. All one's principles (or at least all the most significant ones) are acquired in a single package.
2. One's ES's are not subject to rational modifications (or modification in any other way).

IX

We have been exploring some of the ways in which psychological research conflates LLW's and HLW's and have been considering the possibilities of disentangling the two. But it may be doubted that this is needed. As Cattell says (1957), with reference to his 'motivation components', they 'are delivered in the same package'. So long as the total achievement or prestige W can be ascertained, why bother to determine how much is LL and how much HL? Whatever the composition, the total W will push the agent in the same direction.

This challenge can only be met by showing that the difference *does* make a difference. Of course there is no question of *showing* this here. But I can mention a few ways in which it would be reasonable to expect that differences in the composition of the total W would make themselves felt.

1. The operation of HLW's requires more special conditions.

It is quite obscure just what is needed to set the mechanisms of SI into operation, the matter never having been properly investigated. But it is clear from common experience that whereas LLM is in operation during all one's working hours (and in sleep as well, if Freud is to be believed), SI is by no means always occurring, even in those periods in which the trend of one's LLM is running counter to some ES.

2. LLW's are more reliable.

If it is a more 'delicate' matter to arouse HLW's, a strong LLW for achievement is more likely, *ceteris paribus*, to produce frequent and vigorous strivings for achievement, than a strong HLW for achievement. This is in line with common experience. Ask yourself whether you would expect more attention to the needs of others from a person who delights in helping others, or from one who takes no delight in this but feels strongly that he *ought* to be doing it.

There is another reason for the greater reliability of LLW's. Not only is a LLW more likely to be frequently activated; a strong LLW is more likely to be successful when activated than a strong HLW. For a HLW is activated only when there is strong opposition; it comes into the game only with the bases loaded; it is never given a large lead to protect. No matter how skillful a late innings relief pitcher, he can't be expected to compile as good a won–lost record as an equally skillful starting pitcher. (The LLW will often be activated when there are no strong opposing W's in the field, and so it will win those contests hands down, even though it may also sometimes have strong opposition.) This is not to deny that *some* persons are so duty-oriented that the HLW's are generally dominant when activated (and are very frequently activated).

3. If we are trying to change behavior, it is necessary to identify the main source.

If we are trying to bring a person to abandon, or ease off on, his achievement strivings, it is important to know their sources. If the main source is a strongly held principle, and if his SI mechanism is finely tuned and easily activated, it will not be useful to attach aversive affect to achievement by 'counter-conditioning' techniques or to attach positive affect to incompatible goals. For a duty-ridden person is inured to persistently pursuing unpleasant goals. If, on the other hand, the LLW is more important, these techniques are appropriate.

4. The balance of HL and LL in W's generally, or for some particular W, may be an important dimension of individual differences.

I won't attempt to elaborate on this. It seems clear that the extent to which a person is either given to control his inclinations by considerations of principle, or given to do what he feels like doing at the moment, is a difference that ramifies widely. It has appeared in personality theory under a variety of guises, but the present distinction gives us a different, and perhaps more useful, way of construing it.

In summary, my suggestion is that once we fully accept the fact of SI and think through its implications, we will be led to certain fundamental complications of our thought about motivation and personality, and everything related to these fields.

William P. Alston
University of Illinois

REFERENCES

ALLPORT, G. W. The Ego in Contemporary Psychology', *Psych. Rev.* 50 (1943), 451–78.

ALLPORT, G. W. *Becoming: Basic Considerations for a Psychology of Personality*. New Haven: Yale University Press, 1955.

ARONFREED, J. *Conduct and Conscience: The Socialization of Internalized Control over Behavior*. New York: Academic Press, 1968.

ATKINSON, J. W. *An Introduction to Motivation*. Princeton: Van Nostrand, 1964.

ATKINSON, J. W. & BIRCH, D. *The Dynamics of Action*, New York: Wiley, 1970.

BALDWIN, J. M. *Social and Ethical Interpretations of Mental Development*. New York: Macmillan, 1906.

BANDURA, A. & WALTERS, R. *Social Learning and Personality Development*. New York: Holt, Rinehart & Winston, 1963.

BANDURA, A. & ROSENTHAL, T. L. 'Vicarious Classical Conditioning as a Function of Arousal Level.' *J. Pers. Soc. Psych.*, 1967, **7**, 111–16.

BERGER, S. M. 'Conditioning through Vicarious Instigation,' *Psych. Rev.*, 1962, **69**, 450–66.

CAMPBELL, C. A. 'The Psychology of Effort of Will,' *Proc. Arist. Soc.*, 40 (1940), 49–74.

CATTELL, R. B. *Personality and Motivation: Structure and Measurement*. Yonkers-on-Hudson: World Book, 1957.

CHEIN, I. 'The Awareness of Self and the Structure of the Ego,' *Psych. Rev.*, 1944, **51**, 304–14.

DOLLARD, J. & MILLER, N. E. *Personality and Psychotherapy*. New York: McGraw-Hill, 1950.

EDWARDS, W. 'The Theory of Decision Making,' *Psych. Bull.*, 1954, 51, 380–417.

FREUD, A. *The Ego and the Mechanisms of Defence*. New York: International Universities Press, 1946.

FREUD, S. *The Ego and the Id*. London: Hogarth Press, 1923.

FREUD, S. *New Introductory Lectures on Psychoanalysis*. New York: Norton, 1933.

FREUD, S. 'Mourning and Melancholia' (1917), in *Collected Papers*, Vol. IV. London: Hogarth, 1946.

HALL, C. S. & LINDZEY, G. *Theories of Personality*. New York: Wiley, 1957.

HARTSHORNE, H. & MAY, M. A. *Studies in the Nature of Character*. Vol. I. *Studies in Deceit*. New York: Macmillan, 1928.

HILGARD, E. R. 'Human Motives and the Concept of the Self.' *Amer. Psych.*, 1949, **4**, 374–82.

HOBBES, T. *Leviathan* (1651). London: J. M. Dent & Sons, 1914.

KOHLBERG, L. 'Stage and Sequence: the Cognitive-Developmental Approach to Socialization,' in D. Goslin, ed., *Handbook of Socialization Theory and Research*. Chicago: Rand McNally, 1969. (a)

KOHLBERG, L. *Stages in the Development of Moral Thought and Action*. New York: Holt, Rinehart & Winston, 1969 (b)

LEWIN, K. *The Conceptual Representation and the Measurement of Psychological Forces*. Durham, N. C.: Duke University Press, 1938.

MACKINNON, D. W. 'Violation of Prohibitions,' in H. A. Murray, Explorations in Personality. New York: Oxford University Press, 1938, 491–501.

MCCLELLAND, D. C. *Personality*. New York: William Sloane, 1951.

MCCLELLAND, D. C., et al. *The Achievement Motive*. New York: Appleton-Century-Crofts, 1953.

MEAD, G. H. *Mind, Self, and Society*. Chicago: University of Chicago Press, 1934.

MILL, J. S. *Utilitarianism*. (1863), London: J. M. Dent & Sons, 1910.

MISCHEL, W. 'Theory and Research on the Antecedents of Self-Imposed Delay of Reward,' in B. A. Maher, ed., *Progress in Experimental Personality Research*, 1966, **3**, 85–132.

MISCHEL, W. *Personality and Assessment*. New York: Wiley, 1968.

MISCHEL, W. 'Processes in Delay of Gratification,' in L. Berkowitz, ed., *Advances in Social Psychology*, **7**. New York: Academic Press, 1973.

MISCHEL, W. & MISCHEL, H. N. 'Self-Control and the Self.' This volume.

MOWRER, O. H. *Learning Theory and Personality Dynamics*. New York: Ronald, 1950.

MOWRER, O. H. *Learning Theory and the Symbolic Processes*. New York: Wiley, 1960.

MURPHY, G. *Personality: a Biosocial Approach to Origins and Structure*. New York: Harper, 1947.

PARKE, R. D. & WALTERS, R. H. 'Some Variables Influencing the Effectiveness of Punishment for Producing Response Inhibition,' *Monog. Soc. Res. Child Develop.*, **32** (1967), Whole no. 109.

PIAGET, J. The Moral Judgment of the Child (tr. M. Gabain), Glencoe, Illinois: Free Press, 1960 (French original, 1932).

ROGERS, C. R. *Client-centered Therapy: its Current Practice, Implications and Theory*. Boston: Houghton, 1951.

ROTTER, J. B. *Social Learning and Clinical Psychology*. New York: Prentice-Hall, 1954.

SEARS, R. R. 'Identification as a Form of Behavioral Development,' in

D. B. Harris, ed., *The Concept of Development*. Minneapolis, University of Minnesota Press, 1957, 149–61.

Sears, R. R., Rau, Lucy, and Alpert, R. *Identification and Child Rearing*. Stanford University Press, 1965.

Sherif, M. & Cantril, H. *The Psychology of Ego-Involvements*. New York: Wiley, 1947.

Symonds, P. M. *The Ego and the Self*. New York: Appleton-Century-Crofts, 1951.

Syngg, D. & Combs, A. W. *Individual Behavior*. New York: Harper 1949.

Taylor, C. 'What is Human Agency?' This volume.

Tolman, E. C. *Purposive Behavior in Animals and Men*. New York: Century, 1932.

Tolman, E. C. 'The Determiners of Behavior at a Choice Point,' *Psych. Rev.*, 1938, **45**, 1–41.

Tolman, E. C. 'A Psychological Model,' in T. Parsons and E. A. Shils, ed., *Toward a General Theory of Action*. Cambridge, Mass.: Harvard, 1951.

Tolman, E. C. 'Principles of Performance,' *Psych. Rev.*, 1955, **62**, 315–26.

Tolman, E. C. 'Principles of Purposive Behavior,' in S. Koch, ed., *Psychology: A Study of a Science*, **2**. New York: McGraw-Hill, 1959.

Toulmin, S. 'Self-Knowledge and Knowledge of the "Self".' This volume.

Walters, R. H., Leat, M. & Nezei, L. 'Response Inhibition and Disinhibition through Empathetic Learning,' *Canad. Journ. Psych.*, 1963, **17**, 235–43.

Walters, R. H. & Parke, R. D. 'The Influence of Punishment and Related Disciplinary Techniques on the Social Behavior of Children: Theory and Empirical Findings,' in B. A. Maher, ed., *Progress in Experimental Personality Research*, 4 (1967), 179–228.

4 What Is Human Agency?

CHARLES TAYLOR

Section One

I

I'd like to explore in this paper what is involved in the notion of a self, of a responsible human agent. What is it that we attribute to ourselves as human agents which we would not attribute to animals?

This question takes us very far indeed, and into several issues of capital importance in philosophy. I am not even going to try to sound them all. But I'd like to make a preliminary exploration of the terrain, using as my guide a key notion which has been introduced recently by Harry Frankfurt, in order to see how well the territory of the self may be mapped with its aid.

The key notion is the distinction betwen first- and second-order desires which Frankfurt makes in his 'Freedom of the Will and the Concept of Person' (1971). I can be said to have a second-order desire when I have a desire whose object is my having a certain (first-order) desire. The intuition underlying Frankfurt's introduction of this notion is that it is essential to the characterization of a human agent or person, that is to the demarcation of human agents from other kinds of agent. As he puts it,

> Human beings are not alone in having desires and motives, or in making choices. They share these things with members of certain other species, some of which even appear to engage in deliberation and to make decisions based on prior thought. It seems to be peculiarly characteristic of humans, however, that they are able to form . . . second order desires . . . (1971, p. 6)

Put in other terms, we think of (at least higher) animals as having desires, even as having to choose between desires in some cases, or at least as inhibiting some desires for the sake of others. But what is distinctively human is the power to *evaluate* our desires, to regard some as desirable and others as undesirable. This is why

> no animal other than man . . . appears to have the capacity for reflective self-evaluation that is manifested in the formatioin of second-order desires. (1971, p. 7)

I agree with Frankfurt that this capacity to evaluate desires is bound up with our power of self-evaluation, which in turn is an essential feature of the mode of agency we recognize as human. But I believe we can come closer to defining what is involved in this mode of agency if we make a further distinction, between two broad kinds of evaluation of desire.

Thus someone might be weighing two desired actions to determine the most convenient, or how to make different desires compossible (for instance, he might resolve to put off eating although hungry, because later he could both eat and swim), or how to get the most overall satisfaction. Or he might be pondering to see which of two desired objects attracts him most, as one ponders a pastry tray to see if one will take an éclair or a mille feuilles.

But what is missing in the above cases is a qualitative evaluation of my desires; the kind of thing we have, for instance, when I refrain from acting on a given motive—say, spite, or envy—because I consider it base or unworthy. In this kind of case our desires are classified in such categories as higher and lower, virtuous and vicious, more and less fulfilling, more and less refined, profound and superficial, noble and base. They are judged as belonging to qualitatively different modes of life: fragmented or integrated, alienated or free, saintly, or merely human, courageous or pusillanimous and so on.

Intuitively, the difference might be put in this way. In the first case, let us call it weak evaluation, we are concerned with outcomes; in the second, strong evaluation, with the quality of our motivation. But just put this way, it is a little too quick. For what is important is that strong evaluation is concerned with the qualitative *worth* of different desires. This is what is missing in the typical cases where I, e.g., choose a holiday in the South rather than the North, or choose to go to lunch at the beach rather than now in town. For in these cases, the favoured alternative is not selected because of the worth of the underlying motivation. There is 'nothing to choose' between the motivations here.

But this does not mean (a) that in weak evaluation the motivations are homogeneous. We may not be weighing two objects of the same desire, or put somewhat differently, two outcomes with the same desirability characterization. Take the example of someone who is hesitating between taking a holiday in the South or in the North. What's going for the holiday in the North is the tremendous beauty of the wild, the untracked wastes, etc. etc.; what's going for the South is the lush tropical land, the sense of well-being, the joy of swimming in the sea, etc. Or I might put it to myself that one holiday is more exhilarating, the other is more relaxing.

The alternatives have different desirability characterizations; in this sense they are qualitatively distinct. But what is missing in this case is a distinction between the desires as to worth, and that is why it is not a strong evaluation. I ultimately opt for the south over the north not because there is something more worthy about relaxing than being exhilarated, but just because 'I feel like it'.

It follows *a fortiori* (b) that weak evaluations are not simply quantitative either. That is, the alternatives cannot necessarily be expressed in some common units of calculation and in this sense rendered commensurable. This has often been obscured by the recurring ambition of our rationalist civilization to make practical reflection over as much as possible into calculation, an ambition whose major expression has been the doctrine of utilitarianism.

The bent of utilitarianism has been to do away with qualitative distinctions of worth on the grounds that they represent confused perceptions of the real bases of our preferences which are quantitative. The hope has been that once we have done away with strong evaluation we will be able to calculate. Utilitarianism has, I believe, been wrong on both counts. For decisions between alternatives which are not distinguished as to worth are not necessarily amenable to calculation—for instance, the choice between the two holidays above is clearly not so amenable, or only in part (or *some* of the considerations relevant to my choice of holiday might be quantifiable in a strict sense, e.g., cost). Nor is there any calculation when I stare at the pastry tray and try to decide whether I'll have an éclair or a mille feuilles.

All these weak evaluations are only 'quantitative' in the weak sense that they do not involve qualitative distinctions of worth. We sometimes explain our choices of this kind by saying that one alternative was 'more fun', or 'better value'; but there is no genuine quantification behind these expressions; they are just cover terms for 'preferred'. Utilitarians are certainly right from their own standpoint in rejecting strong evaluation, for doing away with this is a necessary condition of reducing practical reason to calculation. But it is far from being a sufficient condition.

Nor can we say (c) that weak evaluation is only concerned with outcomes, and never with desires; that all cases of second-order desires are strong evaluations. For I can have what Frankfurt calls 'second-order volitions' on the basis of weak evaluations. I have a second-order volition when I want certain first-order desires to be the ones which move me to action. Now I can want the desire to lunch-and-swim-later to be prepotent, because I know that I'll have a better time all things considered, though I fear that I will break down now that you're offering me lunch now. And I can have second-order desires on the same kind of basis: I might want my addiction to rich desserts to abate so that I can control my weight. But in both of these cases by hypothesis the alternatives would not be distinguished in that one of the desires was unworthy or base, or alienating, or trivial, or dishonourable, or something of the sort; in short there would be no qualitative distinction of the worth of the motivations.

And just as one can desire not to have a desire one has on the basis of weak evaluation, so one can desire a desire one hasn't got. Roman banqueters had and acted on this kind of second-order desire when they went to the vomitorium, so as to restore appetite and be able to go on eating with pleasure. This contrasts sharply with the case where I aspire to a desire out of a strong evaluation, where I see it as admirable, for instance, as when I want to be capable of a great and single-minded love or loyalty.[1]

The distinction between the two kinds of evaluation, then, doesn't simply turn on that between quantitative and qualitative evaluation,

[1] We might add a forth reservation and protest that strong evaluation is generally not of desires or motivations, but of qualities of action. I eschew some action because that is a cowardly way to *behave*, or a base *action*. The point is well taken if we mean that we are not speaking of desires alone, but we are seriously mistaken if we think that what is evaluated here are actions *as distinct from* motivations. Cowardly or other kinds of base behaviour are such partly in virtue of their motivation. So that strong evaluation necessarily involves a qualitative distinction of desires. To evaluate them by outcomes, that is, from a consequentialist or utilitarian standpoint.

or on the presence or absence of second-order desires. It concerns rather whether desires are distinguished as to worth. And for this we can perhaps set out two interlocking criteria.

(1) In weak evaluation, for something to be judged good it is sufficient that it be desired, whereas in strong evaluation there is also a use of 'good' or some other evaluative term for which being desired is not sufficient; indeed some desires or desired consummations can be judged as bad, base, ignoble, trivial superficial, unworthy, and so on.

It follows from this (2) that when in weak evaluation one desired alternative is set aside, it is only on grounds of its contingent incompatibility with a more desired alternative. I go to lunch later, although hungry now, because then I shall be able to lunch and swim. But I should be happy to have the best of both worlds: if the pool were open now, I could assuage my immediate hunger as well as enjoying a swim at lunch-time.

But with strong evaluation this is not necessarily the case. Some desired consummation may be eschewed not because it is incompatible with another, or if because of incompatibility, this will not be contingent. Thus I refrain from committing some cowardly act, although very tempted to do so, but this is not because this act at this moment would make any other desired act impossible, as lunching now would make swimming impossible, but rather because it is base.

But of course, there is also a way in which we could characterize this alternative which would bring out incompatibility. If we examine my evaluative vision more closely, we shall see that I value courageous action as part of a mode of life; I aspire to be a certain kind of person. This would be compromised by my giving in to this craven impulse. Here there is incompatibility. But this incompatibility is no longer contingent. It is not just a matter of circumstances which makes it impossible to give in to the impulse to flee and still cleave to a courageous, upright mode of life. Such a mode of life *consists* among other things in withstanding such craven impulses.

That there should be incompatibility of a non-contingent kind here is not adventitious. For strong evaluation deploys a language of evaluative distinctions, in which different desires are described as noble or base, integrating or fragmenting, courageous or cowardly, clairvoyant or blind, and so on. But this means that they are characterized contrastively. Each concept of one of the above pairs can only be understood in relation to the other. No one can have an idea what courage is unless he knows what cowardice is, just as no one can have a notion of 'red', say, without some other colour terms with which it contrasts. It is essential to both 'red' and 'courage' that we understand with what they are contrasted. And of course with evaluative terms, as with colour terms, the contrast may not just be with one other, but with several. And indeed, refining an evaluative vocabulary by introducing new terms would alter the sense of the existing terms, even as it would with our colour vocabulary.

This means that in strong evaluation, we can characterize the alternatives contrastively; and indeed, it can be the case that we must do so if we are to express what is really desirable in the favoured alternative. But this is not so with weak evaluation.[2] Of course, in each case, we are free to express the alternatives in a number of ways, some of which are and some of which are not contrastive. Thus I can describe my first issue above as between going to lunch *now* and going to lunch *later;* and this is a contrastive description in that it is essential to the identity of one of these alternatives that it not be the other. This is because the term 'now' only has sense through contrast with other terms like 'later', 'earlier', 'tomorrow', and so on. Indeed given the context (e.g., that one cannot decide to lunch in the past), and the contrastive background necessary to 'now', it would be enough to pose my issue to ask myself, 'shall I lunch now?' (or perhaps, 'shouldn't I better lunch later?).

But if I want to identify the alternatives in terms of their desirability, the characterization ceases to be contrastive. What is going for lunching now is that I'm hungry, and it is unpleasant to wait while one's hungry and a great pleasure to eat. What's going for eating later is that I can swim. But I can identify the pleasures of eating quite independently from those of swimming; indeed, I may have enjoyed eating long before swimming entered my life. Not

[2] It might be objected that utilitarians too make use of a qualitative contrast, i.e., that between pleasure and pain. But this is precisely not a qualitative contrast of *desires* of desired consummations, which is what we are considering here. Only pleasure is what is desired, according to utilitarian theory; pain we are averse to. Of course, we might want to contrast the *avoidance of pain*, which in one sense of the term we desire, and pleasure. But it is exactly this contrast which utilitarians have notoriously failed to make.

being contrastively described, these two desired consummations are incompatible, where they are, only contingently and circumstantially.

Reciprocally, I can describe the issue of my strong evaluations non-contrastively. I can say that the choice is between saving my life, or perhaps avoiding pain and embarrassment, on one hand, and upholding my honour on the other. Now certainly I can understand preserving my life, and what is desirable about it, without any acquaintance with honour, and the same goes for avoiding pain and embarrassment. And even if the reverse is not quite the case, no one could understand 'honour' without some reference to our desire to avoid death, pain, or embarrassment, for while one preserves honour, among other things, by a certain stance towards these—still saving one's honour is not simply contrastively defined with saving one's own life, avoiding pain and so on; there are many cases where one can save one's life without any taint to honour, without the question even arising.

And this non-contrastive description may even be the most apposite for certain purposes. Since there are certainly contingent conditions underlying my being faced with this dread choice of death or dishonour: if only the colonel hadn't sent me to the front line at just that moment when the enemy were attacking.... It is indeed in virtue of a contingent set of circumstances that I must now risk my life to avoid dishonour. But if I focus again on what makes the alternative to be rejected undesirable, i.e., that running away here is incompatible with honour, the incompatibility is no longer a contingent one: honourable conduct just consists in standing in face of such threat to life when this kind of issue is at stake. Or to put it in one word, running is to be eschewed because it is 'cowardly', a word which carries the sense of a non-contingent conflict with honourable conduct.

Thus while another pair of alternatives can be described either contrastively or non-contrastively, when we come to the desirability (or undesirability) characterizations in virtue of which one alternative is rejected, the alternatives in strong evaluation must be contrastively described. For in strong evaluation, where we deploy a language of evaluative distinctions, the rejected desire is not so rejected because of some mere contingent or circumstantial conflict with another goal. Being cowardly doesn't compete with other goods by taking up the time or energy I need to pursue them, and it may not alter my circumstances in such a way as to prevent my pursuing them. The conflict is deeper; it is not contingent.[3]

2

The utilitarian strand in our civilization would induce us to abandon the language of qualitative contrast, and this means, of course, abandon our strong evaluative languages, for their terms are only defined in contrast. And we can be tempted to redefine issues we are reflecting on in this non-qualitative fashion.

For instance, let us say that I am addicted to over-eating. I find it hard to resist treating myself to rich desserts. Now as I struggle with this issue, in the reflection in which I determine that moderation is better, I can be looking at the alternatives in a language of qualitative contrast. I can be reflecting that someone who has so little control over his appetites, that he would let his health go to pot over cream-cake, is not an admirable person. I yearn to be free of this addiction, to be the kind of person whose mere bodily appetites respond to his higher aspirations, and don't carry on remorselessly and irresistibly dragging him to incapacity and degradation.

But then I might be induced to see my problem in a quite different light. I might be induced to see it as a question of quantity of satisfaction. Eating too much cake increases the cholesterol in my blood, makes me fat, ruins my health, prevents me from enjoying all sorts of other desired consummations; so it isn't worth it. Here I have stepped away from the contrastive language of strong evaluation. Avoiding high cholesterol content, obesity, ill-health, or being able to climb stairs, and so on, can all be defined quite independently from my eating habits. Someone might even invent some drug which would allow me to go on eating rich desserts and also enjoy all those other goods, whereas no drug would allow me to eat my cake and attain the dignity of an autonomous, self-disciplined agent which I pined after on my first reading of the issue.

It may be that being talked around to see things in this non-qualitative light may help me solve my problem, that somehow it was too deeply disturbing when I put it in terms of dignity versus

[3] I am indebted for the present formulation of this point to the vigorous objections of Anne Wilbur Mackenzie against the whole enterprise of distinguishing strong from weak evaluation.

degradation, and now I can come to grips with it. But this is a separate question from which way of putting it is more illuminating and true to reality. This is a question about what our motivation really is, how we should truly characterize the meaning things have for us.

This is a conflict of self-interpretations. Which one we adopt will partly shape the meanings things have for us. But the question can arise which is more valid, more faithful to reality. To be in error here is thus not just to make a misdescription, as when I describe a motor-vehicle as a car when it is really a truck. We think of misidentification here as in some sense distorting the reality concerned. For the man who is trying to talk me out of seeing my problem as one of dignity versus degradation, I have made a crucial misidentification. But it is not just that I have called a fear of too high cholesterol content by the name 'degradation'; it is rather that infantile fears of punishment or loss of parental love have been irrationally transferred on to obesity, or the pleasures of eating, or something of the sort (to follow a rather vulgar-Freudian line). My experience of obesity, eating, etc. is shaped by this. But if I can get over this 'hang-up' and see the real nature of the underlying anxiety, I will see that it is largely groundless, i.e., I do not really incur the risk of punishment or loss of love; in fact there is a quite other list of things at stake here: ill health, inability to enjoy the out-door life, early death by heart-attack, and so on.

So might go a modern variant of the utilitarian thrust, trying to reduce our qualitative contrasts to some homogeneous medium. In this it would be much more plausible and sophisticated than earlier variants which talked as though it were just a matter of simple misidentification, that what people sought who pined after honour, dignity, integrity, etc. were simply other pleasurable states to which they gave these high-sounding names.

There are of course ripostes to these attempts to reduce our evaluations to a non-qualitative form. We can entertain the countersurmise that the rejection of qualitative distinctions is itself an illusion, powered perhaps by an inability to look at one's life in the light of some of the distinctions, a failure of moral nerve, as it were; or else by the draw of a certain objectifying stance towards the world. We might hold that the most hard-bitten utilitarians are themselves moved by qualitative distinctions which remain unadmitted, that they admire the mode of life in which one calculates consciously and clairvoyantly as something higher than the life of self-indulgent illusion, and do not simply elect it as more satisfying.

We can't resolve this issue here. The point of introducing this distinction between strong and weak evaluation is to contrast the different kinds of self that each involves. In examining this it will, I think, become overwhelmingly plausible that we are not beings whose only authentic evaluations are non-qualitative as the utilitarian tradition suggests.

A subject who only evaluates weakly, i.e., makes decisions like that of eating now or later, taking a holiday in the North or in the South, such a subject we might call a simple weighter of alternatives. And the other, who deploys a language of evaluative contrasts ranging over desires we might call a strong evaluator.

Now we can concur that a simple weigher is already reflective in a minimal sense, that he evaluates courses of action, and sometimes is capable of acting out of that evaluation as against under the impress of immediate desire. And this is a necessary feature of what we call a self or a person. He has reflection, evaluation and will. But in contrast to the strong evaluator he lacks something else which we often speak of with the metaphor of 'depth'.

The strong evaluator envisages his alternatives through a richer language. The desirable is not only defined for him by what he desires, or what he desires plus a calculation of consequences; it is also defined by a qualitative characterization of desires as higher and lower, noble and base, etc. Reflection is not just a matter, where it is not calculation of consequences, of registering the conclusion that alternative A is more attractive to me, or draws me more than B. Rather the higher desirability of A over B is something I can articulate if I am reflecting as a strong evaluator. I have a vocabulary of worth.

In other words, the reflection of the simple weigher terminates in the inarticulate experience that A is more attractive than B. I am presented with the pastry tray, I concentrate on it, hesitate between an *éclair* and a *mille feuilles*. It becomes clear to me that I feel more like an *éclair* now, so I take it. Of course, one can say a lot more about the attractiveness of the alternatives in other cases of simple weighing. For instance, when I was choosing between a holiday in the North and one in the South, I will talk about the tremendous beauty of the North, of the wild, the sense of untracked wastes, etc. etc., or the lush tropical land, the sense of well-being, the joys of swimming in the sea, etc. All this can be expressed. What cannot be is what makes the South, my ultimate choice, superior.

Thus faced with incommensurables, which is our usual predicament, the simple weigher's experiences of the superiority of A over B are inarticulable. The role of reflection is not to make these articulate, but rather to step back from the immediate situation, to calculate consequences, to compensate for the immediate force of one desire which might not be the most advantageous to follow (as when I put off lunch to swim-with-lunch later), to get over hesitation by concentrating on the inarticulate 'feel' of the alternatives (do I really feel like an *éclair* or a *mille feuilles*?).

But the strong evaluator is not similarly inarticulate. There is the beginning of a language in which to express the superiority of one alternative, the language of higher and lower, noble and base, courageous and cowardly, integrated and fragmented, and so on. The strong evaluator can articulate superiority just because he has a language of contrastive characterization.[4]

So within an experience of reflective choice between incommensurables, strong evaluation is a condition of articulacy, and to acquire a strongly evaluative language is to become (more) articulate about one's preferences. I can't tell you perhaps very volubly why Bach is greater than Liszt, say, but I am not totally inarticulate: I can speak of the 'depth' of Bach, for instance, a word one only understands against a corresponding use of 'shallow', which, unfortunately, applies to Liszt. In this regard I am way ahead of where I am in articulating why I now prefer that *éclair* to the *mille feuilles*; about this I can say nothing (not even that it tastes better, which I could

[4] It is because the alternatives are characterized in a language of qualitative contrast that strong evaluative choices show the feature we mentioned above, that the rejected alternative is not rejected because of some merely contingent or circumstantial conflict with the goal chosen. To have a language of qualitative contrast is to characterize the noble essentially as in contrast to the base, the courageous to the cowardly, and so on.

With this in mind we can see right away how the holiday preference could become articulate, too. We might decide to go South rather than North because we will have a more humanly meaningful or uplifting experience in visiting some ancient civilization than in being away from any traces of man. With this example we can also see that languages of strong evaluation don't have to be exclusively ethical, as one might have surmised from the examples above; they can also be aesthetic and of other kinds as well.

say, for instance, in explaining my preference for *éclairs* over brussels-sprouts; but even this is on the verge of inarticulacy, cf. our replying above that Bach 'sounds better'). And I am also way ahead of where I might be if I had never arquired any language to talk about music, if it were a quite inarticulable experience for me (of course, it would then be a very different experience).

To be a strong evaluator is thus to be capable of a reflection which is more articulate. But it is also in an important sense deeper.

A strong evaluator, by which we mean a subject who strongly evaluates desires, goes deeper, because he characterizes his motivation at greater depth. To characterize one desire or inclination as worthier, or nobler, or more integrated, etc. than others is to speak of it in terms of the kind of quality of life which it expresses and sustains. I eschew the cowardly act above because I want to be a courageous and honourable human being. Whereas for the simple weigher what is at stake is the desirability of different consummations, those defined by his *de facto* desires, for the strong evaluator reflection also examines the different possible modes of being of the agent. Motivations or desires don't only count in virtue of the attraction of the cosummations but also in virtue of the kind of life and kind of subject that these desires properly belong to.[5]

[5] To be a strong evaluator is thus to see desires in an additional dimension. And this is in fact essential to our important evaluative distinctions. It has been remarked for instance that the criteria of a courageous act cannot be given simply in terms of external achievement in a given context. Someone may rush the machine-guns out of stupidity, or drunk with frenzy, or because he has had too much of life. It is not sufficient just that he see the danger, a condition which is met in the last two cases. Or suppose a man is driven with some uncontrollable lust, or hatred, or desire for revenge, so that he runs out into danger. This isn't courage either, so long as we see him as *driven*.

Courage requires that we face danger, feel the fear which is appropriate, and nevertheless over-rule the impulse to flee because we in some sense dominate it, because we are moved by something higher than mere impulse or the mere desire to live. It may be glory, or the love of country, or the love of some individuals we are saving, or a sense of our own integrity. Implicit in all of these is that the courageous man is moved by what we can at least think of as seen by him to be higher. If someone for instance thought that there was nothing higher than life and the avoidance of pain, and believed that no one could sanely and responsibly think otherwise, he would have no place in his vocabularly for physical courage. Any act that might appear to qualify for this title would have to be classified by him as foolhardy, mad, or moronically insensitive to reality, or something of the kind. If we can think of gangsters as being heroic it is because in this post-Romantic age we see something

But this additional dimension can be said to add depth, because now we are reflecting about our desires in terms of the kind of being we are in having them or carrying them out. Whereas a reflection about what we feel like more, which is all a simple weigher can do in assessing motivations, keeps us as it were at the periphery; a reflection on the kind of beings we are takes us to the centre of our existence as agents. Strong evaluation is not just a condition of articulacy about preferences, but also about the quality of life, the kind of beings we are or want to be. It is in this sense deeper.

And this is what lies behind our ordinary use of the metaphor of depth applied to people. Someone is shallow in our view when we feel that he is insensitive, unaware or unconcerned about issues touching the quality of his life which seem to us basic or important. He lives on the surface because he seeks to fulfil desires without being touched by the 'deeper' issues, what these desires express and sustain in the way of modes of life; or his concern with such issues seems to us to touch on trivial or unimportant questions, e.g., he is concerned about the glamour of his life, or how it will appear, rather than the (to us) real issues of the quality of life.

The compleat Utilitarian would be an impossibly shallow character, and we can gauge how much self-declared utilitarians really live their ideology by what importance they attribute to depth.

3

Thus the strong evaluator has articulacy and depth which the simple weigher lacks. He has, one might say, articulacy about depth. But

---

admirable in people living some grand design to the ultimate end, whatever it be.

In other words the criteria of courage, of a courageous act, include the motivation of the act; and judging the motivation here involves reference to higher and lower motives. At the very least an act of courage must be an act of self-domination, it cannot be done out of uncontrollable craving, or frenzy; and the condition of our using 'courage' in connection with this act is that we see self-domination in the name of some responsible goal as higher than mere uncontrollable craving, or frenzy; that we think it a higher form of life, a better type of subject, to be able so to direct one's self towards some responsible goal than to be in the grips of craving or frenzy. If someone really thought that the highest in life was to let it all go all the time ('let it all hang out man') then he couldn't see the same acts as courageous, but just as compulsive, hung up, insensitive.

where there is articulacy there is the possibility of a plurality of visions which there wasn't before. The simple weigher may hesitate, as before the *éclair* and *mille feuilles*, and his momentary preference may go back and forth. But we wouldn't say that he envisages his situation of choice now one way now another. But with strong evaluation there can be and often is a plurality of ways of envisaging my predicament, and the choice may be not just between what is clearly the higher and the lower, but between two incommensurable ways of looking at this choice.

Let us say that at the age of 44 I am tempted to pick up, abandon my job and go to some other quite different job in Nepal. One needs to renew the sources of creativity, I tell myself, one can fall into a deadening routine, go stale, simply go through the motions of teaching the same old courses; this way is premature death. Rather rejuvenation is something one can win by courage and decisive action; one must be ready to make a break, try something totally new; and so on, and so on. All this I tell myself when the mood is on me. But then at other moments, this seems like a lot of adolescent nonsense. In fact nothing in life is won without discipline, hanging in, being able to last through periods of mere slogging until something greater grows out of them. One has to have a long breath, and standing loyalties to a certain job, a certain community; and the only meaningful life is that which is deepened by carrying through on these commitments, living through the dead periods in order to lay the foundations for the creative ones; and so on.

We see that, unlike the choice between *éclair* and *mille feuilles*, or the vactions North and South, where we have two incommensurable objects attracting us, we have here 'objects'—courses of action—which can only be characterized through the qualities of life they represent, and characterized contrastively. It is part of the desirability characterization of each that it has an undesirability story to tell about the other. But the struggle here is between two such characterizations, and this introduces a new incommensurability. When I am feeling that the break to Nepal is the thing, my desire to stay is a kind of pusillanimity, a weary enmiring in routine, the growing action of a sclerosis that I can only cure by splitting. It is far from being the quietly courageous loyalty to an original line of life, hanging in during the dry period to permit a fuller flowering. And when I am for staying my trip to Nepal looks like a lot of

adolescent nonsense, an attempt to be young again by just refusing to act my age, hardly great liberation, renewal and all that.

We have here a reflection about what to do which is carried on in a struggle of self-interpretations, like our example above of the man struggling against his addictions to rich desserts. The question at issue concerns which is the truer, more authentic, more illusion-free interpretation, and which on the other hand involves a distortion of the meanings things have for me. Resolving this issue is restoring commensurability.

Section Two

I

Starting off from the intuition that the capacity for second-order desires, or evaluating desires, is essential to human agency, I have tried to distinguish two kinds of such evaluation. I hope the discussion has also served to make this basic intuition more plausible, if indeed it lacked any plausibility at the outset. It must be clear that an agent who could not evaluate desires at all would lack the minimum degree of reflectiveness which we associate with a human agent, and would also lack a crucial part of the background for what we describe as the exercise of will.

I should also like to add, but with perhaps less certainty of universal agreement, that the capacity for strong evaluation in particular is essential to our notion of the human subject; that without it an agent would lack a kind of depth we consider essential to humanity, without which we would find human communication impossible (the capacity for which is another essential feature of human agency). But I will not try to argue this case here. The question would revolve around whether one could draw a convincing portrait of a human subject to whom strong evaluation was quite foreign (is Camus' Mersenne such a case?), since in fact the human beings we are and live with are all strong evaluators.

But for the remainder of this paper, I should like to examine another avenue of the self, that of responsibility, with the aid of the key notion of second-order desire. For we think of persons as responsible as well, in a way that animals are not, and this too seems bound up with the capacity to evaluate desires.

There is one sense of responsibility which is already implicit in the notion of will. A being capable of evaluating desires may find that the upshot of such evaluation is in conflict with the most urgent desire. Indeed, we might think of it as a necessary feature of the capacity to evaluate desires that one be able to distinguish the better one from the one that presses most strongly.

But in at least our modern notion of the self, responsibility has a stronger sense. We think of the agent not only as partly responsible for what he does, for the degree to which he acts in line with his evaluations, but also as responsible in some sense for these evaluations.

This sense is even suggested by the word 'evaluation', which belongs to the modern, one might almost say post-Neitzschean vocabulary of moral life. For it relates to the verb 'evaluate', and the verb here implies that this is something we do, that our evaluations emerge from our activity of evaluation, and in this sense are our responsibility.

This active sense is conveyed in Frankfurt's formulation where he speaks of persons as exhibiting 'reflective self-evaluation that is manifested in the formation of second-order desires'.

Or we might put the suggestion another way. We have certain *de facto*, first order desires These are given, as it were. But then we form evaluations, or second-order desires. But these are not just given, they are also endorsed, and in this sense they engage our responsibility.

How are we to understand this responsibility? An influential strand of thought in the modern world has wanted to understand it in terms of choice. The Nietzschean term 'value', suggested by our 'evaluation', carries this idea that our 'values' are our creations, that they ultimately repose on our espousing them. But to say that they ultimately repose on our espousing them is to say that they issue ultimately from a radical choice, that is, a choice which is not grounded in any reasons. For to the extent that a choice is grounded in reasons, these are simply taken as valid and are not themselves chosen. If our 'values' are to be thought of as chosen, then they must repose finally on a radical choice in the above sense.

This is of course, the line taken by Sartre in *L'Être et le Néant*, in which he takes the line that the fundamental project which defines us reposes on a radical choice. The choice, Sartre puts it with his characteristic flair for striking formulae, is 'absurde, en ce sens, qu'il est ce par quoi . . . toutes les raisons viennent à l'être' (1943, p. 559). This idea of radical choice is also defended by an influential Anglo-Saxon school of moral philosophers.

But in fact we cannot understand our responsibility for our evaluations through the notion of radical choice. Not if we are to go on seeing ourselves as strong evaluators, as agents with depth. For a radical choice *between* strong evaluations is quite conceivable, but not a radical choice *of* such evaluations.

To see this we might examine a famous Sartrian example, which turns out, I believe, to illustrate the exact opposite of Sartre's thesis, the example in *L'Existentialisme est un Humanisme* of the young man who is torn between remaining with his ailing mother and going off to join the Resistance. Sartre's point is that there is no way of adjudicating between these two strong claims on his moral allegiance through reason or the reliance on some kind of overarching considerations. He has to settle the question, whichever way he goes, by radical choice.

Sartre's portrayal of the dilemma is very powerful here. But what makes it plausible is precisely what undermines his position. We see a grievous moral dilemma because the young man is faced here with two powerful moral *claims*. On one hand his ailing mother may well die if he leaves her, and die in the most terrible sorrow, not even sure that her son still lives; on the other side the call of his country, conquered and laid waste by the enemy, and not only his country, for this enemy is destroying the very foundation of civilized and ethical relations between men. A cruel dilemma, indeed. But it is a dilemma only because the claims themselves are not created by radical choice. If they were the grievous nature of the predicament would dissolve, for that would mean that the young man could do away with the dilemma at any moment by simply declaring one of the rival claims as dead and inoperative. Indeed, if serious moral claims were created by radical choice, the young man could have a grievous dilemma about whether to go and get an ice cream cone, and then again he could decide not to.

It is no argument against the view that evaluations do not repose on radical choice that there are moral dilemmas. Why should it even be surprising that the evaluations we feel called upon to assent to may conflict, even grievously, in some situations? I would argue that the reverse is the case, that moral dilemmas become inconceivable on the theory of radical choice.

Now in this hypothetical case the young man has to resolve the matter by radical choice. He just has to plump for the Resistance, or for staying at home with his mother. He has no language in which the superiority of one alternative over the other can be articulated; indeed, he has not even an inchoate sense of the superiority of one over the other, they seem quite incommensurable to him. He just throws himself one way.

This is a perfectly understandable sense of radical choice. But then imagine extending this to all cases of moral action. Let us apply it to the case that I have an ailing mother and no rival obligation. Do I stay, or do I go for a holiday on the Riviera? There is no doubt I should stay. Of course, I *may* not stay. In this sense, there is also a 'radical choice' open: whether to do what we ought or not (although here I might put forward all sorts of rationalizations for going to the Côte d'Azur, I owe it to myself, after all I've faithfully taken care of her all these years while my brothers and sisters have gone off, and so on). But the question is whether we can construe the determination of what we ought to do here as issuing from a radical choice.

What would this look like? Presumably, we would be faced with the two choices, to stay with my mother or go to the South. On the level of radical choice these alternatives have as yet no contrastive characterization, that is, one is not the path of duty, while the other is that of selfish indulgence, or whatever.

This contrastive description will be created by radical choice. So what does this choice consist in? Well, I might ponder the two possibilities, and then I might just find myself doing one rather than another. But this brings us to the limit where choice fades into non-choice. Do I really choose if I just start doing one of the alternatives? And above all, this kind of resolution has no place for the judgement 'I owe it to my mother to stay', which is supposed to issue from the choice.

What is it to have this judgement issue from radical choice? Not that on pondering the alternatives, the sense grows more and more strongly that this judgement is *right*, for this would not be an account of radical choice, but rather of our coming to see that our obligation lay here. This account would present obligations as issuing not from radical choice but from some kind of vision of our moral predicament. This choice would be grounded. What is it then for radical choice to issue in this judgement? Is it just that I find myself assenting to the judgement, as in the previous paragraph I found myself doing one of the two actions? But then what force has 'assenting to the judgement'? I can certainly just find myself saying 'I owe it to my mother', but this is surely not what it is to assent. I can, I suppose, find myself feeling suddenly, 'I owe this to my mother'; but then what grounds are there for thinking of this as a choice?

In order for us to speak of choice, we cannot just find ourselves in one of the alternatives. We have in some sense to experience the pull of each and give our assent to one. But what kind of pull do the alternatives have here? What draws me to the Côte d'Azur is perhaps unproblematic enough, but what draws me to stay with my mother cannot be the sense that I owe it to her, for that *ex hypothesi* has to issue from the choice. It can only be a *de facto* desire, like my desire for the sun and sea of the Côte d'Azur. But then the choice here is like the choice of the two holidays in the previous section. I feel the attraction of these two incommensurable alternatives, and after I ponder them I find that one begins to become prepotent, it draws me more. Or perhaps, the matter obstinately refuses to resolve itself, and I say at one moment, 'what the hell, I'll stay'.

The agent of radical choice has to choose, if he chooses at all, like a simple weigher. And this means that he cannot be properly speaking a strong evaluator. For all his putative strong evaluations issue from simple weighings. The application of a contrastive language which makes a preference articulate reposes on fiat, a choice made between incommensurables. But then the application of the contrastive language would be in an important sense bogus. For by hypothesis the experience on which the application reposed would be more properly characterized by a preference between incommensurables; the fundamental experience which was supposed to justify this language would in fact be that of the simple weigher, not of the strong evaluator. For again by hypothesis, what leads him to call one alternative higher or more worthy is not that in his experience it appears to be so, for then his evaluations would be judgements, not choices; but rather that he is led to plump for one rather than the other after considering the attractiveness of both alternatives.

But of course, even this account of choice would not be acceptable to the theorist of radical choice. He would refuse the assimilation of these choices to such decisions as whether to go South or North for my holiday. For these choices are not supposed to be simply the registration of my preferences, but radical choices. But what is a radical choice which is not even a registration of preference? Well, it may be that I just decide, just throw myself one way rather than another. I just say, 'what the hell, I'll stay'. But this, of course, I can do in the holiday choice case, where, for instance, I can't seem to make up my mind which is preferable. This doesn't distinguish the two cases.

Perhaps then it is that in radical choice I don't consult preferences at all. It is not that I try to see which I prefer, and then failing to get a result, I throw myself one way or the other; but rather, this kind of choice is made quite without regard to preferences. But then with regard to what is it made? Here we border on incoherence. A choice made without regard to anything, without the agent feeling any solicitation to one alternative or the other, or in complete disregard of such solicitation, is this still choice? What could it be? Well, suddenly he just goes up and takes one of the alternatives. Yes, but this he could do in a fit of abstraction. What makes it a choice? It must be something to do with what he is thinking out of which this act comes. But what could that be? Can it just be that he is thinking something like 'I must take one of them, I must take one of them', repeating it to himself in a fever? Surely not. Rather he must be pondering the alternatives, be in some way considering their desirability, and the choice must be in some way related to that. Perhaps he judges that A is by all criteria more desirable, and then he chooses B. But if this is a choice and not just an inexplicable movement, it must have been accompanied by something like: 'damn it, why should I always choose by the book, I'll take B'; or maybe he just suddenly felt that he really wanted B. In either case, his choice clearly relates to his preference, however suddenly arising and from whatever reversal of criteria. But a choice utterly unrelated to the desirability of the alternatives would not be intelligible as a choice.

The theory of radical choice in fact is deeply incoherent, for it wants to maintain both strong evaluation and radical choice. It wants to have strong evaluations and yet deny their status as judgements. And the result is that on close examination, it crumbles; in order to maintain its coherence the theory of radical choice in fact mutates into something quite different. Either we take seriously the kinds of consideration which weigh in our moral decisions, and then we are forced to recognize that these are for the most part evaluations which do not issue from radical choice. Or else we try at all costs to keep our radical choice independent of any such evaluations; but then it ceases to be a choice of strong evaluations, and becomes a simple expression of preference; and if we go farther and try to make it independent even of our *de facto* preferences, then we fall ultimately into a criteria-less leap which can't properly be described as choice at all.

In fact the theory maintains a semblance of plausibility by surreptitiously assuming strong evaluation beyond the reach of radical choice, and that in two ways. First, the real answer to our attempted assimilation of radical moral choice to the mere preference of a simple weigher is that the choices talked about in the theory are about basic and fundamental issues, like the choice of our young man above, between his mother and the Resistance. But these issues are basic and fundamental not in virtue of radical choice; their importance is given, or revealed in an evaluation which is constated not chosen. The real force of the theory of radical choice comes from the sense that there are different moral perspectives, that there is a plurality of moral visions as we said in the previous section, between which it seems very hard to adjudicate. We can conclude that the only way of deciding between these is by the kind of radical choice that our young man had to take.

And this in turn leads to a second strong evaluation beyond the reach of choice. If this is the predicament of man, then it plainly is a more honest, more clairvoyant, less confused and self-deluding stance, to be aware of this and take the full responsibility for the radical choice. The stance of 'good faith' is higher, and this not in virtue of radical choice, but in virtue of our characterization of the human predicament in which radical choice has such an important place. Granted this is the moral predicament of man, it is more honest, courageous, self-clairvoyant, hence a higher mode of life, to choose in lucidity than it is to hide one's choices behind the supposed structure of things, to flee from one's responsibility at the expense of lying to oneself, of a deep self-duplicity.

When we see what makes the theory of radical choice plausible we see how strong evaluation is something inescapable in our conception of the agent and his experience; and this because it is bound up with our notion of the self. So that it creeps back in even where it is supposed to have been excluded.

2

We can see this from another angle if we consider another way of showing the theory of radical choice to be wrong. I mentioned in the last section that strong evaluators can be called deep because what weighs with them are not only the consummations desired but also what kind of life, what quality of agent they are to be. Now this is closely connected with the notion of identity.

By 'identity' I mean that use of the term where we talk about 'finding one's identity', or going through an 'identity crisis'. Now our identity is defined by our fundamental evaluations. The answer to the question, what is my identity? can't be given by any list of properties of other ranges, about my physical description, provenance, background, capacities, and so on. All these can figure in my identity, but only as assumed in a certain way. If my being of a certain lineage is to me of central importance, if I am proud of it, I see it as conferring on me membership in a certain class of people whom I see as marked off by certain qualities which I value in myself as an agent and which come to me from this background; then it will be part of my identity. This will be strengthened if I believe that men's moral qualities are to a great extent nourished by their background, so that to turn against one's background is to reject oneself in an important way.

So my lineage is part of my identity because it is bound up with certain qualities I value, or because I believe that I must value these qualities since they are so integrally part of me that to disvalue them would be to reject myself. In either case, the concept of identity is bound up with that of certain strong evaluations which are inseparable from myself. This either because I identify myself by my strong evaluations, as someone who essentially has these convictions; or else because I see certain of my other properties as admitting of only one kind of strong evaluation by myself, because these properties so centrally touch what I am as an agent, that is, as a strong evaluator, that I cannot really repudiate them in the full sense. For I would be thereby repudiating myself, inwardly riven, and hence incapable of fully authentic evaluation.

Our identity is therefore defined by certain evaluations which are inseparable from ourselves as agents. Shorn of these we would cease to be ourselves, by which we do not mean trivially that we would be different in the sense of having some properties other than those we now have—this would indeed be the case after any change however minor—but that shorn of these we would lose the very possibility of being an agent who evaluates; that our existence as persons, and hence our ability to adhere as persons to certain evaluations, would be impossible outside the horizon of these essential evaluations, that we would break down as persons, be incapable of being persons in the full sense.

Thus, if I were forced by torture or brainwashing to abandon these convictions by which I define my identity, I would be shattered, I would no longer be a subject capable of knowing where I stood and what the meanings of things were for me, I would suffer a terrifying breakdown of precisely those capacities which define a human agent. Or if, to take the other example, I were somehow induced to repudiate my lineage, I would be crippled as a person, because I would be repudiating an essential part of that out of which I evaluate and determine the meanings of things for me. Such repudiation would both be itself inauthentic and would make me incapable of other authentic evaluations.

The notion of identity refers us to certain evaluations which are essential because they are the indispensable horizon or foundation out of which we reflect and evaluate as persons. To lose this horizon, or not to have found it, is indeed as terrifying experience of disaggregation and loss. This is why we can speak of an 'identity-crisis' when we have lost our grip on who we are. A self decides and acts out of certain fundamental evaluations.

This is what is impossible in the theory of radical choice. The agent of radical choice would at the moment of choice have *ex hypothesi* no horizon of evaluation. He would be utterly without indentity. He would be a kind of extensionless point, a pure leap into the void. But such a thing is an impossibility, or rather could only be the description of the most terrible mental alienation. The subject of radical choice is another avatar of that recurrent figure which our civilization aspires to realize, the disembodied ego, the subject who can objectify all being, including his own, and choose in radical freedom. But this promised total self-possession would in fact be the most total self-loss.

3

What then is the sense we can give to the responsibility of the agent, if we are not to understand it in terms of radical choice? Do we have to conclude that we are not in any sense responsible for our evaluations?

I think not. For there is another sense in which we are responsible. Our evaluations are not chosen. On the contrary they are articulations of our sense of what is worthy, or higher, or more integrated, or more fulfilling, and so on. But as *articulations*, they offer another purchase for the concept of responsibility. Let us examine this.

Much of our motivation—our desires, aspirations, evaluations—is not simply given. We give it a formulation in words or images. Indeed, by the fact that we are linguistic animals our desires and aspirations cannot but be articulated in one way or another. Thus we are not simply moved by psychic forces comparable to such forces as gravity or electro-magnetism, which we can see as given in a straightforward way, but rather by psychic 'forces'[6] which are articulated or interpreted in a certain way.

Now these articulations are not simply descriptions, if we mean by this characterizations of a fully independent object, that is, an object which is neither altered in what it is, nor in the degree or manner of its evidence to us by the description. In this way my characterization of this table as brown, or this line of mountains as jagged, is a simple description.

On the contrary, articulations are attempts to formulate what is initially inchoate, or confused, or badly formulated. But this kind of formulation or reformulation doesn't leave its object unchanged. To give a certain articulation is to shape our sense of what we desire or what we hold important in a certain way.

Let us take the case above of the man who is fighting obesity and who is talked into seeing it as a merely quantitative question of more satisfaction, rather than as a matter of dignity and degradation.

[6] I put the expression in quotes here because the underlying motivation which we want to speak of in terms of psychic 'forces' or 'drives' is only accesible through interpretation of behaviour or feeling. The line here between metaphor and basic theory is very hard to draw. Cf. Paul Ricoeur (1965), and my discussion (1975).

As a result of this change, his inner struggle itself becomes transformed, it is now quite a different experience.

The opposed motivations—the craving for cream cake and his dissatisfaction with himself at such indulgence—which are the 'objects' undergoing rediscription here, are not independent in the sense outlined above. When he comes to accept the new interpretation of his desire to control himself, this desire itself has altered. True, it may be said on one level to have the same goal, that he stop eating cream cake, but since it is no longer understood as a seeking for dignity and self-respect it has become quite a different kind of motivation.

Of course, even here we often try to preserve the identity of the objects undergoing redescription—so deeply rooted is the ordinary descriptive model. We might think of the change, say, in terms of some immature sense of shame and degradation being detached from our desire to resist over-indulgence, which has now simply the rational goal of increasing over-all satisfaction. In this way we might maintain the impression that the elements are just re-arranged while remaining the same. But on a closer look we see that on this reading, too, the sense of shame doesn't remain self-identical through the change. It dissipates altogether, or becomes something quite different.

We can say therefore that our self-interpretations are partly constitutive of our experience. For an altered description of our motivation can be inseparable from a change in this motivation. But to assert this connection is not to put forward a causal hypothesis: it is not to say that we alter our descriptions and then *as a result* our experience of our predicament alters. Rather it is that certain modes of experience are not possible without certain self-descriptions. The particular quality of experience in the obesity case where I approach the alternative purely as a balance of utility, where I am free from the menace of degradation and self-contempt, cannot be without my characterizing the two rival desires in this 'deflated' way, as two different kinds of advantage. This deflated description is part of the objectifying, calculative way I now experience the choice. We can say that it is 'constitutive' of this experience, and this is the term I shall use for this relation.

But the fact that self-interpretations are constitutive of experience says nothing about how changes in both descriptions and experience are brought about. It would appear in fact that change can be brought about in two different ways. In some circumstances, we are led to reflect, on our own or in exchange with others, and can sometimes win through to a new way of seeing our predicament, and hence a change in our experience. But more fundamentally, it would appear that certain descriptions of experience are unacceptable or incomprehensible to some people because of the nature of their experience. To someone who strongly experiences the fight against obesity in terms of degradation, the 'deflated' descriptions appear a wicked travesty, a shameless avoidance of moral reality—rather as we react to the hiding of political crime through Orwellian language, e.g., renaming mass murder a final 'solution'.

That description and experience are bound together in this constitutive relation admits of causal influences in both directions: it can sometimes alow us to alter experience by coming to fresh insight; but more fundamentally it circumscribes insight through the deeply-embedded shape of experience for us.

Because of this constitutive relation, our descriptions of our motivations, and our attempts to formulate what we hold important, are not simple descriptions, in that their objects are not fully independent. And yet they are not simply arbitrary either, such that anything goes. There are more or less adequate, more or less truthful, more self-clairvoyant or self-deluding interpretations. Because of this double fact, because an articulation can be *wrong*, and yet it shapes what it is wrong about, we sometimes see erroneous articulations as involving a distortion of the reality concerned. We don't just speak of error but frequently also of illusion or delusion.

We could put the point this way. Our attempts to formulate what we hold important must, like descriptions, strive to be faithful to something. But what they strive to be faithful to is not an independent object with a fixed degree and manner of evidence, but rather a largely inarticulate sense of what is of decisive importance. An articulation of this 'object' tends to make it something different from what it was before.

And by the same token a new articulation doesn't leave its 'object' evident or obscure to us in the same manner or degree as before. In the fact of shaping it, it makes it accessible and/or inaccessible in new ways. This is in fact well illustrated by our example of the man fighting obesity.

Now our articulations, just because they partly shape their objects, engage our responsibility in a way that simple descriptions do not.

And this in two related ways which correspond to the two directions of causal influence mentioned above.

First, because our insights into our own motivations and into what is important and of value are often limited by the shape of our experience, failure to understand a certain insight, or see the point of some moral advice proferred, is often taken as a judgment on the character of the person concerned. An insensitive person, or a fanatic, cannot see what he is doing to others, the kind of suffering he is inflicting on them. He cannot see, for instance, that this act is a deep affront to someone's sense of honour, or perhaps deeply undermines his sense of worth. He is proof to all remonstrating on our part.

He cannot listen to us because he has closed off all sensitivity to questions of honour, or perhaps to the sense of personal worth, in himself, say; and this might in turn be related to earlier experiences which he has undergone. These earlier experiences account for a shape of his current experience in which these issues figure as specious and of no account, and this current shape makes it impossible for him to allow the insights we are pressing on him. He cannot admit them without his whole stance towards these matters crumbling; and this stance may be motivationally of deep importance to him.

But in this kind of case we take the limits of the man's insight as a judgement on him. It is because of what he has become—perhaps indeed, in response to some terrible strain or difficulty, but nevertheless what he has become—that he cannot see certain things, cannot understand the point of certain descriptions of experience. In the sense of 'responsibility' where we only attribute it to people in relation to outcomes that they can presently encompass or avoid, we should not speak of responsibility here. And even if we take account of what the agent could have done differently in the past, the responsibility in this sense may be very attenuated, e.g., when people have been marked by truly harrowing early experiences.

But in another sense of 'responsibility', one older than our modern notions of moral agency, we hold them responsible, in that we judge them morally on the basis of what they see or don't see. So that a man may condemn himself by giving his sincerely held view on the nature of experience that he or others are living through, or on what is of importance to himself or what he sees as important to men in general.

This is one sense in which we think of people as responsible for their evaluations, and in a way which has nothing to do with the theory of radical choice. But we also think of ourselves as responsible for them in a more straightforward 'modern' sense.

This has to do with the other direction of causal influence in which we can sometimes alter ourselves and our experience by fresh insight. In any case, our evaluations would always be open to challenge. Because of the character of depth which we saw in the self, our evaluations are articulations of insights which are frequently partial, clouded and uncertain. But they are all the more open to challenge when we reflect that these insights are often distorted by our imperfections of character. For these two reasons evaluation is such that there is always room for re-evaluation.

Responsibility falls to us in the sense that it is always possible that fresh insight might alter my evaluations and hence even myself for the better. So that within the limits of my capacity to change myself by fresh insight, within the limits of the first direction of causal influence, I am responsible in the full direct, 'modern' sense for my evaluations.

What was said above about the challengeability of evaluations applies with greatest force to our most fundamental evaluations, those which provide the terms in which other less basic ones are made. These are the evaluations which touch my identity in the sense described in the previous section. There I spoke of the self as having an identity which is defined in terms of certain essential evaluations which provide the horizon or foundation for the other evaluations one makes.

Now precisely these deepest evaluations are the ones which are least clear, least articulated, most easily subject to illusion and distortion. It is those which are closest to what I am as a subject, in the sense that shorn of them I would break down as a person, which are among the hardest for me to be clear about.

Thus the question can always be posed: ought I to re-evaluate my most basic evaluations? Have I really understood what is essential to my identity? Have I truly determined what I sense to be the highest mode of life?

Now this kind of re-evaluation will be radical; not in the sense of radical choice, however, that we choose without criteria; but rather in the sense that our looking again can be so undertaken that in principle no formulations are considered unrevisable.

What is of fundamental importance for us will already have an articulation, some notion of a certain mode of life as higher than others, or the belief that some cause is the worthiest that can be served; or the sense that belonging to this community is essential to my identity. A radical re-evaluation will call these formulations into question.

But a re-evaluation of this kind, once embarked on, is of a peculiar sort. It is unlike a less than radical evaluation which is carried on within the terms of some fundamental evaluation, when I ask myself whether it would be honest to take advantage of this income-tax loophole, or smuggle something through customs. These latter can be carried on in a language which is out of dispute. In answering the questions just mentioned the term 'honest' is taken as beyond challenge. But in radical re-evaluations by definition the most basic terms, those in which other evaluations are carried on, are precisely what is in question. It is just because all formulations are potentially under suspicion of distorting their objects that we have to see them all as revisable, that we are forced back, as it were, to the inarticulate limit from which they originate.

How then, can such re-evaluations be carried on? There is certainly no metalanguage available in which I can assess rival self-interpretations, such as my two characterizations above of my ambition to go to Nepal. If there were, this would not be a radical re-evaluation. On the contrary, the re-evaluation is carried on in the formulae available but with a stance of attention, as it were, to what these formulae are meant to articulate and with a readiness to receive any gestalt shift in our view of the situation, any quite innovative set of categories in which to see our predicament, that might come our way in inspiration.

Anyone who has struggled with a philosophical problem knows what this kind of enquiry is like. In philosophy typically we start off with a question, which we know to be badly formed at the outset. We hope that in struggling with it, we shall find that its terms are transformed, so that in the end we will answer a question which we couldn't properly conceive at the beginning. We are striving for conceptual innovation which will allow us to illuminate some matter, say an area of human experience, which would otherwise remain dark and confused. The alternative is to stick stubbornly to certain terms and try to understand reality by classifying it in these terms (are these propositions synthetic or analytic, is this a psychological question or a philosophical question, is this view monist or dualist?).

The same contrast can exist in our evaluations. We can attempt a radical re-evaluation, in which case we may hope that our terms will be transformed in the course of it; or we may stick to certain favoured terms, insist that all evaluations can be made in their ambit, and refuse any radical questioning. To take an extreme case, someone can adopt the utilitarian criterion and they claim to settle all further issues about action by some calculation.

The point has been made again and again by non-naturalists, existentialists, and others that those who take this kind of line are ducking a major question: should I really decide on the utilitarian principle? But this doesn't mean that the alternative to this stance is a radical choice. Rather it is to look again at our most fundmental formulations, and at what they were meant to articulate, in a stance of openness, where we are ready to accept any categorical change, however radical, which might emerge. Of course we will actually start thinking of particular cases, e.g., where our present evaluations recommend things which worry us, and try to puzzle further. In doing this we will be like the philosopher with his initially ill-formed question. But we may get through to something deeper.

In fact this stance of openness is very difficult. It may take discipline and time. It is difficult because this form of evaluation is deep in a sense, and total in a sense, that other less than radical ones are not. If I am questioning whether smuggling a radio into the country is honest, or judging everything by the utilitarian criterion, then I have a yardstick, a definite yardstick. But if I go to the radical questioning, then it is not exactly that I have no yardstick, in the sense that anything goes, but rather that what takes the place of the yardstick is my deepest unstructured sense of what is important, which is as yet inchoate and which I am trying to bring to definition. I am trying to see reality afresh and form more adequate categories to describe it. To do this I am trying to open myself, use all of my deepest, unstructured sense of things in order to come to a new clarity.

Now this engages me at a depth that using a fixed yardstick does not. I am in a sense questioning the inchoate sense that led me to use the yardstick. And at the same time it engages my whole self in a way that judging by a yardstick does not. This is what makes it uncommonly difficult to reflect on our fundamental evaluations. It is much easier to take up the formulations that come most readily to hand, generally those which are going the rounds of our milieu or society, and live within them without too much probing. The obstacles in the way of going deeper are legion. There is not only the difficulty of such concentration, and the pain of uncertainty, but also all the distortions and repressions which make us want to turn away from this examination: and which make us resist change even when we do re-examine ourselves. Some of our evaluations may in fact become fixed and compulsive, so that we cannot help feeling guilty about X, or despising people like Y, even though we judge with the greatest degree of openness and depth at our command that X is perfectly all right, and that Y is a very admirable person. This casts light on another aspect of the term 'deep', as applied to people. We consider people deep to the extent, inter alia, that they are capable of this kind of radical self-reflection.

This radical evaluation is a deep reflection, and a self-reflection in a special sense: it is a reflection about the self, its most fundamental issues, and a reflection which engages the self most wholly and deeply. Because it engages the whole self without a fixed yardstick it can be called a personal reflection (the parallel to Polanyi's notion of personal knowledge is intended here); and what emerges from it is a self-resolution in a strong sense, for in this reflection the self is in question; what is at stake is the definition of those inchoate evaluations which are sensed to be essential to our identity.

Because this self-resolution is something we do, when we do it, we can be called responsible for ourselves; and because it is within limits always up to us to do it, even when we don't—indeed, the nature of our deepest evaluations constantly raises the question whether we have them right—we can be called responsible in another sense for ourselves whether we undertake this radical evaluation or not.

4

I have been exploring some aspects of a self or human agent, following the key notion that a crucial feature of human agency is the capacity for second-order desires or evaluation of desires. In the course of the discussion, it will have become more and more plausible, I hope, that the capacity for what I have called strong evaluation is an essential feature of a person.

I think that this has helped to cast light on the sense in which we ascribe reflection, will and also responsibility to human agents. But our conception of human agency is also of crucial importance to any potential science of the human subject, in particular to psychology.

In concluding, I'd like to sketch a few of the consequences for the study of psychology of this conception. First, it evidently means that a concept like 'drive', used in motivational theory as a psychic force operating in abstraction from any interpretation, cannot find a fruitful application. The idea of measuring drive like a force in natural science is in principle misguided. Instead we would have to accept that those branches of psychology which attempt to account for fully motivated behaviour must take account of the fact that the human animal is a self-interpreting subject. And this means that these branches of the discipline must be 'hermeneutical' sciences.

I have discussed some of what is involved in this elsewhere (Taylor, 1973). But one consequence, which has been touched on in this symposium, is for the study of personality. For if we take the view that man is a self-interpreting animal, then we will accept that a study of personality which tries to proceed in terms of general traits alone can have only limited value. For in many cases we can only give their proper significance to the subject's articulations by means of 'idiographic' studies, which can explore the particular terms of an individual's self-interpretations. Studies exclusively in terms of general traits can be empty, or else end up with baffling inconsistencies. I believe that there is some common ground here with a point made by W. and H. Mischel in their very stimulating paper in this volume, that such functions as self-control are carried out more discriminatively than we can account for in terms of something like 'a unitary trait entity of conscience or honesty'.

But perhaps the most valuable fruits of a more fully developed conception of the self on the above lines, which avoided the reductiveness of drive theory, would come in dialogue with those strands in psycho-analysis which are particularly concerned with the development of the self, of which Ernest Wolf's paper gives an extremely interesting account. For evidently any theory of the ontogenesis of the self, and any identification of its potential breakdowns, must also both draw and draw from, implicitly or explicitly, a portrait of the fully responsible human agent. The attempt to explore our underlying notion of responsibility could thus both help and be helped by a study of the growth and pathologies of the self.

Thus I believe that there are links between the rather groping remarks about identity in this paper and the much more fully developed notion of a 'cohesive self' that Kohut and Ernest Wolf have introduced. These links would greatly repay further exploration. They are made all the closer in that Kohut and Wolf are not working with a drive or psychic 'force' view of motivation. Thus sexual libido is not seen as a constant factor, but rather sexual desire and excitability have a very different impact on a cohesive self than on one which has lost its cohesion (see Wolf, this volume).

The prospect of a psycho-analytic theory which could give an adequate account of the genesis of full human responsibility, without recourse to such global and reified mechanisms as the super-ego, and with a truly plausible account of the shared subjectivity from which the mature cohesive self must emerge, is a very exciting prospect indeed.

REFERENCES

FRANKFURT, H. 'Freedom of the Will and the Concept of a Person,' *Journal of Philosophy*, LXVII, no. 1, Jan. 1971, pp. 5–20.

MISCHEL, W., & MISCHEL, H. N. 'Self-Control and the Self.' This volume.

RICOEUR, P. *De L'Interprétation*, Paris: Editions du Seuil, 1965.

SARTRE, J. P. *L'Être et le Néant*, Paris: Gaillimard, 1943.

TAYLOR, C. 'Peaceful Coexistence in Psychology,' *Social Research*, 40, no. 1, Spring 1973, pp. 55–82.

TAYLOR, C. 'Force et Sens,' in G. Madison, ed., *Sens et Existence*, Paris: Editions du Seuil, 1975.

WOLF, S. E. 'Irrationality in a Psychoanalytic Psychology of the Self.' This volume.

PART III Self-Knowledge

5 The Social Construction of Self-Knowledge*

KENNETH J. GERGEN

Common parlance strongly suggests that the ancient search for self-knowledge continues to be of paramount concern in society. We are all familiar with such questions as 'who am I', 'what are my real values', 'do I really love him or her', 'what am I trying to hide or protect myself from', 'am I really a calloused person', 'what are my real intentions', and so on. It is commonly thought that without a certain degree of self-knowledge, one's life is likely to be fraught with difficulty. People often try to 'find themselves' and seek professional guidelines for this. Erik Erikson makes 'self-identity' a criterion for psychological maturity;[1] the aim of Rogerian therapy is to enable the individual to acquire true experience of self, and psychoanalysis is similarly oriented in its emphasis on the motivational springs behind aberrant or maladaptive behavior. Others have used the Wanderyahr, lysergic acid, meditation, the armed services, the primal scream, transactional analysis, or leaves of absence for much the same purpose. The search, then, seems to be for a stable and unifying core of existence, a firm touchstone which can provide us with a sense of authenticity and coherence, and which can serve as a criterion for action. It is my present aim to demonstrate that the search for self is largely misconceived. It does not yield knowledge in the traditional sense, but rather, provides a means of rendering action socially intelligible.

In order to establish more clearly the grounds for colloquy, it will

* All research by the present author reported in this paper was conducted with funds made available by the National Science Foundation. I am indebted to Mary Gergen for her critical comments during the drafting of the paper.

[1] Erikson, E. *Childhood and society*. Chicago: W. W. Norton, 1963.

be useful to make explicit several assumptions underlying the traditional quest for self-knowledge. The following propositions appear fundamental to the common view of self-identity:

1. All human beings of normal constitution are capable of conscious experience or sensation.
2. At a minimum such experience may be roughly divided into two major categories: self and not self. That is, there is a class of experience which the individual can identify as personal or intrinsic to his own individual existence. This class may be distinguished from experiences which seem extrinsic or separated from the individual. Within the class of self-experience may be included the emotions, iconic images, sentiments, feelings of right and wrong, sensations of pleasure and pain, desires, both overt and covert physical movement, memories, and so on.
3. Over time, a unified core or gestalt of self-relevant experiences is developed. Once crystallized, this core self, or sense of identity, remains stable over time and across diverse circumstances, and provides a useful basis for social conduct. For example, an individual may develop a clear, dependable set of experiences of himself as male and this will guide his behavior across varying circumstances and will inhibit his behaving in ways that contradict his core experience.
4. One of the most important types of self-experience is evaluative in character. From early childhood, the individual comes to experience himself along a dimension of good vs. bad. The core set of experiences that emerge is commonly viewed in terms of self-esteem. Level of self-esteem is of major significance in determining one's actions; if it is sufficiently low, various forms of maladaptive behavior may be anticipated.
5. Various features of the social surroundings may prevent the individual from having direct access to such experiences of self as would occur in an unencumbered state of nature. By introjecting others' values, fearing their retaliation or punishment, or acquiring their habits of thought, the individual may 'lose touch with himself', as it were. Self-experience may become unavailable in its natural form, with the result that the individual may be self-deceived or unrealistic.

Although these various assumptions are based on a rich intellectual and cultural tradition, and although they pervade modern culture together with its restorative institutions, the present paper will provide an alternative orientation, one that contradicts or fundamentally modifies virtually all of these assumptions. This is not to say that my major aim is simply to replace what seems a misconceived analysis of self-knowledge. More fundamentally, it is my hope to elaborate a particular orientation toward self, one which has epistemic, scientific, therapeutic, and socially significant implications. Essentially, the position I wish to set forth may be termed *socio-cognitive*. The orientation may be traced in large measure to the seminal work of George Herbert Mead. However, inquiry in sociolinguistics, attribution theory in social psychology, and the ethnomethodological movement in sociology all contribute to the present analysis.[2]

I shall initially provide a brief synopsis of the socio-cognitive orientation to self, and then move on to discuss in detail several lines of research that bear on this orientation. This empirically oriented discussion will first center on the development and change of self-understanding, and then shift its focus to the problem of personal volition or self-will. At this point, it will be possible to return to the traditional tenets previously outlined and to argue that the traditional position is obfuscating in implication. Finally, I will touch on the implications of this analysis for a science of self.

A Socio-Cognitive Orientation to Self

William James assumed that the experiential world of the infant is largely a 'booming, buzzing confusion'; from moment to moment the infant is confronted with ever-changing patterns of essentially undifferentiated and meaningless stimuli. Adaptive action within such a chaotic environment requires that the individual come to differentiate among kinds of stimulus inputs and to relate these classes of inputs with one another. Thus, in order to secure nurturant care, it may be necessary to differentiate a class of stimuli which may later be called 'mother' from the remainder of the stimulus array. A class of liquid substances may be singled out for the pleasure which they seem to produce when ingested, and a class of actions we call 'crying' seems to bring forth the presence of living beings.

[2] Contributions by Rom Harré and by George McCall to the present volume are also largely consistent with the present analysis.

In order to cope with the otherwise overwhelming array of stimulation, the individual learns to engage in a cognitive batching process that we commonly view as conceptualization.

It seems clear that the particular form in which this batching takes place is largely under the influence of the social world. The child learns through observation, for example, to differentiate a class of objects we call 'chairs' from other objects, and observes that people normally engage in certain classes of actions (e.g., sitting on, moving toward or away from a table, etc.) toward this particular set of objects. Once the child has developed a rudimentary grasp of the language, the efficacy of the learning process is increased manifold. Although imperfectly, the language of the culture reflects the common inventory of 'What there is', i.e., the relevant groupings of significance within the culture, and enables the individual to assimilate rapidly large amounts of information about the relationships among such classes. In the simple directive, 'Never hit your mother', the individual quickly learns the relationship (in this case, negative) between two classes of events, 'hitting' and 'mother', a relationship which might otherwise have required numerous and painful instances to learn *in vivo*. In effect, through exposure to the contingencies of social interaction and to the linguistic medium, the individual acquires a conceptual system that provides (1) a virtual inventory of the relevant and functional classes of events or phenomena within the culture, (2) rules concerning the conditions under which these concepts are to be applied, and (3) the manner in which these classes are to be related. More generally, the individual acquires an 'intelligibility system' which enables him to 'make sense' of the stimulus world and to participate 'meaningfully' with other members of the culture.

Although these observations are not particularly challenging in themselves, they begin to acquire a cutting edge when applied to the self. The infant may rapidly learn to differentiate a class of experiences that may later be called 'self' from the surrounding environment. He may also learn that certain of his behaviors are to be singled out as 'bad' and others as 'good'. By adolescence, the social milieu will have also furnished the individual with a host of concepts with which he may classify his internal states. States of 'pleasure', 'pain', 'love', 'hate', 'anger', and so on, must be differentiated if the individual is to function adequately within this milieu. He must master such differentiations as well as the proper circumstances in which the relevant concepts are to be employed in self-understanding. Further, whether an individual perceives himself as 'willing' his own behavior, whether he believes he possesses a soul, whether he perceives himself to harbor certain attributes or capabilities, should depend on the meaning systems into which he is socialized. Thus, through social observation, interaction, and language acquisition the individual acquires an inventory of self-attributes or conceptions, and knowledge as to their relationship with other relevant classes of stimuli. In more general terms, what there is to understand about the self and how one is to go about it, follows a normative rule system governing concept usage. Only through mastering such rules can the individual render himself intelligible to himself and to others.

If I impute a certain arbitrary character to the intelligibility system which the individual comes to acquire, it is not by accident. The particular way in which we come to segment the world of experience is certainly not sacrosanct and it could be otherwise. Immense anguish is generated over the question of whether one is sufficiently principled, warm and accepting, spontaneous, ambitious, intelligent and so on, and seldom does one question the arbitrary character of the questions themselves. The existence of such distinctions, the value placed upon them, and the precise range of particulars that may be encompassed by each concept is subject to gross alteration both through time and across circumstance.

This brief introduction requires extensive elaboration. Such elaboration must be selective, and in the present case we shall confine our focus to two major lines of inquiry. First, we shall inquire more deeply into the linkage between self-understanding and the social milieu in order to make clear the various means through which one acquires self-understanding. More particularly, on what psychological processes does the individual rely in order to make him or herself intelligible within ongoing social circumstances? The discussion will shift then to the concept of personal volition and the conditions governing its attribution. What are the rules by which we make decisions concerning the source of our decisions? Each of these discussions will allow us to scan the results of various empirical demonstrations that lend substance to the present position.

The present orientation distinguishes between raw sense data and the symbolic conceptualization of these data. Thus, we may say that the organism is exposed to a continuous stream of sense data, and that the process of conceptualization exists as an artificial overlay or template employed in making sense or codifying the otherwise chaotic aspects of this experience. In this context, it is misleading to view the individual in quest of self-knowledge as trying to discover some truth or reality; to borrow William James' phrasing, we are not confronted with a searching 'I' and the discovered 'me'. Rather, we may view the process of knowing as one of fitting a conceptual template to experience. There is nothing to be discovered; the sense data are essentially given. The 'experience of discovery', of self-revelation or insight, is essentially the realization that an alternative template is also applicable to the same experiential complex. Our orienting premise is thus that self-knowledge is best understood as the application of a conceptual system, imbedded as it is within the social system, to a given field of sense data. To make this clear, we will examine four means to self-knowledge, each of which rests upon these orienting assumptions.

Communication and Conceptualization

In Nigel Dennis' novel, *Cards of Identity*, a shattering story is unfolded in which an altogether normal adult is abducted and placed in an entirely alien environment. He is given a new name, different clothing, is housed in a separate domicile, and most importantly, is treated as a servant by all members of his new environment. There is no escape. Unsettlingly, within a short period the protagonist comes to feel perfectly at home in his new identity. He gains perfect authenticity within a life-circumstance jarringly inconsistent with his entire past. The question raised by Dennis is whether normal identity, that indelible core of self-relevant experience (as it is commonly considered) can be obliterated so easily. Is our hold on personal reality so very tenuous? Of course, one can dismiss Dennis' account as purely fictional. But this does not escape the question: Erving Goffman again brings it to our attention in his analysis of the mental patient.[3] As he demonstrates, by ordering the patient about, locking him in, examining him without his consent, speaking to him as an alien and so on, the patient learns a new identity, that of being 'mentally ill'. When the individual exists in a closed institu-

[3] Goffman, E, *Asylums*. New York: Doubleday Anchor, 1963.

tion, one in which the social and physical environment consistently reinforces a specific identity, there is virtually no escape because there is no alternative identity into which one can step. Neither the individual's view of himself in the here and now, nor his past behavior which led him into the institution, provide an incentive for departure. Mental illness is a secure niche in which the individual may remain—often 'til death.

It is also possible to dismiss Goffman's analysis. We cannot be certain that, like any good social analyst, he didn't select out of a complex set of incidents only those which confirmed his particular predilections. But, the question remains: is common identity so fragile that it will readily capitulate to social influence? From the socio-cognitive viewpoint, we might fully anticipate such flexibility in self-identity. If we may define identity as a sub-set of highly salient concepts which the individual most frequently utilizes in thinking about himself or his activities, then any means by which concepts in general can be altered should apply in no lesser degree to self-identity. Accordingly, if the social environment continues to define a given individual in a specified manner, we may reasonably anticipate that, without countervening information, the individual will come to accept the publicly provided definition as his own. This view, of course, does not differ essentially from that developed by George Herbert Mead in the 1920s. As Mead maintained, 'We are in possession of selves just insofar as we can and do take the attitudes of others toward ourselves and respond to those attitudes'.[4] The relevance of Mead's account to ours is assured with the simple substitution of concepts for attitudes. Further, if we liberalize Mead's notions concerning the means by which others' concepts of oneself are introjected, if we can agree that taking the role of the other is only one means by which the individual may incorporate others' views of himself, then Mead's theory of self-development and change may be considered wholly consistent with the present treatment.

In this context, let us consider research on alterations in self-esteem. It is commonly held, within the mental health tradition and by the public more generally, that the individual develops over time (and typically within the first six years of life) an essential mode of self-evaluation. He comes to attach a basic value to his identity, which may vary from extremely positive (in which case he might

[4] Mead, G. H. The genesis of self and social control. *International Journal of Ethics*, 1925, *35*, 251–73.

be labelled an egotist) to extremely negative (in which case it was once popular to say that he suffered an inferiority complex). It is generally argued that the individual carries such evaluative sets with him across time and circumstance and that they are highly significant in molding his social behavior. Numerous means of assessing basic self-esteem have been developed over the years, and an immense number of experimental studies have attempted to isolate the behavioral correlates of persons differing in basic self-esteem. Therapy in both the neo-Freudian and Rogerian traditions may be specifically directed toward altering this basic sense of self-esteem.

From the present standpoint, self-esteem may be understood in terms of our knowledge of the relationship between concepts and affect. Experimental psychology has provided a number of wide-ranging experiments demonstrating that through association learning, affect may become associated with specific objects or our concepts of them. Once such associations are developed it is possible to stimulate affect by calling the concepts to mind. Various forms of lie detection, in fact, owe their success to this line of experimentation. What is traditionally termed self-esteem may thus be viewed in terms of the affective associations accompanying the individual's central array of self-relevant concepts. However, from this vantage point, there is little reason to suspect a strong degree of trans-situational coherence in self-esteem. Unlike the picture of enduring levels of self-esteem found in the clinical annals, we might anticipate that the stability of self-esteem is importantly dependent on the consistency of the social environment. As the messages received from others concerning one's worth are varied, one's concepts of self (along with their valuational associations) may be changed. Self-esteem may thus be regarded, not as an enduring sub-stratum of experience, but as inextricably linked to the social context and fully dependent on it for its strength.

Consider some research findings related to this line of thinking. Undergraduate women volunteered to help in a training program for clinical graduate students.[5] As part of the program each woman found herself in an interview in which the graduate student asked her various questions about herself. The questions were primarily

[5] Gergen, K. J. Interaction goals and personalistic feedback as factors affecting the presentation of self. *Journal of Personality and Social Psychology*, 1965, *1*, 413–24.

of a self-evaluative nature, so that the interviewee had to rate herself on a variety of characteristics, including her intelligence, facial beauty, sociability, and so on. During the 45 minute interview, the interviewer showed subtle signs of agreement (smiles, nods, 'I agree', etc.) whenever the student made a positive evaluation of herself. When the self-ratings were negative, however, the interviewer showed signs of disagreement (frowns, 'I don't see it that way' etc.). As the interview progressed the participants thus learned that the interviewer's conception of them was highly positive in character. Would their self-appraisal begin to mirror the social context? A systematic study of the self-ratings revealed that as the interview progressed the participants' ratings of themselves became steadily more positive. No such increase in self-esteem was evidenced in a control condition.

It is possible, of course, that the self-ratings may have been adopted for the benefit of the interviewer and so may not have been an accurate reflection of what the subjects thought about themselves at the time. Would the enhanced self-evaluation be found on a subsequent test of self-esteem, administered after the interview was complete? To test this the women were given, in private, a set of self-esteem items and asked to rate themselves as honestly as possible; they were advised that the interviewer would not be privy to these evaluations, and that their candor was important to the success of the project. When the self-ratings of the experimental group were examined, it was found that the interview had a marked and significant effect. These women retained the enhanced self-image developed in the interview. The control group showed no such effects.

Further illustrations of the ways in which social communication can alter self-conception are abundant in the social psychological literature.[6] One's identity in general, and self-evaluation in particular, thus seem importantly wedded to social circumstance. As the social environment shifts its definition of the individual, self-definition may be altered accordingly.

[6] Gergen, K. J. *The concept of self.* New York: Holt, Rinehart and Winston, 1971

The Evidence of Action

The research presented above is closely wedded to the symbolic interactionist position, and may be somewhat limited in its emphasis on social communication. One's conception of self may be influenced by virtually any source of information and one major source of self-relevant information is provided by one's own actions. As Bem has argued we are more or less continuously in sensory contact with our own behavior, and through observation of such behavior we may draw conclusions as to our identity.[7] The view that our overt behavior furnishes us information about what we feel, believe, desire, will, and so on, has substantial empirical support. Over the past thirty years, social psychologists have provided numerous demonstrations of the effects of role playing on an individual's attitudes and feelings. If one can be induced (though not coerced) into taking a disagreeable public stance on an issue, one typically finds that his private opinion is subsequently changed in the direction of the public commitment.[8] In order to explore the relevance of this work for self-conception, my colleague, Margaret Gibbs, and I arranged a situation in which undergraduate females were to apply for a job.[9] In one condition, the women were asked to formulate a talk about themselves which would enable them to gain the positive regard of a prospective employer. They were encouraged to present themselves as positively as they could, and after spending fifteen minutes formulating their talks they recorded them for the ostensible purpose of later playing them to the prospective employer. Subsequently each participant was asked to help in validating some clinical test materials, including a standardized test of self-esteem; this test had been administered to the same group approximately six weeks earlier in a large classroom setting. An examination of self-esteem change revealed that the role-playing subjects evidenced a striking increase in self-esteem ratings. This enhanced level of

[7] Bem, D. An experimental analysis of self-persuasion. *Journal of Experimental and Social Psychology*, *1*, 199–218.

[8] Brehm, J. W. A dissonance analysis of attitude-discrepant behavior. In C. I. Hovland & M. J. Rosenberg (Eds.), *Attitude organization and change*. New Haven: York University Press, 1960.

[9] Gergen, K. J. & Gibbs, M. S. Role playing and modifying the self-concept. Presented at the annual meeting of the Eastern Psychological Association, 1966.

self-esteem was not found in a control group which did not participate in the role-playing procedure. Positive presentation seemed to generate positive self-conception.

Other research on self-observation has been concerned with the definition of one's emotional states. Traditionally, it had been supposed that various types of emotional states that we experience are coordinated with specific physiological states. Thus, one might expect that feelings of love can be differentiated in terms of physiological coordinates, from admiration, infatuation, and so on. To know what one is 'truly' feeling from this viewpoint requires that one harken sensitively to his internal nudgings. Physiology tells no lies.

However, as arguments by Stanley Schachter and his colleagues demonstrate, there is little physiological support for this classic position.[10] Little physiological differentiation is revealed as one moves through the range of emotional experience, and it is virtually impossible to map a finely differentiated emotional vocabulary onto a set of physiologically discriminable states. Rather, the nervous system seems to operate primarily in terms of gross arousal. Differentiations may be made between positive and negative emotional states and between such states as intense fear and anger, but beyond such gross differences the physiologist is unable to predict, on the basis of information about the nervous system, when we experience hostility, as opposed to envy, vengefulness, or frustration. If such scant information regarding emotional state is furnished by the nervous system, what is the source of our differential experiences? The answer provided by Schachter and his colleagues is highly compatible with the present analysis. Through socialization, the individual comes to acquire an emotional vocabulary along with knowledge of the proper cues (either social or situational) concerning the proper utilization of such labels. Early work by Schachter and others indicated that precisely the same state of physiological arousal could give rise to experiences of anger or humor, depending on the situational context in which the arousal occurred. In effect, the situational cues provided the individual with the proper concepts to be used in understanding what he 'truly' felt in the situation.

In one of the more interesting extensions of these investigations,

[10] Schachter, G. & Singer, J. E. Cognitive, social and physiological determinants of emotional state. *Psychological Review*, 1962, 69, 379–99.

males were exposed to slides of attractive, partially clothed females.[11] As they viewed the slides, they were also allowed to hear an amplification of what was purported to be their heartbeats. In actuality, the frequency of the heartbeat as controlled by the experimenter. By design, participants found that their heart appeared to undergo a rapid increase in rate on certain slide presentations, but not others. The particular instances in which such increases were experienced were randomly selected. Attractiveness ratings of the slides then revealed that those photographs which had ostensibly produced an increase in heart rate were viewed as more attractive; these effects remained when the participants were tested again two months later. Thus, subjects seemed to use their bodily cues to label their emotional reaction to the stimulus—they judged their preferences by observing and labelling their bodily reactions.

While highly compelling, this line of thinking does raise worrisome problems concerning the limits of the socio-cognitive approach. Our initial premise was that self-knowledge is primarily a socially mediated and essentially arbitrary construction of experience. Since such constructions are virtually interchangeable, the notion of 'true' knowledge of self becomes chimerical. However, if we admit that one's behavior furnishes information concerning the state of the self; then it might be concluded that some conceptual templates are superior to, or possess greater validity than, others. One's own behavior becomes the crucible against which we may assess the true value of various self-constructions.

Against this view, it may be proposed that one's own behavior, in itself, is not informative because it provides raw sensation that has no inherent meaning. Whatever meaning is found in the behavior must essentially be 'read into' it. A similar argument is often made against the naive realist view of the development of scientific laws. As the naive realist would have it, the scientist discovers laws by observing regularities that are inherent in nature. But this view has been largely discredited within philosophical circles on the ground that nature in itself provides little information and that lawfulness is largely created through the human application of conceptual biases. Thus, comprehension depends on a pre-existing repertoire of concepts at the individual's disposal. What conclusions are reached regarding one's behavior depends on what concepts have

[11] Valens, S. Cognitive effects of false heart-rate feedback. *Journal of Personality and Social Psychology*, 1966, 4, 400–8.

been supplied through socialization and which happens to be salient at the time of behavior scanning.

This analysis suggests that, in principle, it should be possible for the individual to confirm virtually any concept of self at any time.[12] If I pause to consider the possibility that I am a passive person, not very comfortable in social situations, I can probably locate enough instances in my behavioral production to confirm this suspicion. Yet, at another time, I might be able to find evidence convincing me that I am active and socially at ease. The major limitation to complete relativism in self-understanding is provided by social consensus. That is, if a given behavioral act is univocally defined as active or passive, and the individual observes himself engaging in this behavior, he may be unable to reach any conclusions about himself other than that provided by the unanimous social milieu. Still, however compelling such self-evaluations may appear, they do not constitute knowledge of 'true self'. A decade ago, a male who engaged in certain acts with others of his kind would have been labelled 'homosexual' by virtually everyone, including himself. If he observed himself engaged in such actions, the conclusion that he was homosexual would be virtually inescapable. Today, the same acts may be labelled 'bisexual', 'self-actualizing', or 'liberated'; the action is equivalent, but 'self-knowledge' has been altered.

Self-Other Comparisons

Self-knowledge, the process of conceptualizing oneself, may be molded not only by direct communication from others and through self-labelling, but also by observations of other persons which have implications for self-labelling. It has been maintained that through learning, various concepts become associated with particular behavioral configurations. Such configurations may not only be evidenced in one's own behavior, but in the actions of others as well. When relating to others, much of our attention is focused on their behavior; we attempt to make sense of their actions by translating them into a conceptual structure. Intermittently we are also cognizant of our own actions, and the continuous shifting of attention

[12] This line of argument is also consistent with Willard Day's reasoning in the present volume concerning the dependency of self-knowledge on the self-descriptive repertories engendered by the surrounding verbal community.

between self and other lends itself to the ascription of similarity and difference. Such comparisons contain further implications as to how we might conceptualize our own behavior. For example, if we confront someone who seems jocular or waggish, and self-other comparison indicates strong differences in patterns of behavior, we may conclude that we are, after all, a more reasonable, circumspect, or unspontaneous sort of person. If we find a close match between the behavior patterns, we might conclude that we are also a jocular or waggish sort of individual.

This process has been documented in research conducted with Stanley Morse.[13] Participants in this research were students at the University of Michigan who answered an advertisement for part-time jobs in the Institute for Social Research. When each applicant arrived for the preliminary screening, he was seated in a room by himself and asked to complete a number of self-rating forms, including a battery of approximately thirty self-evaluation items carefully designed by Coopersmith to tap basic level of self-esteem. After each applicant had completed the various measures, the secretary entered the room, bringing with her another 'applicant' for the job who was, in fact, a collaborator. For some forty applicants, the collaborator was obviously very desirable as a potential employee. He wore a dark business suit and carried an attache case which he opened to remove several sharpened pencils, at the same time revealing copies of books on statistics and philosophy. The remaining applicants were exposed to a dramatically different experience. Here the competitor entered wearing a smelly sweatshirt, torn trousers and no socks; he appeared generally dazed by the procedure and tossed onto the table a worn copy of a cheap paperback novel. After several minutes of silent exposure to the newcomer, the original applicant was given additional forms to complete, including a second battery of items assessing level of self-esteem.

This study showed that the mere presence of the other person was sufficient to alter the manner in which the applicants conceptualized their own self-worth. Applicants exposed to the impressive individual demonstrated a sharp drop in self-evaluation; those who sat face-to-face with the bumpkin showed a significant increase in their evaluations of self. The implications of such findings are far reach-

[13] Morse, S. J. & Gergen, K. J. Social comparison, self-consistency and the presentation of self. *Journal of Personality and Social Psychology*, 1970, *16*, 148–56.

ing, as they suggest that personal identity is in important measure dependent on the immediate or continuing social milieu. One need never come in direct communication with such surrounds; mere presence may be sufficient to cause elation or depression. What is 'true' about self depends on those available for comparison. In the presence of the devout, we may 'discover' that we are ideologically shallow; in the midst of dedicated hedonists, we may gain awareness of our ideological depths.

Concept Association: Identity by Implication

Concepts may become associated not only with particular experiential events but also with each other, a fact utilized in the free association method. When presented with a string of words and asked to respond to each with the first word that enters the mind, the split-second response that occurs reveals the underlying associational structure. In part, this structure may depend on the frequency of various associations within the language of the culture. If we hear a man described as 'tall' and 'dark', the word 'handsome' is likely to come to the tip of our tongue. In addition, the configuration of associations may reflect patterns of behavior as they are commonly perceived. If we observe that behavior we term 'aggressive' often produces behavior we term 'anger' in the target of the aggression, a strong association between the concepts of aggression and anger may develop and influence our expectations. Thus, if we observe person *X* treating *Y* in an aggressive manner, we may be primed to anticipate that Y's subsequent behavior will reveal anger. As much early research on perceptual biases has shown, we may be inclined to label the behavior as 'anger' even when a variety of other labels would be equally credible.

This enables us to understand additional influences on the way in which one interprets oneself: it may be that (1) we utilize others' behavior in order to interpret our reaction to them, and (2) we use others' reactions to us to understand our behavior or feelings toward them. In support of (1), it may be argued that we can often readily identify or label what another has done to us, but are less able to categorize our reaction. A person may realize that a friend is angry with him, but his reaction to this anger may be an emotional swim, unclear and diffuse. Since we have numerous associations regarding what type of behavior (A) leads to what reaction (B), the presence of A in another's behavior toward us may bring to mind its associated concept *B* which is then used in judging our reaction. If 'fond expressions' on the part of one person have frequently been associated with 'fond feelings' on the part of the individual to whom they are directed, then confronting an ardent suitor may cause one to label his or her diffuse emotional reaction as 'fondness'. The question is not whether one *actually* feels fond or not; it is misleading to ask about true feelings. The major issue is what concept has been called into play by the surrounding conditions.

We are hampered by a lack of direct empirical support for this particular line of reasoning. However, a study by Brehm,[14] concerned with the degree to which we like or dislike various foods lends itself to the case. Are such preferences intrinsic and knowable, or can they be understood as mobile conceptual constructions? High school students were offered a prize for eating a small amount of spinach, a vegetable for which they had previously expressed an antipathy. One group of students was then informed that they would be writing home indicating what vegetable they had eaten; the letter was stated in such a way that the student could fully expect to be served much more of this vegetable. Thus, through a *fait accompli*, they found themselves committed to a good deal of spinach eating in the future. The major question was whether this information about their 'fated future' would have an effect on their subsequent liking for the vegetable. In terms of concept association, eating a great deal of any food is typically associated with liking it. If the environment is arranged so that we are to receive a great deal of spinach, we might well look at ourselves for evidence of a positive reaction; given the vagaries of human taste, we are most certain to find such evidence. Although multiple interpretations are possible, the results do lend ample support to this position. The knowledge of what they were to receive was sufficient to *decrease* the students' dislike of the vegetable as measured in subsequent ratings. No such change was found in a control group of students who did not receive the information about their future. Thus, the knowledge that the unwanted food was often to be served influenced the students to increase their liking for it.

[14] Brehm, J. W. Increasing cognitive dissonance by a *fait accompli*. *Journal of Abnormal and Social Psychology*, 1959, *58*, 379–82.

What about (2), the claim that we use our categorizations of others' reactions to us in interpreting our behavior or feelings toward them? In most relationships, we speak without necessarily planning what we are going to say, and our feelings are often evanescent and ambiguous. We do not at each moment conceptualize our behavior and our feelings, but when we must decide what it is we are doing to the other or how it is we are feeling, the process of concept association may be quite important. If we are unable to identify our behavior *A* toward a person, but we can label his reaction, *B*, then relying on the structure of association including *A* and *B*, we may infer the existence of *A*, given the existence of *B*. If we observe another reacting to us in a 'friendly' way, we may conclude that our behavior toward him has been friendly or that we are a friendly sort of person. If another reacts in a 'submissive' manner, concept association would suggest that we tend to be dominating. The actual state of our behavior or affect may be the same in all cases; our comprehension of it may vary markedly depending on inferences made from others' reactions.

Again, though there is no precise documentation, an experiment conducted with E. E. Jones and K. Davis provides interesting insight.[15] In this study, women students took part in a clinical interview about their academic life and various personal aspirations and values; after the interview, they learned the interviewer's impressions of them. These impressions were systematically constructed so that half of the students found the interviewer was uniformly impressed by them, conveying feelings of warmth, comfort and admiration in the written impression. For the remaining half of the participants, the interviewers' reactions were lukewarm and more carefully guarded. The participants were then asked to rate the honesty of their behavior during the interview. How candid were they; to what extent did they reveal a true picture of their personality in the interview? From the present standpoint, one's true personality is primarily a function of the label we happen to assign, and in this case, the label might be inferred through concept association. If the response is clearly guarded, it may be inferred that the picture one has presented has been less than accurate. This is precisely what the experimental results revealed. Those students who found the

[15] Jones, E. E., Gergen, K. J. & Davis, K. Some reactions to being approved or disapproved as a person. *Psychological Monographs*, 1962, *76*, Whole No. 521, No. 2.

interviewer's reaction wholly positive, rated their presentation in the interview as significantly more honest and candid than those who received the neutral reactions. Essentially, one may not know whether he has been honest or authentic until he learns of others' reactions.

Memory Scanning and Other Forms of Cognitive Processing

Thus far, we have viewed the process of self-conceptualization as actively molded by the actions and appearances of others and ourselves. However, self-conception may occur in relative isolation from the immediate givens of ongoing relations. That is, at any given point one may be moved to engage in some form of symbolic functioning, the results of which may yield an altered conceptualization of who one is, of one's true identity or true feelings. Such processing may serve to strengthen or weaken already existing conceptual structures, or it may provide altogether novel constructions of one's identity.

While complete account of such processing is beyond the scope of this paper, it may be useful to document the effects of one such process, namely memory scanning, in altering self-knowledge. While one may adopt a variety of different strategies in recalling the past, one mode of recall involves using a concept as a criterion of memory scanning. That is, the individual utilizes a given concept, such as 'strong-principled', 'intelligent', 'physically attractive', or the like, and examines his or her memory for instances that may verify or falsify the application of the concept to self. Unless one is particularly systematic, there is good reason to suspect that the products of such memory scanning will be biased toward confirmation. Past experience is usually rich enough to provide confirming instance of virtually any self-relevant concept. Thus, if one commences his search with a given concept in mind, it should be relatively easy to discover confirming evidence and, once satisfied that the concept applies to the self go no further; if the concept is desirable, further search for disconfirmations may be less than appealing. In many cases, then, memory scanning may succeed in convincing the individual that the concept is an accurate description of self.

Evidence from an extension of the role playing study described earlier is relevant here.[16] As will be recalled, women in this study had to develop a speech that would impress a potential employer; women who presented the self-congratulatory talk subsequently came to evaluate themselves more positively. Within this experimental context, a further group of some fifteen women simply engaged in the process of developing the talk; it was never actually presented. In order to develop the talk, the women had to think of various accomplishments of the past which would enable them to present a positive image of themselves. The women were thus engaged in a biased scanning of their past history. Later, when a standardized test of self-esteem was administered, it was found that these women also evidenced a striking increase in self-esteem scores, an increase not found in a control group. It appeared, then, that the biased scanning of memory was sufficient to alter the conception of self operating at that moment. What we believe to be true of ourselves at any instant thus depends importantly on the particular machinations of memory in which we are engaged.

Memory scanning is only one of a number of cognitive processes through which self-conception may be fashioned; each of the environmentally dependent processes discussed thus far probably has an environmentally independent counterpart. Thus, just as others' opinions may influence self-conception at any given time, so may the memory of past communications from others, or the imagined communication that might take place should others witness our present or anticipated actions. Likewise, we may consider ourselves in comparison with groups that are not immediately present, groups from the past or from an imagined future. Each of these ratiocinative processes may yield a particular conception of self that may appear both compelling and valid at a particular time.[17]

The Rules of Freedom

Our analysis has emphasized the close interdependency between cognitive processes and social milieu: the ways in which society, either directly or indirectly, fashions the conceptual divisions within the

[16] Gergen, K. J. & Gibbs, M. S. op. cit

[17] Other cognitive processes of potential significance in altering self-conception have been detailed elsewhere in this volume. Charles Taylor's discussion of self-definition through radical choice is particularly relevant.

world of experience, provides an indication of what exemplars are to be included within each concept domain, and indicates the relationship holding among concepts. To view the process through another lens, we may say that the society provides a set of loosely constructed rules concerning the way in which reality is to be interpreted if one is to function adequately within the society. Thus, our cognitive functioning typically follows a set of rules unintentionally generated by the society for its own maintenance. Although the full implications of this argument cannot be examined here, it is significant to realize that traditional psychology has tended to view the processes of cognition as locked into the physiological system. That is, our neurological makeup virtually insures the operation of certain types of cognitive processes. Inquiries into association learning, short-term memory, problem solving, information processing, Piagetian development, and the neural basis of language, have all tended to make such an assumption. From the present vantage point, we have reason for sufficient doubt in such matters. It is quite possible that in all such cases the form of mental processing may be the psychological counterpart of social rules. We learn, process, remember, shift stages of cognitive development, and so on, not because of physiological givens but because it is socially adaptive to do so. Should this position be sustained we might well witness a revolution in the character of experimental psychology.

For the present we must be content with preliminary inquiries into particular forms of psychological functioning. In particular, our concern will be with the process of self-determination, an issue of immense importance to a full theory of self. There is widespread conviction within Western culture that the individual is endowed with volitional power, that is, the ability to make free (that is undetermined) decisions concerning his conduct. We say, 'I decided on my own to do it', 'I am determined to do it', 'I did it of my own free will', 'John chose not to act', 'Mary is certainly self-determined', 'He has strong will power', 'I don't intend to pay', and so on. The supposition of will is spelled out even more clearly in our legal codes which make clear distinctions between acts that are under the person's control and those which are not. The person is held 'responsible' for the former and receives stiffer penalties accordingly.

From the viewpoint of scientific determinism in general, and Skinnerian behaviorism in particular, this belief in free will is viewed as misguided if not pernicious. But whether or not we accept the idea that people are free to act voluntarily, we cannot avoid the fact that people do seem to make widespread use of the notion; this fact remains an important phenomenon for study. We may frame our inquiry in terms of the rule systems governing the use of the concept of personal volition. Under what circumstances is the concept likely to be employed in coming to understand oneself or others? In effect, what are the rules of freedom?[18]

Our analysis must be tentative because a more extensive body of relevant data is needed and we are relying primarily on studies dealing with the attribution of causality to other persons rather than to the self. To date, concern with social perception has been greater than with self-perception. However, it may be ventured that the concept of volition is used similarly in attributing volition both to self and to others. Our analysis will distinguish four particular rules commonly utilized in ascribing volition, though we cannot, at this point, be certain whether all four rules must be in operation or whether some particular combination is sufficient to generate the ascription of volition.

When the individual's attention is drawn to surrounding circumstances or when reasonable causes for his behavior are otherwise made salient, he is less likely to attribute his actions to his own volitions. One's perception of will thus seems to depend on the extent to which one's behavior may be understood as resulting from external factors which appear to push one actively toward some end, or which lure or attract one to a particular goal. There is strong experimental support for this. In the case of self-perception, deCharms[19] reports studies in which children as well as high school students built mechanical models. In one condition the students were given no directives for completing the model, and in a second they were given instructions outlining each step of the construction. Subjects in the latter condition rated

[18] The same rules influencing the naive perception of others may also be represented by the more formal attempt of the theorist to account for social behavior. For example, in Secord's contribution to this volume, 'personal intention' plays a key role in his account of social action. The assumption of intention, in this case, should follow the model outlined here. Social science 'accounts' or intelligibility systems are typically derivatives of the naive accounts common to the culture. If they were not, they would be little understood. Toulmin's contribution to this volume deals extensively with his argument.

[19] deCharms, R. *Personal causation*. New York: Academic Press, 1968.

themselves as feeling significantly less free, as if their behavior were guided by forces beyond their control. Interestingly enough, they also enjoyed their work to a greater extent when unencumbered. In turning to the perception of others we find similar results. Steiner and Field[20] had subjects participate in three-man discussion groups dealing with racial integration. In some groups the experimenter publicly assigned one of the members (actually an experimental confederate) the task of presenting the pro-segregation side of the argument. For other groups, the confederate took the same pro-segregationist position, but in this case it was not apparent that he was instructed to do so. Ratings of the confederate made after the discussion showed that where the pro-segregationist position appeared to be adopted out of duress, subjects were much less trusting of his opinions. In effect, his opinions did not appear to be self-determined or voluntary, and thus, not really his own.

Just as past history and present circumstance may be viewed as 'pushing' one toward some end, so future rewards may be seen as 'pulling' one in spite of his will: we see an action as less willful if done for great reward. It is quite fitting to respond to a superior who is questioning one about why he is departing for another post with, 'the offer is just so attractive that I am forced to take it'. The reply suggests that the act is unwilled and thus not subject to criticism. Research findings support this line of argument. In a study conducted with Walter Swap, students were given several situation-sketches to read.[21] For example, they were to imagine themselves in a juvenile gang, and as a result of group pressure forced into committing a certain crime. They were then asked to rate the extent to which they would feel their behavior to be a true expression of will and the amount of responsibility they would feel for their actions. Consistent with our discussion, there was a high degree of correlation between rated willfulness and responsibility. The ratings also demonstrated that increasing the attractiveness of a goal significantly decreased subjects' feelings of will and responsibility. In the case of the juvenile gang situation, for instance,

20 Steiner, I. D. & Field, W. C. Role assignment and interpersonal influence. *Journal of Abnormal & Social Psychology*, 1960, *61*, 239–45.

21 Gergen, K. J. & Swap, W. as described in 'The perception of others and oneself'. (K. Gergen), for *Basic issues in social psychology*, K. Back (Ed.). New York: John Wiley, in press.

subjects rated their feelings of will when the value of the object stolen was low, and then again under conditions in which the object was of great value. In the former case significantly more involvement of will was indicated.

Similar findings emerge when we turn to the perception of others. E. E. Jones and his colleagues listen to tape recordings in which two students, *A* and *B*, each gave their opinions on a variety of issues.[22] For each topic covered, *A* gave his opinion and *B* followed. In one portion of the study, subjects found *B*'s opinion to be consistently close to *A*'s. Regardless of topic, *B*'s opinion never varied significantly from what *A* had said. One group of subjects, however, heard this sequence take place under conditions in which it was highly profitable for *B* to show agreement with *A*. If *A* liked him, the two would have the opportunity to earn a considerable sum of money while doing some interesting work. For a second group of subjects there was little apparent reason for *B* to conform. Ratings of *B* subsequently showed that when the value of conformity was high, his opinions were seen as far less trustworthy, less likely to be voluntary expressions of true opinion. Subjects also liked *B* less in this condition, even though what he said was precisely the same as in the condition where conformity was of no consequence. In all these studies it is important to note that the rule of environmental rationale seems to operate without respect to the actual state of the individual. That is, as long as one's actions can be explained in terms of environmental pushes and pulls, one is not likely to view these actions as voluntary.

The second rule accounting for attribution of freedom stems from the common distinction between mind and body. Given the pervasiveness of this dichotomy in Western culture, it may be ventured that the greater the degree to which an action may be attributed to mind (and to the ratiocinative processes in particular), the greater the probability of volitional attribution. Or, in obverse form, behavior perceived to be under the influence of bodily needs or emotions is not likely to be perceived as willful. This mode of thinking is most evident within our system of jurisprudence which holds individuals less responsible for crimes preceded by rage rather than rational planning; in Italy, a 'crime of passion' may be excused altogether. Flattening another with one's automobile may be

22 Jones, E. E., Jones, R. G. & Gergen, K. J. Some conditions affecting the evaluation of a conformist. *Journal of Personality*, 1963, *31*, 270–78.

'manslaughter' if one is under the influence of alcohol, but the same act, if rationally considered, would be 'homicide'.

A study by E. E. Jones and his colleagues[23] provides more systematic evidence. Since people tend to think of the mentally unbalanced as not acting willfully, but as being driven by irrational or emotional impulses, they are less affected when treated badly by someone who is mentally disturbed; they feel that he does not really intend his actions and would act differently if he possessed his full rational capacities. To explore this possibility female college students were placed in a situation in which they received criticism from another student. One group of students was led to believe that the person who criticized them was maladjusted; another group felt that their critic was quite normal. The actual criticism was the same for both groups. Both groups subsequently rated their critic, and these ratings were compared with ratings of the derogator made by bystanders. The results showed that when criticized subjects rated the maladjusted critic they were less negative than the bystanders. In effect, they seemed to forgive the maladjusted girl because she couldn't help it. On the other hand, in rating the well-adjusted critic, the results were reversed. The criticized women were much more retaliatory than the bystanders. They were seemingly 'stung' as a result of the intentional assault of the other.

In the case of self-attribution, supportive evidence may be found in the study with Swap cited above. In the case of the criminal act, for example, respondents were asked about their feelings of willfulness if the robbery had been carried out after having consumed a large quantity of alcohol: rated willfulness and feelings of responsibility decreased significantly. When subjects were asked about their feelings if rational planning had been taken place prior to the crime, rated willfulness and responsibility increased significantly.

The third major rule stems from our conception of *effort:* the greater the perceived effort accompanying a given action, the greater the probability that willfulness will be attributed to another or oneself. This connection was noted as early as 1920 when Wheeler[24] argued from his data that the concept of volition should be entirely

[23] Jones, E. E., Hester, S. L. Farina, A., & Davis, K. E. Reactions to unfavorable personal evaluations as a function of the evaluator's perceived adjustment. *Journal of Abnormal and Social Psychology*, 1959, *59*, 363–70.

[24] Wheeler, R. H. Theories of will and kinesthetic sensation. *Psychological Review*, 1920, *27*, 351–60.

equated with feelings of physical strain. But common usage also reveals the connection. When we see a person doggedly persist at a task we speak of his being 'strong-willed' or 'determined'. With actions of little effort, brushing a fly from one's hand, snuffing a cigarette, there is little inclination to attribute intention or decision. There are supporting data for this in the study with Swap, where respondents were asked about their feelings of will and responsibility under conditions in which effort was either high or low. In one case the robbery required great physical stress, in another it was done casually; a race at a track meet was said to be very difficult to win, or very simple; an examination was difficult to pass, or very easy. In each of these cases respondents rated their actions as being a greater expression of will under the high effort conditions.

The fourth and final rule can be linked to our earlier discussion of the role of perceived rationality. Implicit in our ordinary conceptual structure is the assumption that people normally utilize rationality in the service of self-gain; this is made explicit in various contemporary elaborations of hedonism, as well as in the psychoanalytic theory of ego functioning. If rationality is generally utilized in the service of self-gratification, it may be inferred that actions which are not self-gratifying in their consequences are not rational in origin. Since actions which are not rational are not generally perceived as volitional, it may be concluded that actions producing negative consequences are not volitional in origin. The interesting implication of this line of reasoning is that the attribution of volition may be altered as the consequences of one's actions are played out. As the consequences improve, one may begin to see one's actions, retrospectively, as personally chosen; as one's fortunes dip, renewed scanning may reveal that one's volition did not play a central role in determining action after all.

Evidence for this has been generated by investigators at Purdue,[25] who arranged a simulation study in which student teams worked together to solve the problems of a revolution-torn nation. They took the role of government administrators, received various types of information and were called upon to make decisions about the best course of action for the nation to follow. A random number of teams went through various periods in which their decisions met with

[25] Streufert, G. & Streufert, S. Effects of conceptual structure, failure, and success on attribution of causality, and interpersonal attitudes. *Journal of Personality and Social Psychology*, 1969, *11*, 137–47.

almost continuous success, while other teams, facing the same decision problems, were told with alarming regularity that their decisions failed. At the end of these critical periods, each team member was required to make a series of evaluations concerning the previous hour's activities, including ratings of the extent to which they had been responsible for the consequences of their actions, the extent to which the revolutionaries had been responsible, and the extent to which their outcomes were due to chance. The results revealed that where success was maximal, almost 70 per cent of the responsibility for the team's outcomes was attributed to the team's decisions. Where the team's decisions ended in failure, however, exactly the reverse was true: less than 40 per cent of the responsibility was attributed to self.

Similar results have also been discovered in the educational setting. In one study teachers rated whether student performance in their classes was due primarily to the child's efforts and abilities or to their own teaching performance[26] The ratings revealed that when a child did poorly, the teacher attributed the behavior to the low intelligence or low motivation of the child. In contrast, when a child showed marked improvement, the teachers perceived the child's behavior to be the result of their own efforts as teachers. In effect, one judges oneself as personally responsible when the results of one's actions succeed, but seldom when they meet with failure.

Summary and Implications for a Science of Self

We can now re-examine the assumptions which underlie the common quest for self-identity. The traditional view of self-knowledge is initially premised on the assumption that all human beings of normal constitution are capable of conscious experience or sensation. The present orientation is essentially similar in this respect. Traditionally such experience is subdivided into self (emotions, thoughts, memories, desires, etc.) vs. not self. At this point the present analysis began to deviate. Rather than viewing these experiences as intrinsically separated within experience, it was argued that such separations were accomplished through a conceptual process typically guided by social learning. The fact the emotions are singled out as

[26] Johnson, T. J., Feigenbaum, R., & Weiby, M. Some determinants and consequences of the teacher's perception of causation. *Journal of Educational Psychology*, 1964, 55, 237–46.

part of oneself, the variety of emotions we believe to exist, and the conditions under which they are to be attributed to self, are all based on socially derived conceptualization. While the tradition emphasizes personal identity as a unified core of self-relevant experience which provides an essential criterion for conduct across time and circumstance, there is little reason to suspect such a core from the sociocognitive standpoint. Rather, it appears that the individual harbors a multitude of self-relevant concepts, many of which are inconsistent if not diametrically opposed. Thus, the same experience of self may be coded differently from one situation to the next, or different self-experiences may be conceptualized as similar. In this sense, the individual may feel at one moment that he is truly sensitive as a person, but at another that he is brutishly calloused in his relations with others. He may feel that each of these concepts of self is truly correct and experience full authenticity in each case.

This argument also challenges the traditional assumption regarding basic self-esteem. Rather than assuming that people possess some essential core level of self-evaluation, the present approach calls attention to the various ways in which an individual may evaluate himself as he moves through the social world. From the sociocognitive viewpoint, therapy designed to enhance one's self-esteem is not likely to have long-term impact. Essentially, the individual may learn to adopt a particular conceptualization of self within the therapeutic hour, but whether this particular stance will be maintained as the individual confronts other groups whose opinions and characteristics are different, or who bring to mind other types of self-relevant memories, is quite another matter.

Finally, the present position differs from tradition in its assumptions about distortions in self-understanding. The tradition holds that beneath the patina of social circumstance lies a source of true knowledge about self. It is said that some of us have distorted images of ourselves, some defend against the truth, some have lost touch with themselves; and, according to the tradition, continued scientific study should reveal how such individuals might be helped to regain contact with themselves, to find true self-knowledge. From the present stance, that orientation is misguided. Self-conceptualization is essentially an arbitrary process, and to speak of valid or invalid self-perception is to do so primarily in terms of the social context. If the social rules dictate the application of particular concepts to particular experiences in specified situations, then rule violations may be said to constitute invalid or distorted self-perception. Such distortions must be viewed with a full appreciation for their social relativity. For other persons, at other times or at other places, those attributions favored within contemporary society would be viewed as invalid or distorted. 'True self' is essentially a label and no intrinsic or objective criteria are available to guide the manner in which it is stuck.

This line of thinking has important implications regarding the potential for a science of self. It is commonly assumed that we may construct theoretical principles covering the development of self (including self-esteem) and its functioning within daily relationships. Such principles should be open to empirical test, and through continued study our knowledge of self should steadily be improved. Such an assumption is widely shared both in psychology and sociology, and has many adherents in psychiatry, anthropology, and political science. However, from the present standpoint, such assumptions are problematic. In traditional form, the ultimate crucible for scientific theory is provided by a common data base, that is, a series of relevant observables. While scientific theory may contain many terms which are not linked operationally to concrete particulars, a theory is not testable until such linkages are constructed. But the present analysis suggests that in the case of self-knowledge there is virtually nothing to know.[27] That is, there is little in the way of factual data that lies waiting to be discovered, explored or assessed. Rather than factual data, we are confronted with a series of social rules or intelligibility systems employed in the process of personal explanation. But such rule systems are tied imperfectly, if at all, to internal psychological or physiological events. From this viewpoint, the proper concern of a science of self may be with the current intelligibility systems rather than with an underlying psychological data base.

To place this in a broader context, we may ask more generally what it means for a given experience to qualify in society as a fact. That is, we term some events factual, and consider them the proper

[27] The contrary position is represented in this volume by D. W. Hamlyn, who posits a self-knowledge which is factually grounded and beyond mere belief or opinion (conceptualization). What he views as 'true insight', I would consider the application of socially derived intelligibility systems; his conditions for 'genuine self-knowledge' are primarily a formalization of our common rules for interpreting or describing social action.

subject of scientific study, while others are viewed as fiction, fantasy, myth and so on, and are ruled out of science. Science may concern itself with plants, trees, water, and neurons but not with the man in the moon, the spirit of God, or with unicorns. What is it about the former class of experiences which differentiates it from the latter? While the answer to this question may initially seem obvious, it is not. Closer scrutiny indicates that we are confronted, not with a simple bifurcation of fact vs. fantasy, but with a continuum. Some experiences clearly qualify as fact, and others as fancy, but between the two poles the applicability of scientific analysis is often in question. In the case of poltergeists, communication with plants, life after death, astrology, and communication with a divinity, to name but a few, it is simply unclear whether science should be brought to bear. In the case of flying saucers, for example, the American government has mounted major research into the question of whether there are any facts (outside of aberrant states of consciousness) worthy of scientific study. Given what we may view as a *continuum of factuality*, the question then arises as to what criterion or set of criteria are typically used in the placement of experiences or events along the continuum. By what standards do we in Western culture presently determine the degree to which a given experience is a reflection of reality?

The question of how we may trust our senses to map reality is, of course, an immensely complex one and has long been a chief concern within epistemology. However, for philosophers the question has primarily been one of establishing proper grounds for the determination of factuality: what *should* we take as the proper basis for establishing reality? But the question can also be asked descriptively: for good or ill, what criteria are currently pressed into service by the populace? Although such criteria may change from one historical era to another, they should be open to documentation. People do seem to sort experiences along a factuality continuum, and the following criteria seems to be operative, at least in our culture:

1. *Neural engagement.* The greater the engagement of the nervous system within a delimited period of time, the greater one's confidence in the factual basis of his experience. A loud roar, a bright flash, seem more indicative of factuality than a faint rumble or a brief flicker. 2. *Modality increment.* The greater the number of sensory modalities which are simultaneously engaged, the greater one's confidence in the factual basis of a given experience. One is most confident in the existence of a reality corresponding to his experiences

when he can simultaneously see, taste, smell, touch, and hear. 3. *Discriminability*. The greater the degree to which a given experience may be differentiated spatio-temporally from other experiences, the greater one's confidence in its factuality. When the neural system is highly engaged, the accompanying experiential state typically (but not always) differs from its predecessors. If a given experience cannot be differentiated with certainty from its spatio-temporal surroundings, one may have little confidence that he is apprehending reality. 4. *Repeatability*. To the extent that an experiential state can be replicated, one's confidence in the factuality of the experience is increased. Since recurrence seems to enhance factuality, *duration* may be viewed as continuous repetition. The longer the duration of an experience, the greater one's confidence in its factual basis. 5. *Inter-observer exposure*. To the extent that a given experience can be replicated in the experience of other persons, our confidence in its factuality is increased.

In the case of flying saucers, factuality is in doubt because neural impact is often very meager and typically is limited to the visual modality; discriminability is often problematic because flying saucers may not be easily differentiated from comets, aircraft, etc.; the experience is seldom repeated for the same individual, is of brief duration, and is only available to a minor segment of the population.

In light of this, what are the prospects for a science of the self? In many respects, the saucer cults may have a stronger claim to scientific respectability. To the extent that self-psychology is concerned with internal states, that is, with evaluative feelings, wants, hopes, aversions, tastes, attitudes, emotions, beliefs, volition and the like, the prospects for a cumulative science seem dim. With the possible exception of emotions, neural engagement is often at a very low level; most sensory modalities are not called into play by internal states and one is virtually limited to interoceptive cues. Further, in the case of internal states, discriminability is often exceedingly difficult for the individual, and repeatability is often small. Finally, there is no opportunity for inter-observer exposure.

With so little in the way of factual underpinnings, the possibilities for an exact science of mental life in general, and a science of self-experience in particular, seem limited. In the main, those internal states bearing no reference to external events do not meet the common criteria for factuality. In an important sense, then, when considering self-knowledge it is unclear what there is to know. Yet, the search for self-knowledge continues, and people do experience 'breakthroughs' in self-understanding. From the present vantage point, such breakthroughs are primarily in one's capacity to master an intelligibility system as it applies to one's own behavior.[28] Self-knowledge is not thereby increased; it is only constructed anew.

[28] In this sense, the man on the street may indulge in the kind of 'diagnostic-descriptive' breakthroughs found within the scientific domain and as described by Toulmin in his contribution to this volume.

6 Self-Knowledge

DAVID W. HAMLYN

I have the impression that someone who wished to sum up recent philosophical and psychological work in the area of self-knowledge and understanding might justly say that those investigating this area have had much to say about various aspects of our knowledge *about* ourselves, but comparatively little about self-knowledge proper. Let me explain what I mean by this. First the philosophers. I shall have something to say directly about the historical philosophical traditions that have thrown up problems about the self. In recent times, at least within what might be called the broadly analytical tradition of philosophy, there has been almost an obsession, if an understandable one, with problems stemming from Cartesian privacy. I mean by the last roughly what Descartes maintained when he said that we have a clearer and more distinct idea of our own states of mind than we have of our bodies, let alone other things. Wittgenstein's concern (Wittgenstein 1953) with the conditions for a public understanding of the concepts of states of mind which are in a certain sense private —concepts such as that of pain or other sensations—has led to a preoccupation with the conditions for speaking, if we *may* so speak, of knowledge of those states of mind. Thus one of the few books in this tradition of philosophy in recent times which has the words 'self-knowledge' in its title—Sydney Shoemaker's *Self-knowledge and Self-identity*—is, to the extent that it is concerned with self-knowledge at all, concerned with this aspect of knowledge about ourselves. Yet, even if considered at the level of knowledge *about* ourselves, this might well seem to psychologists a rather minor aspect of that knowledge, even granted the point that in self-characterization, as opposed to the characterization of others, a good deal of weight is put upon personal experiences and how things appear to us.[1]

[1] cf. one of the contributions to the last symposium of this kind, P. F. Secord and B. H. Peevers, 'The development and attribution of person concepts', in T. Mischel (ed.), 1974, pp. 117–42.

The fact that recent philosophical concerns with the self have been limited in scope should not necessarily, however, be taken as a criticism of those philosophers. Philosophical concerns, however minute they may seem at first sight, usually have at the back of them large-scale traditional issues. It might indeed be said that it is these alone which in the end mark off the more limited concerns as philosophical. By 'large-scale traditional issues' I mean and have in mind such matters as the place of man within nature in general, a philosophical concern that goes back almost to the beginnings of philosophical thought in Greece. I am inclined to say that the form of a philosophical problem can be set out as 'How is X possible?', and the possibility of man being construed either as a part of nature or as set apart in some way from the rest of nature is an issue which generates a whole mass of other problems which in one way or another provide a challenge to the understanding. A concern with one aspect of this large-scale issues is understandable if it provides a particularly pressing challenge to the understanding.

Apart from the Cartesian thesis of which I have spoken, together with various reactions against it, there have, however, been other philosophical issues that have affected such concern with self-knowledge as there has been. There has, for example, been a philosophical puzzlement about the status of the 'I', originating perhaps in Hume's inability to find an impression of the self, together with Kantian reactions which lay emphasis on the correlativeness of the ideas of the self and non-self. There is also the connected issue of the distinction between self and other which is to be found in, for example, Hegel. There may be other themes of this kind, and in some philosophers one can find amalgamations of more than one theme. There is thus in Ryle's discussion of the systematic elusiveness of the self in the *Concept of Mind* a blend of the Hume/Kant theme with an anti-Cartesianism; while in Sartre's claim in *Being and Nothingness* that consciousness is a nothingness and his doctrine of the transcendence of the ego one might also find the Hume/Kant theme together with certain preoccupations with questions about self and other. I think that it is generally true that philosophical treatments of self-knowledge have been overladen with concerns of this kind, concerns which are in a genuine sense metaphysical; and there has been little in the way of an attempt to get at self-knowledge pure, so to speak. Is it possible to do this, to divorce a philosophical treatment of self-knowledge from these more general metaphysical concerns? And if so, are recent inquiries by psychologists relevant, whether in themselves or in providing a stimulus towards a shift in point of view?

So, to the psychologists. I am no expert here, but a relatively casual survey of the literature seems to reveal a preoccupation with such things as the self-concept. (There is an ambiguity here that ought to be noted. Sometimes, perhaps even generally, what seems to be meant by the self-concept is not what philosophers have in mind when they speak of the concept of the self, as opposed to, say, that of others—not, that is, the conception of what it is for something to be a self at all—but rather the conception of oneself as a certain *kind* of person, the picture that people have of themselves.) Connected with this seems to be a concern with the attribution to oneself of various characteristics, its conditions and basis, and its relation to the attribution of similar characteristics to others. Finally, although by no means exhaustively, there is the matter of the presentation of oneself to others and the place of other people's attitudes in one's picture of oneself. The notion of something like the picture of oneself (even if this is not the term generally used) seems to have a large place in this. To be concerned with this, however, is in effect to be concerned with one's *beliefs* about oneself and about the way in which those beliefs are formed. Many, if not all, of those beliefs have to do with relationships with others, and that is particularly so in connection with the presentation of the self, where the notion of roles has a large part to play. One might say, therefore, that a good deal of the psychological literature in this area is concerned with the beliefs that people have about themselves in a social context, and the way in which the beliefs about the sort of person one is affects one's general behaviour. That does not amount to self-knowledge.

There is perhaps some tendency to invert what I have said and to see the beliefs as arising from the behaviour rather than vice versa. At the extreme that would amount to the thesis that our beliefs about the kind of person we are are the product of the interrelationships of behaviour that we are involved in; so that what we take ourselves to be is simply what interaction with others makes us believe. An even more extreme thesis would be that we *are* no more than that; we are not merely what society makes us but what society makes us believe ourselves to be. There are suggestions of this point of view in G. H. Mead, to whom references are often made in writings in this area. Mead saw the notion of the self as social in origin, and what he called the 'me' he defined as 'the organized set of attitudes of others which one himself assumes' (Mead, 1934, p. 175). The assuming of these attitudes is what promotes self-consciousness. Hence as far as the 'me' is concerned 'that is the self that immediately exists for him in his consciousness' (ibid.). That is not perhaps the very extreme view that I have mentioned, but it is an easy step from it to that view, and I believe that others may have taken it under his inspiration. Mead in any case distinguished between the 'me' and the 'I' that reacts to it, although he did speak of the 'me' as a kind of 'censor' on the 'I', so setting limits to its expression (Mead, 1934, p. 210). I shall return to something of this issue later. It is sufficient for now to indicate that it is not a large step from this to the Goffmanesque position that what I am is determined by the set of roles that I take up and that these are determined by my interactions with others.

However all this may be, it is natural that a psychological concern with the self should be a concern with the beliefs that one has about oneself, how one sees oneself or thinks about oneself, and the relevance of all this to behaviour, particularly social behaviour. For how people see themselves has clearly a large bearing on our understanding of that behaviour. Yet it has to be said that an inquiry into the acquisition of the self-concept, into the attribution of characteristics to ourselves, or into the ways in which we see ourselves, is not as such an inquiry into self-*knowledge*. While it may be an inquiry into *a* way or *some* ways in which we understand ourselves, such understanding may not amount to knowledge. My concern in this paper is with *knowledge;* it is arguable whether such knowledge is commensurate with complete understanding, but I do not have to take a stand on that issue here. It is enough to indicate that the approaches that I have mentioned are concerned with our understanding of ourselves to the extent that, but only to the extent that, they are concerned with the beliefs, it may well be true beliefs, that we form about ourselves. Whatever more there is to complete understanding of ourselves, this must fall short of knowledge since true belief is never sufficient for knowledge. (I shall return to this point in the next section.) One might perhaps express my concern in this paper by putting the issues that I have mentioned so far alongside the Delphic saying that Socrates welcomed and insisted upon—'Know thyself'. What was Socrates asking of us and what has it to do with any of the philosophical and psychological issues that I have mentioned? Was he indeed asking us to embark upon a wild-goose chase?

I do not think that the answers to these questions are at all obvious. Socrates clearly thought that the possession of self-knowledge would have moral consequences, and indeed that self-knowledge was a necessary condition of true virtue. I do not think, however, that he believed that the self-knowledge in question could come about by any kind of self-analysis or any kind of psychological inquiry into, say, the nature of one's personality, although it may well be unrealistic to suppose that we can have self-knowledge without *some* knowledge of that kind about ourselves. Indeed in some cases it may be necessary to know a great deal of that kind. It is equally clear, however, that too much attention to facts about oneself may lead, not to self-knowledge in any sense that Socrates can have been concerned with, but to self-consciousness in the colloquial sense that Laing describes as implying both an awareness of oneself by oneself and an awareness of oneself as an object of someone else's observation, if not more than this (Laing, 1965, p. 106). It might even be said that self-consciousness in this sense is antithetical to self-knowledge. Someone who has true insight into himself needs to be aware of what he is to others, but he does not need to be looking over his shoulder all the time to see how others are regarding him; to do so would inhibit a concern for and a commitment to what he is engaged in and thus one of the essential conditions of self-knowledge proper would be missing. To say this is, however, to anticipate what I have to say later. Let us first try to get clearer about the relationship between knowledge of self and knowledge about oneself by considering what we ordinarily mean by those words.

Knowledge of and Knowledge About Self

I said earlier that what is often discussed under the heading of the 'self-concept' is certain beliefs about oneself, in particular beliefs about the kind of person that one is. Such beliefs would of course be parasitical upon having the concept of a person in general and upon some kind of understanding of the notion of the self both as opposed to what is not oneself in general and as opposed to other persons in particular. These latter issues have, as I noted earlier, been of concern to philosophers in the past and are still with us as philosophical issues. But the issues that are of immediate concern are: what is the relationship, given my possession of those concepts, of the beliefs that I have about the kind of person I am to knowledge about myself, and what is the relationship of this to self-knowledge?

The first of these questions is relatively easy to answer—formally at any rate. The relation between belief about oneself and knowledge about oneself is the same as that between belief and knowledge generally. I said that it was easy to answer the question formally because the exact relation between knowledge and belief has been the subject of much philosophical discussion lately. It is sufficient for present purposes to say, what is in any case true, that for a belief to amount to knowledge it must be true and it must be no accident that it is what is true that is believed. There is, however, a further point that is for present purposes more important—that if one's beliefs about oneself are to be considered rational they must be founded in some way on knowledge that one has about oneself. Moreover, it is implausible to suppose, perhaps even inconceivable, that one should have beliefs about oneself but no knowledge about oneself. People often have a false conception or picture of themselves, or so we say. But what we generally mean by this is that their beliefs about themselves are false in certain very important ways. It is perhaps rarer for people to have beliefs about themselves which are merely accidentally true, but similar considerations would apply. It would be impossible to say what proportion of people's beliefs about themselves are usually false or merely accidentally true; nor do I see any grounds for claiming that knowledge about oneself is in some sense the norm. The claim that I wish to make is a much weaker one—that a person could have no beliefs at all about himself if he knew *nothing* about himself; he must know, for example, that he is the sort of thing that can have beliefs.

The second question, about the relation between knowledge about oneself and self-knowledge is more difficult and more complex. It seems clear, for example, that to have self-knowledge it is not enough to have knowledge about oneself *of any kind whatever*. The notion of self-knowledge is more restricted in its application than that, and some kinds of knowledge that one may have about oneself seem irrelevant to the question whether one has self-knowledge proper. For example, knowledge about one's looks does not seem to the point in this context unless one's looks affect other things about oneself. Cyrano de Bergerac's long nose was rightly portrayed as affecting very considerably his character and personality, so that it had a considerable place in the pattern of his life; he could scarcely be said to have known himself at all if he did not know about his nose. The same would not be true of some much less prominent physical characteristic which had no appreciable affect on a person's life. Not any old facts about oneself are material to self-knowledge.

Can one, then, go straight to the character and personality of which I have spoken, and say that to have self-knowledge a man must know about these things as they affect himself? The answer depends to some extent on that 'as they affect himself'. If I know something about my character and personality I will know such things as that I am cheerful and honourable, or morose and unreliable. Suppose that I know a lot of things of this kind, to the extent that I can produce what is in effect a profile of my character and personality. It would not necessarily follow that it would be right for someone to say of me 'He knows himself all right'. Suppose that while I can indeed produce this profile of myself, a profile that seems to others accurate enough, I show no ability to apply this knowledge to the particular circumstances of life. Suppose, for example, that in particular exchanges with others I show no signs of recognizing that unreliability which I avow to in general and which in general holds good for me (I say 'Suppose'!); I behave on the contrary as if it is clear that I shall keep my promises, do what I say I shall, and so on. There will in that case be a gap between what I seem to know about myself in a general way and what I seem to know of myself in a more practical and particular way. I say 'seem to know' because the conflict of evidence might cast doubt on the extent to which it is appropriate to speak of knowledge proper in these circumstances. One way to put the matter might be to say that while I do indeed know a great deal about myself, including what kind of character and personality I have, I do not really know myself; the general knowledge about myself that I have is not somehow cashed in the ordinary course of my life. Hence, there certainly seems to be a sense in which I may know a great deal about myself, and attribute to myself characteristics that I undoubtedly have, without having self-knowledge; my conception of myself is in one sense quite right in these circumstances, but that is not enough.

There is also what might well be regarded as the opposite tendency. Suppose that certain person has a kind of knack in practical affairs and in intercourse with others, so that he seems to know exactly how far he is likely to go and can go, how seriously he should be taken, how reliable his faculties are, and so on. Thus, as far as concerns himself, all his affairs are conducted in what appears to be a well-oiled way; and insofar as failures occur they arise not from any inability to estimate his own potentialities properly, but from a simple failure to foresee what others may or may not do (and there are clearly limits to anyone's ability in that respect). Yet he is quite unable to produce any account of his general character and personality. It is not just that he is modest about it or that he cannot find the words; his success in practice simply has nothing to do with any general views of himself that he may have, if indeed he has any. His practical success in life is an extension of that kind of success which may be achieved by athletes who know just how far to push themselves and how far they can go in their efforts. If we are at all inclined to say that such a person knows himself, it is in the sense that we should say such things about the athlete—meaning that he has things nicely judged as far as concerns himself. This could not be in any full sense what we expect of self-knowledge, since he lacks any explicit self-insight. At the extreme such cases correspond to that of the so-called 'holy fool', the person who has a complete sense of right and wrong and of his position in that respect, but who is quite incapable of spelling out what is involved and appears in a certain sense not to know this.

It may be said that there is a certain artificiality in my procedure up to this point, in that I have been relying on intuitions which may not be shared by others, and on a sense of the ordinary use of words like 'self-knowledge' which may be idiosyncratic and may well not be relevant to our purposes. It may well be that in ordinary parlance we *would* say of the athlete that 'he certainly knows himself', meaning that he knows the limits and extent of his physical capabilities. But our judgment would be confined to that particular context. If we wished to extend the scope of the judgment in asking what a man has to have in order to have self-knowledge in a fuller sense, would it be enough to add to the knowledge of the physical capabilities knowledge of potentialities and dispositions of other kinds—for example those already mentioned that go to make up a person's personality, temperament and character? It could not reasonably be denied that a successful athlete must know much of these things too in regard to himself. Yet if the knowledge in question still manifested itself simply in what he did and was disposed to do, it would amount at best to a knowledge of 'what he would do if...', and a knowledge that he might not be able to express to himself or others. Thus while we may sometimes limit our concerns in speaking of self-knowledge to one particular dimension of a person's life, e.g., his practical skills and concerns, it has to be admitted that there is more to a person, and therefore more to the possibilities of self-knowledge, than that.

Earlier in this section I asked whether, in seeking what is required for self-knowledge, one could go straight to the knowledge that a man might have of his personality and character (and now one might add other capacities) as they affect himself. I said that the answer depended to some extent on what was involved in the words 'as they affect himself'. I have since then discussed two contrasting ways in which such knowledge might *not* affect the possessor, first in not carrying over into his practical life, and second in being in effect confined to this. Yet there is an asymmetry between the two cases, as was in effect indicated by the fact that there seemed to me some inclination to say that the second man did have self-knowledge if only in a limited way and with limited scope. A relevant point is that the first man undoubtedly had knowledge *about* himself, even if that knowledge did not carry over into his more practical life; the second man could not really be said to have knowledge *about* himself at all, or at least not to any great extent. His knowledge was of a quite different kind, that one might call 'practical' (it is not the only relevant sense of the term, as we shall see later). This does not necessarily suggest that knowledge about oneself is antithetical to self-knowledge, or knowledge of oneself, but it does suggest that knowledge *about* oneself is nothing if it has no relation to one's life in general—nothing, that is, as far as self-knowledge is concerned. That would suggest in turn that certain models of self-knowledge, which regard it in terms of information-getting are on the wrong track. We should not approach self-knowledge in the first place through the idea of getting knowledge about ourselves, or at any rate not through this to the extent that the knowledge is construed like that of other things—and that is what the story about information-getting suggests.

Blindness to Self

It does not seem quite right to say of the hypothetical persons whom I discussed in the last section that to the extent that they failed to have self-knowledge they revealed ignorance of self. The last phrase is not one, in any case, that is in common use. There is no problem about a person being ignorant about himself. To say that he is this is simply to say that he lacks knowledge of things about himself that he may or may not be in the position to know. Ignorance *of* oneself is another matter. We can be ignorant of other people, if they have never, so to speak, come within our ken; but that makes no sense in regard to ourselves, to the extent that we have a conception of ourselves at all. If we wish to speak of a failure of self-knowledge, if we wish to speak of that to which self-knowledge may be opposed, self-ignorance does not seem to be the right term, whether or not it is a term which is used in ordinary parlance. Moreover, even 'ignorance about oneself' suggests merely a failure of diagnosis that others have made or could make; someone who is ignorant about himself fails to know what others know or could know, and the knowledge that he lacks is thus a form of knowledge that others must be able to have in principle at least, such as a knowledge of general characteristics and the like. There are other forms of knowledge of himself that a person may lack. The failure to possess them may reveal itself in his behaviour and in the general conduct of his life, so that to speak of the failure as a failure of diagnosis may be quite wrong. An athlete who was the converse of the one whom I mentioned in the last section, an athlete who regularly failed to pull it off because of misjudgments of various kinds about himself need not have failed in any self-diagnosis; for he need never have made any diagnosis of himself at all, or felt it relevant to do so, preferring to rely on a kind of practical knowledge of himself—a knowledge that, as it turns out, he lacks.

One might speak of this kind of failing as a form of blindness to self. Blindness is what Aristotle called a 'privation'—the lack of a quality by something or someone which things or people of the kind in question normally have or may be expected to have. A successful athlete may be expected to have some sense of his own powers, if only on the practical level that I have mentioned. A failure to have that sense on the part of a practising athlete may therefore be set down as a privation, in the way that blindness in the literal sense is for ordinary human-beings (although not, Aristotle believed, for moles!). A blindness to self may, however, take many forms, not simply this impercipience in action which is reflected in a lack of skill. There is, for example, the blindness to self which comes from overriding attention to other things, with perhaps as a correlate a complete lack of concern for one's own position in the matter. There is also, though perhaps arguably, self-deception.

Let me take the latter first. I have argued elsewhere (Hamlyn, 1971b) that the self-deceiver does not really make himself ignorant of what he is or of what he is up to, but rather that he somehow prevents himself from being conscious of what he in fact knows. I have also argued that it is a mistake to think that the deception involved is always to be construed on the model of that form of deception of others in which we deceive them by giving them false information. Indeed false information need not necessarily constitute deception; the person receiving it has to take a certain attitude to it and to the person who gives it. Similarly, it is impossible to understand self-deception without taking into account other attitudes that a person may have to himself. All this obviously fits in with the strictures that I have put on construing self-knowledge in terms of getting information about oneself; that would, for one thing, leave out the place that that information might have in relation to the attitudes that we have to ourselves. I shall not argue these points again here, but it may be as well to point out some of their implications.

In the first place, the position that I have maintained about self-deception does not preclude the possibility that by putting out of consciousness something that he knows about himself a man may eventually come, even if he could not produce that result intentionally and directly, to be in a state equivalent to that of one who is ignorant of the same thing about himself. That is to say that by, so to speak, blinding himself to a certain point a man may with luck, if that is the right word, come to be in a state in which he is quite incapable of recognizing that point. He will be so incapable not simply because he will not allow himself to be capable of recognizing it, as may be the case during the initial stages of self-deception, but because he has become like one who has genuinely forgotten. The item has passed not only out of his consciousness, but out of, if we may speak, his knowledge. He began by blinding himself to the issue, and he has ended up as good as blind to it. If this comes about, however, it will be, as I have said, by 'luck' and not as a result of his direct and intentional agency. Unless and until this comes about, the self-deceiver may blind himself to certain things about himself, but the blindness is not a genuine and proper blindness; rather it is more like the hysterical blindness of one who cannot see something because he does not wish to do so, fears to do so, or cannot bear to do so. (I do not of course adduce the case of the hysteric as more than a parallel; in itself it raises as many problems as that of the self-deceiver, and may in fact be considered as a special case of that.)

A further point is whether there are any restrictions on the possible range of objects for self-deception, the things that one can possibly be deceived about. Can one be deceived about *anything* in regard to oneself? I think that the answer to this question is that nothing in logic restricts the range of possible objects of this kind, but that if something is to be such an object it has to satisfy certain conditions which would make it very implausible that certain things *should* be in the range in question. What I mean is the following. If it is the case that self-deception involves one's putting out of consciousness something that one in fact knows, it is inevitable that it should presuppose a certain conflict in oneself. For, suppose that one is self-deceived in believing p; then one must know that not-p but one must have put that fact out of consciousness. Otherwise the belief that p would amount to wishful thinking only and not self-deception proper. But to know that not-p one must have some concern for the truth, while if one wishes to put the fact that not-p out of consciousness one must have a concern of a different and opposing kind about the truth of not-p. Hence opposing concerns must be involved. This means in turn that it is possible to be deceived about something only if it is in one way or another the object of differing concerns, and that it is not possible to be self-deceived about something that cannot in any way be this.

The next question that arises is whether there are any restrictions in the range of things or of truths that can be a possible matter for concern. In this one is up against the kind of issue that Elizabeth Anscombe raised in asking whether it is possible to want a saucer of mud (and this simply, and not because, for example, one wanted to use it for some purpose) (Anscombe, 1951, p. 70). If it is asked whether anything at all could be a matter of concern for us, the answer must be that there comes a point at which we should find it unintelligible that the thing in question could be so—at least in the sense that if someone did claim to find it a matter for concern we should have to say that we did not understand *him*. Thus it seems to be the case that if in ceasing to be self-deceived one gains a kind of insight into oneself, that insight must have regard to what it is that is a matter for concern for oneself. The self-deception itself must involve an obscuring of that concern.

This suggests that what is important for self-knowledge, at least in the sense of this that is involved when we speak of freedom from self-deception, is what one puts value upon. The man who knows himself in this way, and who is not subject to self-deception, knows, without obscuring the fact from himself, where his values lie, what he truly wants, and where he stands in relation to those wants. I do not think that such knowledge can plausibly be construed in terms of knowledge of 'what he would do if . . .'. It is of course true that one way of finding out whether one wants a certain thing is to ask oneself what one would do if one were deprived of it or if one were presented with the opportunity of getting it but only at the cost of other sacrifices. Doing this, however, is really to employ a kind of heuristic device, an imaginative way of giving concreteness to a choice by putting oneself in the position of making a hypothetical decision. Nevertheless, what is demanded is a *decision*, not a prediction about oneself. In such circumstances we should not be passing a judgment about ourselves as to what we should do in hypothetical situations: rather we should be using those hypothetical situations to give body to a decision. Moreover, in making the decision explicit to ourselves we should be gaining knowledge of ourselves that we did not previously possess. It is very often the case that it is only in the context of an actual decision that we become really conscious of where our values and true wants lie; for in those circumstances we may become aware of what really matters to us. In abstraction from contexts of decision, speculation about 'what we should do if . . .' may become idle because it is divorced from any real concern about the objects and matters in question.

What this means is that although I have been discussing the kind of blindness that is involved in self-deception in terms of the self-deceiver blinding himself to certain things *about* himself, there must inevitably lie behind this another kind of blindness to self. This latter blindness, or rather blinding of oneself, is more akin to a refusal to commit oneself to a line of action or perhaps even to make a decision on the course of one's life—or at any rate it must be seen in a context of that kind. A similar point emerges from a consideration of the other example of blindness to self that I instanced earlier—that which comes from an overriding attention to other things. I suggested at the outset that this might be correlated with a lack of concern for the person's own position in the matter. There are of course people with a genuine lack of concern for themselves in comparison with others, but what we expect of such people is really a concern for themselves which is limited to what is necessary for the promotion of the concerns of others. If someone had a completely overriding lack of concern for himself he would be likely to be thought of as a liability—his lack of concern for himself would certainly not be anything like a complete virtue. For it to be anything approaching this the lack of concern for self must be both relative and positive, not the negative thing involved in a privation. It should be clear, however, that this blindness to self, to whatever degree, is not a simple blindness about oneself and could not be construed simply in those terms. Whereas behind self-deception there lies perhaps a refusal to commit oneself to one single course of action, a refusal to recognize this as one's course, the blindness to self that I have been concerned with now involves a failure to see oneself as having a place in any course of action. The important thing in this is the reference to action. One would expect of one who revealed any degree of blindness to self that his life and course of action would lack a continuous sense. I shall return to this point and its converse later.

Self-knowledge and Self-involvement

The opposite of being blind to oneself would be something that corresponded to having one's eyes open to oneself, a form of self-awareness, but not one that amounts to self-consciousness in the colloquial sense of which I spoke earlier. I said in an earlier paper ('Person-perception and our understanding of others' in T. Mischel (ed.), 1974) that a condition of knowing something is that we should stand to the object of knowledge in relations which are appropriate to things of that kind. If that is true, how does it apply to self-knowledge? In what sort of relations can one stand to oneself? One negative thing should be clear from what I have said already—that one must be neither blind to oneself nor in some sense standing back from or apart from oneself. The failures of self-knowledge that I discussed in the last section amount to these two alternatives. Indeed the self-deceiver, by standing back and apart from himself, may well blind himself to himself and so put himself in the position of the person who is blind to himself *simpliciter*. So much for the negative side of the problem. What, however, can be said on the positive side about the attitudes appropriate to oneself as a condition of self-knowledge.

The major problem here, as it often is in philosophy, seems to be to find a form of words that sums up what is the case. To employ the wrong words would be in effect to have recourse to a model which would be misleading. In an earlier version of this paper I used the notion of 'acceptance' to express the attitude to oneself that is a condition of self-knowledge. I do not think, however that that is quite right, even apart from the conservatism and quietism that the notion suggests in this context. There is, however, a tradition in the history of thought which connects self-knowledge and self-understanding with a freedom which itself involves an acceptance of oneself in one way or another. I should like to go into that tradition a little.

One strand of it—represented, for example, by the Greek Atomists, the Stoics, and Spinoza, though in rather different ways—lays emphasis on the idea that freedom comes through an acceptance of oneself as part of nature and through an understanding of just how one is part of nature. (Those whom I have mentioned had different conceptions of nature, but that does not affect the general point.) There is another strand, however, which emphasizes the idea of knowledge of, commitment to and perhaps acceptance of whatever one is engaged in as a conscious agent. There is something of this, for example, in what Hegel has to say about the connection between self-consciousness and freedom (where of course 'self-consciousness' is *not* being used in the colloquial and pejorative sense). In modern Anglo-Saxon philosophy the idea is to be found in, if I understand them correctly, the writings of Stuart Hampshire, although he, I think, also connects what he has to say with Spinoza. For he puts a premium on a rational understanding of our actions, so that the more that we understand and know of what we are up to the greater our freedom. The self-knowledge that this involves is thus, in part at least, practical. As Hegel puts it, 'Actual free will is the unity of the theoretical and practical mind' (Hegel, ed. J. N. Findlay, 1971, p. 238, S. 481). For Hampshire, as I interpret him, self-knowledge and freedom equally depend upon an increased consciousness of the reasons for our actions, so that what we do becomes to the maximum extent intentional. This means that the increased consciousness in question must not be seen as external to the actions; it is correlative with increased involvement in what we are engaged in. If this is put together with the idea that it is possible to recognize more and more aspects of our life as involving intention, then the involvement of which I have spoken has acceptance of what we are as a natural corollary.

Freud has sometimes been seen as an ally in this, just as he has sometimes been seen as a preacher of self-knowledge.[2] I think that this is a wrong view on both counts. The 'historical' aspects of psychoanalysis, the suggestion that the analysis has to do with the past history of the patient, loom larger in Freud's early writings, or at any rate have a more obvious rationale there, than they do later. The views expressed in Freud's middle-period and later writings, after the 'discovery' of the fictitious nature of reports of infantile seductions, with the emphasis on instinct theory, the primary and secondary processes and the like, really amount to something like a theory of human nature. In the theory of analysis that goes with this the notion of 'transference' plays an all-important part, a fact which in itself makes it impossible to construe analysis as having self-knowledge as its primary goal. Indeed Freud sometimes speaks of analysis as a kind of education for life (e.g. *Introductory Lectures on Psychoanalysis*, ch. 27). Although changes in the theory of human nature that Freud brought forward changed the theory of analysis itself to some extent (the influences are evident in *Inhibitions, Symptoms and Anxiety*), analysis remained for him a kind of education for life in conformity with his conception of human nature. It is not at all clear that self-knowledge as such plays a central part in all this, and I think that to that extent one popular view of psychoanalysis is wrong. Indeed it might be argued that it is at least consistent with Freud's theory that too much self-consciousness is a bad thing.

The same is true of the more special view that psychoanalysis has

[2] See e.g. S. N. Hampshire, 1959, p. 255.

as its aim the bringing to consciousness of the reasons for our actions in the light of the revelation that more of our life than had previously been supposed is governed by reasons. This view has been criticized on the grounds that what psychoanalysis reveals as governing our actions is not generally or strictly speaking reasons.[3] In one way at least this line of criticism seems to me correct. If Freud indicated that more than had previously been supposed is intentional, he also indicated that not all that is intentional is conscious and perhaps more importantly still for present purposes that it is not all rational or capable of being so. He was quite definite, at least in his mature years, that the irrational and unconscious parts of the mind, those corresponding to the primary process, are not as such capable of being made conscious and rational. What therefore has to be aimed at is a control, though often of necessity a tenuous control, of our irrational instincts on the part of the ego. This may involve a kind of 'know how', which may itself be based on some kind of insight into one's past self; but it is scarcely true that what it produces is an increased consciousness of the reasons for our actions. (I should perhaps add that I am not so much concerned here with the truth of what Freud had to say as with its bearing on considerations about self-knowledge).

Moreover, even if it were true that psychoanalysis was concerned to produce self-knowledge of the kind in question and that this is correlative with an increased freedom on our part, the notions of self-knowledge and freedom that this would involve would surely be severely limited ones. As far as freedom is concerned, it is important to recognize that one does not stand alone; there are of course other people. Thus Hegel, for example, says (1971, S. 431, *Zu.*), 'I am only truly free when the other is free and is recognized by me as free', and he elaborates this conception in what he has to say about the master–slave relation, and the restrictions on the master's true freedom imposed by the relationship. Hegel's treatment of this in the *Phenomenology* has sometimes been looked at as a brilliant piece of social analysis. It is scarcely that, brilliant though it is; for it has no particular connection with any actual cases of human relationships. It is rather a metaphysical exposition of certain aspects of the concepts of a person and personal relationships as they arise from Hegel's view of the self and self-consciousness.

[3] See P. Alexander, 1962 and the reply by T. Mischel, 1965.

This becomes clear from his parallel treatment of the matter in the *Encyclopaedia*, although that treatment is much less elaborate and brilliant. He does not simply say there that one cannot have a clear view of oneself without taking into account how one stands to others (although that is no doubt true); he says that 'in that other as ego I behold myself' (1971, S. 430), and in the accompanying *zusatz* he emphasizes the universality of the 'I'. Nevertheless, Hegel's conclusions may have considerable interest for us, irrespective of the grounds on which they rest. There would be, to say the least, an extreme artificiality in the claim that one can attain self-knowledge and thereby acquire a certain freedom by seeking an increased awareness of one's intentions in and reasons for action; for that would presuppose a view of oneself as cut off from all else. At the worst this would involve not merely an artificiality but an arrogance of attitude.

It would thus be quite wrong to think that how one stands to others had nothing to do with oneself or that knowledge of how one stands to others had nothing to do with self-knowledge. If self-knowledge involves some kind of involvement in what we are engaged in (a notion that is connected with the emphasis on intention that we have noted), it is also true that in very many aspects of life what we are engaged in cannot be separated from what we are to others and what they are to us. That is one important implication of Hegel's master–slave case; one cannot be a master and cannot be engaged in being a master without others being involved—a truistical point, perhaps a boring one, but an important one for present purposes all the same.

Self-knowledge and Others

It might be said that the master–slave relation presents a very special case. Why should we extrapolate from it to the conclusion that self-knowledge inevitably presupposes something about how one stands to others? Does a hermit, for example, have no possibility of self-knowledge or do we have to treat an absence of relations to others as one kind of relation to others? There is some plausibility in the suggestion that the answer to the last question is 'Yes', but in order to get a clear view of the situation it is necessary to disentangle various different issues here. There are, first, issues concerning what is presupposed in the possibility of acquiring self-knowledge at all. And there are, second, issues concerning the extent to which someone who fulfils the conditions under the first head is capable of having self-knowledge without regard to others. It is the second set of issues to which the consideration about the master–slave relation belongs, and I shall return to it and similar issues later. For the time being I wish to concentrate on the first set of issues.

Negatively the moral of the considerations that I wish to raise under this first head is the same as one to which I drew attention earlier in the paper—the impossibility of construing self-knowledge or even self-understanding as coming about simply via the consideration of information about oneself. While it is the same in this respect, it is so, however, for different reasons. It is not just a matter of our being unable to come to an understanding of self-knowledge on this model alone because of the practical side to our lives and the practical nature of the knowledge that must be presupposed; the model is inadequate any way if treated as an account of how self-knowledge comes about or can come about in the first place. Roughly, it can be said that, if that were all that there was to it, it could never amount to knowledge, nor, since understanding involves knowledge, understanding either. The point is a familiar one to philosophers since Wittgenstein, and it is one that I have made use of elsewhere.[4] Simply put, the point is that if something is to count as knowledge it must be true (or in some sense correct), and if someone is to have knowledge he must know what it is for things to be true or what it is to be correct. But truth, though it is not identical with intersubjective agreement, depends on it in the sense that the concept of truth would get no intelligible application except through it. Hence anyone who knows what truth is must at least know what it is to be in agreement with others. (The same applies analogously to correctness.) It follows therefore that the possession of knowledge implies this also, and if this is true of knowledge in general something like it must be true of self-knowledge. Self-knowledge is possible only for one who has stood to others in the kind of relation that makes agreement possible; for only by so standing could he understand what it is to do so. (This

[4] See Hamlyn, 1973. A more extended account of the matter is to be found in my book *Experience and the growth of understanding* which is forthcoming.

presentation of the argument is excessively brief, and for a longer version I must refer to the references given.)

Thus while someone could gain information about himself, given that the other conditions are satisfied, it would make no sense without that; for in that case self-consideration could not produce anything that could function as *information*. That is not to say that when a person does get information about himself it is *ipso facto* information about how he stands to others. It is rather to say that he could not be said to have knowledge unless he did stand in some way to others, and in particular in a way that gives application to the notion of agreement with them in some ways. I have argued elsewhere that such agreement must be founded ultimately on agreement in emotional attitudes or attitudes involving feeling. Once given this and the gradual acquisition of a set of concepts in terms of which knowledge of oneself is to be expressed, one can by attending to oneself in various ways come to acquire information about oneself that may amount to self-knowledge of a kind, if only of a kind. This too might take place under conditions of isolation from others, but could not take place unless there had been some initial contact with others. To this extent, but to this extent alone, self-knowledge must necessarily presuppose a social context. All this is in effect an extension of Wittgenstein's point that one could not gain an understanding of, say, pain simply by considering the sensation that one is now having (Wittgenstein, 1953, I. 314). A public, social context is presupposed in the understanding of any given concept, since the knowledge that is involved in having that concept is itself public. Without sharing in a public and shared form of life, or at least being in the position to do so, one could not have knowledge. Hence, much else has to be understood before one can begin to think of self-knowledge in terms of getting information about oneself.

The act of a hermit, therefore, in removing himself from society is clearly in one sense a social act, and it is quite fair to consider his consequent lack of relations with others as one kind of relation to them. To say this, however, is merely to say that his act of removing himself or keeping himself apart from others is, to the extent that he knows what he is doing, an intentional act under that description; and even if he does not construe his act as having anything to do with others, he could have knowledge of what he is doing only if he is one who once had things to do with others.

Hence, his state as a hermit is a privation of one relationship with others, not a simple negation of all such relationships. Nevertheless, and this takes me to the second issue, if someone takes himself into the desert in isolation in order to seek self-knowledge through contemplation, he thereby deprives himself of certain possibilities of self-knowledge, or at least of knowledge about himself. He cannot see himself in other people's eyes any longer, and for this reason he cannot get those kinds of information about himself that are usually obtainable only through others—how he is to others. Nor can he reliably gain knowledge of what he would do and how he would be in a variety of social contexts and roles. Such knowledge would be of the kind 'what would be the case if . . .', and I tried to indicate earlier that this cannot be all that self-knowledge consists in. It may nevertheless be relevant. If knowledge about oneself is not entirely confined to what one is to others and the like, some part of it must have to do with this.

It is important, however, not to confuse the two points that I have discussed. The fact that self-knowledge, along with other knowledge, presupposes relationships with others, is not to be taken as implying that what one knows must be set out in terms of those relationships, even if some, perhaps much, of what one may come to know about oneself may be construable in those terms. To suppose that would be to confuse the conditions for a kind of knowledge with its content. I suspect that this mistake is made by Mead in his social view of the self. He says, for example (Mead, 1934, p. 138), 'The individual experiences himself as such, not directly, but only indirectly, from the particular standpoints of other individual members of the same social group, or from the generalized standpoint of the social group as a whole to which he belongs. For he enters his own experience as a self or individual, not directly or immediately, not by becoming a subject to himself, but only insofar as he first becomes an object to himself just as other individuals are objects to him or in his experience; and he becomes an object to himself only by taking the attitudes of other individuals toward himself within a social environment or context of experience and behavior in which both he and they are involved'. Some of this might imply that all that there is to be known about oneself is what is available to others, and that one can acquire knowledge of oneself only by taking on the attitudes of others. That, however, does not seem to be true. It *is* true that the existence of a social context is necessary for the initial acquisition of knowledge about oneself, it may sometimes be true that one can get to know certain things about oneself only through the attitudes of others, and it may be true that our own attitudes to ourselves may be considerably influenced by the attitudes of others. None of that, however, adds up to the point that Mead seems to want to make—that knowledge of myself is simply the knowledge that others have of me. That does seem to involve a confusion of the conditions of knowledge with its content.

What I have been discussing, however, is in the main knowledge *about* oneself, and it is necessary to bring these considerations into relation with self-knowledge in the full sense. Before embarking on a discussion of the place of others in knowledge about oneself, I was concerned with the idea that self-knowledge can be connected with some kind of commitment to oneself. My initial reason for embarking on a discussion of our relations to others was to counter the suggestion that one could think of self-knowledge as concerned primarily with a knowledge of one's reasons for action and perhaps as connected thereby with the idea of a commitment to that line of conduct. I suggested that the idea would involve, as it stands, a kind of arrogance, to say the least, a lack of interest in or concern for others and what we are to them. My succeeding discussion was meant to provide a warning against going to the other extreme and suggesting that self-knowledge is entirely a matter of our relations with others in one way or another. Given this, let us return to the main theme.

Being Oneself

One objection to a concentration on knowledge of one's own reasons for acting or what one is intentionally engaged in as a key to what self-knowledge involves is that such knowledge seems to be a one-sided diet. It might reasonably be held that a concentration on one's own doings and the reasons for them may be inhibitory of spontaneity; there would inevitably be an element of rationalization in the process, a rationalization that might well prevent natural and spontaneous reactions to situations. It does not seem to me at all obviously desirable that people should continually try to make explicit to themselves the reasons for their actions, and if this were what self-knowledge consisted in it might be said that it is not necessarily a good thing. To say that, however, would be to make a comment on the moral desirability of this kind of self-awareness, and while I believe that there are many interesting implications for ethics in this point, my present concern ought to be with its implications for self-knowledge. My main point is that a concentration on making explicit the reasons for our actions must inevitably involve a kind of detachment from oneself, which at the worst can produce that bad kind of self-consciousness which I referred to in connection with Laing. It would of course be wrong to imply that it *must* produce that kind of self-consciousness. It is, however, very likely that it will do so, and to the extent that it involves detachment from oneself it must in any case prevent one being oneself.

How then could it be supposed that concentration on the reasons for our actions and our intentions in acting is the paradigm of self-knowledge, and equally the key to the kind of freedom that this may produce? I indicated earlier that, as I understand him, Stuart Hampshire is one of the main proponents among Anglo-Saxon philosophers of this point of view. He might say that the kind of knowledge of reasons for action that I have been considering is theoretical and not the practical knowledge that he has in mind. For he insists with some emphasis that the knowledge that he has in mind is practical. It is so in the sense that what we know in doing something intentionally is what we are doing *in doing it*; we do not have to watch ourselves in order to get the knowledge, or anything like that. To do something intentionally is to do it knowing what we are doing, but this does not involve any observational knowledge of our actions, as might be involved if we were to suppose that we had to stand back from ourselves in order to have the knowledge. I think that the basic premiss in all this is correct—the knowledge involved in doing something intentionally, the knowledge of what we are doing, is not a knowledge gained from observation of ourselves, nor one that is in any way like that. One might wonder, however, why in that case it has anything to do with self-knowledge. I think that the mediating link in Hampshire's theory is provided by the belief that the knowledge must be conscious and to that extent displayed to ourselves, as it were, even if it is, as he puts it, non-propositional.

It is not clear to me that the non-theoretical character of the knowledge entails that it is non-propositional. The knowledge might be expressible in propositional form even if it were not in fact so expressed. As far as concerns the point about consciousness, it might be argued that when we act with full consciousness of what we are up to there must be a kind of reflexiveness about that consciousness; we are not only conscious of what we are engaged in, we are conscious of *that* and what it involves as well. I am not sure that this is in fact true, since it would imply that the deliberation must take in not only the immediate circumstances of the action but also its larger significance for our lives and its place in our conception of ourselves. While this may sometimes be true it is by no means clear that it must always be true. Even so, if what I have said about self-deception is right, it cannot be said that intentional action in general always involves such a consciousness of what we are up to; for knowledge of what we are doing does not necessarily imply consciousness of what we are doing.[5] Thus, although it may be true that someone who does something intentionally does it knowingly and is in some sense responsible for what he does, there need be no implication that he is aware or conscious of what he is up to, let alone that his knowledge brings with it anything that deserves the title 'self-knowledge'. And if in making himself increasingly aware of what he is up to someone thereby increases the control that he has over his actions, his self-knowledge may nevertheless remain very limited. This has large implications for psychoanalysis.

My final point in this connection is that a concentration on the knowledge involved in intentional action, whether or not as a key to self-knowledge, ignores the whole passive side of our mental life. The Spinozistic tradition, within which Hampshire to some extent operates, associates passivity with irrationality and with ignorance or confused consciousness. But the ideal of a rationality that goes with an activity of mind which can transcend the confusedess of passivity has little to do with anything human. Our emotional life, for example, which has to do with the passivity in question, is not just an area of irrationality which increasing awareness can diminish. We are dependent on it in all sorts of ways, and a theory of self-knowledge must take that into account. The supposal that one could be alive to what one is by bringing more and more of one's activities under intention is a likely recipe for self-deception; it would certainly entail an abstention from being oneself—something which, as it seems to me, is a necessary condition of self-knowledge.

[5] See Hamlyn, 1971a, 1971b.

What I have said is, I admit, excessively dogmatic, and in taking Hampshire as my target for criticism I may have seriously misunderstood what he has to say. There may, however, be general morals to be abstracted from it all. What it suggests is the extent to which genuine self-knowledge presupposes that we must *be* ourselves and not be in the position of standing back from ourselves in any way. We shall be in that position either if we insist on regarding ourselves theoretically all the time or if, under the influence of a theory, we concentrate our consciousness and attention on one part of ourselves. This does not mean that for self-knowledge we have no need to know all sorts of facts about ourselves, any more than that the thesis which I defended on the last occasion of this kind—that knowing other people presupposes standing in certain relations to them—entails that we do not need to know all sorts of facts about them. No matter what the object of knowledge is, knowledge of it of course involves knowledge of many things about it; the point is simply that it does not involve *just* that. It is obvious enough that there are many attitudes which one can take up towards oneself that will prevent self-knowledge—and this may be so even if one knows a great many things about oneself. This can certainly happen if, as I indicated earlier, the knowledge is strictly theoretical in the sense that it gets no real purchase in practice. Similarly, I suppose, we might know many things in theory about another person without this knowledge getting any purchase in our practical dealings with them. Yet I have argued in connection with other people that genuine knowledge of this kind is not properly to be construed merely as a practical know-how in our dealings with them, whether or not that know-how is backed up by knowledge of their character, temperament, personality, etc. For people are not merely objects the handling of which demands knowledge of this kind; so that it is important that we should stand to them in relations which are appropriate to them as people. If it is less clear what this means in connection with knowledge of oneself, it is at all events evident that certain kinds of knowledge will not be sufficient, given that the knowledge that has to be explained thereby is knowledge of a *self*. In addition there is the important point that the knowledge in question is knowledge of *oneself* and not another self; for this eliminates the possibility of genuine self-knowledge where there is any tendency to stand back from oneself in such a way as to regard oneself, in part at least, as another person. One must be involved in oneself.

'Know Thyself'

I wish finally to return to the Delphic saying and Socrates' use of it, and then to try to sum up the implications of it all for our present purposes. I suspect (though I can hardly claim to know) that when Socrates invoked the saying he wanted people to make their own decisions about the conduct of their lives and not simply go by rules however derived. To make those decisions people would have to have some insight into their own position, and their capabilities and limitations, in respect of the situation in which they found themselves, a situation which would inevitably involve other people. If in such a situation you were to obey his instruction you would not simply go by any kind of rote or rule; you would have to think out for yourself what you should do. Some of the factors in that decision might well depend on how you *felt* about certain things, so that you could not necessarily present them as considerations that must appeal to all men irrespective of circumstances. There is in all this a demand for a certain kind of integrity (the parallel of which in Kierkegaard, who admired Socrates so much, is purity of heart and freedom from 'double-mindedness'). I am not entirely sure that this must have the ethical consequences that these thinkers demanded; there is a kind of integrity combined with insight which is quite compatible with an evil disposition. The case of Eichmann has sometimes been invoked in this context. It might also be said that as a moral point of view it pays insufficient attention to social considerations. These are arguable points. Nothing in any case can make moral decision easy in *all* circumstances; nothing can ensure that such decisions are always right. The important thing for present purposes, however, is the reference to *decision*, a point on which I remarked earlier in the paper.

For one of the paradoxes about self-knowledge is that it can be mediated by decision; perhaps indeed it must be in the end.[6] We and our lives are constantly changing. Whether or not it is right to think of this as development[7], the changes that take place build on what is past. A decision about the future conduct of our life can alter the whole perspective from which we view ourselves and give a new or different sense to what we have been. That new sense may

[6] I think that I owe much in what follows to Richard Campbell.

[7] For which see Hamlyn, 1975.

involve the taking up of things that we did or which happened to us and which seemed only marginally to do with us, so that they become genuinely ours. That is presumably what some moral philosophers have been getting at when they have spoken of giving sense to our lives as a whole and of a kind of self-deception that may pervade a whole life.[8] I think, however, that it has to be said that it can work quite the other way round or perhaps even in some intervening way; things that seemed of vital concern to us can come to be viewed as merely incidental. Once again there is no recipe for how it has to be. The important point for present purposes is the point that an important decision for the future can utterly change our view of ourselves in relation to our past. A person is not a static thing. If there are some constant things about us (there *is* such a thing as personal identity, and some constants about us may be genetically determined), we are also changing entities with both a history and a possible future. For this reason alone there can be no complete story about what has to be known for adequate self-knowledge. Indeed it might be said that a central fact about self-knowledge is that there is no *thing* to be known.

Is not the same true, however, of knowledge of others? Yes, in a sense. Other people are creatures with a past and a possible future. Yet there is an asymmetry; for in a sense what I am is my own past and future, and I must therefore be involved in this in a way and to a degree different from my involvement in those of others. This affects how and what I know in these cases, if I do. The point is really just a corollary of the point, previously mentioned, that my knowledge of anything has as a necessary condition my standing in relations to it of the kind appropriate to things of that kind (Hamlyn, in T. Mischel, 1974). I cannot therefore construe my knowledge of myself, to the extent that it exists, as parallel to that of others, let alone to that of other kinds of thing. We can decide to some extent what our futures shall be (even if to a limited extent only) in a way that we cannot decide on the futures of others. That is vital to any view of self-knowledge that we can form.

[8] cf. I. Dilman and D. Z. Phillips, 1971, although I would not myself go along with much of the discussion in that book.

Conclusion

All this may seem poles apart from anything that psychologists normally have to do with; and so it is. Yet what I have said must have some implications for the understanding of oneself. There are many respects in which to understand ourselves we may have to view ourselves in ways that are parallel to those which enable us to understand others. But the asymmetry remains even here; and *one* way of coming to understand ourselves—perhaps an all-important way—may be to have to make the kind of decision about our future that I have mentioned, a decision that may bring with it other views of ourselves. That feature, however, need not be taken as undermining the point that within that framework the ways in which we understand others can to some extent be applied to ourselves. We should nevertheless be conscious of the limits involved in this.

I noted near the beginning that most psychological investigations in this area have to do with what are in effect people's beliefs about themselves, under which heading I include how they see themselves, the picture that they have of themselves, all that is included under the notion of the self-concept. To the extent that all this can indeed be put in terms of people's beliefs about themselves, it is feasible to think of the acquisition of such beliefs in terms of getting information; for such beliefs may be acquired in the process of social learning. It is clear that the part played by social factors in a person's forming a picture of himself and in the acquisition of various beliefs about himself should not be underestimated. Our beliefs about ourselves, just as with our beliefs about others, may be founded on stereotypes or they may have a foundation in reality. Part of that reality may be social relationships; for what a person is to others is an important part of what he has to get to know about himself. But self-knowledge as such is, as I have tried to show, quite another thing.

Appendix

Some of the other contributions to this book have connections with what I have had to say, particularly the admirable paper by Charles Taylor. There is a kind of opposition, however, between what I have had to say and some of the things said by some others. In the first place, I have argued as if self-knowledge is inevitably a single thing. I cannot justify that view here in any way that does not mean going over again what I have had to say. Some may think the conception is an illusion, but I do not think that it is. Those views of oneself of which I have spoken do not of course necessarily amount to *knowledge*—they may amount to belief only and in some cases perhaps grossly mistaken belief. Knowledge in this context may be an ideal only, so that it is impossible to say what has to be the case for it to be attained. What remains true, however, is that such knowledge is not possible at all in any full sense without some view of one's practical self, of one's past and future life in general, and without some involvement in this to the extent that division from oneself is ruled out. On the other hand, such involvement is not a sufficient condition of self-knowledge. Moreover, too much self-involvement may be inhibitory of self-knowledge, just as is the case with involvement with others in connection with knowledge of them.

In relation to Kenneth Gergen there is a different kind of opposition, and I shall finish with some brief comments on his contribution. He has stressed the way in which our views of ourselves may be taken from others, and he has given an interesting account of some studies along these lines. I do not believe, however, that any of this amounts to the 'social construction of self-knowledge'. There are two ways in which relations with others are necessary for self-knowledge. First, they are necessary as a condition of that publicity without which understanding and knowledge as such would be impossible. Knowledge is necessarily intersubjective and public in the sense that the standards both of truth and the attainment of truth are public. I can of course know things that nobody else may know, but if it is really knowledge then others can in principle have it. There is no sense in which something may be true for me but not for others. The possibility of someone knowing something, therefore, depends upon his participation and acceptance of public standards of truth, knowledge and understanding. There is no way in which these standards can be constructed simply out of what is so for me. Indeed the beliefs that each of us have must be viewed against these intersubjective standards. The 'I' presupposes a 'we', as it is sometimes put; hence what 'we' know cannot be simply a construction out of what each of us takes to be so.

Secondly, relations with others may be necessary as an important source of self-knowledge, given the fact that men are social creatures, so that a hermit must inevitably deprive himself of that kind of knowledge of himself that might come from his relations with others. To suppose that knowledge of oneself has nothing to do with others might, as I have said, be thought to constitute a kind of arrogance. These truths, however, say nothing for the idea of the social relativity of such knowledge. Many of the *beliefs* that we have about ourselves are no doubt taken from others; there may be some tendency, as the studies reported by Gergen suggest, to see ourselves as others see us (despite Bobbie Burns!). But that does not imply that self-*knowledge* is a social construction. Gergen's acknowledgment of Mead, about whom I made some critical remarks in this connection, is significant, though I am not entirely sure that Mead is a consistent exponent of the view I wish to criticize. It may be true that the *beliefs* that one takes from others about oneself limit the possibilities of independent self-expression—I take it that that is part of what Gergen is saying. But none of that prevents the possibility of some kind of access to oneself that is independent of that. In any case, the thesis seems to be about *beliefs* about oneself, not *knowledge*, or at least that is how it ought to be construed; and, as I have already claimed, knowledge is in a certain sense a prerequisite of such beliefs.[9] At all events the thesis that Gergen derives from Mead certainly does not entail that self-knowledge is simply those beliefs about oneself that society brings about. In that sense it is just false that self-knowledge can properly be viewed as a social construction, even if social factors enter in an important way into its content.

REFERENCES

Alexander, P. 'Rational behaviour and psychoanalytic explanation', *Mind*, LXXI, 1962, 326–41.

Anscombe, G. E. M. *Intention*, Blackwell, Oxford, 1951.

Dilman, I. & Phillips, D. Z. *Sense and Illusion*, Routledge and Kegan Paul, London, 1971.

Freud, S. *Introductory Lectures on Psychoanalysis* (1916–17), S.E. Vols. XV and XVI, Hogarth Press, London, 1953.

Freud, S. *Inhibitions, Symptoms and Anxiety*, S.E. Vol. XXII, Hogarth Press, London, 1953.

9 See also Hamlyn, 1970, pp. 93–5.

Hamlyn, D. W. *The Theory of Knowledge*, Doubleday, New York, 1970 (also Macmillan, London, 1971).

Hamlyn, D. W. 'Unconscious intentions', *Philosophy*, XLVI, 1971a, 12–22.

Hamlyn, D. W. 'Self-deception', *Proceedings of the Aristotelian Society*, Supp. Vol. XLV, 1971b, 45–60.

Hamlyn, D. W. 'Human learning' in *The Philosophy of Psychology* (ed. S. C. Brown), Macmillan, London, 1973, 139–57 (also in *The Philosophy of Education* (ed. R. S. Peters), Oxford University Press, London, 1973, 178–94).

Hamlyn, D. W. 'Person-perception and our understanding of others' in T. Mischel (ed.), 1974.

Hampshire, S. N. *Thought and Action*, Chatto and Windus, London, 1959.

Hegel, G. F. *Phenomenology of Mind* (trans. J. B. Baillie), Allen and Unwin, London, 1910.

Hegel, G. F. *Hegel's Philosophy of Mind* (trans. W. Wallace, ed. J. N. Findlay), Clarendon Press, Oxford, 1971.

Laing, D. *The Divided Self*, Penguin, Harmondsworth, 1965.

Mead, G. H. *Mind, Self and Society*, Chicago University Press, 1934.

Mischel, T. 'Concerning rational behaviour and psychoanalytic explanation', *Mind*, LXXIV, 1965, 71–8.

Mischel, T. (ed.), *Understanding Other Persons*, Blackwell, Oxford, 1974.

Ryle, G. *The Concept of Mind*, Hutchinson, London, 1949.

Sartre, J. P. *Being and Nothingness* (trans. H. E. Barnes), Methuen, London, 1957.

Shoemaker, S. *Self-knowledge and Self-identity*, Cornell University Press, Ithaca, 1963.

Wittgenstein, L. *Philosophical Investigations*, Blackwell, Oxford, 1953.

PART IV Self-Development and Its Failures

7 'Irrationality' in a Psychoanalytic Psychology of the Self

ERNEST S. WOLF

The strongest oaths are straw
To the fire in' the blood.
(The Tempest)

Classical psychoanalysis, i.e., the psychoanalysis created by Sigmund Freud during the decades just before and just after the turn of the century, has filled, more or less satisfactorily, a great void in the consciousness of an educated commercial middle-class: first it provided a *treatment* for neurosis, the stigmatic illness of solid *Buergertum*; second, it developed a *method* for the systematic study of mental activity, a prized accomplishment in a scientific age; and, third, it organized its insights into a *theory* of man, thus seeming to replace discredited religion. The influence of Freudian thought on all aspects of the culture of the West has been so pervasive as to truly justify calling it revolutionary. Ironically, the *raison d'etre* for the birth of psychoanalysis, namely the ubiquitous neurotic patient suffering from hysteria, has become a relative rarity in contemporary mass society. To be sure, now and then, the modern psychoanalyst still encounters a hysterical paralysis or a hand-washing compulsion but, in the main, the patients with these symptoms seem to come out of old fashioned rural environments. Not that psychoanalysts have become unemployed, on the contrary more patients are in treatment than ever before. But today's patients, by and large affluent city dwellers, do not present themselves usually with the typical neuroses as they were described by Freud in his classical case histories. Rather, today's psychoanalyst is sought out for help with depressions, with disintegrating marriages, with incapacitating work inhibitions, with seemingly irremediable hypochondriacal preoccupations, with empty lives lacking zest and joy and seeking escape through addiction to drugs or alcohol, to perversion or delinquency—and even to frenzied life styles, whether in business or the arts.

In retrospect it seems that it was inevitable that, sooner or later, the change in the predominant clinical picture and the therapeutic problems this presented to psychoanalysts, had to lead to new insights and new theoretical conceptualizations. During Freud's time the development of psychoanalysis also had progressed in response to clinical therapeutic difficulties: the phenomena of hysterical symptoms led to the technique of providing symptom relief by emotional catharsis; the difficulties with hypnosis led to the technique of free association; the resistances to free association led to insights into defense mechanisms; the displacements of erotic interest onto the analyst led to the recognition of transference phenomena and this in turn led to the most penetrating therapeutic techniques of transference analysis. One could multiply these examples of the interplay between clinical phenomena and theoretical developments but that would lead too far afield from today's topic. In a science that was so much the creation of one genius it is not surprising that, with Freud's death, this progressive development seemed, at least temporarily, to have come to a halt. Partly this was due to the truly unique quality of Freud's genius, partly to an understandable but nevertheless inappropriately excessive attitude of reverence toward Freud's accomplishments. Psychoanalytic progress slowed down as psychoanalytic investigators restricted themselves to further development of only those lines of thought that had been securely launched by Freud.

During the last decade this self-imposed restriction in the thinking of psychoanalytic scholars seems to have been lifted and there has begun a serious re-examination of some of the major theoretical assumptions of classical psychoanalysis by contemporary investigators, e.g., Klein (1976), Schafer (1973) and Gedo and Goldberg (1973).

While these re-examinations of theoretical assumptions bespeak the renewed spirit of scientific inquiry in psychoanalysis, the most significant recent advances in psychoanalysis have come not from a re-examination of theory, but from the need to solve new or newly prominent clinical problems. Contemporary patients whose symptoms, outlined above, reflect the ups and downs of their self-esteem more than the inhibition of their sexuality, usually do not respond with a great deal of improvement to the analysis and interpretation of their oedipus complex. This does not mean that these patients do not have neurotic conflicts derived from unresolved oedipal conflicts, nor does this mean their neurotic conflicts are unanalyzable. But it does mean that the neurotic conflicts derived from unresolved oedipal fixations are not central to their suffering and that their resolution through classical psychoanalytic treatment is not sufficient to restore adequate functioning. Kohut was the first to conceptualize the central pathology of some of these sufferers from depression and hypochondriasis as a defect in the cohesion of their self, the latter concept an abstraction related to, but not identical with, sense of self. In this paper I will use some of the concepts developed by Kohut (1959, 1966, 1968, 1971, 1972, 1973 1975a,b, 1976, 1977) in his discussion of clinical and theoretical aspects of a psychoanalytic psychology of the self in order to illustrate what the psychoanalyst often understands by neurotic irrationality. (I am excluding psychoses, i.e., insanity.) *Pari passu*, I hope also to illuminate the concepts of Kohut's psychology of the self.

In the clinical context of psychoanalysis, irrationality may mean that a person has come to judge his or her subjective mental state, or even observable behavior, as somehow unreasonable or inappropriate. Such irrationality may be directly associated with psychological discomfort, such as varying degrees of anxiety and depression, or these symptoms may secondarily cause additional discomfort due to their quality of apparent unreasonableness and inexplicability. It is this apprehension that something is not 'right' that brings the prospective analysand to see an analyst. He wants help for his dis-ease. For example, Miss S., a graduate student whose boyfriend had to be away for six weeks on a business trip, noticed that she not only missed him and felt sad but that she could not free herself of the recurrent thought that he would meet and get involved with another woman, forgetting Miss S. In the light of the circumstances of their enforced separation and the solidity of their past relationship, Miss S. judged that the feared loss of her friend was not likely to occur. Moreover, she surmised that if she really did lose his affections she ought to be able to adapt herself fairly quickly, for she was young, attractive and intelligent. But these considerations, she said, did not help her in staving off a growing feeling of discouragement combined with a restlessness. She found herself depressed and tired, yet unable to either sleep well or to function efficiently in her daily work. The she suddenly found herself staring at other women with fantasies of touching and sexual contact, became frightened about herself, wondering whether she was becoming a homosexual, and consulted an analyst. This example illustrates, first, the direct perception of a disturbed state of the self, (depression, restlessness, etc.), and secondly the direct perception of an inappropriate ideational content, e.g., a thought (which may be more or less delusional, like her unsupported conviction of being betrayed) or a fantasy such as touching someone (with or without associated affects that are recognizably sexual). Thirdly, there is a secondary affect of fear in that her perceptions of specific feelings, thoughts and fantasies signalled to her that something was not 'right' within herself—that she might be neurotic, or going crazy, or becoming a pervert—at any rate that she was sick and ought to consult a doctor.

I will not now enter into a discussion of whether such a person is to be regarded as 'sick'. Suffice it to say that one man's painful depression may be another man's satisfying awareness of the depth of his feelings associated with a meaningful loss.[1] Moreover, judgments about the reasonableness or unreasonableness of subjective experiences are not only influenced by individual predisposition, but also by the complex social and cultural milieu. For example, a scientist's conviction that the universe is lawful, or the religionist's conviction of his deity's omnipotence, may be seen as normally appropriate piety when viewed from within the respective subcultural groups, but as delusional when viewed from within a different cultural community.

In psychoanalytic work both analyst and analysand must start by

[1] A consistent use of the concepts 'health' or 'illness' is fraught with much difficulty. Consider, for example, an epidemic of the common cold, a syndrome that occurs in response to invasion of one of a number of viruses. A particular epidemic affects, let us say, 75 per cent of a community. Thus, the average response to the virus includes certain symptoms, such as congestion of mucous membranes that are the results of tissue responses, e.g. the inflammatory reaction, which serve to isolate, destroy and eliminate the invading organisms. Is such a person 'sick' with a cold or 'healthy' with the needed responses that will restore the *status quo ante* the viral invasion? There are instances where the normal bodily defenses do not function, e.g. where an infection does not evoke the normally expected febrile responses and the invading infectious agents overwhelm with resulting death. In the latter situation one can perhaps unequivocally speak of illness leading to death. Usually the situation is more complicated and more usefully analyzed in terms of more or less appropriate adaptive responses. This is particularly so in the area of mental functioning.

assuming the legitimacy of the analysand's psychic experience, whatever it may be, in order to make the psychoanalytic investigation a fruitful one. That is, they both tacitly agree that the analysand's psychological experience is real in that no matter how inappropriate and inexplicable it may *seem*, it can, in principle, be explained. The analytic work, then, consists of attempts to realize the potential explanation. Whether, or to what extent, the achieved insight will alter the analysand's psychological experience depends on a number of other factors, and is not the subject of the present discussion.

Another clinical vignette will help in developing the concepts that concern us. A young man finds that on rather frequent occasions he becomes tense, restless, perhaps somewhat depressed; he is unable to concentrate on whatever he's doing, as he becomes more and more preoccupied with various homosexual fantasies. Eventually, and reluctantly, he will give in to these fantasies and seek out some homosexual contact, usually making a 'pick-up' of some stranger in a public lavatory. Following the consummation he experiences a sense of relief and is able to pursue his everyday activities until the next time. The total sequence of events is seen by him as an unexplained and undesirable intrusion, in spite of the temporary excitement and pleasure derived from the sexual encounter. Not only would he much rather have enjoyed long lasting and satisfying relationships, his inability to do so was felt by him as evidence for there being something terribly wrong with him.

During the course of his analysis it was possible to reconstruct certain events in this young man's early years which allowed us to understand the apparently strange self-experience and behavior which brought him into the analysis. War and persecution had fated him to be without a reliable mother during the early years of his life, notwithstanding the well-meaning intentions of a number of foster mothers. His father's brutality, and the unpredictability of both his parents after his father's remarriage, created an ambience in which the youngster experienced himself as helpless and powerless in a world of unreasoning and unpredictable giants, the adults, who had no empathic understanding for what he was experiencing. The fact that these years were full of dramatic incidents characteristic of the severe trauma that the boy was undergoing is less important than the constant and ubiquitous isolation from an empathically understanding parent. Though there were short-lived periods of closeness to his stepmother, he mainly gained some strength for his enfeebled and slowly developing self from an older cousin who was living in the household. This cousin was not only strong, handsome, well-dressed, but also able to defy the youngster's parents and shake off whatever punishment was visited upon him. Alas, as soon as he could, the cousin left the inhospitable home to make his own way in the world, leaving our youngster bereft and shattered.

During the analysis we were able to establish quite clearly that the irresistable urge to go and 'pick-up' somebody occurred in the context of a real or fancied rejection that left him feeling quite disconcerted and isolated. The 'pick-up' episodes themselves were characterized by mounting excitement, until he got to see the other man's erect penis. Psychologically that was the high point of the sexual contact, the subsequent mutual manipulations being more for the benefit of the partner. We then began to understand that these episodes were repetitive attempts again and again to incorporate the strength that at one time he had received from being close to his admired cousin: through visual incorporation by staring at the beautiful large erect penis and through tactile incorporation, symbolically, by touching and holding the penis in his hand, he now infused himself with strength, similarly as he had as a child. Later during his analysis, this young man recovered memories of his cousin asleep in the same room with the little boy, who admired, awestruck, his cousin's beautiful physique, including his genitals, and slyly tried to touch them.

I will not discuss there the details of the transference manifestations and of the working through process in the analysand. The symptom yielded to the analysis. What is important for our purpose, however, is the light which a case like this, and many others, can throw on the development of 'irrationality'; *pari passu* we may also learn something about the development of 'rationality'.

As indicated earlier, I am only concerned with a very narrow range of 'irrational' phenomena, namely those that are *subjectively* experienced as irrational; thus, e.g., cases of grossly and overtly psychotic behavior, which would doubtlessly be judged as 'irrational' by most observers, but which may not be experienced as such by the afflicted person, are not under consideration. I am thus proceeding from the point of view of psychoanalysis as a strictly introspective psychology, and the relation of that point of view to theory needs to be made clear.

The tremendous prestige of the natural sciences has given the collection of empathic data a faint smell of disrepute, even among many psychoanalysts. Kohut (1959) has outlined the relationship of psychoanalytic theory to psychoanalytic data: the latter are collected by processes of introspection and empathy (vicarious introspection). Other observational methods also yield useful data for psychoanalysis, but their function is mainly to aid in the verification of hypotheses which had been derived from the empathically gathered data (cf. Wolf, 1977). A corollary of the psychoanalytic method is its primary concern with the analysand's mental states. One way of making this an explicit part of psychoanalytic theory is to view psychic phenomena from *within* a postulated psychic apparatus, that is from the point of view of subjective experience. I believe this became implicit in psychoanalysis when Freud began to let his patients associate freely. The technical directions for conducting a psychoanalysis, as given by Freud (1912), make it evident that a combination of the patient's free associations and the analyst's 'evenly-suspended attention' describe a set-up which evokes increasing awareness of inner psychic processes in both analyst and analysand, in other words introspective experiences. Freud formulated his insights into a scientific model and theory within the framework of natural science, i.e., he tried to describe an inner world of subjective experiences as they might be conceptualized by a scientist looking at a world of objects *outside* of himself. Freud's structural model of the id, ego, and superego describes relationships within and among agencies of the psychic apparatus from the point of view of an observer stationing himself *outside* this apparatus. Kohut's self/self-object model, on the other hand, allows conceptualization of insights gained from psychoanalytic data in terms of a model that explicitly recognizes that these data are experienced from *inside* a psychic apparatus; it describes relationships from the point of view of an observer stationing himself *inside* the experiencing apparatus. These alternate ways of conceptualizing empathically gathered psychoanalytic data lead to alternate models of a 'psychic apparatus' and to alternate theories.

Perhaps we can best illustrate these alternatives by again referring to Miss S. In terms of 'classical' psychoanalytic structural theory one might understand Miss S.'s relationship to her boyfriend as being of the narcissistic type, which means a not very stable investment of an object with narcissistic libido. Even the temporary loss of the invested object, the boyfriend, causes the narcissistic libido, a rather unstable form of libido, to be withdrawn, 'introjected' into the ego which is modified to the extent of now containing an 'identification' with the lost object. By virtue of this identification, the ego now becomes the target of the aggression originally directed at the lost object and the ego's suffering of this aggression directed against itself is experienced as depression. The ego tries to remedy this by again extending narcissistic libidinal cathexes e.g., Miss S.'s fantasy of a lesbian relationship. The narcissistic (love because like me) character of the investment is thus revealed, and it would be assumed that the choice of her boyfriend initially also was a narcissistic choice, i.e., he was chosen because he was like Miss S., or like what Miss S. aspired to be. By contrast, true object love is not a variety of self-love, but love of someone for their own and distinct qualities.

How would this be conceptualized in terms of Kohut's self/selfobject model? Here the analyst-observer stations himself inside the analysand's psyche and attempts to conceptualize the analysand's subjective experience. Miss S. apparently was experiencing herself as a more or less well functioning 'me' until the loss of her boyfriend. With his absence she initially began to experience tension, depression and restlessness. It was as if she were in a frantic search of something missing, something with which to soothe herself to restore the previous feeling of calmness and well being.

Kohut postulates that a calm but energetic feeling of well being requires psychologically an enduringly balanced pattern of relationships polarized between a person's largely unconscious ambitions on the one hand, and his similarly unconscious ideals on the other, with native talents serving as mediating structures between these two poles. This total configuration is experienced as a healthy sense of self, it evokes a strong subjective conviction of selfhood and has therefore been termed a 'cohesive self'.

Miss S. had lost her comfortably assured conviction of valued selfhood. She experienced the pain of 'not feeling like her old self'. We would say that the balanced pattern of relationships within her, which we call a 'cohesive self', had become unbalanced with resulting tension; using a structural metaphor, one might say that her 'cohesive self' had fragmented and she was experiencing the painful symptoms of partial fragmentation of the self. The boyfriend had performed a psychological function which became apparent only when he was no longer present: he had somehow lent cohesion to Miss S.'s self, or, in a structural metaphor, he had been experienced by Miss S. as part of herself and in his absence her self was incomplete, it lacked wholeness, structure and strength.[2] An observer would undoubtedly see the boyfriend as an object of Miss S.'s strivings and, of course, to Miss S.'s conscious-intelligence he is a separate person with whom to have a relationship; but at the same time he would, unconsciously, be experienced by Miss S. as an integral part of her self. Thus he is both self and object, or in Kohut's phrase a 'self-object'.

We now can conceptualize Miss S.'s restlessness as a search for a new self-object to replace the missing part of her self and again be a complete self. Her depression is an unpleasant affect accompanying the state of incompleteness of self. Her behavior is governed by the attempt to re-establish the previous perception of her self as whole. This also applies to her fantasy of reaching out for an admired beautiful woman, who embodies the qualities she experiences as missing from her self, qualities which would be experienced as her own if she could establish the kind of close relationship where the admired object becomes part of her self, a self-object.

But what about the libidinal aspects of this fantasy? How can one in using the self/self-object model understand the emergence, so frightening to Miss S., of a sexual excitement in association with her fantasy of touching the beautiful and desirable woman? Kohut has suggested that within the total configuration of a cohesive self are integrated many diverse aspects of the personality, among them the normal components of sexuality which are experienced by the self as normal sexual desires when integrated within a total fabric of social relatedness. But when the cohesion of self is lost, the resulting fragments of the self assume the prominence formerly held by the total configuration. Thus fragments of body-self are experienced as a heightened awareness of body parts, often to the point of painful hypochondriasis. With the loss of cohesion of the self one finds intense sexuality among the disintegration products, as if sexuality had lost its proper function within a harmoniously balanced matrix and now were on its own as sexuality *per se*; it becomes a most

[2] It is not at all unusual in human experience to become aware of an integral aspect of one's functioning or structure *only* when the function or the structure are impaired or even missing. For example one becomes sharply aware of the integral part that oxygen plays in one's total functioning and well being only when it is missing, i.e. when not breathing enough of it. Ordinarily one may not really know about the crucial need without having experienced it: the 'descriptive insight' of one's dependence on oxygen becomes an 'ostensive insight' only through the deprivation.

powerful force which may be an organizing center for the fragmented personality. Subjectively this is experienced as a heightened and intensified sense of sexual driveness in which various behaviors come under the sway of sexual goals. Analysts have sometimes referred to these phenomena as sexualization. A quite common clinical observation is the occurrence of perverse sexual behavior following a self-fragmenting experience, almost as if the sexual excitement and gratification were warding off the feeling of deadness due to the lost cohesion of the self. In Miss S. we have observed an illustration of this pathological sexualization of her yearning for a new self-object.

These considerations also suggest a relationship between certain aspects of psychoanalytic drive psychology and the psychology of the self. The vicissitudes of the drives and their impact on the ego with it defenses have been well worked out by psychoanalysts, beginning with Freud. What is becoming clearer, with increasing knowledge of the psychology of the self, is that it is not drives *per se* that force pathological adaptation upon the ego; it is only when they are wrenched out of their normal matrix within a cohesive self, by the latter's disintegration, that these drives assume pathological intensity which forces the ego into the distortions that we call neurotic symptom formation (cf. Kohut, 1977).

In the above I said nothing about the developmental factors that must have been crucial in leaving Miss S. so vulnerable that she experienced as a major trauma an event which would, to most people, be a passing and mildly painful annoyance. I hope, nevertheless, that is it already becoming evident that drive psychology and the psychology of the self are not mutually exclusive conceptualizations: a psychology of the self, while widening the realm of psychoanalysis, encompasses among its wider dimensions the phenomena of the drives. The drives, however, in this larger context are seen, not as the biological bedrock of untamed sexual and aggressive instincts, but as an integrated aspect of the total self and its healthy functioning. It is when this highly complex configuration breaks down that the simpler constituents, among them the drive elements, become manifest in their pathological forms as disintegration products.

Freud, in his clinical observations, was most impressed by the quality of 'driveness' of his patients. In the brief clinical vignettes which I mentioned earlier, Freud would have been most impressed by the patient's experience of feeling 'driven' to perform various sexually perverse actions. Freud made this observation of 'driveness' the bedrock of his theory. Thus the core of psychoanalytic theory, as developed by Freud, is a theory of libidinal drives; that theory served well to conceptualize many of the phenomena associated with the classical psychoneuroses. These syndromes could be adequately understood and successfully treated when conceptualized as the consequences of the repression of infantile libidinal drives, particularly those that are involved in the Oedipus complex. The theory assumes these infantile sexual drives, their further development, and the involvements of the Oedipus complex to be universal, and assigns to inborn, quantitative factors, the decisive role in whether the resulting conflict will turn out to be pathological or within normal limits.

But the psychoneuroses represent only a small fraction of the psychological disorders of man. Extending libidinal theory to encompass the major psychoses and depressions resulted in somewhat awkward theoretical constructs and required the postulation of 'narcissism', defined as the libidinal drive invested in the self as an object. From the point of view of psychological development, narcissism was seen to be a phase which had to be traversed on the way from autoerotism to object love. Theory thus assigned to self-love and its derivatives, such as self-expression and creativity, a quasi-pathological status. Of course one can discern the influence of our Judeo-Christian *Weltanschauung*, with its strong emphasis on altruism and its equally strong condemnation of egotism, in this conceptualization. While a number of analysts made important clinical observations and attempted limited revisions of classic psychoanalytic theory (e.g., Hartman, Jacobson, A. Reich, Winnicott, E. Bibring, Rapaport, Lichtenstein), Kohut was the first to systematically study the phenomena of narcissism, and to create a new conceptual framework which allows us to encompass drive-phenomena within the new psychology of the self. But Kohut's new insights and conceptualizations are not derived *ab initio* from theoretical considerations; they stem from the discovery within the psychoanalytic clinical situation of two types of transferences that had not been described before.

Kohut noticed that certain analysands experienced a state of well-being and effective functioning when in the presence of the benignly understanding analyst. In the absence of the analyst, or even in his presence if his understanding was defective, the analysand would experience various degrees of discomfort and tension which might lead to varieties of symptomatic behavior. Kohut recognized that these phenomena were the transference repetitions of an early developmental phase, when the child's integrative capacity is as yet insufficient to organize itself into a coherent system unless it is assisted by the various functions performed by the parent, usually the mother. If one conceptualizes the subjective experience of possessing a coherent configuration of smoothly effective psychological functions as a 'cohesive self', then the child's subjective experience of his 'self' includes those aspects of his parents which are necessary for the coherence of the configuration. Similarly the analysand who comes into an analysis with an insufficiently coherent self may begin to utilize aspects of the analyst to achieve a coherent integration of his self. Looked at in a social framework, one can say that aspects of an object are needed by the subject for his efficient functioning; when experienced by the subject as part of his self they are 'self-objects'.

Kohut distinguishes two types of narcissistic transferences which can be schematically outlined as follows. In one type, the analyst lends cohesion to the analysand's self organization by functioning as a confirming psychological mirror ('mirror transference'). In the other narcissistic transference cohesion is brought to the analysand's self by allowing a psychological merger with the analyst's strength, values and ideals ('idealizing transference'). These transferences correspond to early phases in infant development, when a parent's empathic understanding of the child either lends needed support to its sense of self, including its phase appropriate sense of its own grandeur, or, when the parents' apparent greatness infuses the child's feeble sense of self with power, value and cohesion.

Two further clinical vignettes will illustrate. A middle aged businessman told his analyst that his feeling of well-being during the analytic sessions depended on whether the analyst greeted him with a smile or seemed to be ill humored. Though the analyst had thought that he almost always received his analysands in a neutrally subdued but friendly manner, he learned that this particular analysand was sensitive to the slightest cues that revealed an underlying more somber mood in the analyst. The latter was then experienced by the analysand as disinterest or as rejection. Further associative material brought this experience, during the analytic session, into conjunction with childhood experiences when the boy's mother had failed to provide him with the needed confirming recognition of his budding self. One memory stood out as prototypical among innumerable similarly experienced mother–child transactions. For the last day of kindergarten a teacher had arranged a poetry recital by her 'graduating' pupils to which the children's mothers were invited as a suitably appreciative audience. But again, as on many other occasions, the youngster's excited hopes to shine and please, to warm himself in his mother's sparkling glance, were dashed by her coldly critical assessment of his performance. He recalled, on the analytic couch, the feeling of utter dejection—and discovered the identical experience in those occasions when the analyst had seemed to fail him by omitting the confirming smile from his greeting. The analysand had discovered that he had transferred into the present his archaic need for a mirroring response from a self-object in order to feel well and whole. When mirrored he felt himself 'cohesive' or, conceptualized in terms of the self/self-object model, the analyst as a self-object had become part of the analysand. This is termed a cohesive mirror transference.

A different vignette will illustrate the idealizing transferences. Very briefly, this analysand, a lawyer, astonished himself with the recognition that without apparent conscious intent he found himself using words, phrases and other mannerisms copied from his analyst, particularly when he was dealing with his clients in difficult direct negotiations. This occurred in spite of his often bitter and biting depreciation of the analyst's intellectual acuity and linguistic skills. Behind this defensive facade of overt depreciation emerged the unconscious need to admire and to idealize the analyst. This need to idealize turned out to be a residue of the archaic need to be merged with an admired and respected father who, alas, severely disappointed and rebuffed the aspiring youngster. Overwhelmed by the trauma of father's disgust with him, the boy was unable to transform his idealization of the paternal self-object into a securely internalized system of values. He remained dependent on idealized self-objects; the idealizing transference is the repetition of these archaic strivings of the past in the here-and-now of the analytic situation.

Clinical experience with the narcissistic transferences and the reconstruction in psychoanalysis of their genetic precursors led to a revision of the theory of narcissism and a developmental psychology of the self. Kohut defines the self as a structure, but at a different level of abstraction from the id, ego and supergo. In keeping with the link of the psychology of the self to the older theories of narcissism, Kohut also speaks about the cathexis of the self with *narcissistic* libido which he postulates as having a line of development *separate* from *object* libido. Thus one may conceptualize mature forms of narcissistic libido and, in a major deviation from Freud, it is no longer assumed that fully matured libidinal development transforms narcissistic libido into object libido.[3] Self-love is thus elevated to a status equal to that of love of others; among the attainments of a maturely developed narcissism, discussed by Kohut, are such highly valued achievements as creativity, humor, a capacity for empathy, wisdom and the acceptance of transience, i.e., mortality.

What light can such an account of the development of the self cast on the origin of irrationality? If we define one kind of irrationality very narrowly as the kind of self-judgment that may result in a decision to consult a psychoanalyst, then we must assume the existence of a self able to judge itself as having unexplained, unwanted and inappropriate self experiences. These might include a person's anxieties and depressions, his obsessive thoughts, his compulsive actions and even his vague ineffable feelings of unhappiness; reasonably appropriate fears of recognized real dangers, or appropriate sadness and mourning at a recognized real loss, would be excluded. As a matter of fact, the *unexpected absence* of these commonly experienced emotions might strike one as irrational and may well be grounds for consultation. There seems to be a close correlation between the quality of inexplicable unexpectedness and the judgment of irrationality, if and when they are introspectively experienced together with discomforting tension. Some striking analogies with certain patterns of early infantile experiences are suggestive of a developmental relationship.

A newborn infant is born into his world pre-adapted for an average expectable environment. Unless there is an average expectable supply of oxygen, food, warmth, etc., forthcoming the

[3] In the considered judgment of many contemporary psychoanalysts terms such as libido or psychic energy have outlived their usefulness and may even be obstacles that obscure a better understanding of psychological phenomena. Nevertheless, I find the continued use of terms such as 'libido' or 'psychic apparatus' of distinct advantage in selected instances provided their metaphorical nature is kept in mind and no undue conclusions about actual physical energies acting in actual spatial locations are implied. One advantage lies in the ready reference to accepted clinical meanings. Another advantage, to me, is the conceptual link to the accumulated psychoanalytic wisdom and the continuity of a sound and solid tradition.

infant will not survive. Less well known, but no less important, is a similar need for an average expectable psychological environment as conclusively demonstrated by Spitz (1946). Providing all the necessary physical care in the absence of a responsive psychological ambience will not prevent the development of marasmus and eventual death.

Of course, no actual environment will perfectly meet all the physical and psychological needs of the newborn. Minor deviations from the expectations for which the newborn is psychologically pre-adapted will not cause traumatic disruptions, but will serve as stimuli for growth. These minor environmental deficiencies will be experienced by the child as tension producing frustrations. The mother or other caretaking adult ordinarily empathically senses the child's distress and reacts with appropriate responsiveness to soothe (or feed, or whatever is needed). The mother thus becomes part of the total subjective experience of well-being. However, psychological tension states recur, shorter or longer, and are not always totally resolved by the mother's responsiveness. These remaining residual tensions are not intense enough to disorganize the rudimentary psychic apparatus, but because of the latter's plasticity stimulate it to 'stretch' itself to take on the function that the mother has 'failed' to perform, thus in effect soothing itself. In this way repeated experiences of *optimal* frustration in repeated small minimal doses become the major spur to direct the expanding psychological configurations into directions where they increasingly take over the functions formerly performed by the caretaking parent. This is the proto-typical conceptualization for psychological growth. If, however, the frustrations and tensions are of a magnitude which is greater than the capacity to cope by functional expansion, then the existing configurations will be disrupted by the unresolved tensions with various kinds of pathological sequelae.

Much of the finer details of the psychological development from infancy into mature adulthood remains a matter for future empirical research, but the major trends can be outlined. In the early months various psychological functions of the infant, whether inborn or acquired, are not yet organized into a cohesive configuration even by the mother's mediating ministrations. Therefore there can be as yet neither an experience of self or of non-self. However, by thinking and acting towards the infant from the very beginning as if he were already a self-conscious person, the mother subtly encourages certain functions while discouraging other functions and she facilitates the emergence of an encompassing overall organization that is experienced as a sense of self, roughly by the age of eighteen months. The self that emerges around this time, however, still includes the mother's functions as a necessary part of its self experience (i.e., the mother is still needed as an organizing participant to achieve an encompassing configuration of otherwise disparate psychological functions). At the same time, but in a different context, the mother can also be perceived as an object, e.g. visually; she is both self and object, that is a self-object. The initially fragile self becomes sturdier with further development, while at the same time the functions of the self-object are increasingly internalized with growing freedom from dependence on the caretaking parent. This process is mainly completed around age eight or nine, so that one then can usually speak of a cohesive self, relatively autonomous and resistant to irreversible regressions.[4]

The smooth functioning of a cohesive organizing configuration at the center of one's personality is experienced as a sense of self, with a feeling of wholeness and well-being. A fragmentation of the self, that is loss of its cohesive integration, is experienced with extreme discomfort, such as feelings of depression or even deadness. Impending fragmentation causes great anxiety, even panic, and total fragmentation is equivalent to psychosis. Even transient and relatively minor losses of cohesion are manifest by such symptoms as hypochondriasis and disturbances of self-esteem, These painful subjective states act as powerful motivators for remedial action, and these actions may have an addiction-like intensity which overrides control by the judgmental faculties of the healthy part of the personality. The developmental trauma is usually unconscious and hardly ever understood by the subject, so that its link to the current precipitating circumstance is obscure. Seperation from a needed self-object, for example the transient absence of a spouse, is thus usually thought of as trivial and its psychological meaning and im-

[4] Pathogenic traumata that disrupt or arrest the development of self will have characteristic consequences. Development which is arrested during the earliest months, before the emergence of a self, is likely to result in the eventual precipitation of psychotic or borderline syndromes. Arrests in development that occur after the emergence of a self, but before it has achieved an irreversible cohesion, result in syndromes expressive of vulnerable self-organization, that is narcissistic personality disorders. These may take sexualized forms such as perversions.

plications are not recognized by the narcissistically vulnerable person. The sudden emergence of, let us say, depression and an associated irresistible urge to act out a sexual perversion may strike both the afflicted person and his friends as irrational. Irrationality is here compounded of narcissistic vulnerability and the imperative nature of the urge to escape the pain that this vulnerability may entail. Achieving an irreversible cohesive self is concomitant with achieving freedom from the imperative intrusions of narcissistic tensions into the functioning of 'rational' judgment. (It will be recalled that I am limiting the discussion to one type of irrationality, associated with disorders of self-cohesion, and am not concerned with other conditions of gross irrationality, e.g., the psychoses.)

It is also important to remember that a mental state (and associated behavior patterns) which would commonly be judged irrational by an adult, may not be so experienced by a child except by reference to adult standards. For example, the panic when his mother leaves him at home to go shopping may be experienced identically by a five year old or by a fifteen year old child. In both children there may occur a fantasy of infinite abandonment induced by the fragmentation of the self subsequent to the separation from the mother. In the five year old this would occasion little surprise, but in the fifteen year old both the terror and the accompanying fantasy would likely be unexpected and judged to be unreasonable, that is irrational. However, for the observer who is familiar with the fifteen year old's history, pointing to an arrested psychological development, it would not be surprising to see him undergo an experience akin to the small child's. It would make sense. Would it still be irrational? Obviously the answer to the question would depend on the context from which one would choose to make the judgment. If judged from the point of view of that individual's history and how he experienced it, i.e., from *within* his psyche, his mental state would make sense. On the other hand, when looked at with the assumption of average expectable development, i.e. from *outside* this particular individual, a judgment of irrationality would result.

We can summarize as follows. An infant born into the kind of average expectable environment for which he was genetically preadapted will have an average expectable psychological development and manifest an average expectable behavior for that environment. This will be experienced by him, as well as observed by others, as 'rational'. Failure of the environment to be expectably average will likely result in failure of an average expectable psychological development, and be associated with mental states and behaviors which will strike most observers as more or less 'irrational'. The irrationality, however, will begin to make sense with increased understanding based on empathic reconstruction of the pathogenically experienced psychological history.

Since such an account of 'irrationality' is tied to a developmental story, I must give a brief systematic outline of the developmental sequences that lead to the establishment of a cohesive self. Psychology, of course, has little to say about the earliest beginnings of mental functioning as a superordinate organization emerges out of and subsumes the basic neuro-biological organizations of the nervous system. Kohut has presented evidence that indicates a facilitating influence of the caretaking person on the contents of the emerging self system. At any rate, a caretaking person who is empathically in tune with the infant responds to its shifting needs in a somewhat selective manner, encouraging the inclusion of certain contents in the self while causing other contents to be discarded. Little is known about the processes involved, but somehow around the age of 18 months, perhaps, the various disparate nuclei of what later becomes the self seem to come together into an integrated configuration which, however, for a long time still lacks stability. Particularly, tension regulation within this self system is deficient and requires the soothing participation of the caretaking self-object. The self-object's functions, though myriad and changing in step with the age-appropriate needs of the child, can usefully be grouped under two headings: availability for mirroring responses and availability for idealization. A properly empathic self-object will be sufficiently in tune to further the relatively undisturbed development of a cohesive self. This self (cohesive by virtue of the self-object's appropriate availability and responsiveness) consists from the beginning of a nuclear grandiose self and a nuclear idealized self-object. The grandiose part contains the self's blissful experience of itself in a state of unlimited power and beauty, a configuration akin to an exhibitionistic drive demanding recognition and confirmation. Everyone is familiar with a mother's extravagant conviction and praise for her baby's unsurpassed grandeur, now and in the future. It is these confirming responses that strengthen the child's nuclear grandiose self in the face of an otherwise unpleasantly depreciating reality, which gradually forces the abandonment, or at least the modification, of the associated grandiose fantasies of the child. *Pari passu* some of the nuclear grandiose self's diminishing grandeur is replaced by increasing idealization of the admired idealized parent whose strength, wisdom and beauty can be experienced as part of the self, i.e. the idealized self-object. Again, a youngster's need to be proud of his family and his feeling dejected, if not shattered, by a parent's traumatically sudden and severe failure, is familiar enough to everyone. Optimal frustration and gradual disappointments facilitate growth and internalization; maximum frustration and severely traumatic disappointments cause the repression of grandiose fantasies in unaltered archaic form and leave the adult with a still vulnerable self which remains dependent on self-objects.

In the course of normal development, grandiose fantasy and exhibitionism are gradually modified and internalized into healthy ambition and pleasure in one's own functioning. The idealized self-object is gradually de-idealized and its values and ideals become part of the self's value system, i.e. the ego ideal. This process seems relatively complete and stable around early latency, that is by about 8 years of age. However, adolescence seems to provide another opening for re-adjustment, when the whole self temporarily undergoes a period of rapid changes and fluid boundaries. The adolescent transformations of the self are as much influenced by the onset of puberty as they are set in motion by the age-appropriate massive disillusionment with the whole adult world, especially the parents. Idealization of peers or of youthful idols temporarily serves to regulate inner tensions, until the consolidation of newly internalized values and goals, (i.e. sexual, social and vocational identities) result in a stable ego-ideal governing a newly restored cohesive self (cf. Wolf, Gedo and Terman, 1971). Transformations of the self probably continue throughout life, especially in conjunction with the major turning points such as marriage, parenthood, middle age crisis and old age. The details are yet to be studied.

The clinical psychoanalytic situation provides an ambience that encourages regression and the emergence of transference to the analyst. Correct interpretation of the transferences together with reconstruction of the relevant genetic ambience set the stage for the repeated re-experience of the original trauma, albeit in small controlled doses. Under the benignly watchful and empathic guidance of the analyst, these repeated re-experiences, akin to the instances of optimal frustrations which facilitate childhood growth, allow growth of new psychological regulatory self-soothing functions, with a concomitant strengthening of the cohesion of the self and its overall integrative capacity.

REFERENCES

Freud, S. (1912), Recommendations to Physicians Practising Psycho-Analysis. *Standard Edition*, 12, 111–20. London: The Hogarth Press, 1958.

Gedo, J. E. & Goldberg, A. (1973), *Models of the Mind: A Psychoanalytic Theory*, Chicago: University of Chicago Press.

Klein, G. S. (1976), *Psychoanalytic Theory: An Exploration of Essentials*. New York: International Universities Press.

Kohut, H. (1959), Introspection, Empathy and Psychoanalysis. *J. Amer. Psychoanalyt. Assn.*, 7, 459–83.

Kohut, H. (1966), Forms and Transformations of Narcissism. *J. Amer. Psychoanalyt. Assn.*, 14, 243–72.

Kohut, H. (1968), The Psychoanalytic Treatment of Narcissistic Personality Disorders. *The Psychoanalytic Study of the Child*, 23, 86–113. New York: International Universities Press.

Kohut, H. (1971), *The Analysis of the Self*. New York: International Universities Press.

Kohut, H. (1972), Thoughts on Narcissism and Narcissistic Rage. *The Psychoanalytic Study of the Child*, 17, 360–400. New York: Quadrangle.

Kohut, H. (1973), Psychoanalysis in a Troubled World. *The Annual of Psychoanalysis*, 1, 3–25. New York: Quadrangle.

Kohut, H. (1975a), The Future of Psychoanalysis. *The Annual of Psychoanalysis*, 3, 325–40. New York: International Universities Press.

Kohut, H. (1975b), The Psychoanalyst in the Community of Scholars. *The Annual of Psychoanalysis*, 3, 341–70. New York: International Universities Press.

Kohut, H. (1976), Creativeness, Charisma, Group-psychology: Reflections on the Self-Analysis of Freud. *Psychological Issues*, Monograph 34/35, 379–425. New York: International Universities Press.

Kohut, H. (1977), *The Restoration of the Self*. New York: International Universities Press (in press).

Schafer, R. (1973), Action: Its Place in Psychoanalytic Interpretation and Theory. *Annual of Psychoanalysis*, 1, 159–96.

Spitz, R. A. (1946), Anaclitic Depression. *The Psychoanalytic Study of the Child*, 2, 313–42.

Wolf, E. S. (1976), Recent Advances in the Psychology of the Self: An Outline of Basic Concepts. *Comprehensive Psychiatry*, 17, 37–46. New York: Grune and Stratton.

Wolf, E. S. (1977), The Role of Empathy in the Work of Psychoanalysis. (In preparation).

Wolf, E. S., Gedo, J. E. & Terman, D. (1972), On the Adolescent Process as a Transformation of the Self. *Journal of Youth and Adolescence* 1, 257–72.

8 On the Behavioral Analysis of Self-Deception and Self-Development

WILLARD F. DAY, Jr.

In order to deal with this topic, I must first say something about contingencies, about the concept of cause as it functions in Skinner's position, and about the notion of control.

I. CONTINGENCIES

In practice, behaviorism boils down to an analysis of contingencies. There are two kinds of contingencies, first, *contingencies of survival*, which reflect action of the environment in the course of natural selection, and which are taken to explain in a causal way our genetic endowment (Skinner, 1975). It is presumably because of contingencies of survival that the human species finds itself reinforced by the particular events that it does. Contingencies of survival are important to a psychology of the Self because much more needs to be known about the nature of the reinforcing events which people find genuinely valuable, or inherently threatening. *Biological* reinforcers of a *social* nature that *bind* us together within community may, as I shall later point out, be among the most powerful positive reinforcers. Second, *contingencies of reinforcement* are taken to explain in a causal way why we have the particular learned repertoires of behavior that we do. To the extent than an analysis moves away from a discussion of contingencies, it moves away from behaviorism.

Characteristically, contingencies of reinforcement are spoken of as a relationship involving three components: (1) antecedent discriminative stimulation (the environmental situation in which behavior occurs), (2) behavior, and (3) consequent reinforcement. In the interpretation of behavior, the specification of the components said to be part of a contingency of reinforcement generally involves considerable conceptual complexity. This is involved even in the attempt to 'observe' the operation of contingencies in the stream of behavior because the observation of behavior consists solely of discriminative responding to the behavior at hand in its environmental setting, and this discriminative responding is generally under multiple stimulus control. The interpretation of behavior in terms of contingencies is regarded as no more than the emission of discriminative behavior on the part of the interpreter, where the repertoires involved are taken as having been made available to him from his previous reinforcement history. This conceptual complexity makes it inappropriate to regard the identification of controlling contingencies as an attempt at physicalistic or phenomenalistic description.

The relationship between material generated in interpretation and its origins in the history of the speaker is generally very unclear, as is the identification of events that may be operating as reinforcers. In the observation of the stream of behavior, the discrimination of events as operating reinforcers is relatively rare while it is easier to discriminate varieties of antecedent stimulation as functioning in some contingent relation with behavior.

2. THE CONCEPT OF CAUSE

Because of the connection that is often made between an interest in the Self and the problem of agency in the initiation of action, and because the problem of agency is often discussed in a context of concern with theories of the physical determination of behavior, it is important to have a reasonably clear notion of how the concept of *cause* functions in behaviorist thinking. We can restrict attention to the way that concept functions in connection with the class of contingencies of most interest to psychologists, namely, contingencies of reinforcement.

Causation plays a part in contingencies of reinforcement only in connection with the effect of reinforcement. Reinforcement is said to have the power to increase the strength of a pattern of behavior, or the likelihood of its future emission. But the applicability of this conception depends on the capacity of someone (an experimental analyst of behavior in the laboratory or an observer of on-going behavior *in vivo*) to monitor the relevant behavior so that the change in frequency from the baseline can be appreciated. Thus, the *force* of even causal explanations relying upon the concept of reinforcement has an ineradicable phenomenological or descriptive aspect to it.

Skinner (1974) insists that only causal explanations are genuinely explanatory; mentalistic explanations are said not to explain. However, Skinner does not deny that a variety of explanatory practices, including the mentalistic, in fact function successfully in one way or another within the verbal community. All verbal behavior is functionally adaptive in some biological sense, and it is the business of a functional analysis to make clear its adaptive nature. Thus the insistence that only causal explanations are truly explanatory is, in a sense, stipulative. It is not that other forms of explanation do not in some sense function successfully as explanations; it is rather that only explanations of a particular nature are centrally relevant to the aims of a functional analysis.

What is said *to be caused* by the action of reinforcement is nothing more than a strengthening of the capacity for a particular pattern to be functionally adaptive in a particular way. Reinforcement causes a *unit* in the functionally adaptive repertoires, of which an organism's behavior consists, to be set up; it causes the organism to have a new functional unit of behavior, which may then appear again in the on-going business of living life. Thus, reinforcement does not cause the organism to *do* anything. Rather it equips him, it enables him to behave in a new way that is functionally adaptive. Thus Skinner's causal explanations explain why an organism does what it does only in a special way. Specification of contingencies of reinforcement does not answer the question 'Why did he do that?' in the sense of 'What *made* him do that?'; it answers that question in the sense of 'What was he doing when he did that?', 'In what way was that behavior functionally adaptive?', 'How did he come to act in this situation in this way?', or 'What has happened that would have the result that this person does this, rather than something else, in this situation?'

Skinner's thought to date simply does not engage the problem of the initiation of action, which is thought to be a physiological matter, except to oppose very stridently the view that there is some sort of Agent within us which has that capacity. Operant behavior has always been said by Skinner to be *emitted* by the organism. The term *emission*, with its explicit connotation of 'being sent out' (but not by an Agent), contrasts explicitly with the expression *evoked*, which is used for the elicitation of reflexes; the latter is the only place in Skinner's system where the analogue with 17th century views of antecedent mechanical causation may be relevant. Since philosophical discussion of the problem of agency stems from a concern with materialist theories more or less of a Hobbesian nature, they are, in my opinion, simply not relevant to Skinner. Consequently, I shall not be concerned with the problem of agency; in any case, the source of contemporary interest in the concept of the Self lies elsewhere to begin with.

3. THE CONCEPT OF CONTROL

Contingencies are often spoken of as *controlling* contingencies. What does the concept of *control* mean in this context?

The phenomenological grounding of Skinnerian concepts, or if one prefers, their grounding in the discriminative behavior of some particular person, is even more apparent in connection with the concept of control. To be sure, the phenomenology involved is only rarely that of the behaving organism under investigation—which would yield an assessment of the situation from the so-called 'agent's point of view'—but is that of the trained observer or experimental analyst of behavior. The realities of self-deception clearly make a psychology stemming simply from 'the agent's point of view' an unpromising perspective.

When behaviorists speak of *controlling* relations they generally have in mind *antecedent* controlling events, although it is true that consequent reinforcers are also spoken of as controlling variables. Discriminative stimulation (S^D's) constitute the paradigm case. Yet discriminative stimuli are said merely 'to set the occasion for response to be followed by reinforcement'. There is not the slightest suggestion of *force* here; the expression 'set the occasion for' in reference to antecedent controlling stimulation contrasts with antecedent causation of a mechanical nature. The concept of stimulus control remains at present largely undifferentiated. Though 'discriminative stimulation' and 'schedules of reinforcement' find relatively refined application in connection with the laboratory work associated with the experimental analysis of behavior, in the area of the observation of on-going behavior *in vivo* a behavioral phenomenology of the range of classes of relevant antecedent controlling relations has barely begun to be set up. The most explicit differentiation among different classes of antecedent controlling relations remains that contained in Skinner's *Verbal Behavior*. However, one can expect a similar differentiation among classes of antecedent controlling relations to emerge as procedures for the naturalistic, essentially ethological, analysis of on-going behavior continue to be worked out among behaviorists, particularly in the area of verbal behavior (see, e.g., Lahren, 1975; Hemenway, 1975; or Spooner and Bennett, 1975).

It is most certainly not appropriate to map the Skinnerian concept of control onto perspectives derived from 17th century models of antecedent mechanical causation. For what is involved here is the kind of control exercised over us by someone we know who happens to pass us on the street. If we like him, he provides discriminative stimulation for our smiling and saying 'Hello', to be followed by positive reinforcement. If we see someone approaching whom we dislike strongly, 'control' is exemplified by the relation that person bears to our subsequent lowering of our eyes or crossing the street so as not to pass him directly. A third illustration is the approach of someone who possesses and exercises power and authority over us. As he passes we smile and say 'Hello'. We may not be aware of the ingratiating nature of our response, or of how in fact our 'Hello' may be controlled by contingencies of negative reinforcement; we may well tell ourselves how very much we like him and be self-deceived. It should be clear that the approach of someone on the street does not *make* or *force* us to respond in a particular way. Discriminative stimulation does not function in the fashion of mechanical causation; it merely sets the occasion for our response to be followed by the kind of reinforcement that has been associated with it in the past.

The relevance of antecedent stimulation in the control of behavior means that we often call upon discriminative responding to explain behavior. Sometimes we 'phenomenologize' our behavior by speaking 'from the agent's point of view'. For example, one might say, 'Ah, there is X. How happy I am to see him. I know that we like each other. Therefore it is appropriate for me to greet him pleasantly'. Yet actually, in most cases such pseudo-phenomenological reasoning is irrelevant; we simply pass, smile, and say 'Hello'. It is common to say that 'the organism understands, or senses, or knows, that in circumstances of this particular kind such and such consequences are likely to follow', but in most cases this is likely to be mentalism.

The driving force of contemporary behaviorism is its opposition to mentalism, which Skinner (1974) characterizes as taking feelings and inner states for the *causes* of behavior. I have often found it helpful to call attention directly to the mentalism involved in taking it for granted that somehow human functioning must basically be an inherently *reasonable* affair, as if an organism would not do anything unless somehow it made *sense* to him to do so, as if an organism's behavior always followed *rationally* from what it could be assumed to *know*. Philosophers seem constantly to talk about the *assumptions* that an organism somehow *must* make if he is to behave as he does. Yet to a behaviorist, such unravelling of assumptions that can be taken to underlie a given instance of behavior generally has little to do with the actual control of the behavior, since emission of the assumptive chains on the part of the organism is not behaviorally present. Instead, such teasing out of assumptions is no more than verbal behavior on the part of the philosopher, the particulars of which have been strengthened in him by his previous history.

It is not necessary to mentalize the inherent intentionality, purposiveness, or adaptiveness of behavior. I have argued elsewhere (Day, 1976) that the intentionality of behavior is preserved in Skinner's thinking in the functioning of the concept of reinforcement. What the concept of reinforcement does is to transpose the bulk of the opportunities for mentalistic interpretation, which are hidden in one way or another in the conception of the intentionality of behavior, to the consequent term of the controlling contingencies focally of interest, i.e., to the concept of reinforcement. By shifting from the purposive ramifications of traditional mentalistic treatments to the concept of reinforcement, the behaviorist can move more directly to an assessment of the controlling contingencies which can be taken to be manifest in the behavior at hand.

Self-Deception

The first thing to say about Skinner's conception of self-deception is that it forms part of the broad perspective on the nature of knowing, i.e., on what it is for us to know anything at all, that is central to his approach to the understanding of behavior. The basic structure of Skinner's solution to the problem of how we know about ourselves was given in 1945 and contains a reference to self-deception:

> It is, therefore, impossible to establish a rigorous scientific vocabulary for public use, nor can the speaker clearly 'know himself' in the sense in which knowing is identified with behaving discriminatively. In the absence of the 'crisis' provided by differential reinforcement (much of which is necessarily verbal), private stimuli cannot be analyzed....
>
> The contingencies we have reviewed also fail to provide an adequate check against fictional distortion of the relation of reference (e.g., as in rationalizing). Statements about private events may be under control of the drives associated with their consequences rather than antecedent stimuli. The community is skeptical of statements of this sort, and any attempt by the speaker to talk to himself about his private world (as in psychological system-making) is fraught with self-deception. (1945, pp. 274–275)

Notice, first, that knowing is identified with behaving discriminatively. Basically this means that whatever knowledge we can be taken to have consists fundamentally in capacities to respond discriminatively in relevant circumstances. Here is where the 'conceptual equipment' people are taken to have is brought into play. Thinking is generally thought to involve the manifestation of conceptual equipment. The behaviorist makes contact with this rock-bottom of our cognitive and behavioral capacities in the concept of discriminative responding. This is what I was getting at when I said earlier that the control exercised by discriminative stimuli manifests considerable conceptual complexity. At any rate, the behaviorist view is that we cannot be said to know anything that does not exist in us, at a certain strength, as particular capacities for responding appropriately to certain environmental demands.

Second, there is the view that we cannot come to know anything at all unless there has been that particular kind of 'crisis' that is provided in differential reinforcement. It is only by the action of specific differential reinforcement in specific situations that our capacities for behaving are set up, including, of course, those repertoires which lead us to say that we know something in a particular way. Thus a particular person's knowledge is always idiosyncratic to the particular history of differential reinforcement that he has had. Knowledge held in common is possible precisely to the extent that common histories of differential reinforcement exist. Finally, note the connection drawn between 'self-deception', e.g., rationalization, and reinforcing consequences associated with 'drives' which differ in some way from the consequences generally associated with non-fictional reference. What this will boil down to is a primary concern, in connection with self-deceptive repertoires, with contingencies involving negative, as opposed to positive, reinforcement. Said simply, in self-deception people are trying hard to avoid or to get away from something.

Skinner's approach is elaborated in more detail in *Science and Human Behavior* (1953). Chapter XVIII, on the Self, contains a six-page discussion devoted exclusively to the issue of self-deception but does not make use of that expression. Significantly, the issue is discussed instead in a section entitled 'The Absence of Self-Knowledge'. This way of looking at the problem emphasizes the point that there is no knowledge outside of repertoires of responding that people actually have. Thus much of the surprise we may have at how little people seem to know about what they are doing is to be accounted for in terms of the practices of the verbal community, which may simply not shape up very effective repertoires of self-descriptive behavior. People have only that knowledge of their own behavior which the verbal community has enabled them to have. Actually, the major portion of Skinner's concern with self-deception involves an analysis of the variety of ways in which we come to have the particular kinds of self-knowledgeable repertoires that we manifestly have. In dealing with much human blindness concerning their own affairs as a deficit or absence of knowledge Skinner leads us away from the temptation to think that there is something wrong with the personhood of people in their blindness.

Yet Skinner goes on to point out that not all instances of what we would take to be inadequacies in self-knowledge are so benign. He discusses 'repression' (1953, pp. 290–1), noting that for a behavioral analysis there is a connection between self-deception in a malevolent sense (where I try to capitalize on the connotations of *deception*) and contingencies of aversive control; self-deceptive repertoires are considered as having been established through negatively reinforcing consequences.

Essentially the same conception of the nature of self-knowledge is developed again in *Verbal Behavior* (1957, pp. 130ff), and issues pertaining to the self are dealt with along the same lines throughout the central third of Skinner's most recent book *About Behaviorism* (1974). There he says:

> REPRESSION: 'A process or mechanism of ego defense whereby wishes or impulses that are incapable of fulfillment are kept from or made inaccessible to consciousness'. For 'wishes or impulses' read the 'probability of behavior'; for 'incapable of fulfillment' read 'extinguished or punished'; and for 'kept from or made inaccessible to consciousness' read 'not introspectively observed'.... We then have this: behavior which is punished becomes aversive, and by not engaging in it or not 'seeing' it, a person avoids conditioned aversive stimulation. There are feelings associated with this, but the facts are accounted for by the contingencies.
>
> The word 'repression' is part of an elaborate metaphor which gives dynamic character to the effect of punishment. When feelings cannot be expressed, pressure is said to build up until an explosion occurs.... But what is happening when a person 'holds his rage inside him', and what is the 'safety valve' through which most people let off emotional steam? The answers are to be found in the conditions under which behavior becomes very strong because it cannot be emitted.... [Often] we have 'repressed our rage' because we have been punished for 'expressing it'. If something happens suddenly in the manner of an explosion, it is because the situation changes.... 'Toy guns', says a psychiatrist, 'allow children to work out conflicts and ventilate some of their aggressive urges'. We should say instead that they permit children to behave aggressively in unpunished ways. (1974, pp. 155–6)

The point to note is the firm restriction of Skinner's treatment to the analysis of contingencies and the continued linking of the mechanisms of ego defense to contingencies involving punishment, aversive control, or strengthening by negative reinforcement. Conversion and sublimation are treated in a similar way.

The view that, primarily, what are taken to be instances of self-deception in ordinary affairs can be most appropriately conceptualized simply in terms of the absence of self-knowledge continues to be central (e.g., 1974, pp. 29–30). We lack knowledge of the *causes* of our behavior and are essentially at the mercy of the verbal community which determines to what extent, and in what way, we can be regarded as having knowledge of what we are doing, and of what the causes of our behavior are taken to be. From a behavioral standpoint, the central matter is: How has a person come to make sense of behavior in the way that he has? Of special interest here may be those occasions where the verbal community happens to regard a different assessment of the operating causes to be more in line with the facts.

A Personal Illustration

I must try now to give these considerations a more robust sense of behavioral reality. A short time ago, something unpleasant happened. I responded curtly but firmly to a graduate student who had asked for information concerning what to do next in connection with a matter which was our mutual responsibility. On this particular day I was working to meet a deadline: I had committed myself to commenting on an unexpected set of student papers at an informal gathering that night, and I was trying to finish reading them.

There was nothing particularly exceptional about the behavior of any of us in this situation. The behavior of the assistant in asking for the information, and my own behavior in responding, were not all that different as patterns of behavior from those which would be characterized as normal functioning within the department. An attempt to interpret the situation that developed in terms of the interaction of 'personalities', would miss completely the fine grain of the richly variegated interaction which constitutes the reality of our relationship. Although curt and firm, I did not perceive my response as angry. I do not think it is correct to say that I was significantly annoyed by the interruption. The firmness and curtness effectively took care of the situation. I did not perceive that anything out of the ordinary had taken place.

The assistant let me know by his absence that something was wrong. During the time involved, roughly one week, I experienced a lot of feeling. There were many feelings that I associate with being hurt, although they did not set the occasion for much verbal behavior of any kind, either covert or overt. There were feelings which I identify as anxiety, and from time to time feelings that I associate with guilt. However, the most significant feelings, which would surge forth and dominate my consciousness for extensive periods, controlling much covert verbal behavior, were feelings which I would identify as those of righteous indignation. Though these feelings of indignation may have had their source in the biological equipment we all have, to say that I was 'frustrated' is to be so vague as to be unhelpful. From time to time I had feelings of elation and excitement, similar to the satisfactions sometimes experienced as a result of the successful exercise of power. Hovering over all was a feeling of fear, which as time progressed became increasingly more acute.

My covert verbal behavior, associated with the feelings of righteous indignation, dwelt on decisions the assistant had made in the recent past that had worked one or another slight inconvenience on me. As I continued to think about the matter I succeeded in marshalling quite a case against him. Clearly he was at fault, he was to blame; I thought of him as irresponsible and I spoke to myself over and over, of his irresponsibility. But from time to time this talk of irresponsibility would encounter other verbal material occurring within me which contradicted the charges of irresponsibility. This contradictory talk clearly had its sources in the verbal behavior of the departmental community, where the singular and exceptional responsibility of this assistant was often an object of public comment. When my covert talk of irresponsibility encountered such instances of substantial evidence to the contrary, I was left with strong feelings of fear.

I believe I have now provided a classic illustration of self-deceptive behavior involved in the projection of blame. What I have said so far consists largely of the simple description of the behavioral realities involved. While this is consonant with the central role played by description in a behavioral analysis, the *point* of a behavioral analysis becomes clear only when the functioning of *contingencies* is considered. There should be little difficulty seeing how my behavior can be conceptualized as involving contingencies of aversive control, stemming from the aversive stimulation occasioned by the assistant's absence. The covert verbalizations involved in the projection of irresponsibility would be regarded as having been set up by negative reinforcement. But suppose that the controlling contingencies had been only slightly different, e.g., that the assistant had given no indication of his displeasure, or that he had simply flashed in anger, and then continued functioning much as before. Or suppose he had taken my curt and firm statement as an indication of anger on my part, and then become submissive. Any of these responses would have further negatively reinforced the self-deceptive verbal repertoires that I have, and I would have been even more tightly locked in the circle of my existing behavioral equipment.

As it happened, things developed differently and I was enabled not only to see the covert verbal behavior as projection, but to go on to new knowledge of the contingencies operating in my own functioning. How did this 'insight' come about? Undoubtedly an important factor was that my covert verbalizations concerning the assistant's irresponsibility did not get reinforced. I can see in retrospect that this was connected to my concern not to aggravate the situation by speaking to others about it; consequently the covert verbal behavior achieved nothing as far as taking me out of the aversive situation was concerned. Then I found myself wondering what the stimulus control over the assistant's absence might possibly be. This included covert questioning of myself, What had I done? I remembered another student saying that according to the assistant I 'was not interested' in our mutual project. I rejected that at once; *obviously* I was interested. Yet the remark returned over and over again in my consciousness. As the week progressed, my feelings assumed a larger and larger proportion of what I identify as guilt. I had stopped blaming the assistant, and my covert verbal behavior was concerned now almost entirely with trying to figure out what I had done wrong. I was at fault in some deeply important way, though I could not see what it could be

Then the assistant suddenly appeared, functioning again as if nothing had happened. He was affectionate and cheerful; my feeling was that somehow I had been forgiven. Yet I also felt that somehow the situation would never again be the same: I would have to change. I knew that my behavior in the situation would have to change for the better in some important way.

The situation that provided the occasion for what might be regarded as a kind of 'insight' occurred shortly. One evening we had an informal get-together of all my students at one of their houses. The occasion was to be purely social, and the fact that there was no academic material assigned for discussion provided an environmental change that may have been critical in enabling the 'insight' to develop. I remember my feelings throughout the evening very clearly. On the whole, I felt depressed. I was of course relieved that the assistant had returned to the fold, and my behavior in interaction with him was ingratiating. There was an underlying sense of my own guilt, and sadness that I could not move beyond a general sense of my own wrongness.

I tended to be somewhat silent, and did more listening than is usual. I found myself comparing the character of the conversation among the students with that of the persons in my own age-group. I noted how open, spontaneous, gentle, and filled with mutual interest the conversation of the students was, and I contrasted this with the 'social coversation' among my own friends at parties and with the heavy, self-interested 'personal' talk in which we often seemed to specialize. Then I found myself, with the usual heaviness, entering in a self-oriented way into one or another conversation. I remember saying a couple of times out loud, 'I am the most judgmental person that I know'. I remember mapping this on to the episode with the assistant. What had happened, I said to myself, was that I had been my usual judgmental self on some particular occasion that had obviously been too much for the assistant to take, and he had become offended. After that my mood improved; I felt relieved that I now knew what I had done wrong, and knew the general sorts of things I had to do to make my interactions with students more successful. In particular, I remember talking with a student towards the end of the evening, about his plans for a dissertation. I had read a paper by the student in the general area in which he wanted to work, and I had disagreed strongly with its overall conclusion. This time I said that clearly he should pursue the area which so deeply interested him. He replied that he still had to face the very real objections along the line that I had expressed earlier, and I responded that he should not pay any attention to the objections I had raised earlier. 'After all,' I said, 'I would be lucky even to be able to follow your thinking'. His response was, 'Well, you are already beginning to become less judgmental'.

Had I now achieved insight? I would strongly insist, 'No'. For if one were to consider my behavior 'objectively', that is, in terms of some sort of average of the descriptions of my behavior that might be made among the verbal community of people who interact with me most, I would come across as a remarkably 'non-judgmental' person. For me to call myself judgmental is clearly for me to have yet another psychodynamically heavy reaction. My concern with judging others is at least partially controlled by the deep investment of time that I have made in the affairs of our Church; this verbal community makes it very easy for me to conceptualize social problems within the nexus of concepts in which communication among Christians takes place. What so clearly distinguishes the account I have given from anything which one might professionally call 'insight' is the fact that I did not yet have knowledge of the contingencies that were actually operating in the behavior at hand. To speak of the possibility that the assistant had gotten offended at some *judgmental remark* on my part, is not to speak very realistically, or even interestingly, about the behavioral realities actually taking place.

In any event, such self-deprecatory verbalizations concerning my own judgmental nature did not persist for long, though I have little doubt that such verbal behavior could easily have been maintained in strength by appropriate social reinforcement. Instead, I began to note that my behavior in connection with the project with which the assistant and I were involved was different in a number of conspicuous ways, from what it had characteristically been in the past. In other words, *after* the relevant behavior-changes had already taken place I found myself making the discrimination. What I found myself doing was responding at once to the demands for my time as they arose in connection with the project. This differed (I could now see) from my behavior in the past when in similar situations I would get the assistant to take care of it. I found myself telling myself, as the work of the project continued to arise, 'No, I must do that myself'. I now told myself on such occasions that it was not fair to ask the assistant to do it. Then I found myself correcting the earlier covert verbalizations that I had made: 'No, it is not the assistant who is irresponsible; it is I who have been irresponsible in connection with my duties on the project'. And there the matter rested.

I have given an illustration of what would generally be regarded as the projection of feelings of irresponsibility and the course of events involved in becoming able to overcome the self-deception involved. I believe that the account has illustrated the acquisition of a deeper and more accurate understanding of the events that occurred, and it seems to me that it is a much better description of the facts to say that I acquired a more accurate understanding of *my behavior in the situation* than to say that I now understand myself more.

However, my major purpose is to illustrate the analysis of contingencies. Where are the contingencies in this account? Clearly, one central contingency is the relation between the aversive stimulation provided by the assistant's absence and my initial verbal responding about his irresponsibility. This relation illustrates *discriminative control*: the discriminative stimulus (the assistant's absence) *sets the occasion* for the responding which occurs. There is undoubtedly some ordinary language usage of 'cause' that maps onto this relation, as when we say that in some general sense the assistant's absence caused me to speak of him as irresponsible. However in a behavioral analysis causal action is properly restricted to the effects of reinforcement. In this case, causation is properly restricted to the reinforcing circumstances in my own environmental history which make it adaptive for me to respond verbally to aversive stimulation arising from the action of others with a judgment as to their responsibility. For example, my overt verbalization that someone who had annoyed me was irresponsible would be reinforced if the contingencies defining the relationship resulted in the social approval of my own circle of friends, or resulted in the other person's modifying his behavior in my favor in view of my own capacities for aversive countercontrol.

The operating contingencies which led to the fact that I did not verbalize publicly my judgment of the assistant's irresponsibility have already been mentioned. As a result, the judgment was not reinforced, in fashions similar to the past, thereby providing the opportunity for other verbal behavior to become more relevant. Thus the judgment of the assistant's irresponsibility soon became nonfunctional. This is an instance of the paradigm of extinction (which does not mean that such judgmental behavior was thereby removed from my behavioral repertoire).

Another salient contingency involved what was my dominant response to the assistant's absence, a response which is to be separated out from the verbalizations of irresponsibility. Much of my emotional responding was under the control of the fact that the aversive stimulation consisted of the assistant's *absence*. Many people in our culture have learned that an effective way to get across the point that something is seriously wrong in a relationship is to withdraw temporarily from the relationship. This is not to intentionalize the assistant's behavior; the assistant's 'point of view' is irrelevant to an assessment of the contingencies that need to be explained in giving an account of my behavior. My point is that my own previous environmental history has been such that sudden and unaccounted for absence from an otherwise continuous relationship provides discriminative stimulation to me for possible rejection, and important reinforcers, associated with biological equipment involved in social affiliation, become engaged. Thus the basic feeling-tone was that I had done something wrong, and this basic emotional reaction set the discriminative occasion for such verbal contingencies as my covert talking to the effect that 'The assistant is right.' It also set the occasion for bringing into play the self-deprecatory verbal behavior emitted at the student gathering concerning my own highly judgmental nature. But this behavior did not simply follow 'naturally' from the feelings of guilt; the verbalizations concerning my own judgmental nature were under the discriminative control of the social behavior of the students at the gathering. The opportunity for me to make this discrimination was also under environmental control. Had there been a paper assigned for discussion, it is unlikely that any of the self-deprecatory verbal behavior would have emerged.

What were the contingencies involved in the control of the verbalizations that it was I, after all, who had been irresponsible? During the week of the assistant's absence aversive stimulation arose from the ongoing functioning of the project, and I simply responded to it. The relevant repertoires had been established in the past, yet they had not been recently engaged because the contingencies were such that the requirements of the project exercised discriminative control, as they arose, over the assistant's behavior rather than my own. In this way the patterning of my behavior changed, a change which I subsequently discriminated. It was then no more than a matter of emitting a simple verbal description (of tacting the environment, as Skinner would put it) to respond discriminatively to the change by saying covertly that I was now exercising more responsibility in connection with the affairs of the project than I had been. The comparative judgment that it was I who had been irresponsible all along, and that the assistant had not been irresponsible after all, seems to me somewhat more complex. Yet I believe here only other segments of my behavioral repertoire were involved, namely, those engaged by aversive stimulation which leads me to try to avoid 'using other people'.

I am not entirely confident that the preceding account is all that representative of the kinds of behavioral phenomena that would be regarded as clinically significant. But in any case, the direction in which a behavioral analysis of phenomena of self-deception would move is clear. The behaviorist would require, first of all, a detailed description of the actually occurrent behavioral events that can be observed to take place in the behavioral episode taken to be representative of the phenomenon. This means that the phenomena must in fact be discriminable by somebody, and that the description consist of a record of the discriminative responses that the person, offering up the description as an instance of the phenomenon, actually has to make. Of course, the description that happens to be given, that is, the set of discriminative responses that turn out to be reported, is *determined* by the previous history of the person offering the description, where by previous history is meant the practices of differential reinforcement which have happened to take place in his environmental background. Thus, in asking for a behavioral description the first step in a behavioral analysis requires the relevant phenomenology of the behavior involved.

But this phenomenological description of the behavioral events involved must be accompanied by a description of the environmental circumstances within which the behavior occurred. Here again the person offering the description can rely only on the discriminative capacities with which he happens to have been endowed by his history of reinforcement. Thus attention is drawn only selectively to aspects of the environment which are seen by the person making the description as relevant to the behavioral phenomena at hand. Since the phenomenological description of the relevant behavior cannot be given adequately without also describing the relevant environmental circumstances, it is clear that a 'reductive' definition of the phenomenon simply in terms of particular types of behavior cannot be given.

Finally, any behavioral analysis of phenomena of 'self-deception' would move directly to an assessment of the contingencies involved in the behavioral control. Almost all professionals are aware of 'relations' between the behavioral phenomena and environmental circumstances, but it is only the behaviorist professional community which draws focal attention to concentration upon such relations as instances of contingencies. It is also characteristic of the behaviorist professional community to restrict its interpretative account to a display of contingencies that can be seen to be operating.

A difficulty for the general professional community in the assessment of contingencies is the prevailing mentalistic climate within which the professional interpretation of behavior is currently made. Explicit attention to the analysis of contingencies needs environmental support if the underlying discriminations are to be shaped up. The behaviorist community has been slow in bringing its attention to bear directly on the methodological problems involved in the analysis of contingencies operating in on-going human behavior *in vivo*. To some, analysis of the contingencies involved in the control of on-going verbal behavior has seemed to be the obvious place to start (e.g., Day, 1971, 1974, 1975). However, there are currently indications that clinically interested phenomena are coming to be reassessed from a behavioral point of view by such techniques as looking for relevant contingencies in transcripts of tape-recorded sessions of the course of psychoanalytic psychotherapy (e.g., Gibbins, 1975).

The Self

For some a concept of the self is relevant to psychological analysis because it bears on the problem of agency in the initiation of human action (e.g., T. Mischel, 1976; Secord, 1975). To this move the behaviorist is opposed. In a sense, the problem of the 'initiation' of action in the amoeba remains as unexplained as it is in man. It is as reasonable a contemporary view as any that as one moves higher in the evolutionary scale the central nervous system functions largely in an inhibitory way, in the service, as it were of 'the art of not doing things' (Pfeiffer, 1969, p. 35). In any case, a solution to the problem of the initiation of action is likely to come only from the physiologist. In a behavioral analysis we are asked to look at the *occurrence* of behavior as something simply given. Behavior is something that *happens*, or *occurs*. There is little point to trying to spruce up the appeal of personalistic psychologies by philosophical reasoning which purports to deduce human agency as a logical implication of one or another pattern of ordinary language usage. The phenomenological description of behavioral events purporting to demonstrate agency is, of course, another matter; here the behaviorist would resort to the search for explanatory contingencies. However arguments centering around logical implication are likely to be received by behaviorists in a fashion similar to Skinner's treatment of the generation of paradoxes, which is viewed as 'playing with sentences' taken out of the environmental context where they function naturally (Skinner, 1974, p. 98).

But Fingarette's (1969) account of self-deception, which is sophisticated both philosophically and psychologically, bears a significant relation to a behavioral analysis. Fingarette regards as his major innovative move the fact that he takes an *action*-oriented approach to the problem of awareness, as opposed to what he calls the 'cognitive' and 'perceptual' conception of consciousness. This, of course, is very similar to Skinner's approach. The central work is done in this connection by Fingarette's conception of 'spelling-out' as an aspect of a person's 'engagement in the world'. Although Fingarette explains what he means by 'engagement in the world' so that the concept can adapt itself nicely to a purposive existentialism, the behaviorist can sympathetically follow his argument by reading that expression as 'interaction with the environment'.

Fingarette however goes on to regard self-deception as something quite different from simply the absence of relevant repertoires for spelling-out or as socially maladaptive skills at doing so, as the Skinnerian would be inclined to do. Simply put, for Fingarette self-deception involves the dynamically motivated refusal on someone's part to acknowledge aspects of his engagement in the world as part of his own personal identity. He concentrates on the *persistence* with which defenses are sometimes stubbornly maintained and on the *resistance* often encountered in therapy toward developing more appropriate insight. For Fingarette, the picture of self-deception is clearly one of a person in conflict with himself. Yet in contact with the same facts the behaviorist would argue that a self-deceptive person is indeed in conflict, that is, he is indeed *fighting*. Yet he is not fighting himself: he is fighting the environment. In this struggle with the realities of his environment he is responding with the only discriminative behavioral repertoires that he has, and they have been established by negative reinforcement as a consequence of their having served successfully in the past in avoiding or escaping aversive stimulation.

In drawing out the moral implications of his analysis, Fingarette distinguishes between moral responsibility and the ideal of total self-acceptance (or the spelled-out acknowledgment of all one's avowed engagements in the world) as the aim of personal development and growth. He says:

> we need to distinguish between avowal and acceptance of responsibility, between *personal* agency, and *moral* agency.... The distinction in question is that between ... the acknowledgement of an engagement as one's own personal engagement, and, on the

other hand acceptance of responsibility for one's engagements.... Although accepting oneself is the condition for accepting responsibility, the achievement of this condition is not a sufficient condition for becoming responsible. Though personal identity normally leads imperceptibly to a significant degree of personal responsibility, in some cases it hardly does at all, and in general the achievement of each varies greatly among individuals.

We must now recognize that although self-acceptance is a spiritual ideal, it is not from the moral point of view a comprehensive or ultimate ideal, for moral responsibility must be a further fruition of self-acceptance. (1969, pp. 146–50)

For the behaviorist such a concentration on the self has the defect of obscuring almost completely the enormous relevance of the environment to issues bearing on the aims of personal development and moral responsibility. Clearly the function of something similar to 'spelling-out' is of central importance, yet it is still the environment, specifically the differential reinforcing practices of particular verbal sub-communities, which determine the particular skills at spelling-out that any given individual will possess. The extent to which an individual appears to be able to 'synthesize' in an 'internally consistent identity' his range of engagements in the world depends upon the extent to which the reinforcing and punishing practices of his environment are themselves consistent. When an individual 'disavows' a particular engagement in the world, the disavowal is made with repertoires which have been found successful in minimizing aversive stimulation in the past. If the 'refusal' to spell-out relations betwen one's behavior and its controlling environment in a fashion more consonant with the assessment of other members of the verbal community is regarded as socially maladaptive, this is because the verbal community is wishfully and magically expecting the behavior-controlling contingencies to be other than what they are. It is one thing to say that a defensive person has trouble accepting himself as he really is, and then go on, in view of the fact that developments in the environment can lead almost anyone into defensive behavior, to encourage the acceptance of oneself as a 'spiritual ideal'. But if what we know of ourselves is what we are told by the environment to make of our engagement with the environment, then the problem of accepting ourselves can be viewed more simply and directly as a problem of accepting the environment.

Given the environment in which we live, one might want to advise someone that the best way to deal with the problems of our environment is to learn to live with them, to learn to accept them for what they are. Such a solution, the analogue of the solution of self-acceptance, has a long and respected tradition as a spiritual ideal. But other contrasting perspectives, e.g., 'standing up for oneself', 'fighting for one's rights', are now becoming increasingly attractive as guideposts to personal fulfilment. In any case the behaviorist moves in yet another direction, away from a concern to change people in themselves and towards a concern to change the environment in which they have to live. Rather than looking at self-deception as the problem of people who have to be helped, or judged, or changed, what we take to be the behavioral indices of self-deception can be viewed as symptoms of environmental inadequacy or stress. For example, one of the simplest things one can try to do, in having to 'deal with' an overly defensive person, is to bring one's thinking and planning to bear, not on the distasteful qualities of the other person in behaving defensively, but upon what one can do to be sure that the aversive discriminative stimulation which sets the occasion for the defensive behavior does not arise. One can think less of one's 'personal rights', or one's own dignity in the situation, and more about what one can do to help the environmental *situation*.

There are moves to make with respect to moral responsibility other than to look at it as a special kind of personal or behavioral achievement. Issues of moral responsibility are often connected to concerns for responsibility to society, or responsibility to others. The behaviorist would advocate turning at once to a consideration of the behavioral realities of the group life in which we actually function for clarification of ways in which one might be interested in 'responsibilities', while at the same time maintaining a focal interest in the 'fulfilment' of individual lives. What makes moral responsibility important is the genuineness of the underlying importance that all of us have for each other as members of a group. Moral responsibility is difficult when the environmental realities of the group in which we function are such that reinforcement is not available to enable us to find personal fulfilment as a member of a group. The reinforcers here are undoubtedly biological and very strong, even though they may only indirectly be connected with sexuality. When reinforcers of this kind are functioning effectively, the sense of obligation to be loyal to others may be replaced by a rich sense of the reality of one's tight affiliation with a group. Under such circumstances a concern with the moral responsibility of individuals may be replaced by a concern with no more than the long-range personal and social welfare of all of us together as members of a group.

Current work in the more relaxed versions of the psychoanalytic traditions may provide useful material for dealing with the Self in an interesting way. For example, Progoff's work is derived from the Jungian tradition (see, e.g., Progoff, 1956, 1959, 1973), and is connected with the most esoteric concerns of psychology. In Progoff's curent work at 'Dialogue House', participants are 'led into meditative states and various psychological exercises'; they are 'asked to chart their experiences and feelings into a carefully organized journal ... for recording dreams, group experiences, life transitions, dialogues with others and dialogues with the self' (see Progoff, 1975). In order to clarify the meaning which the concept of Self actually has for clinicians, one should examine the behavioral phenomena associated with such work. Of course, the challenge to behaviorism is the extent to which such phenomena can be incorporated within a 'natural', biological account. To do this, the behaviorist would move, once again, from a phenomenological description of the behavioral realities involved, to an attempt at giving an account in terms of genetic and reinforcing contingencies. Indeed, Progoff himself stresses the importance of incorporating the central concepts of depth-psychology within a thorough-going biological naturalism (see Progoff, 1959). Progoff's concentration on practical *techniques* for maximizing one's innate potentialities for personal fulfilment, techniques which apparently do not involve personal interaction with a therapist at all, would appear to lend itself particularly well to a systematic attempt to assess the relevant behavioral contingencies.

A great many people these days are interested in personal change, and they conceptualize this in ways that seem to hinge centrally on a concept of the self. People are interested in 'fulfilling their human potential', in 'increasing their self-awareness', in 'becoming more genuinely themselves as a unique person', in capitalizing on the personal advantages of meditative and other techniques for achieving altered states of consciousness, etc., all with a view to self-development. Underlying all this, in my opinion, is basically an interest in a redistribution of the range and kinds of reinforcement that effectively operate in the maintenance and control of one's behavior. Fundamentally, this is an interest in a change away from predominantly aversive patterns of behavioral control. When one begins to look at what people do, and what people say to each other, simply as manifestations of the behavioral equipment that they happen to have, and then begins to consider what the practices of reinforcement must have been in the various social sub-communities within which we function to have established such defensive and self-protective repertoires, the 'human condition' must surely appear as truly appalling. Even in lives which appear 'successful', the behavioral repertoires actually manifest can be seen to have been established by negative reinforcement, or they function in relation to 'positive reinforcement' in grasping and possessive ways. It is in an effort to move away from controlling contingencies of this kind that many people find themselves involved in one or another project hopefully leading towards self-development.

Now it is a significant fact that many people find that such steps towards self-development are, at least to some extent, successful. What does it mean to be successful in moving towards self-development? It seems to me too simple to look at the process as *simply* a redistribution in the relative amounts of negative and positive reinforcement. The aim is not pleasure but spontaneity. Many common positive reinforcers are related to environmental circumstances of deprivation, and the particulars of the schedule of reinforcement under which behavior is maintained must be taken into account: schedules of intermittent positive reinforcement are often associated with behavior 'strain'. One program aimed at self-development puts it this way: 'Another reason for doing something is because it is a response to another's love for us which is given freely, no matter what we do. We don't *have to* do, we *simply do it*'. The point here is not to emphasize agency, i.e., that *we* do something; the emphasis is on the naturalness, the spontaneity, or the simplicity with which we respond. But clearly the matter of spontaneous responding is not simply one of emitting only behavior which has been positively reinforced. Responding naturally in anger with behavior which may have been negatively reinforced is sometimes regarded as an indication that self-development is taking place. Instead, spontaneity seems to have more to do with the density of the demands that are placed upon us by our environment. In many ways the desirable aim of behavioral spontaneity may best be pursued by thinking rationally about the environmental circumstances under which we function, rather than thinking about what we can do to change ourselves.

In my view, a very great amount of the behavior involved in any search for self-development centers around a particular variety of reinforcement, namely that involved in our biological equipment for social affiliation. Man is not only inherently intelligent; he is inherently *social* as well. People involved in projects of self-development might be more accurately regarded as searching, not so much for themselves, as for a *group* which successfully engages their capacities to participate in contingencies of reinforcement derived from our biological needs for social affiliation. In our culture, successful personal development is often associated with the concept of love: one passes from habits of dependent and possessive love to the capacity 'to love others for their own sake'. But in trying to biologize the concept of love, it is a mistake to turn too exclusively to our current conceptions of 'sexuality'. The biological basis of our social affiliation is just now beginning to be put into a perspective based on biological research (see, e.g., Wilson, 1975), and the nature of the contingencies involved in our 'need for others' will undoubtedly have to be reconceptualized in this light. Other concepts generally associated with an agency account, and often peripherally involved with the complex issues associated with self-development, could be similarly expected to gain greater clarity with continued investigation of the biological reinforcers involved in social affiliation. I am thinking here, for example, of such concepts as *respect*. In searching for ourselves we do not need simply to be accepted for the person that we are by just any group that happens to be available. We need to function effectively as a member of a group that we can respect. But I am confident that even such ethically-laden concepts as respect and dignity will ultimately be seen to be grounded in the struggles of the verbal community to deal with the realities of human interaction which have their basis in biologically determined reinforcers.[1]

[1] An interesting current development that bears on a behavioral approach to the concept of the self is the emergence of 'behavioral jurisprudence'. The difficulties of the legal profession in making clear in a practical sense the boundaries of the concept of personal responsibility, in the face of increasing awareness of the relevance of operating psychological factors, is becoming

What is the Self? To a behaviorist, there is no such thing. 'A person is not an originating agent; he is a locus, a point at which many genetic and environmental conditions come together in a joint effect' (Skinner, 1974, p. 168). What is progress towards self-development or personal fulfilment? It is progress towards creating an environment in which one is successfully affiliated with a group and where the occasion for negatively reinforced behavior rarely arises. What is a behavioral analysis? It is an analysis of the contingencies of survival and reinforcement that are manifest in the functional adaptation of any organism, including the human, to its environment.

REFERENCES

DAY, W. F. Methodological problems in the analysis of behavior controlled by private events: Some unusual recommendations. Paper presented at the annual meeting of the American Psychological Association, Washington, D.C., September, 1971.

DAY, W. F. Ethical philosophy and the thought of B. F. Skinner. Paper presented at the Behavior Analysis and Ethics Conference, West Virginia University, June, 1975.

DAY, W. F. Contemporary behaviorism and the concept of intention. *Nebraska Symposium on Motivation*, 23, Lincoln: *University of Nebraska Press*, 1976.

FINGARETTE, H. *Self-deception*. New York: Humanities Press, 1969.

GIBBINS, J. Dissertation prospectus. Department of Psychology, University of Nevada, Reno, 1975.

---

increasingly apparent under the pressure of the current conditions of our society. The legal profession has begun to look to what behaviorists have to say about the analysis of behavior-controlling contingencies as a possible new angle to take in dealing with difficulties of this kind. As Wexler put it at the First Bi-Annual Law-Psychology Conference, 'lawyers and behavioral psychologists have reached the stage where they may begin cooperating to formulate a "behavioral jurisprudence". Such a jurisprudence could involve "contingency consciousness raising" with regard to the legal system, applying behavioral principles in analyzing and revising that system, clarifying vague cognitive legal concepts by attempting to re-define them in behavioral terms, and explaining from a behavioral perspective the existence of rights and rules'. (1975a, p. 21) See also Wexler 1975b.

HEMENWAY, R. A behavioristic analysis of phenomenological data. Paper presented at the annual meeting of the American Psychological Association, Chicago, September, 1975.

LAHREN, B. Analysis of the discriminative control of controlling variable statements. Paper presented at the annual meeting of the American Psychological Association, Chicago, September, 1975.

MISCHEL, T. Psychological explanations and their vicissitudes. *Nebraska Symposium on Motivation*, 23, Lincoln: University of Nebraska Press, 1976.

PFEIFFER, J. E. *The emergence of man*. New York: Harper & Row, 1969.

PROGOFF, I. *The death and rebirth of psychology*. New York: McGraw-Hill, 1956.

PROGOFF, I. *Depth psychology and modern man*. New York: The Julian Press, 1959.

PROGOFF, I. *Jung, synchronicity, and human destiny*. New York: Dell Publishing Co., 1973.

PROGOFF, I. *At a journal workshop*. New York: Dialogue House Library, 1975.

SECORD, P. Contingency control and self-control. Grant application to The History and Philosophy of Science section, National Science Foundation, 1975.

SKINNER, B. F. The operational analysis of psychological terms. *Psychological Review*, 1945, 52, 270–77, 291–94.

SKINNER, B. F. *Science and human behavior*. New York: Macmillan, 1953.

SKINNER, B. F. *Verbal behavior*. New York: Appleton-Century-Crofts, 1957.

SKINNER, B. F. *About behaviorism*. New York: Knopf, 1974.

SKINNER, B. F. The shaping of phylogenic behavior. *Journal of the Experimental Analysis of Behavior*, 1975, 24, 117–20.

SPOONER, D., & BENNETT, M. The identification of controlling variables: The behavioral reality. Paper presented at the annual meeting of the American Psychological Association, Chicago, September, 1975.

WEXLER, D. Criminal commitment contingency structures. Paper presented at the First Bi-annual Law-Psychology Research Conference, University of Nebraska-Lincoln, October, 1975a.

WEXLER, D. The surfacing of behavioral jurisprudence. *Behaviorism*, 3, 172–76, 1975b.

WILSON, E. O. *Sociobiology: The new synthesis*. Cambridge: Harvard University Press, 1975.

9 Making Oneself Behave: A Critique of the Behavioral Paradigm and an Alternative Conceptualization*

PAUL F. SECORD

While there are many psychological systems for explaining human behavior, those aiming at a scientific explanation adopt as an 'ideal' a system in which behavior can be fully explained by identifying with rigor and precision the conditions that bring about a line of action. The greater the certainty with which such conditions can be identified, and the more they can be seen as directly causing the behavior, the greater the approximation to the ideal. This view underlies the major thrust of various behavioristic approaches, which emphasize what can be observed externally, although physiological states and processes and even mental states are allowed into some behavioristic systems. But that behaviorism achieves that ideal is only an illusion.

Operant behaviorists assume that we emit those behaviors which have been previously reinforced, when confronted with situations similar to those occurring during the earlier history of reinforcement. Typically these 'situations' are identified in terms of discriminative stimuli; that is, stimuli which were salient during the reinforcement process and identified with it. It is common parlance among operant behaviorists to speak of behavior as 'under the control of' such stimuli. Indeed, operant learning is essentially conceived of as bringing a response under the control of discriminative stimuli, which are a component of 'contingencies of reinforcement'. (Skinner, 1975)

The phrase 'under the control of' is ubiquitous in the operant research literature and deserves analysis. Behavior that is regular

* Preparation of this paper was facilitated by a grant from the History and Philosophy of Science Section of the National Science Foundation (SOC 75–14077).

or lawful is always thought of as under the control of *external* conditions or stimuli, and never under the control of internal states of the individual. That is, lawful behavior is due to a learning history; it comes about through the pattern of reinforcement contingencies that have occurred naturally or that have been manipulated by the experimenter. This emphasis on control by external stimuli, on the identification of external *causes* as sources of behavior, is entirely consistent with Skinner's distaste for explanations which appeal to cognitive process, memory, personality trait, biological drive, or any other inner locus.

But 'under the control of' is a metaphor which is probably as misleading as many of the Freudian metaphors that Skinner detests so much. For to place all of the 'control' of a learned response in a discriminative stimulus is to ignore the fact that the changes actually took place in the individual during the process of learning, and that it is the individual's changed nature that accounts for the new response in the presence of the stimulus. Even familiar tropisms, e.g., the moth attracted to the flame, are not cases where the sole control over the organism lies in an external contingency. For while moths almost invariably fly toward a flame or light, this is explained in terms of a bio-chemical mechanism operating within the moth. So to speak of the moth as being under the control of the flame is only a manner of speaking. More correct might be: because of his nature, a moth flies toward a flame. In the much more complex human learning situations, *what* has changed during the course of learning is not at all clear, but it is indisputable that the individual is now in a different state.

This point is important because behavior therapists, most of whom stem from the operant tradition, have in recent years become intensely interested in what has been variously labeled self-control, self-regulation, self-direction, and self-reinforcement. The idea here is that people can somehow gain sufficient control over their behavior so as to change it. But how can the idea of self-control or self-regulation be reconciled with the belief, vigorously espoused by behavior modification specialists, that the locus of control lies in external contingencies? I will argue that the introduction of self-control into a system which has operant behaviorism as the core theoretical construct amounts to opening Pandora's box and to the death of the theory.

Behavior Therapy and Self-Control

In the early 1970s about a half-dozen books and hundreds of articles have been published on the uses of self-control in behavior research and therapy. But the theoretical constructs proposed in these publications must surely be the despair of those operant behaviorists who, like Skinner, require consistency and clarity in dealing with the constructs involved in contingencies of reinforcement. To some extent, conceptual confusions about the nature of self-control on the part of behavior therapists may be excusable, since their aim is wholly pragmatic; they use whatever procedures seem to work with their clients, whether or not these procedures fit the mold of operant behaviorism. And since they have gone very far afield, indeed, their activities can stimulate thinking along new theoretical lines.

Self-control applications are typically worked out in collaboration between the therapist and the client. Instead of the standard behavior modification approach, in which the therapist applies certain patterns of reinforcement to change the frequency of desired or undesired actions, the therapist teaches the clients to apply these to themselves. The general approach commonly used is well summarized by Watson and Tharp (1972, p. 48):

1. The basic idea in self-modification is to arrange situations so that desirable behavior is positively reinforced and unwanted behavior is not reinforced.
2. Reinforcement is made contingent, which means that it is gained only if some particular behavior (the target) is performed.
3. The steps in self-modification are:
   a. Specifying the target in terms of behavior in a specific situation.
   b. Making observations on how often the target behavior occurs, the antecedents that precede it, and the consequences that follow it.
   c. Forming a plan to intervene by contingently reinforcing some desirable behavior and by arranging situations to increase the chances of performing that behavior.
   d. Maintaining, adjusting, and terminating the intervention program.

Thoreson and Mahoney (1974) note that there are two basic forms of behavior here. The first involves environmental planning, and the second, behavioral programming. In *environmental planning*, the client changes environmental and situational factors so as to modify the reinforcement contingencies that ordinarily occur, prior to executing the target behavior. A smoker trying to give it up might leave the house in the morning without cigarettes and without money to buy them, and he might enlist his friends in the effort to discourage his smoking. *Behavioral programming* involves self-administered consequences after the target behavior occurs. Individuals modify the consequences that normally follow the target behavior, by punishing themselves if they smoke, or rewarding themselves if they refrain from smoking.

Notice that the entire emphasis lies on contingencies of reinforcement as they affect the target behavior. The control of the target behavior is seen as lying in the external circumstances and also in the consequences that follow the action. Moreover, the means of changing the target behavior are also seen as residing in the events and consequences that the clients produce, rather than in the clients themselves. It is the reward or punishment of one's own acts that changes the frequency of their occurrence. The theoretical idea is that behavior can only be changed through changing contingencies of reinforcement and that people are controlled by such contingencies.

But if people are controlled by external contingencies, how can they make the appropriate changes in their environment and in their behaviors so as to bring about change in the target behavior? The problem is that planning and arranging are themselves forms of behavior. Behavior therapists focus on contingencies of reinforcement, adopting them as a central principle in their model of human behavior. But they do this mainly in connection with the target behavior, while at the same time using commonsense or pragmatic notions in connection with the client as a planner and arranger. In this context they treat the client as an individual with some autonomy, capable of making choices, modifying opportunities, and making commitments. But there is a paradox in treating clients as capable of rearranging reinforcement contingencies and, at the same time, viewing their behavior as rigorously controlled by reinforcement contingencies. Failure to recognize this paradox results in a gross caricature of what is taking place when successful self-regulation occurs. What is needed instead is a single set of theoretical constructs that will allow us to deal with all phases of what goes on under the name of self-control or self-regulation.

Self-Direction and Self-Intervention

The phenomenon of special interest to behavior therapists working with self-regulation consists of those behavior changes which are intentionally brought about through the active efforts of the client. People adopt a specific objective or goal, such as dieting, or giving up smoking, and attempt to reach that objective. Since many self-directed actions are not problematic (e.g., getting from one place to another), the cases of special interest are those which require directed efforts that are difficult to carry out because they represent a substantial departure from one's customary way of behaving.

Not all of the terms used to describe this phenomenon are equally satisfactory. 'Self-control' is too broad since it has been widely used by psychologists to cover such processes as housebreaking pets or toilet training infants; such inhibitions seem to be acquired by a learning process not requiring verbalization or understanding on the part of the individual (e.g., operant conditioning). But individuals who go to behavior therapists have in mind making an intentional change in the way they behave. Thus, we need a term for talking about intentional behavior, and a term for making intentional changes in one's behavior. The requisite concepts are *self-direction* and *self-intervention*, and these concepts cannot be handled within the narrow paradigm of operant behaviorism.

Self-directed behavior refers to a line of action that is aimed at a particular object or goal. Individuals are aware of the goal and its connection to their actions, and they monitor their progress toward it. In a word, self-directed behavior is under the control of the actor or agent or person (P). He can change direction or stop the action.

Self-intervention is the assumption of control by P over a line of action that otherwise would have taken a different course. P initiates a new line of behavior which differs from that which normally would have occurred, or aborts his customary way of behaving.[1]

[1] In all cases of self-intervention discussed here, I am assuming that the individual is strongly motivated to change a line of action. Though a similar

Before examining self-intervention, note that the following requirements must be met by a model of human behavior that would allow for self-direction:

1. P must have reflective awareness of his desires; he must be able to appraise them. This does not mean that some desires could not be below the level of awareness, or that he may not make mistakes in assessing the strength of a desire. But without awareness of at least some desires, P could not specify any goal that he wanted to attain but could not reach.

2. P must have the ability to monitor and make assessments of action patterns. In one type of self-directed behavior the goal is achieved only at the end of a series of actions; in another, each action is cumulative. The former requires the ability to execute the series of actions correctly in order to achieve the goal (e.g., solving a problem, like repairing an auto engine which has broken down). The latter requires a certain accumulation of actions adding up to a total which reaches a threshold of sufficiency (e.g., enough studying for an examination so that the desired grade is attained). Successful execution of such action patterns is further complicated by the nature of everyday behavior. We rarely perform a single set of actions at a time; more often our activities consist of several sets of actions being performed within the same period of time, often with much shifting from one to the other.

3. P must be able to allocate time appropriately to various actions, so that they can be completed within appropriate periods. Moreover, some actions may have interfering characteristics—features that make it more difficult to execute certain other actions.

4. Since these activities all have goals or ends recognized by P, P must be able to keep the goals in mind and to maintain appropriate motivation for performing the activities. If he forgets where he is going, or loses interest in getting there, self-direction fails.

There is nothing particularly remarkable about self-directed behavior: going to the grocery store to buy food, or to the library to get a book, are simple examples. But since operant behaviorists

---

assumption must be made by behavior therapists if they are to deal with self-intervention, they do not make this assumption explicit if they are operant behaviorists. The role of motivation in self-intervention is very complex; for a discussion of this problem, see W. Alston's contribution to this volume.

usually refuse to admit mental states into their system, they cannot identify self-directed behavior in terms of beliefs and goals. This, together with their failure to recognize the concept of a *person*, makes it difficult to see how they can conceptualize self-directed behavior at all. Since they insist on describing behavior from the point of view of the external observer, it is hard to see how they could possibly distinguish between a series of actions that are performed habitually, without thinking, and the same series executed deliberately with the intention to achieve some effect. Moreover, they see the source of control in external conditions and events (and additionally, for some of them, in the neuro-physiology of the individual), while the concept of self-direction implies that control over the line of action lies in the person.

Self-intervention typically occurs when attempts at self-direction fail. The individual turns his attention to his failure, and tries to bring his behavior under his control; different forms of self-intervention correspond to different forms of failure in self-direction. There are several paradigm cases of such failures:

1. P desires to do X, but instead does Y. For example, P may desire to diet and lose weight by eating only low-calorie foods, but repeatedly fails to achieve his objective because he frequently eats high calorie foods.

2. P desires to do X, but is not able to do so, although he does not do any particular Y in place of X. This may occur because of lack of knowledge, an inability to organize behavior properly, or it may occur because of fear, anxiety, or other liabilities.

3. P desires *not* to do X, but nevertheless does X. For example, he may want to give up biting his fingernails, but continues to do so.

Later I will discuss particular strategies of self-intervention that are used to deal with these paradigm cases of failure in self-direction. But my general thesis is that behavior therapists who adopt operant behaviorism as a conceptual scheme place themselves in a logical box which does not allow them to talk about self-directed behavior without being totally inconsistent or paradoxical. Instead, my analysis proceeds in reverse fashion, adopting a different model of human behavior. People are viewed as knowing what they are doing much of the time, as having certain ends in view, and as performing actions that accomplish these ends. They reflect upon their needs, and they monitor their behavior so as to satisfy those needs. This deliberately anthropomorphic view of human behavior has been spelled out in detail and defended as a scientific approach by Harré and Secord (1972).

This approach removes the problem of self-direction in one bold stroke: successful instances of self-direction need no special explanation. If P adopts a goal of losing ten pounds by dieting and exercising, and successfully carries out this program, no special explanation is required. But further analyses, even causal ones, of why the goal might have been adopted, are not excluded. For example, P might have adopted this goal because of external circumstances, like inactivity enforced by a long period of inclement weather, which might have led to a weight gain which in turn made his clothes fit too tightly, leading to the adoption of the goal. But note that the goal itself is self-consciously adopted, and a rational plan followed to achieve it.

While self-direction is no problem for an anthropomorphic model, the model does raise a new problem: we now need to explain those cases where we fail to change our own behavior, where self-direction fails. Sometimes we do things in spite of ourselves. Occasionally we are 'carried away', by anger or love. Or we may be depressed and unable to function. We may perform some acts having underlying motives of which we are unaware. Can an anthropomorphic model of human behavior explain these exceptions, and, can it explain self-intervention—the deliberate taking over by P, to place these recalcitrant behaviors under his own control? The concept of liabilities is especially helpful for understanding how this is done.

Liabilities, Self-intervention and Helplessness

Liabilities are dispositions to act in ways that are not under one's control (Harré and Secord, 1972). Thus, one may be liable to be afraid when alone in the dark. One may be liable to provocative situations of various kinds. For example, one may be liable to drink, to drugs, to gambling, to forgetting, to overeating. Behaviors that are not self-directed are, typically, the result of liabilities.

Liabilities are attributed to a temporary or permanent internal state of the agent. These states may involve neurophysiology as well as certain learning histories; frequently, the states may not be fully described or understood, but the liability is identified through behavioral observations carried out in situations where the liability is expressed in behavior. Behavior therapists have dealt in a practical way with such common liabilities as fear or anxiety that is aroused in specific situations; for example, a morbid fear of snakes, or fear of entering the enclosed space of an elevator.

Controlling liabilities seems a 'natural' application of self-intervention, for, by definition, liabilities are things that happen to a person, and to control them, individuals take over management of themselves and their situation. But while behavior therapists talk about changing contingencies of reinforcement, including self-applied reinforcements, they do not conceptualize the means by which P is able to arrange and manage his behavior. This is done only in a pragmatic, commonsense manner which has implicit in it the model of self-directed behavior which I have outlined, rather than the operant behavior paradigm.

An apparent exception to the notion that self-intervention is a matter of controlling liabilities is provided by those instances where individuals desire to shape up some positive behavior. An example would be increasing the time that students spend in studying, in order to raise their grades. Quite possibly, however, the key to successfully establishing the positive behavior is again the control of liabilities. Presumably, if students were sufficiently motivated to study, they would simply do so. But what happens is that they are liable to distractions and to engage in competing activities. Even when they sit down to study, they may be unable to concentrate, their thoughts may wander, irrelevant ideas may come to mind, etc.; they cannot study because competing liabilities create interfering behaviors.

If this is true, then what is really involved is not the establishment of the positive behavior, but rather control of the liabilities to engage in competing behaviors. It would be significant, indeed, if all instances of self-intervention turned out to be the elimination of liabilities, and none could be identified as the shaping up of desirable behavior; the latter may only seem to be a separate case because of the vague use of 'self-reinforcement'. This is not to suggest that instances of learning a skill, for example, consist solely in controlling liabilities to perform incorrectly. While this might occasionally be the case, there surely are straightforward cases of self-direction that involve learning a skill or a performance. But the emphasis in our discussion is on failures of self-direction—situations where individuals are having difficulty shaping or directing their behavior along desired lines. It is these problematic instances where behavior therapy has been offered as a remedial device, and where self-intervention comes into play. And it could well be that these are all instances where liabilities get in the way of adequate performances.

To this point we have put aside the question of the exact nature of a liability. But it may well be that this question must be answered in specific instances, if self-intervention is to be successful. Whether cigarette smoking is physiologically addictive, or whether it is merely a habit, has important implications for controlling it. A particularly interesting question is whether some liabilities have as their core a particular belief which prevents people from making attempts to perform certain acts.

In recent years, some excellent related research has been carried out on helplessness (Seligman, 1975). This is directly relevant to self-intervention because helplessness has been conceived as the opposite of self-direction: helplessness is a state where outcomes are *independent* of one's own acts. No matter what acts one performs, outcomes follow their own course, in a manner totally unrelated to one's actions. For example, if the steering linkage of your car became disconnected, then no matter how you turned the wheel you would be helpless to control its path. Similarly, if another person were bound to some course of action, so that no matter what you said or did he would continue along the predetermined course, then you would be helpless to affect outcomes.

While helplessness can be described behaviorally, in terms of inability to affect outcomes, one is strongly inclined to presume that a belief in one's helplessness, a feeling of lack of control or even of hopelessness, underlies human helplessness. It is not simply that individuals fail to try to affect outcomes; rather, they believe that attempts would be useless, so they do not try. The strength of this state of helplessness, whether expressed behaviorally, or in terms of beliefs, is clearly brought out by Seligman's research program.

Seligman (1975) set up a paradigm using a two-sided chamber in which a dog escaped or turned off electric shock by jumping over a barrier to the other side. Naive dogs, placed in the box for the first time, ran about frantically when they received the first shock, until they accidentally scrambled over the barrier. After sufficient experience with the box, the dogs remained calm, and simply jumped the barrier as soon as the signal for the shock was received, avoiding the shock.

Some dogs, however, received prior training. They were placed in a restraining hammock, where they received a signal followed by inescapable shock delivered according to a random pattern. When these dogs were later placed in the shuttle-box, they moved about for only about 30 seconds, failing to escape from the shock, and then lay down on the shock grid. On successive trials, they became increasingly passive, making no attempt to escape the shock. Seligman suggests that they had learned that their responses have no effect on outcomes, so that they gave up.

What is especially striking about this outcome is the depth or strength of the passivity or helplessness. Seligman and his colleagues found it extremely difficult to retrain the dogs. First, they took the barrier out of the shuttle-box. This made no difference, the dogs just lay on the shock side. The dogs were made hungry, and salami was dropped on the other side; experimenters tried to coax the dogs away from the shock grid by calling them. But the dogs just lay there. Finally, they decided to force the dogs to respond. Using long leashes, they began to drag the dogs to the other side (an act which turned off the shock). But it took from 25 to 200 draggings before the dogs began to respond on their own. Eventually, however, they learned to escape and were no longer helpless.

Seligman's explanation of helplessness is that the dogs learned that outcomes were *not* contingent upon their behavior. They acquired the *expectation* that their actions would not affect the delivery of the shock. Seligman states:

> .... the expectation that an outcome is independent of responding (1) reduces the motivation to control the outcome, (2) interferes with learning that responding controls the outcome; and, if the outcome is traumatic, (3) produces fear for as long as the subject is uncertain of the uncontrollability of the outcome, and then produces depression. (Seligman, 1975, p. 56)

Helplessness, based on the belief or expectation that one's actions have no relation to outcomes, is thus one paradigm for a disabling liability. The belief that one's efforts are hopeless appears to be the central core in this type of liability. Seligman discusses at some length various other experiments and observations, including many with human participants. He suggests that many familiar phenomena may fit the helplessness paradigm, e.g., childhood failures to learn certain specific skills which persist into adulthood, certain types of situational anxieties, states of ennui found among some inactive retired people, and reactive depression. All are characterized by a feeling of lack of control over one's fate.

The implications of this concept for self-intervention are clear. Many liabilities comprising an 'inability' to perform may be a function of believing that one's efforts would invariably fail. To overcome such liabilities people must repeatedly experience control over outcomes; through such experience they eventually come to give up their beliefs of impotence and their feelings of hopelessness.

The possibility that helplessness is based on a hopeless expectation leads to consideration, in the final section, of various cognitive processes that might be employed in self-intervention. But before turning to these, I want to show that *self*-reinforcement—the core concept used by behavior modification specialists to deal with self-intervention—is inconsistent with the operant behavior paradigm.

Self-reinforcement

The following is an example of self-reinforcement: A young man characteristically smoked about 20–30 cigarettes per day. Reading about lung cancer convinced him that he should give up smoking. He decided to tear up a dollar bill and discard the pieces each time he smoked more than 15 cigarettes a day. After each five-day period, he progressively reduced the number of cigarettes he allowed himself to smoke before he would have to destroy a dollar bill. At the end of 50 days, he had stopped smoking entirely, and two years later, had not resumed (Axelrod, Hall, Weis, and Rohrer, (1974).

This simple case is cited as an example of the use of self-reinforcement for changing one's own behavior. In this instance, the individual punished himself, but often reinforcers are positive. For example, one might reward oneself for successfully dieting by allowing oneself some favorite activity or indulgence (other than food). Self-reinforcements may take a great variety of forms and be used in many circumstances. But in each instance, positive self-reinforcers are seen as increasing the frequency of desirable behavior, and aversive self-reinforcers are thought to reduce undesirable behavior. Essentially, self-reinforcements are viewed as functioning in exactly the same way as externally applied reinforcements: they are events contingent on the act and their occurrence alters the probability of the act.

What does it mean for an event to be contingent upon an act? Skinner (1969, 1974) has insisted that contingencies can only be identified by examining their effect upon probability of response. Contingencies are those consequences (of a response) that result in a change in the frequency with which that response occurs. He recognizes that this is a tautology, but considers it to be a useful one; it is the most objective, preferred 'meaning' of reinforcement contingencies.[2]

But this tautology only provides an *empirical* criterion; it does not enable us to identify contingencies in terms of semantic or substantive content. We do not really know what meaning 'contingency' has if we can identify contingencies only through their empirical effect upon a response. The problem with this is that the complex reinforcing sequences alleged to characterize human behavior, particularly sequences that are 'self-reinforcing', are left open to a wide variety of interpretations or re-interpretations.

If an event is to be *contingent* upon an act, then it is clear that the contingency must in some fashion *follow from* the act. This is also suggested by the repeated reference to the contingency as a *consequence* of the response. But what is meant by 'follow from'? One possible meaning is that individuals perceive their act as producing this contingency. Herrnstein, a behaviorist, rather surprisingly says that the rat 'figures out' the connection between the act and the contingency (Brown and Herrnstein, 1975, p. 188). But this is tantamount to giving up entirely Skinner's conception of contingencies of reinforcement. If we stay within a behavioristic framework, the idea that the act *produces* the contingency must be consistent with a view of reinforcement as a 'mechanical', 'automatic', 'stamping-in' of the act. The act and its accompanying conditions *cause* the contingent event, or, somewhat more weakly, the act is a *sufficient condition* for the contingent event to occur. In the hundreds of experiments conducted with animals, and in many

[2] In his earlier book, *Verbal Behavior*, he does introduce some classes of reinforcers, e.g., *tacts* and *mands*. But his later works do not contain any general classification system of reinforcers. (Skinner, 1974)

conducted with children and adults, reinforcement appears to be used in this sense. Some 'obvious' contingency is chosen, like food, water, or candy, and made to follow the behavior, so as to increase or decrease the frequency with which that act occurs.

Thus, what is meant by contingency in cases of external reinforcement is simply that the contingency follows the act and that it is a sufficient condition for reinforcing the act, if repeated according to an appropriate schedule.[3] Essentially this argument is based upon default—to the extent that radical behaviorism does not specify any conditions for contingencies except that they follow the act, we are forced to regard them as sufficient conditions without semantic content.

Now when we examine *self*-reinforcement, the nature of the connection between the target act and the contingencies becomes crucial. Consider two possible kinds of 'self-reinforcement'. Suppose that an archer shoots an arrow which hits the center of the bullseye at 60 yards. The act of shooting is immediately followed by the contingency of the arrow piercing the bullseye. Hitting the bullseye is an achievement meeting a self-imposed standard, and the archer may well experience elation at his success. The elated feeling is a consequence having an intimate connection, not just with the act of shooting, but with shooting successfully, i.e., hitting the bullseye. Contrast this contingency with a second kind of 'self-reinforcement', praising oneself or giving oneself something desirable. This kind of self-reinforcement, often used by behavior therapists, lacks the intimate causal connection with achievement. The successful accomplishment of the act of shooting and the elation experienced on hitting the bullseye is contingent upon a certain level of skill, whereas self-praise or giving oneself a treat are made contingent only by adopting an arbitrary rule.

The crucial difference between the two cases is that, in the second one, individuals have control over the reinforcement *independently* of whether or not they achieve a self-imposed standard. Archers have it within their power to praise themselves or to give themselves privileges *whether or not* they hit the bullseye. They are

[3] The concept of the reinforcement schedule is an important part of radical behaviorism not dealt with here. Single reinforcements have little meaning; what is crucial is the pattern of reinforcements over time. Some schedules of reinforcement are more effective than others, but dealing with this is not crucial to the arguments presented here.

following an arbitrary rule if they reward themselves when they succeed; should they choose to do so, they could break this rule. But they do not have the same arbitrary control over hitting the bullseye. Often they fail. Hitting the bullseye is directly contingent upon performing the act in an especially skillful way. There is a causal connection between performing the act in a particular way and hitting the bullseye. Archers cannot arbitrarily decide to hit the bullseye; they can only decide to try, and then succeed or fail.

Now it is by no means clear that this type of reinforcement can be called a *self*-reinforcement. For the archer is reinforced by his achievement and that achievement is not self-delivered. It is a consequence of shooting the arrow in a certain way, but it is not a second act (of reinforcement) performed by the archer, which is required if we are to call it a self-reinforcement. If we were to consider hitting the bullseye a self-reinforcement, then we could as easily consider the food pellet following the bar-press of the rat as a self-reinforcement, because the rat is bringing the consequence about. To be logically consistent, we must consider these consequences mere reinforcements, *not* self-reinforcements.

On the other hand, the 'self-reinforcements' which are under the control of the agent and which are arbitrary because they lack connection with achievement may not be reinforcements at all. There is, in fact, a boot-strapping absurdity inherent in the idea of self-delivered contingencies as automatically reinforcing. For self-reinforcements under our own control, if they worked, would enable us to 'make ourselves' do virtually anything. The only reservation would be that we would have to be able to emit the act at least once, so that we could reinforce it. To caricature the notion, we could carry around a pocketful of favorite candies, and pop one in our mouth every time that we wanted to increase the frequency of an act that we performed. There is no reason to suppose that such self-delivered rewards can be effective reinforcements, like the archer's scoring a bullseye. And if we cannot regard such 'self-reinforcements' as *reinforcements*, then it may well be that 'self-reinforcement' cannot be conceptualized at all within the operant paradigm used by behavior modificationists.

In an analysis conducted independently of the present one, and published after my analysis was essentially complete, Catania (1975) arrived at a similar conclusion, and states that self-reinforcement is a myth. He shows that in most instances of so-called self-delivered reinforcements, it would be more correct to speak of the target act as a discriminative stimulus for the subsequent reinforcement. His example is that of a student who is using self-delivered reinforcements for completing an assignment. Catania notes that, in order for the student to give himself a reward, he would have to discriminate whether or not he had completed the assignment. But then the completing of the assignment is itself reinforcing, and the extra self-delivery of a reward would seem to have little point. The case of the archer is exactly parallel. He discriminates whether or not he made a good shot, but then his achievement is the reinforcement, and self-praise is superfluous. Catania notes further that praising *oneself* is not the same as reinforcing one's *act*, a fact which casts more doubt on self-praise as a reinforcer.

Perhaps one reason that this point has been missed for so long is that in most of the work on self-intervention, the two kinds of reinforcement (contingencies connected with successful achievement and self-controlled contingencies) have been confounded. They always occur together, as they do in the archery example. When they hit the bullseye, the archers give themselves a reward in accordance with instructions, but they also are successful, which may well be the crucial reinforcing contingency.

A second reason why this difference has been overlooked is the behaviorist's insistance on ignoring the perceptions of the individual, whether animal or human. The 'connection' between the action and the reinforcing contingency may often be a perceived one, but if the individual's perceptions are not taken into account, then such connections cannot be brought into the system. For example, it might be argued in objection to the line of reasoning offered here that rats are arbitrarily given food pellets for pressing a bar according to a certain schedule; and rats do learn when given such reinforcements, demonstrating their effectiveness. But the connection is arbitrary only from the point of view of the experimenter. Once the rat has learned that food pellets are regularly forthcoming for certain bar-pressing performances, the connection as perceived by the rat may be as compelling as the connection between shooting an arrow in a certain way and hitting the bullseye. And, of course, the delivery of reinforcements is not totally under the rat's control. He cannot receive pellets whenever he desires, he has to enact a successful performance to get them.

In sum, though 'self-reinforcement' is the key concept which behavior therapists use to deal with self-intervention, that concept does not seem to be intelligible within the operant behavior paradigm. For insofar as the contingency that follows from the act is not perceived by the individual as connected with successful achievement, it is hard to see why it should be reinforcing. But insofar as it is connected with successful achievement it is not self-controlled in the sense that it can be self-delivered under any circumstances.

Processes of Self-intervention

This section will identify some of the processes that occur during self-intervention. Suppose a person has a liability to behave in some way that constitutes a failure in self-direction. If this behavior is not under P's control, how can self-intervention bring it under P's control? Two concepts are especially useful in conceptualizing self-intervention: *enabling* and *constraining conditions*. Such conditions may be either external circumstances or internal states; enabling conditions make it easier to perform an act, constraining conditions make it harder. The advantage of using these concepts is that they do not require exact knowledge of the nature of a liability. Since enabling and constraining conditions are identified in terms of their effects, they may be discovered empirically, without knowing whether these conditions have been established through habit, conditioning, emotional states, or what have you.

For example, some behavior therapists help individuals gain knowledge of the target liability, and then assist them in establishing enabling and constraining conditions for intervening. Stuart and Davis (1972) have worked this out for obese people. They help them to identify the most tempting situations they encounter, and to discover the circumstances under which they are most apt to overeat. Then they develop plans for avoiding or changing these provocative situations, and a regimen which will prevent the troublesome bodily or mental states from occurring. Again, fear may be dealt with by desensitization procedures. This involves instruction in deep relaxation, a state which is incompatible with fear, and exposure to situations which are greatly attentuated versions of the target fear-arousing situation. The situations are represented in progressively less and less attenuated forms, until the client is ultimately able to handle the full-strength, fear-arousing situation.

Enabling and constraining conditions typically affect the pattern of choices available. A constraining condition may be a form of giving up options to behave in certain ways, or in order to not-X. Consider the murderer who begs to be put in prison so that he won't commit any more murders; or, less dramatically, the individual who leaves home without cigarettes or money in his pocket, so that he won't smoke. Note that there are two ways of giving up options: making the act physically impossible, and denying it through adopting a rule or procedure. The murderer who is imprisoned has made murder physically impossible. But the individual who left home without money and cigarettes can probably borrow cigarettes or borrow money to get them. His constraining condition requires that he simultaneously exercise denial—that he put an option out of consideration. The device frequently used by behavior therapists, a box in which one locks one's cigarettes, which are then rationed one at-a-time at intervals, also requires self-restraint in order to work. Otherwise one could simply carry an additional packet of cigarettes, and smoke whenever one pleased. Another technique, the 'smoking chair', involves adopting a rule that one will smoke only while sitting in that chair. This requires marked self-restraint.

When giving up an option does not require continued self-restraint, but is accomplished through some mechanical means, intervention may be seen as *less* self-directing. For in that case P has fixed the situation so that now he has *no choice:* he is incapable of performing the undesired action because of circumstances. He is not learning to resist temptation, but is simply not performing the undesired action. Nothing in current research makes clear whether this approach is the best one. It could well be that self-direction is best learned through its active exercise. On the other hand, in cases where an undesired behavior is accentuated by some physiological process, as in drug addiction, constraints not requiring active self-restraint might be necessary, until sufficient changes have occurred in the relevant biochemical factors.

A related process that is especially important in self-intervention is *commitment.* When P decides to carry out an action at some future time, a first step is taken toward control of his future behavior. Although social psychologists have studied commitment (Kiesler, 1971; see also the large research on dissonance theory), the failure to appreciate fully the role of the person in controlling his own behavior has severely limited these contributions. How are commitments, the decisions people often make to bring about changes in their behavior, to be characterized, and what role do they play in self-intervention? Rachlin (1974), an operant behaviorist, has suggested that commitment is quite simply a choice which places constraints upon a future act, and that it characterizes rats and pigeons as well as men and women. He claims that commitment works because it introduces constraints on behavior at a time when the reinforcement for the behavior is at some distance in time beyond the present moment. For example, individuals shopping for food four hours before mealtime can better honor their commitment to diet and resist tempting purchases than if they shop immediately before a meal. During their shopping trip, they are in effect making commitments to eat foods that they buy (rather than the ones they would buy if they were hungry).

Rachlin and Green (1972) experimented with pigeons placed in a cage, one at a time, pecking lighted red or green keys that produced certain consequences. If pigeons are presented with either an immediate small reward, or a delayed large one, they almost always choose the immediate one. A more complex arrangement was then set up, involving successive choices. The pigeons now had two initial alternatives to choose from. One alternative produced a ten-second delay followed by the choice of either a small immediate reward or a further delay followed by a larger reward; the immediate, small reward following the ten-second delay was almost always chosen. But the other initial alternative produced a ten-second delay, followed by another four-second delay and a larger reward (no other choice was available after the ten-second delay). Rachlin and Green were interested in the eventual behavior of the pigeons after they had had considerable experience with these arrangements.

What they found was that the fourteen-second delay with the larger reward was chosen about 85 per cent of the time. In other words, when presented with the initial choice, the pigeons chose the longer delay in order to get the larger reward. They *committed* themselves to this longer delay, in order to get the larger reward. Rachlin suggests that this is exactly what happens in the human case of commitment.

Both Herrnstein (1975) and Ainslie (1975) have attempted to generalize this phenomenon to explain the control of impulsiveness solely in terms of reinforcement. They call attention to the well-known fact that, the more distant in time a reinforcing event, the weaker its effect at the moment. They note further that a small, *immediate* reinforcement is probably stronger than quite large reinforcements distant in time, and the act that provides the former will probably be performed. But they note further, that if both reinforcements are somewhat removed in time, there will be a point at which the tendency to perform the act leading to the larger reinforcement will be stronger than the tendency to perform the act leading to the smaller reinforcement. This is true because the gradient for the larger reinforcement is less steep than the gradient for the smaller reinforcement. So, at that particular time, individuals will be able to resist the impulsive choice of immediate gratification, and will commit themselves to waiting for the larger reward.

While this explanation works for the pigeon experiment just described, it encounters certain difficulties in the human case. Both Herrnstein and Ainslie are equivocal with respect to the role of cognitive factors. At times, they clearly imply that individuals calculate in a rational way the reinforcement values of acting now or later. If this is indeed the case, it opens the way for other cognitive factors to influence the choice, and a strict reinforcement interpretation is considerably weakened.

An even stronger objection to extending the pigeon paradigm to the human case comes from the nature of human commitments. We must ask how the commitment exercises constraints upon the individual in both cases. The most notable thing about constraints in the pigeon apparatus is that the pigeon has absolutely no choice once it has made the decision leading to the fourteen-second delay; there is no way of breaking this 'commitment'. But most human commitments are not like that. Some, of course, may be costly to break or to reverse. A groom who fails to show up for his wedding would be terribly embarrassed; but he *could* back out and fail to appear. And many commitments that are made to oneself and which do not involve other people are not very costly to break. So, it commitment helps people to carry out their intentions, the important question to ask is why? Rachlin might be quite right in suggesting that commitments are made at a time when what is forgone is still remote in time—one agrees to start the diet *tomorrow*, but not *right now*. But what needs to be determined is whether commitments which could be reversed are kept, and what needs explaining is why they are kept.

What is overlooked in the Rachlin version of commitment is the fact that, in human situations, P must often sustain an active dedication to the achievement of the goal to which he has committed himself. This may consist of doing X while refraining from doing Y, doing X in spite of difficulties or obstacles, or doing not-X. Doing not-X is a pure case of giving up an option (like smoking) but it can be considered a commitment to the positive goal of not smoking (or protecting oneself from cancer by not smoking). Commitment always involves giving up some options; if one commits oneself to a goal like learning to play the piano, or writing a novel, one must give up those activities that might have been carried out instead, and sometimes it invokes other costs as well. Making promises of various sorts grant to the recipient various sorts of rights—on one's time, services, support, or even the right to monitor the keeping of the promise and the right of reproach for failure to do so. But commitment almost always involves allegiance to a positive goal as well.

What are the psychological processes that might make commitments work? Some possible elements are the following:

1. ALLOCATION OF TIME. Typically people block out at least some of the day's activities; portions of the week may also be allocated, and some longer-time allocations made. When a commitment is made, the decision allocates a new activity to the future. It becomes a part of what the individual expects to do.

2. BINDING OF ALLOCATIONS. Allocations of future activities may be *bound* in varying degrees. By *binding* we mean that certain costs will be incurred if the commitments are broken. Work, school, personal appointments like doctor or dentist, family obligations like cooking dinner or shopping, dates with friends, are obvious examples. These allocations are binding because of the sanctions they carry for failure to keep them. They also carry a sense of obligation, which if violated, creates guilt feelings. Becker (1960) has referred to such 'bindings' as 'side-bets'.

3. FORMATION OF AN ACTION PLAN. The weakest commitment is a mere statement of intention, without an action-plan (for a discussion of action-plans, see Miller, Galanter, and Pribram, 1960; Boden, 1972, 1973). Action-plans consist of the contemplated series of actions by which the individual means to carry out his intention; they may be simple or they may be elaborate schemes consisting of

a series of sub-plans. Most action-plans are much-repeated routines, like getting from place to place or preparing and eating meals. New action-plans are more troublesome—they may have hitches or unforeseen obstacles. Presumably the more complete the action-plan, the more likely it is that the intention or commitment will be carried out. Without the formation of an action-plan, execution may be impossible because many actions require planning or preparation. No action-plan, or an incomplete action-plan, may result in failure to carry out the commitment.

4. BLOCKING OF ALTERNATIVES. Partly carrying through an action plan may eliminate certain competing alternatives from consideration. This may occur because engaging in certain actions excludes the possibility of engaging in others. A college junior who has been majoring in English and who wishes to change his major to pre-medicine usually finds that it is too late, for he failed to take the basic science courses required for pre-medicine.

5. INVESTMENT IN ACTION-PLANS. Often the execution of an action-plan involves a considerable investment of energy, effort, money, and 'self'. To abandon it before reaching the ultimate goal is to lose one's entire investment. Typically one struggles mightily to complete the action plan successfully so as to avoid losing the investment.

An important feature of commitment, then, is the formation of adequate action-plans. Too many commitments, perhaps lack a plan. Like New Year's resolutions, they are vague promises to oneself to change in some way. All too often there is no effort to put them into action, by devising a plan for bringing the changes about. The reasons for this failure are varied: one may lack the requisite knowledge or skill, other competing desires may be stronger, environmental constraints may be too great—one is too busy, other persons make too many demands upon one's time, and so on. A comprehensive action-plan would recognize these difficulties, and contain procedures for overcoming them.

In conclusion, it is only by allowing for such cognitive processes that we can understand how it is possible to make oneself behave, how there can be cases of self-direction and self-intervention. Such phenomena cannot be conceptualized as 'self-reinforcements' which fit the paradigm of operant behavior theory.

REFERENCES

AINSLIE, G. Specious reward: A behavioral theory of impulsiveness and impulse control. *Psychological Bulletin*, 1975, **82**, 463–96.

AXELROD, S., HALL, R. V., WEIS, L., & ROHRER, S. Use of self-imposed contingencies to reduce the frequency of smoking behavior. In M. J. Mahoney & C. E. Thoresen (eds), *Self-control: Power to the person*. Monterey, CA: Brooks/Cole, 1974, 77–85.

AYERS, M. R. *The refutation of determinism: An essay in philosophical logic*. London, Methuen, 1968.

BECKER, H. S. Notes on the concept of commitment. *American Journal of Sociology*, 1960, **66**, 32–40.

BODEN, M. A. *Purposive explanation in psychology*. Cambridge, Mass.: Harvard University Press, 1972.

BODEN, M. A. The structure of intentions. *Journal for the Theory of Social Behavior*, 1973, **3**, 23–46.

BROWN, R., & HERRNSTEIN, R. J. *Psychology*, Boston: Little, Brown, 1975.

CATANIA, A. C. The myth of self-reinforcement. *Behaviorism*, 1975, **3**, 192–99.

HERRNSTEIN, R. J. Action and value in society. Chapter 4 in R. Brown and R. J. Herrnstein, *Psychology*. Boston: Little, Brown, 1975, 163–198.

HARRÉ, R., & SECORD, P. F. *The explanation of social behaviour*, Oxford, England: Basil Blackwell, 1972.

KIESLER, C. A. *The psychology of commitment: Experiments linking behavior to belief*. New York: Academic Press, 1971.

MILLER, G. A., GALANTER, E. A., & PRIBRAM, K. H. *Plans and the structure of behavior*. New York: Holt-Dryden, 1960.

RACHLIN, H. Commitment and self-control. *Behaviorism*, 1974, **2**, 94–107.

RACHLIN, H., & GREEN, L. *Journal of the Experimental Analysis of Behavior*, 1972, **17**, 15–22.

SELIGMAN, M. E. P. *Helplessness: On depression, development, and death*. San Francisco, Cal.: Freeman, 1975.

SKINNER, B. F. *Verbal behavior*. New York: Appleton-Century-Crofts, 1957.

SKINNER, B. F. *Contingencies of reinforcement*. New York: Appleton-Century-Crofts, 1969.

SKINNER, B. F. *About behaviorism*. New York: Knopf, 1974.

STUART, R. B., & DAVIS, B. *Slim chance in a fat world: Behavioral control of obesity*. Champaign, Ill.: Research Press, 1972.

THORESEN, C. E. & MAHONEY, M. J. *Behavioural self-control*: New York: Holt, Rinehart & Winston, 1974.

WATSON, D. L., & THARP, R. G. *Self-directed behavior: Self-modification for personal adjustment.*

10 The Social Looking-Glass: A Sociological Perspective on Self-Development*

GEORGE J. McCALL

I. The Looking-Glass Self

The concept of the social self has played a central role in American social psychology throughout the past eight decades. Indeed, the sociological strain of social psychology has been and remains today literally founded on the principles of self and society sketched out by Charles Horton Cooley (1902) and George Herbert Mead (1934). Even through the dark days of learning-theory hegemony, the psychological variety of social psychology made extensive use of the ideas of self introduced by William James (1890) and James Mark Baldwin (1897), through the sometimes courageous stands of men like Gordon Allport (1943).

The notions of self, others, and social interaction developed by these figures varied significantly in thrust and detail, to be sure. Yet all represent elaborations of basic views developed by the Scottish moral philosophers, particularly Adam Smith (1759) and David Hume (1751), concerning social and moral consequences of the Kantian duality of self as the knower and the known, subject and object of consciousness. This reflexiveness of mind—the ability to see oneself as he sees others, to become an object to oneself much like other persons—is the core of the concept of self.

The Scottish moralists and the early American philosopher-psychologists added one important dimension to this core property, *viz.*, that the central means through which a person sees himself is in the reactions of others to himself. Making capital of the common etymology of *reflexion* and *reflection*, Smith and Cooley in particular relied heavily on the metaphor that the reactions of others are a

* Prepared, in part, through support as Visiting Scientist, Center for Studies of Crime and Delinquency, National Institute of Mental Health

mirror held up to a person, reflecting an image of self which he might appraise in much the same fashion as he would appraise another person seen directly. Cooley called this social self 'the reflected or looking-glass self' and said:

> A self-idea of this sort seems to have three principal elements: the imagination of our appearance to the other person; the imagination of his judgment of that appearance; and some sort of self-feeling, such as pride or mortification. The comparison with a looking-glass hardly suggests the second element, the imagined judgment, which is quite essential. The thing that moves us to pride or shame is not the mere mechanical reflection of ourselves, but an imputed sentiment, the imagined effect of this imagination upon another's mind.... We always imagine, and in imagining share, the judgments of the other mind. (Cooley, 1902, pp. 184–185)

From this metaphor derive many of the most familiar terms of social psychology—self-image, self-concept, self-appraisal, and terms for various feelings of self-worth (e.g., self-esteem).

In the principle of the 'looking-glass self', in the ability of the person to see himself through the reactions of others and thus to appraise and react to himself as an object like other persons, these early theorists felt they had identified the basis at once for disciplined thought-process, coordination of individual lines of action, and an objective moral order. The sociologist Robert E. Park, drawing on ideas formulated by Mead, held that human conduct must be distinguished from behavior that is merely reflexive, instinctive or habitual. Conduct is 'that form of behavior we expect in man when he is conscious of the comment that other men are making, or are likely to make, upon his actions' (Park, 1931, p. 36). As a result

> ... the individual in society lives a more or less public existence, in which all his acts are anticipated, checked, inhibited, or modified by the gestures and intentions of his fellows. It is in this social conflict, in which every individual lives more or less in the mind of every other individual, that human nature and the individual may acquire their most characteristic and human traits. (Park, 1927, p. 738) ... [Moreover] a new and more intimate type of solidarity is made possible; a solidarity which enables societies to coordinate

> and direct the acts of their individual components in accordance with the interests and purposes of the society as a whole,... a more intimate form of association based on communication, consensus, and custom. (Park, 1939, p. 21)

Over the intervening decades, the guiding ideas of the 'looking-glass self' social psychology have been sustained through extensive research on role-taking ability (e.g., Stryker, 1957; Dymond, 1949; Piaget, 1932) and on the dependency of self-conceptions on the reactions of others (e.g., Videbeck, 1960; Backman and Secord, 1962; Quarantelli and Cooper, 1966). The force of this social psychology is still manifest, both in theory (e.g., reference-group theory, social comparison theory) and in practice (e.g., the widespread use of role-playing and videotape self-confrontation techniques to increase role-taking ability).

II. Identities and Choices

Contemporary theoretical accounts of the social self, particularly in sociological social psychology, are frequently framed in the dramaturgical model sketched by Park in the following way:

> One thing that distinguishes man from the lower animals is the fact that he has a conception of himself, and once he has defined his role he strives to live up to it.... Being actors, we are consciously or unconsciously seeking recognition, and failure to win it is, at the very least, a depressing, often a heartbreaking, experience. This is one of the reasons why we all eventually conform to the accepted models and conceive ourselves in some one or other of the conventional patterns.
>
> The consequence of this, however, is that we inevitably lead a dual existence. We have a private and a public life. In seeking to live up to the role which we have assumed, and which society has imposed upon us, we find ourselves in a constant conflict with ourselves. Instead of acting simply and naturally, as a child,... we seek to conform to accepted models.... In our efforts to conform, we restrain our immediate and spontaneous impulses, and act, not as we are impelled to act, but rather as seems appropriate and proper to the occasion.

> Under these circumstances our manners, our polite speeches and gestures, our conventional and proper behavior, assume the character of a mask. . . . In a sense, and in so far as this mask represents the conception we have formed of ourselves, the role we are striving to live up to, this mask is our 'truer self', the self we would like to be. So, at any rate, our mask become at last an integral part of our personality; becomes second nature. (Park, 1927, pp. 738–39)

Erving Goffman (1957), for example, distinguishes three analytically separable aspects of self—self as performer, self as audience to that performer, and self as the character performed. The first two aspects correspond, respectively, to the 'I' and the 'me' in Mead's (1934) classic formulation of the twin aspects of self. What the dramaturgical model of self adds to the classical model is a critical recognition of the conventionalizing influence of the social looking-glass. By taking the attitude of the other toward himself, the behavior of an organism becomes the conduct of a person—a sophisticated performance, as in theater, calculated to create a proper impression. The individual strives to appear a person proper and appropriate to his role and to the social situation. If this implication of the looking-glass idea is valid, a person's conduct cannot be correctly understood without taking due account of the character (mask, persona) he is seeking to sustain.

The notion of *identity* relates to the notion of self not so much in the aspects of self as performer or as audience but in the aspect of self as character. Identity is closely related to an answer to the question, 'Who am I?', and when people are asked this question, they have been found to answer preponderantly in terms of social positions they occupy (or aspire to occupy) or in terms of social roles they perform (or aspire to perform) (Kuhn and McPartland, 1954). That is, when asked to identify themselves, people name their masks (characters, personas). Since a person occupies a number of social positions and performs a number of social roles, especially in modern societies, it follows that he would have a number of social identities (masks, characters). Indeed, when asked to make twenty separate answers to the question, 'Who am I?', virtually every responding subject named a substantial number of masks; many, in fact, named twenty different masks (Kuhn and MacPartland, 1954; Kuhn, 1960).

Despite plural identities, most persons sustain some subjective sense of (and display some objective evidence for) an important degree of personal integrity, of personal continuity across situations (James, 1890). This represents a second, 'personal' sense of identity and poses a theoretical problem for self-theory of this type. The device generally posited is some sort of dynamic, hierarchically organized system of social identities as the core structure of a person (McCall and Simmons, 1966; Stryker, 1964; Turner, 1970).

One integrating principle in such identity-sets that helps to sustain personal integrity and continuity is that persons importantly adapt each mask to their other masks in a sort of contextual effect. That is, a mask has not only a name but also semantic content; that content is largely conventional and consensual but importantly permits considerable idiolectical variation. Since performers vary in their fitness to perform a given role and, in pluralistic societies, perform this role before disparate audiences, they see themselves through somewhat different mirrors and thus conceive the character in somewhat different fashions (Strauss, 1958). Given this flex in any particular mask, the individual is thought to bend each of his masks a bit to achieve some better fit among them as a set adapted to his own performer characteristics and his own set of audiences.

A rather elaborated account of these processes is presented in some of my previous work (e.g., McCall and Simmons, 1966). There, an adapted mask is referred to as a *role-identity*, the person's imaginative view of himself as he likes to think of himself being and acting as an occupant of a particular social position. The individual's set of role-identities is seen as organized through a joint function of two interdynamic hierarchical principles—the prominence and the salience of his various role-identities.

The prominence of a given role-identity in an individual's thinking about himself is thought to be determined by a weighted average of average past levels of several types of reinforcement for its performance. These include his commitment to and investment in that identity, the extrinsic and intrinsic gratifications earned through performance of that identity, and the degree to which his performances have been judged by himself and others to have fully sustained and confirmed the semantic content of that role-identity. (This last factor will hereafter be referred to as 'quantity of role-support', except that on occasion it is necessary to differentiate 'self-support' and 'social support' of a role-identity.) The slow-changing prominence hierarchy of role-identities corresponds to what some have called the 'ideal self' and makes possible some sense of personal integrity and continuity.

The salience of a role-identity to the person, on the other hand, may change from moment to moment, in close interdependence with his performance. Salience of a given role-identity is taken to be a resultant of several factors—its prominence, the degree to which it is currently deficient in role-support, the person's need or desire for the kinds and amounts of intrinsic and extrinsic gratifications ordinarily gained through its performance, and the perceived degree of opportunity for its profitable enactment in the current situation. The salience hierarchy of role-identities (or 'situational self') represents their relative order of priority as potential sources of performance in the situation.

The concept of *choice*, like that of identity, is entailed in the ideas of the social looking-glass. Of course, organisms without selves may in some sense be said to choose, as among bowls of food, but it is doubtful that they may be said to make choices. Making choices (or, better, *decisions*) seems bound up with the socialized intelligence derived from the social looking-glass. But even if, say, rats were taken to make choices, as between running a maze or running an exercise wheel, I imagine that most serious men would take the choice to be made only on the basis of the relative expected utilities of the alternatives in terms of simple intrinsic and extrinsic gratifications. In the case of persons making decisions, however, self theories of the type described here give explicit and important place to an additional calculus of value, i.e., the need for role-support (McCall and Simmons, 1966). (*Cf.* the treatment of action intended to obtain role-support in Goldman, 1970, pp. 56–63 and pp. 104–9.)

Self, in the sense of personal identity, is most profoundly revealed (if not discovered) in the context of moral decision. The salience hierarchy, shaped in good part by immediate needs and pressures, may incline the performer toward a certain line of conduct. In the capacity of audience to his own performance, the person may judge that conduct to be discrepant with his prominence hierarchy, to be inconsistent with the sort of person he likes to think of himself as being. 'My fellow patrolman might think me foolish not to take home some of this recovered loot, but what would my family think of me? I shouldn't want to take the stuff'. Self-awareness through the anticipated reactions of various audiences thus facilitates self-control, and the variable success of self-control efforts importantly indicates to the individual what sort of person he really is.

III. Research on Identity and Choice

We have touched on two senses of identity in relation to the self: (1) social identity (mask, character), framed in terms of response to the question, 'Who am I?' and ultimately glassed as *role-identity;* (2) personal identity, framed in terms of personal integrity and continuity across role-performances, and glossed as the person's adaptively organized *prominence hierarchy* of role-identities.

The two senses of identity have been importantly cross-cut by a distinction between cognitive self-appraisal and judgmental self-appraisal. Sociological social psychologists seem to have focused on the more cognitive aspects of identity, i.e., what it is that a person believes he is supposed to be like. Such cognitive notions of identity are employed to understand and interpret relatively long-term patterns of free interaction in everyday life—patterns such as encounters (Weinstein and Deutschberger, 1964; M. M. McCall, 1970), relationships (G. J. McCall, 1970, 1974), family dynamics (Stryker, 1964; Turner, 1970), and careers (McCall and Simmons, 1966). Such interaction patterns, of course, represent patterns of important choices among activities, among persons, among structural roles, and among alternative allocations of life-resources.

In the psychological tradition, on the other hand, primarily judgmental notions of identity (i.e., how worthy the person feels himself to be) are used to explain the impact of evaluations by others on performance and attitudes, particularly affective preferences regarding the evaluators (Shrauger, 1975; Wilson, 1965; Jones, 1966, 1968). Identity terms most commonly employed in this tradition are 'self-esteem' and 'aspiration level' or 'performance-expectancy'.

While choice, as such, has rarely been the central focus in most of this work, one recent line of research does take the relations betwen identity and choice as its explicit focus. *Situated identity analysis* (Alexander and Knight, 1971; Alexander and Sagatun, 1973; Alexander and Epstein, 1969), which represents a convergence of the sociological and psychological strains in social psychology, attempts to explain the choice behaviors of subjects in the constrained opportunity-structures of laboratory settings by reference to the implications of available alternative actions for subjects' identities. The core idea of situated identity analysis is that

> ... when a person acts, he communicates information about the kind of person he presumes to be and obliges others to regard him as being that kind of person. In Mead's terminology, behaviors are 'constituted' into action, because they have implications for the creation, affirmation, or transformation of an actor's situated identity. The social situation is conceptualized, from an actor's perspective, as a range of possible identities entailed by the behavioral alternatives he confronts ... (B)ehavior can be predicted if the situated identity that results from the choice of one action is more socially desirable than those associated with alternative actions.... (Alexander and Knight, 1971, p. 66).

In an impressive series of empirical investigations, classic patterns of results from a range of established experimental situations have been successfully explained as being a function of situated identities, rather than of the putative efficacy of the manipulated independent variables.

The attempt to explain experimental behavior in terms of the situated identities associated with alternative responses also receives some support from research on facework—the tactics of saving face or personal identity. Following the sociological studies of Goffman (1955) and Gross and Stone (1964) on facework and embarrassment, several psychological experiments (Modigliani, 1968; Brown, 1968, 1970; Archibald and Cohen, 1971; Blumstein, 1973) have shown that subjects will knowingly pay a very high price, in intrinsic and extrinsic rewards forgone, in order to maintain face or identity despite experimenter demands.

A related line of research is represented by Heise's (unpublished) control-system theory of attitudes and action, derived from Meadian social psychology and subject-verb-object (*SVO*) models of attitude dynamics (Gollob, 1968, 1974; Heise, 1969). Heise is concerned not only with the implications of choice for identity (i.e., 'What kind of person (*S*) would perform act *V* toward a person of social identity *O*?'), but also with the implications of identity for choice (i.e., 'What kind of act (V) would a person of social identity *S* perform toward a person of social identity *O*?'). Based solely on independent, aggregate attitudes toward several hundred social identities and toward several hundred social acts, Heise's control-system equations predict answers to these two questions with rather surprising success.

Recent research along these lines provides more direct empirical support for the self-theory contention that identity and choice are mutually entailed in conduct and in self-appraisal.

IV. *Self-Development and Its Failures*

Self-control is made possible through awareness (in the form of anticipations of the reactions of various audiences) of the identity-implications of behavioral choices. Accounts of the development of self-awareness and self-control—i.e., of the emergence of ability to take the role of another toward oneself—have long been generally familiar (e.g., Mead, 1934; Piaget, 1932; McCall and Simmons, 1966). Correlative accounts of the *failure* of self-control have been relatively neglected within the social looking-glass tradition, but the few exceptions have principally focused on inaccuracies in role-taking emerging from various structural constraints on the role-taker's relationships with relevant audiences (e.g., Stryker, 1957).

An alternative account of the triumphs of impulse over socialized conduct, however, does not require the uniform assumption that such triumphs of impulse represent failures of either self-control or self-development. In a provocative article, which develops the concept of the 'propriateness of self' emphasized by James, Cooley and Allport, Ralph H. Turner (1976) argues that 'among the various feelings and actions that emanate from my person' I distinguish those which are 'expressions of my real self' from those which 'seem foreign to the real me' so that I take little credit or blame for them (1976, p. 989). Thus:

> To one person, an angry outburst or the excitement of extra-martial desire comes as an alien impulse that superficially beclouds or even dangerously threatens the true self. The experience is real enough and may even be persistent and gratifying, but it is still not felt as signifying the real self. The true self is recognized in acts of volition, in the pursuit of institutionalized goals, and not in the satisfaction of impulses outside institutional frameworks.

To another person, the outburst or desire is recognized—fearfully or enthusiastically—as an indication that the real self is breaking through a deceptive crust of institutional behavior. Institutional motivations are external, artificial constraints and superimpositions that bridle manifestations of the true self... [which] consists of deep, unsocialized, inner impulses.

To varying degrees, people accept as evidence of their real selves either feelings or actions with an *institutional* focus or ones they identify as strictly *impulse*. (Turner, 1976, pp. 990, 991–9)

In this formulation, the identity-implications of feelings and actions are still seen as controlling, but the self-conception is not required to be lodged in the institutional nexus. Rather, some persons predominantly (and perhaps all persons to some degree) conceive the kind of person they are, or want to be, not so much in terms of social roles as in terms of other, non-institutionalized modes of action and feeling (e.g., as a 'free spirit' or 'soul wanderer').

If impulse as well as institution is thus considered a locus of self-appraisal, the notion of self-development takes on a somewhat different cast, stressing that the individual 'develops at least a vague conception by which he recognizes some of his feelings and actions' (Turner, 1976, p. 1011). Some of the key differences in criteria for self-appraisal corresponding to the institutional and impulse loci of self are summarized in Table 1.

The complex dynamics of self envisioned in micro-sociological theories depend only on the fact that the individual employs criteria for self-appraisal, not on the content of those criteria. Theories emphasizing the *social* looking-glass assert the overriding importance of the criteria associated with the institutional locus of self. If, however—as Turner suggests but others might deny—the past two decades have witnessed an erosion of institutional locus and a rise in impulse locus, such sociological theories of self will need some revision to illuminate the more contemporary relations between individual impulse and the institutional order.

Table 1.
Criteria for Self-Appraisal Associated with Institutional and Impulse Loci of Self (adapted from Turner, 1976)

	Institution Locus	*Impulse Locus*
Real self is revealed when the person:	Adheres to a high standard, especially in the face of serious temptation.	Does something not because it is good, etc., but because he spontaneously wants to.
Real self is something:	To be attained, created, achieved.	To be discovered.
Real self is revealed:	Only when the person is in full control of his faculties and behaviors.	Only when inhibitions are lowered or abandoned.
Hypocrisy consists of:	Failing to live up to one's standards.	Asserting standards and adhering to them even if the behavior is not what one wants to do and enjoys doing.
An admired performance is:	A polished, error-free one in which audience forgets the actor and sees only the role played.	An imperfect one which reveals the actor's human frailties.
Time perspective emphasizes:	Future; making commitments.	Present; freedom from past commitments.
Individual integrity is threatened by:	Social pressures on the side of mediocrity and abandonment of principle.	Social pressures in league with a system of arbitrary rules and false goals.
Social structure is viewed as:	Values.	Arbitrary and restrictive norms.

REFERENCES

Alexander, C. N., and Epstein, J. Problems of dispositional inference in person perception research. *Sociometry*, 1969, **32**: 381–95.

Alexander, C. N., and Knight, G. W. Situated identities and social psychological experimentation. *Sociometry*, 1971, **34**: 65–82.

ALEXANDER, C. N., and SAGATUN, I. An attributional analysis of experimental norms. *Sociometry*, 1973, **36**: 127–42.

ALLPORT, G. W. The ego in contemporary psychology. *Psychological Bulletin*, 1943, **50**: 451–78.

ARCHIBALD, W. P., and COHEN, R. L. Self-presentation, embarrassment, and facework as a function of self-evaluation, conditions of self-presentation, and feedback from others. *Journal of Personality and Social Psychology*, 1971, **20**: 287–97.

BACKMAN, C. W., and SECORD, P. F. Liking, selective interaction, and misperception in congruent interpersonal relationships. *Sociometry*, 1962, **25**: 321–35.

BALDWIN, J. M. *Social and Ethical Interpretations in Mental Development*. New York: Macmillan: 1897.

BLUMSTEIN, P. W. Audience, Machiavellianism, and tactics of identity bargaining. *Sociometry*, 1973, **36**: 346–65.

BROWN, B. R. The effects of need to maintain face on interpersonal bargaining. *Journal of Experimental Social Psychology*, 1968, **4**: 107–22.

BROWN, B. R. Face-saving following experimentally induced embarrassment. *Journal of Experimental Social Psychology*, 1970, **6**: 225–71.

COOLEY, C. H. *Human Nature and the Social Order*. New York: Scribner's, 1902.

DYMOND, R. F. A scale for the measurement of empathic ability. *Journal of Consulting Psychology*, 1949, **13**: 127–33.

GOFFMAN, E. On face-work: an analysis of ritual elements in social interaction. *Psychiatry*, 1955, **18**: 213–31.

GOFFMAN, E. *The Presentation of Self in Everyday Life*. Garden City, N.Y.: Doubleday, 1957.

GOLDMAN, A. I. *A Theory of Human Action*. Englewood Cliffs, N.J.: Prentice-Hall, 1970.

GOLLOB, H. F. Impression formation and word combination in sentences. *Journal of Personality and Social Psychology*, 1968, **10**: 341–353.

GOLLOB, H. F. The subject-verb-object approach to social cognition. *Psychological Review*, 1974, **81**: 286–321.

GROSS, E., and STONE, G. P. Embarrassment and the analysis of role requirements. *American Journal of Sociology*, 1964, **70**: 1–15.

HEISE, D. R. Affective dynamics in simple sentences. *Journal of Personality and Social Psychology*, 1969, **11**: 204–13.

HEISE, D. R. Attitudes, expectations, and social action: recent and planned research. Unpublished manuscript.

HUME, D. *An Enquiry Concerning the Principles of Morals*. London: A. Millar, 1751.

James, W. *Principles of Psychology*. New York: Holt, 1890.

Jones, S. C. Some determinants of interpersonal evaluating behavior. *Journal of Personality and Social Psychology*, 1966, **3**: 397–403.

Jones, S. C. Expectation, performance, and the anticipation of self-revealing events. *Journal of Social Psychology*, 1968, **74**: 189–97.

Kuhn, M. H. Self attitudes by age, sex, and professional training. *Sociological Quarterly*, 1960, **1**: 39–55.

Kuhn, M. H., and McPartland, T. S. An empirical investigation of self-attitudes. *American Sociological Review*, 1954, **19**: 68–76.

McCall, G. J. The social organization of relationships. In G. J. McCall (ed.), *Social Relationships*. Chicago: Aldine, 1970. Pp. 3–34.

McCall, G. J. Asymbolic interactionist approach to attraction. In T. Huston (ed.), *Foundations of Interpersonal Attraction*. New York: Academic Press, 1974. Pp. 217–231.

McCall, G. J., and Simmons, J. L. *Identities and Interactions*. New York: Free Press, 1966.

McCall, M. M. Boundary rules in relationships and encounters. In G. J. McCall (ed.), *Social Relationships*. Chicago: Aldine, 1970. Pp. 35–61.

Mead, G. H. *Mind, Self, and Society*. Chicago: University of Chicago Press, 1934.

Modigliani, A. Embarrassment and embarrassability. *Sociometry*, 1968, **31**: 313–26.

Park, R. E. Human nature and collective behavior. *American Journal of Sociology*, 1927, **32**: 733–41.

Park, R. E. Human nature, attitudes, and mores. In K. Young (ed.), *Social Attitudes*. New York: Holt, 1931. Pp. 17–45.

Park, R. E. Symbiosis and socialization: a frame of reference for the study of society. *American Journal of Sociology*, 1939, **45**: 1–25.

Piaget, J. *The Moral Judgment of the Child*. New York: Harcourt, Brace, & World, 1932.

Quarantelli, E., and Cooper, J. Self-conceptions and others: a further test of Meadian hypotheses. *Sociological Quarterly*, 1966, **7**: 281–97.

Shrauger, J. S. Responses to evaluation as a function of initial self-perceptions. *Psychological Bulletin*, 1975, **82**: 581–96.

Smith, A. *The Theory of Moral Sentiments*. London: A. Millar, 1759.

Strauss, A. L. *Mirrors and Masks*. New York: Free Press, 1958.

Stryker, S. Role-taking accuracy and adjustment. *Sociometry*, 1957, **20**: 286–96.

Stryker, S. The interactional and situational approaches. In H. T. Christensen (ed.), *Handbook of Marriage and the Family*. Chicago: Rand McNally, 1964. Pp. 125–70.

Turner, R. H. *Family Interaction*. New York: Wiley, 1970.

Turner, R. H. The real self: from institution to impulse. *American Journal of Sociology*, 1976, **81**: 989–1016.

Videbeck, R. Self-conception and the reactions of others. *Sociometry*, 1960, **23**: 351–59.

Weinstein, E. A., and Deutschberger, P. Tasks, bargains, and identities in social interaction. *Social Forces*, 1964, **42**: 451–56.

Wilson, D. T. Ability evaluation, postdecision dissonance, and co-worker attractiveness. *Journal of Personality and Social Psychology*, 1965, **1**: 486–89.

PART V The Meanings of 'Self' and the Multiplicity of Selves

11 Self-Knowledge and Knowledge of the 'Self'

STEPHEN E. TOULMIN

I

In evaluating the role (or roles) of the term 'self' within psychology we cannot afford to limit our attention to technical uses of the term while ignoring its more familiar, pre-scientific meaning and implications. Even within psychology—as we shall see in this paper—the term has at least two distinct *kinds* of technical senses. These have branched off from the every day, pre-scientific sense at different points and in different directions, and a good deal hangs on the differences between them. In clarifying the goals of any 'psychology of the self', we should therefore begin by acknowledging the existence of three distinguishable concepts of *self*, or uses of the term 'self'—

(1) 'self-' and '-self', treated as reflexive, auxiliary prefixes or postfixes in everyday colloquial language;
(2) 'self', treated as the name of a hypothetical entity, or intervening explanatory variable, in speculative psychological theories; and
(3) 'self', treated as a diagnostic term, in clinical psychotherapy and comparable, non-medical modes of psychological description.

—and go on to consider the relations between these three concepts. Specifically, we shall need to see how the second and third, which correspond to two distinct ways of using the independent free-standing noun 'self', respectively connect up with the first, in which the word 'self' figures as one part of a number of compound words: i.e. how (2) the hypothetical-explanatory concept of *self* in theoretical psychology, and (3) the diagnostic-descriptive concept of *self* in clinical psychology, respectively arise out of and connect up with (1) everyday perceptions of reflexive human activity and attitudes, as involving (e.g.) 'self-awareness', 'self-understanding' and/or 'self-control'.

At the outset, we must be clear about the differences between the two psychological concepts of *self*. In terms of concept (2), our knowledge of the existence and attributes of the 'self' is like our knowledge of the existence and attributes of any novel theoretical entity: i.e. it is an intellectual kind of knowledge, based on the abstract theoretical interpretation of human behavior, viewed as a general collection of phenomena. We have to establish the presence in those phenomena of regularities demanding explanation in terms of such an 'entity', and providing evidence of its 'existence', as was done in physics (say) in the case of radio waves and electrons. In terms of concept (3), by contrast, our knowledge of the 'self' is a practical, personal kind of knowledge, based on direct experience of, and interaction with, specific human beings. This kind of descriptive clinical understanding is not strictly intellectual, let alone merely cognitive. It is not arrived at as a result of the psychologist *distancing himself from* the human agents he is studying, and treating their acts as neutral phenomena, to be observed (as it were) from behind a 'blind': on the contrary, the clinical psychologist arrives at his understanding precisely as a result of *interacting with* his subjects.

What, indeed, would it be like to regard human conduct as a 'natural phenomenon', in the strict sense of that phrase? To begin with, it would involve treating that conduct as an entirely *non-responsive* object of study, which cannot be substantially affected by interaction with the observer-like the fall of a rock or the movement of a planet. This is the method of study we adopt quite naturally and properly in the case of 'things'.

When scientists deal with totally insensate objects, they can deal with them in an entirely 'unfeeling' way. It makes no realistic difference to an astronomer's expectations about the movements of (say) a binary star whether or not he feels any emotional involvement in them, since there is no conceivable way in which the star could reciprocate those feelings and modify its behavior in response to them. In this respect, physics and its related sciences are based on a *systematic abstraction of the cognitive*—which Goethe and Blake passionately condemned, even so. In other fields of study, however, this method of investigation may be even less appropriate, let alone exhaustive. It is highly doubtful, for instance, whether recent advances in our understanding of the mental capacities of chimpanzees could have been achieved by investigators whose methods of study were systematically abstract and cognitive; while a psychology that interprets human interactions as 'natural phenomena', entirely on a par with the movements of binary stars, can fairly be charged with the sin of 'mechanomorphism'—i.e. the converse of 'anthropomorphism'.

Our practical understanding of individual human beings is, in fact, arrived at in ways that are far from being purely 'cognitive'. Thus, a young child begins to develop his capacities for such practical understanding by interacting with other human beings: initially, his mother, later his father, siblings and others. The interaction within which he learns to 'read' the feelings and motives of others are not merely the cognitive operations of a detached observer: rather, they involve communicative exchanges and joint activities with family and friends, of kinds that are quite as much 'affective' and 'volitional' as 'cognitive'. In this way, the child comes to recognize what he can expect of other human beings; and this 'expecting of' goes far beyond any simple predictive 'expecting that' they will behave in one way rather than another. (What we *expect of* the loving parent or loyal colleague is what we may confidently hope for, and rely on in our own actions, not just what we may correctly predict.)

If we distinguish between 'knowledge of phenomena' and 'knowledge of persons' in these terms, how then are these two kinds of knowledge related, and which of the two provides the better analogy for the self-knowledge at which we aim, in the everyday sense (1)? The narrowly 'cognitive' or 'conceptual' type of knowledge is—evidently—a special and somewhat artificial case, which has been developed only over the last three hundred years, precisely as a means of organizing and accounting for our experience of the non-responsive 'objects' studied in the natural sciences; but it has only a limited relevance to the understanding of human conduct, human interactions, and specifically of human self-awareness.

Human beings normally deal with one another in ways that engage their entire personalities without regard to abstract distinctions between 'cognition', 'affect' and the rest. It takes a quite deliberate act of 'witholding oneself' for any human agent to view (form expectations about/deal with) another human agent in an entirely 'unfeeling' manner—strictly, as a 'thing'—and to avoid investing any emotion, or practical trust whatever in that other human being's response. And there is much that we can learn about our fellow-humans, only in the context of those normal, *un*detached interactions and dealings, within which our 'expectations' of one another embrace the full complex of predictive belief, hope and trust alike.

It remains to be seen just how far we can hope to arrive at a satisfactory 'psychology of the self' by choosing to take the 'objective' route first—i.e. by treating all human behavior as a 'natural phenomenon'—and then seeking to reintroduce, subsequently, the elements that are abstracted out by that initial choice. Certainly, this is not the route taken by most clinically-oriented psychologists, least of all by psychoanalytically-oriented clinicians. Nor is it a program that provides a very helpful first step for arriving at an understanding of 'self-knowledge', in the colloquial, auxiliary sense (1) of that phrase. Our everyday self-knowledge is not the intellectual product of detached self-observation alone: as though I set out to keep quasi-astronomical records of my own performances and to develop the cognitive skills required in order to predict, by extrapolation, what it may be 'expected that' I would do next! Rather, we learn what we can 'expect of' ourselves in a practical way, through living reflectively and so critically, and seeing what we can reasonably and desirably try 'to make of our lives'. Self-knowledge in this sense is a product both of self-study and of self-creation. The question, 'What should I expect of myself?', is not a narrowly cognitive or intellectual (i.e. predictive) question: it is an affective-volitional question, to be paraphrased as, 'What should I *hope for* and/or *demand of* myself?'

In this respect—as we shall see—the initial link between knowledge of the 'self' in the everyday sense (1) and in the clinical sense (3) is closer than the link between sense (1) and the abstract, theoretical sense (2). Clinical understanding of the development of the 'self' carries further, in sophisticated technical ways, the kind of practical understanding we acquire—whether of other people or of ourselves—in our everyday dealings with them. So, the terminology of the 'self' in clinical psychotherapy remains—as we may put it—the language of psychic integration and autonomy; and the broader intellectual tasks facing psychological theories about the development of the self are those of unraveling, and accounting for,

(1) the typical ontogenetic sequences by which a human infant, child or adult comes to achieve the kinds and degrees of integration and autonomy he does; and
(2) the different types of vicissitudes as a result of which this achievement of integration and autonomy is liable to be distorted, limited, or entirely frustrated.

It would be a mistake to suppose that, even on the level of general clinical theory, the corresponding uses of the term imply claims about the existence or non-existence of some hypothetical, explanatory entity (the *self*) which functions as an 'intervening variable' in the traditional sense. Such clinical theories begin, in fact, at a point where the meaningfulness and applicability of the term 'self' are already beyond doubt, and the question of 'existence', as such, does not arise. Instead of being distracted by the speculative issue of 'existence', we shall therefore do better to consider how this clinical language reapplies, and extends, the everyday terminology of the 'self': i.e. the uses of the term in the context of such reflexive phrases as 'self-command', 'self-control', and/or 'self-understanding'—uses which entail no speculative empirical claims about any hitherto-unknown theoretical entity, to be called the 'self'.

The colloquial currency of reflexive idioms embodying the terminations, 'self-' and '-self', may not by itself validate (or give a sense to) any uses of the freestanding noun, 'self'. Still, such idioms do provide a solid base from which, *by extension of meaning*, we can move in directions that can subsequently give a sense to that freestanding noun. The problem is to get clear about the question of just what such extensions of meaning do, and do not, imply.

II

Consider the everyday, idiomatic uses of the term 'self'; or, to be more exact, the everyday, idiomatic uses of the prefix 'self-' and the postfix '-self'. Digesting the rich complexities in the seventeen columns of the Oxford English Dictionary entry for the word 'self', and the further forty columns of derivative compound words, ranging from 'self-abased' to 'self-yew', we can begin with some first, rough generalisataions.

In their primary senses, the terms 'self-' and '-self' figure not as separate, freestanding nouns, but as reflexive, auxiliary *parts* of compound nouns and/or verbs, adjectives and/or adverbs: *viz.* 'myself' or 'self-confident', rather than the supposed noun, 'self', standing alone—or, as we would say, 'by itself'. Etymologically, the term is the English representative of a wider family of prefixes, terminations, reduplications, etc., embracing also the German *selbst*, the Latin *se-* and *-se* (cf., *ipse*), and the French third-person pronoun *se* (cf., *il se dit* = he says to himself). Functionally, the English 'self-' is also homologous to such familiar forms as the Greek *auto-*, which similarly marks off reflexive actions, attitudes, etc. (An 'autobiography' is a *self*-biography.)

In their detailed usages, the different European languages display no universal pattern or consistency in their use of 'self' idioms. Set the standard English forms alongside corresponding forms in other European languages, and you will find many alternative words, some of them derived from quite other roots—meaning (e.g.) such things as 'own', 'same', or even 'me/my, you/your, he/his' etc.—others indicating reflexiveness by the use of a reduplicative form, as with the Greek *seautos* (= 'he himself'). However, this seeming looseness does not affect the colloquial meanings of these idioms since, in their primary contexts, nothing stands or falls on our ability to treat 'self' as a freestanding noun.

Consider, (e.g.) the English forms of reflexive personal pronoun. At first glance, we might be tempted to construe the first and second-person forms, 'myself' and 'yourself', as compound words uniting the possessives 'my' and 'your' to a hypothetical noun, 'self', naming some independent entity; which would make these forms equivalent to 'my self' and 'your self'. By contrast, the third-person singular masculine form, 'himself', apparently combines the accusative pronoun 'him' with a reflexive termination, '-self', strictly comparable to the French *-même*, meaning 'same', to yield a compound meaning 'him-same'.[1] Matters become even more confused when we note the complementary dialect forms, 'meself' and 'hisself', which are entirely interchangeable with the standard forms in practice, although they reverse the apparent metaphysical over-

[1] This prompts the question, whether the English word 'selfsame' may not be, in effect, merely an intensive reduplication, equivalent to 'same-same'.

tones—'me-same' and 'his self'. Indeed, the sole effective ground for preferring the standard forms is probably euphony: the words 'myself' and 'himself' *sound* better than 'meself' and 'hisself'. Similar considerations are probably responsible for eliminating the grammatically possible French forms, *me-même* and *mon-même*, as words for 'myself', in favor of the current standard form, *moi-même*.

In French, the reflexive personal pronouns are formed on quite a different pattern. Thus, the compounds *moi-même* and *soi-même* (lit., 'to-me-same' and 'to-one-same') are formed from *moi* and *soi* by adding the French word for 'same' as a termination, and so contain no element corresponding exactly to the English '-self'. They therefore provide no ostensible basis for postulating the existence of an independent *self*; as a result, the philosophical issues lumped together, in English, as 'the problem of the *self*', present themselves to French-speaking thinkers in quite different terms, and with quite a different classification. The problem of the self is no longer the problem of the *même*: rather, it is the problem of the *moi* or the *soi*. It is as though the forms 'myself' and 'oneself' prompted English philosophers to raise the problem of the 'my' or the 'one', not the 'self'. Given this different starting-point, French philosophers also continue their analysis along different lines. Having raised the issue in terms of personal pronouns which posses a variety of cases, rather than in terms of a case-neutral 'self', they are led to postulate alternative entities (different 'selves') corresponding to the different cases of the pronoun: e.g. the nominative, *je*, and the dative, *moi*. So, one very early step in French discussions of the self is to question the relations between the *je* and the *moi*—i.e., between one supposed 'self', which serves as the essential agent (*je*), and another supposed 'self', which serves as the essential patient (*moi*).

Such examples could, no doubt, be multiplied. If the philosophical issues about the 'self' appear so different in French and in English, imagine what we might find if we compared the standard English 'self-' and '-self' idioms with their conterparts in (say) Basque or Japanese. The variety and heterogeneity of these linguistic idioms, of course, establishes no positive conclusions about the nature of the 'self', but it may warn us against jumping to conclusions: against moving with unguarded speed, for instance, from the superficial appearance of words like 'myself' (? = 'my self') to any philosophical conclusion whatever. There is a serious risk that drawing such conclusions may represent no more than a play upon words.

For, given only the evidence of idiomatic forms such as *moi-même*, we could equally well have postulated a distinct and intelligible 'same'![2]

One other point of English grammar also deserves attention at the outset. The available forms of our indicative verbs display a basic contrast between the two *voices*, active and passive. Yet, this division is neither inescapable nor universal, as any student of classical Greek knows. Ancient Greek had in fact not two, but three voices: active, passive and middle. Thus, there were classical Greek verb-forms equivalent in most contexts to our familiar active and passive forms (as in the sentences 'Plato struck/contradicted/shaved Aristotle', and 'Plato was struck/contradicted/shaved by Aristotle'); but, in addition, the Greeks employed a third, distinct set of verb-forms for reflexive actions, attitudes etc. These are translatable into current English only by the addition of our auxiliary pronouns, e.g. 'myself' and 'himself', as in 'Plato struck/contradicted/shaved himself'. By using the middle voice, the Greeks absorbed many of the auxiliary functions of the English 'self-' and '-self' forms *directly into the verb*. It was as though, instead of 'Plato struck/contradicted/shaved himself', modern English-speakers were to say 'Plato sestruck/secontradicted/seshaved'.

Once again, of course, these grammatical facts do not by themselves *prove* anything about the nature, existence and/or status of an independent, autonomous, more-or-less coherent 'self', nor about the role of any such entity in human action. But, by recognizing them, we can help to remove some of the 'underbrush' that, in Locke's phrase, 'stands in the way of knowledge', and so clear the ground for a more constructive discussion of the *self*. The late J. L.

[2] Can such elementary matters of idiomatic usage have any real philosophical relevance? In my own view, the study of *comparative philosophy*—i.e., of the varied ways in which philosophical issues are formulated within different cultures and within different languages—has been sorely neglected, so that we have no way of estimating that relevance. To offer another illustration: when Ferruccio Rossi-Landi was translating Gilbert Ryle's book, *The Concept of Mind*, into Italian, he had no serious difficulty in finding colloquial Italian idioms to stand in for the homespun English of Ryle's particular examples. On a more abstract, philosophical level, however, he met real obstacles. For there is no systematic correspondence on that level between the two languages—terms like 'mind', 'soul', 'person', and 'self', do not tie up in any consistent manner with *mente*, *spirito*, *uomo*, *personalità*, *etc*. The very title of Ryle's book thus proved untranslatable, and Rossi-Landi fell back on a compromise paraphrase, *Lo Spirito come Comportamento*.

Austin used to speculate that the currency of a middle voice in fifth and forth century B.C. Athens, alongside the active and passive voices, helped to spare classical Greek philosophers from the virulent mind-body dichotomy that afflicted their seventeenth-century successors, and this speculation is highly suggestive. Certainly, one experiential basis of philosophical problems about human agency lies in the familiar contrast between *doing* and *being done to*; and it is a short philosophical journey from this experiential contrast to the belief that what is *active* (mind/soul/spirit/je) is, properly speaking, a distinct 'substance' from what is *passive* (matter/body/flesh/*moi*).

The availability of a third, distinct set of verb-forms for reflexive actions and attitudes helps avert premature closure at this point. By focusing the minds of philosophers on the distinctive character of reflexive conduct, it discourages them from assuming that reflexive conduct must necessarily be subsumed under, or made a special case of, the two more familiar types, *viz*. 'action' and 'passion'; and so from concluding prematurely that reflexive conduct necessarily involves a division of the personality into 'self-as-agent' and 'self-as-patient' (*je* and *moi*) or that the sole question to be settled is the consequential one, how the *je* 'interacts with' the *moi*. This assumption is gratuitous. As Aristotle pointed out in *Physics* II.8, our familiarity with cases of intentional, teleological conduct in which the agent and the patient are separate—like a shipbuilder, and the ship he is building—tempts us to universalize the distinction without any real warrant. Yet many of the most 'natural' cases of teleology or intentionality involve purely reflexive conduct, where there is no evident separation between 'agent' and 'patient' at all. To quote Aristotle:

> The best illustration of this is a doctor doctoring himself: Nature is like that.

The availability of a middle voice might also have helped to spare twentieth-century British philosophers from another perplexing and scandalous problem: *viz*. the Paradox of the Barber, formulated by Bertrand Russell as support for his well-known 'theory of types'. The problem is easily summarized:

> Suppose that the barber shaves all those, and only those, who do not shave themselves. Who then shaves the barber?

We apparently have to say, *either*, that the barber shaves the barber, *or else*, that someone other than the barber shaves the barber; and both alternatives land us in trouble. If the barber shaves the barber, this goes against the statement, 'The barber shaves *only* those who do not shave themselves'. If someone other than the barber shaves the barber, this goes against the statement, 'The barber shaves *all* those who do not shave themselves'. Either way, as a result, our initial formulation generates a contradiction.

But must we really construe all episodes of shaving as being either active ('A shaves B') or passive ('A is shaved by B')? If we could mark off *reflexive* shaving from both *active* and *passive* shaving by using a distinct middle-voice form ('A seshaves'), we could immediately avoid Russell's paradox. Restating Russell's problem in these new terms, we obtain the question:

> The barber (actively) shaves all those, and only those, who do not seshave. Who then (actively) shaves the barber?

And the answer to that question, as re-stated, is unparadoxical: *viz.* Nobody (actively) shaves the barber. The barber seshaves. Given a threefold distinction, we are spared any immediate inferences from the middle-voice statement, 'The barber *seshaves*', to any active or passive conclusion, whether 'the barber *shaves* the barber', or 'The barber *is shaved by* the barber'. The barber actively shaves all those, and only those, who do not seshave. In addition, the barber also seshaves; but that is another matter.

By explicitly acknowledging reflexive activity, attitudes etc. as a distinct species of conduct—to be equated neither with outward action *on* the world, nor with passive being-acted on *by* the world—we can therefore protect ourselves against any inclination to assume an exhaustive dichotomy between agents (e.g. 'shavers') and patients (e.g. 'shaved'), and establish the legitimacy of a third, unambiguous status (e.g. 'seshavers') captured grammatically by the use of middle-voice forms.

III

So much for preliminary linguistic and grammatical issues: the currency of 'self-' and '-self' idioms, which derive their sense from our familiar experience of reflexive conduct, defines the starting-point and context from which we are free to move in directions that can be used—by extension of meaning—to *give a sense to* the free-standing noun, 'self'. How can this be done? There are two possible and different ways of making the step, and we should now try to spell out the difference between them.

(1) When scientists introduce new nouns, as names of ostensible 'entities', the existence of these entities must at first be treated as conjectural; and it must be asked, separately, how far such a conjecture helps us to explain phenomena that were previously inexplicable. Wittgenstein in his lectures at Cambridge discussed the example of *invisible light.* If somebody talks to us about 'invisible light' entirely out of the blue, when we have never heard of such a thing, the appropriate response is to reply not, 'How amazing!', but 'What do you mean?' In its primary sense, the term 'light' refers to visible phenomena only; and, before we can put any other sense on it, we need to have it explained how, and under what circumstances, this *extension of meaning* is possible. We need to be told (e.g.) about experiments in which ultra-violet and infra-red radiation produce perceptive effects—heating, etc.—beyond the ends of the spectrum, analogous to the secondary effects of visible light, and we may then understand what fresh meaning is being attached to the phrase 'invisible light'. Once this has been done, we shall at any rate see how the 'existence' of these novel types of radiation could be demonstrated, not just as a conjecture, but as a scientific fact.

In such cases, the question of *existence* is evidently primary and basic. We encounter novel phenomena (e.g. heating effects beyond the two ends of the normal light spectrum) which would be straightforwardly explicable given certain novel entities—e.g. types of radiation having frequencies to which the human eye is insensitive—whose properties were otherwise similar to those of more familiar entities, e.g. visible electromagnetic radiation. Our range of understanding can then be extended, if only we may make good our initial, hypothetical claims about the novel entities, and so provide a secure basis for reapplying to the new class of phenomena patterns of scientific explanation already established elsewhere.

(2) Alongside this 'hypothetical-explanatory' mode, however, there is another way of introducing new technical terms into our language, which we are here calling the 'diagnostic-descriptive' mode. The

novel discoveries made by scientists, physicians and others, involve only occasionally the recognition of brand-new types of phenomena to be accounted for by appeal to hitherto-unsuspected 'entities'. Often, they arise instead from rethinking our ideas about phenomena and entities whose existence is quite familiar, and whose authenticity is not in doubt. When a botanical taxonomist establishes that the genus *Asparagus* is closely related to the lilies, or a clinical pathologist demonstrates that rickets is a nutritional not an infectious disease, he certainly increases the richness of our scientific understanding; but he does not thereby reveal to us the existence of some new class of 'entities'. And this remains true, even if he takes the occasion to introduce some new theoretical noun, or noun-phrase, into his account: e.g., 'spathe' or 'calcium metabolism'. Here, the use of neologisms embodies a fresh understanding of phenomena *within* the earlier range of our experience, rather than providing names for novel objects of study *outside* that previous range.

What, then, about the uses of the noun 'self' in psychology? Is the existence of the *self* a conjectural hypothesis comparable to the existence of invisible light? Was the term introduced to help us explain newly-observed phenomena outside the normal range of our psychological experience? Or should psychological discussions about the self be understood rather in the alternative diagnostic-descriptive mode? Do psychologists give a meaning to the free-standing noun 'self' (that is to say), not to serve as the name of a hitherto-unsuspected entity, but rather to mark new complexities and relationships within psychological phenomena that have, in less exact and detailed terms, been long familiar?

The first alternative—*viz.*, that the *self* is an hypothetical explanatory entity, introduced into psychology for the same kind of speculative reasons that justified introducing the terms 'atom' and 'electron' into physics—may, perhaps, underlie certain philosophical arguments about 'personal identity'. Thus, we might read David Hume's arguments about the 'hidden thread' supposedly linking all of an individual's sense-impressions, so as to guarantee that they are all alike 'his', as pointing towards a conjectural 'self' lying behind the immediate flux of our sensory experience. But the objections to this view are well known; and it is no wonder that Kant countered Hume's position by claiming that any philosophically-acceptable *self* must be the *transcendental subject* of any possible experience, rather than an *empirical object* discovered in particular actual experiences. On the second, diagnostic-descriptive interpretation, however, questions about the existence or non-existence of the self are not of primary concern. On this account, there will be no implication that the phenomenon in question—*viz.* reflexive conduct—manifests the action of some hidden 'entity'. Rather, the concept *self* will now be understood as expressing insights into the complexities and relationships within reflexive conduct of kinds that elude expression in less sophisticated language. From this point of view, our present task is not to inquire how the existence of the self was first guessed at, then demonstrated: instead, it is to show how—by careful extension of meaning—the everyday practical language of reflexive conduct ('self-' and '-self') provides the grounding for, and in due course develops into, the fully-fledged terminology of the 'self', as it figures in clinical theory, psychiatric diagnosis and/or psychoanalytic interpretation.

One further comparison can also help to make our present task clearer. In his correspondence with Samuel Clarke, Leibniz set out to explicate the physicist's theoretical concept of Space in a new way. Thinking about *space* as a hypothetical entity coexistent with the 'particles or 'corpuscles of *matter* (Leibniz argued) can lead only to confusion. Instead, the philosopher should begin by studying everyday colloquial language about spatial relations: asking what is meant by saying (e.g.) that one object *B* is now 'in the same place' that another object *A* previously occupied. Our scientific language about *space* may be a highly sophisticated theoretical extension of such everyday colloquial locutions, but (as Leibniz showed) it never loses touch with those practical origins. Accordingly, the philosopher's task is not to 'prove the existence of' Space, but rather to show how the criteria for identifying 'the same place'/'equal speeds'/'increases of acceleration' etc. are made more perceptive, discriminating, quantitative, and universal, as theoretical physics develops.

So in our case, too: the language of psychological description and psychoanalytic diagnosis, within which the freestanding noun 'self' acquires one of its characteristic uses, is not a completely fresh invention, detached from all pre-existing modes of thought and speech. On the contrary: like the *Space* of the physicists, the *Self* of the clinical psychologists acquires its sense within a repertory of theoretical idioms whose intellectual filiations lead back to pre-existing everyday locutions about reflexive, 'self-oriented' conduct;

and these filiations are as demonstrable as those by which Leibniz traced sophisticated questions about (say) the finitude of space back to colloquial locutions about (say) the relationship 'in the same place as'.

IV

Tracing these filiations from 'self' back to 'self-' involves picking our way through issues of some delicacy: issues over which *ethical* and *epistemological* issues overlap to an unusual extent. For, in the nature of things, a person's 'self-knowledge'—that is, his reflexive knowledge—is as much practical as theoretical. Socrates' injunction, 'Know thyself', was not just an exhortation to increase our detached, theoretical knowledge *about* ourselves (our 'self-understanding') but equally a call to improve our active, practical knowledge *of* ourselves. Correspondingly, any satisfactory philosophical analysis of self-knowledge must focus on the virtues of self-command as well as on the criteria of self-understanding; and, most of all, on the *interdependence* of self-understanding and self-command. The difficulty of separating practical from theoretical self-knowledge is evident even in our initial colloquial idioms. If we describe someone as 'not knowing his own mind', for instance, we are commonly remarking not on his incompetence as a self-observer but rather on his indecisiveness or vacillation: on his inability (say) to account clearly and consistently for the relations between his declared intentions and his manifest actions.

The subtleties of colloquial idiom embody—I would argue—a great reservoir of human experience with antedates, and gives a first foothold to, the enterprises of clinical psychology and psychotherapy. Even in advance of any convincing explanations of the phenomena, common observation show us that human beings are frequently unable to 'give a good account of themselves', so betraying confusion and even incoherence in their ostensible motives and intentions. Similiarly, we know that with most people this confusion shows up only locally, over specifically 'touchy' topics; so that there is a clear contrast between those broader areas of life in which their self-knowledge is adequate, and those particular situations in which they display confusion about themselves/lose control/fall apart etc. (Notice the close connection between these last idioms.)

How, then, do we make the conceptual move from this general, practical, common-sense grasp of self-knowledge and its vicissitudes to a more discriminating and perceptive account, informed by the professional accumulation of clinical observation and therapeutic experience? A detailed account of that move would be as laborious as a detailed account of the transition from everyday idioms like 'in the same place as' to the sophisticated physical terminology of 'space-time'. It will be enough to show, here, how the clinical psychology of the *self* draws a legitimate sense from its roots in everyday idiom and experience, in its clinical application to actual cases.

Notice, for a start, that the everyday idea of *self-knowledge* embraces, and unites, several distinguishable sub-notions. To list a few of these, we can distinguish:

(1) Knowing your own mind—i.e. having settled, consistent, explicit and preferably realistic intentions;
(2) Knowing your own capacities and propensities—i.e. being able to judge realistically how far you are in fact likely, and able, to carry through your declared intentions,
(3) Recognizing your standing as one agent among others—i.e. being able to perceive clearly the relations between your own needs/wishes/hopes/plans/feelings, and those of the other agents with whom you deal, particularly those to whom you are emotionally 'close';
(4) Being in command of yourself—i.e. being able, in actual practice, to match your conduct to your intentions, capacities and perceived situations.

Failures in 'self-knowledge' are of correspondingly different kinds. (1) Since coherent intentions and a settled plan of life are normally regarded as merits, inconsistency, vacillation and other forms of 'indecisiveness' are seen as shortcomings. (2) Again, our conduct is commonly expected to be—at least—broadly proportioned to our true situation and capacities, so that 'unrealistic' conduct represents a second class of failings or shortcomings. Similarly, with the other two components: (3) Since 'knowing oneself' involves understanding the proper boundaries between your own plans and feelings and those of other human agents, any tendency to misconstrue those limits—whether by drafting other agents into your own intentional life, or needlessly denying your own right to plans and wishes on a par with those of others—represents a significant failure in 'self-perception'. (4) Finally, on the level of sheer 'know-how', a certain minimum level of self-command is regarded as an indispensable virtue; so any tendency to lose control, blow up, clam up, or otherwise fall apart—in ways that we confessedly 'cannot help'—constitutes a final variety of defective self-knowledge.

This analytical taxonomy of the varieties and vicissitudes of self-knowledge would not be difficult to extend. In the first place, each of these four initial categories covers a broad range of cases, whose differences might well prove to be as important as their resemblances. In the second place, there are some other categories, or aspects of self-understanding, which could very plausibly be added to these first four. (Perhaps, for instance, we should see human self-knowledge as involving the capacity for forming a 'self-representation' or 'self-image'.) But, for our purposes, the most significant point is the possibility of developing such a taxonomy at all: in particular the recognition that, in actual practice, the epistemic and ethical aspects of self-knowledge (self-understanding and self-command) interdigitate at every point. After all, we demonstrate our self-knowledge most characteristically, by *acting* realistically; and 'realistic' action, so understood, presupposes both adequate self-appraisal and effective self-control.

So much for the underlying reservoir of common-sense experience about self-knowledge: to follow the move from this everyday starting-point to the professional 'psychology of the self', we should focus on the internal relationships *within* this common-sense experience. For, in our everyday practical lives, we are far less clear about the manner in which these different aspects of self-knowledge *interact* than we are about the separate aspects themselves: most particularly, we have little occasion in our everyday affairs to discover how failures in one direction are bound up with shortcomings in others. Even without going outside this everyday notion of self-knowledge, however, we can formulate a series of questions that arise directly from the internal complexity of that notion; and the sense of those questions is evident—regardless of their possible answers—merely from unpacking the implications of our everyday conceptions.

(1) Consider, first, our ability to form consistent intentions and coherent plans of life. If we are unable to act decisively and consistently in certain areas of life, that shortcomings may—if taken in isolation—appear merely perverse or unintelligible. So it is worth

asking: 'Is the inability to know-our-own-minds related to, or directed by, shortcomings in the other varieties of self-knowledge? If so, how, to what extent, and in what respects?' May that indecisiveness not be related, for instance, to an agent's misperception of his own status *vis-à-vis* other agents: e.g., to his propensity to suppress his own wishes in favor of the supposed—but mysterious—wishes and plans of his immediate associates? (2) Again, our ability to judge our own capacities and propensities realistically may—if taken in isolation—be too easily over-intellectualized. Why should we find it so hard to act as dispassionate observers, when the agents whose characteristics we must judge are ourselves? So, we might do better to regard self-appraisal as a skill quite distinct from normal character assessment, and ask 'Are our difficulties in self-appraisal bound up with (say) our confused intentions, emotional misperceptions, and/or failures of self-command? If so, how, to what extent, and in what respects?'

(3) Likewise, for failures in our self-perception: if taken in isolation, an individual's tendency to act manipulatively or self-effacingly may appear simply inexplicable, infuriating, or even perverse. By relating this tendency to other aspects of self-knowledge, we can once again raise worthwhile questions: e.g. about the links between the inability to perceive clearly the boundaries between one's own goals and plans and those of others and (say) confused intentions, inaccurate self-appraisals, and/or failures of self-control. (4) Finally, for failures of self-command: if we consider these in isolation, we may not be able to understand why any given individual breaks down, blows up, retires into his shell, or otherwise 'falls apart' at the particular moments he does. Yet, viewing such failures of his self-command in their proper context, we can at once raise significant questions about their relations to his self-perception, self-understanding, and the rest, so hinting at possible connections between (say) a person's uncontrollable temper and his inadequate self-esteem. In all these different ways, an analysis of the inner complexities within the everyday notion of 'self-knowledge' serves to define a coherent, self-consistent field of inquiry, with its own characteristic set of questions.

Three brief comments are desirable at this point. Firstly: though this field of inquiry may be self-consistent, it is not necessarily self-contained. It may not prove possible to account for the vicissitudes of self-command (for instance) exhaustively and in every case in terms of the other vicissitudes of self-knowledge alone. It is simply our business here to raise the question in what respects, and to what extent, these things prove to be connected in practice. In some cases, factors of other kinds (genetical predispositions, cultural conventions, or hormonal imbalances, say) may be needed to complete any convincing account. Still, to the extent that some systematic pattern of relations can be found between successes and failures in the different kinds of self-knowledge, we have scope for psychological investigations whose subject-matter is directly linked to the everyday kinds of reflexive conduct.

Secondly: this problem-area substantially overlaps the area of contemporary psychoanalysis and clinical psychotherapy about which Heinz Kohut, Ernest Wolf and others have written illuminatingly, under the title of 'the analysis of the self'. If their clinical discussions of 'the self' are to be read, not as speculative hypotheses about an additional entity lying behind human conduct and brought to light by psychoanalysis, but rather as compact and sophisticated ways of characterizing psychological interrelations *within* the reflexive conduct of human beings, this can help to make them that much the less mysterious. If this conclusion is well-founded, it is no wonder that attempts to construe the *self* as an hypothetical 'intervening variable' in psychological theory have appeared so lame and off-the-point. For in clinical contexts, the point of invoking the *self* is not to speculate about concealed mechanisms, but rather to elucidate confused motivations.[3] On this clinical level, theories about the *self* 'cash in for' a special class of empirical relations within the whole spectrum of reflexive 'self-' phenomena: self-esteem, self-control, self-understanding, etc., etc.

Thirdly: the sources of these clinical/empirical phenomena do much to explain the attractions of an image, or idiom, that plays a large part in current discussions of the self. The central questions in

[3] The purpose of psychological descriptions or diagnoses framed in terms of the 'self', in sense (3), is accordingly *not* to bring to light the *causes* of human actions. So the use of the term 'self' in this diagnostic-descriptive manner involves no claims that the self is an 'inner cause (or source of causes) of human action'; so that behaviorist arguments against the legitimacy of such claims, such as those advanced by Willard Day elsewhere in this volume, miss the point. Nor need dissatisfaction with such claims lead us to look away from all questions about the 'self', so as to pursue the 'true causes' of action into the surrounding world of contingencies, stimuli or reinforcements, either, so that move misses the point equally!

the clinical theory of the self are frequently stated as questions about 'integration' or 'fragmentation'. To be mature (or free from psychological troubles) is to have a 'cohesive, well-integrated' self: to suffer from psychological immaturities (or difficulties in the area of self-knowledge) is to have a 'fragile, fragmented and/or incompletely-cohesive' self. Here again, there is a fruitful interaction between familiar, everyday insights, as embodied in colloquial idiom, and the more carefully formulated analyses of clinical theory. Under particular stress, psychologically-troubled agents are notoriously liable to 'crack up' or 'fall apart'. Their plans are disrupted; their declared intentions become incoherent; they lose the capacity to judge their own capabilities, or to perceive their positions *vis-à-vis* other agents realistically; they are liable to behave in erratic, unexpected, even uncontrollable ways. And the business of clinical theory is to analyze such incoherences more carefully and explicitly than we have occasion to do in the course of everyday life.

So understood, the *integration* of the 'cohesive self' is a compendious label for the coherence of feelings and motives, intentions, and actions, typical of a psychologically trouble-free agent. First and foremost, the cohesive integration of the self is manifested—perhaps, even consists chiefly—in a rational coherence between the different components in his 'self knowledge': in an agent's self-evaluation and self-esteem, his perception of the relations between himself and others, his command over his own reactions, and the like. Conversely, 'fragmentation' of the self and similar failings are first and foremost manifested—even perhaps consist—in the absence of intelligible coherence between these different reflexive characteristics of the agent's conduct.

V

In this paper, of course, we have taken only a single first step away from the everyday experience and language of reflexive conduct ('self-' and '-self') towards a full scale 'psychology of the self', in which 'self' has become an independent, freestanding noun. Filling in the other steps would mean reconstructing the complex technical and historical stages by which clinical psychoanalysis have deepened their understanding of the issues involved in the development and expression of self-understanding, self-perception, and self-command.

All that concerns us here, however, is the general character of the resulting problems.

These problems comprise: (1) Clinical questions, about the manner in which, in different situations, individual agents fail to display a coherent, integrated pattern of self-knowledge. (2) Developmental questions, about the normal sequences by which the young child develops a realistic conception of himself as an autonomous agent, with a limited 'sphere of influence'; about the ways in which he comes to appreciate the proper boundaries—physical, emotional, and practical—between his own 'sphere of influence' and those of other agents; and about the traumas or vicissitudes by which those normal, sequences may be frustrated, distorted or otherwise limited. (3) Theoretical questions about the nature of the so-called 'self', construed as an expression of the agent's capacity to handle himself in a coherent, well-defined manner, to develop a single, consistent personality and life-plan, and to recognize the autonomous existence and legitimate rights of other, co-equal agents. However far such questions are pursued, and however technical the associated intellectual constructions become, the resulting theories of the self will retain an empirical meaning and application *just to the extent that* their implications can be 'cashed in for' reflexive auxiliary descriptions of the everyday kind.[4]

[4] In connection with the developmental group of questions (2), one point should be touched on here, arising out of Rom Harré's discussion (this volume) of the 'dramaturgical' or 'social role' aspect of human conduct. Whether we speak of our own 'self-understanding', or describe the experience of others in terms drawn from some clinical theory of the 'self', we have the choice of describing individual development in either *social* or *individual* terms. The question, 'What has So-and-So made of himself?', can be given two different kinds of sense:

(1) 'By improving his understanding of, and his command over, his own talents and aptitudes, he has made himself a first-rate concert pianist',

(2) 'By improving his understanding of, and his command over, his own psychic limitations and vulnerabilities, he has made himself a much more self-reliant person'.

A 'dramaturgical' account of human conduct, such as Harré gives, too easily leaves one with the impression that all 'self-knowledge' and 'knowledge of the self' is of the first type, and that all 'ethogeny' is, correspondingly, a matter of entering into certain public social roles. Yet surely (one might ask) we can factor out all such social roles and still have room to talk of self-knowledge and self-development in terms that refer to an individual's personality alone?

To go further: the diagnostic-descriptive terminology of clinical psychology uses the freestanding noun, 'self', as the key term in the *language of autonomy*. There are certain deep connections between the spectrum of clinical terms for an individual agent's self ('well-integrated/more-or-less cohesive/more-or-less fragile/fragmented') and the family of practical notions that have to do with freedom and responsibility (i.e. the different kinds and degrees of autonomy/freedom/compulsiveness/control). An understanding of psychological complexities within 'self-knowledge', as developed into a full-scale theoretical psychology of the self, can help us to see more clearly *in just how many different ways* our effective autonomy as human agents may be facilitated and/or restricted: i.e., in just how many different respects our current psychic strengths and vulnerabilities, together with their developmental roots in the vicissitudes of early life, shape our capacity to live our own lives.

Thus: (1) an agent who does 'know his own mind' can put his declared intentions into effect coherently and consistently, over a substantial period of time, while one who does not will act vacillatingly or inconsistently, and will not be able to 'give an account of himself' in case those discontinuities are challenged. Again, (2) an agent with a realistic 'self-understanding' can act smoothly and effectively in his dealings with the real world, while one who lacks such 'self-understanding' is forever liable to over-reach himself or to stop short of his true capacities. Alternatively, (3) an agent who perceives clearly how his own needs and plans properly relate to those of his co-agents can act 'realistically' and 'objectively', in both the moral and the practical sense of those terms, while one whose perception is in these respects clouded or distorted will be driven by 'unrealistic' and 'subjective' fantasies, rather than by a true grasp

---

It may be the case (as Harré remarked in discussions) that it is only in our own modern Western culture that any great store is set by 'individuality', in this latter sense; so that it is only in our own cultural context that the question of 'self-development' would naturally be interpreted in that personal, rather than social sense. And we might even conceive that the current emphasis on 'individuality' may in certain respects be exaggerated; still more, that the goal of living a life such as Rilke called for, which would have a single unitary sense informing it throughout, is a completely unrealizable ideal. Yet the idea of 'personality development' in the *individual* sense remains nonetheless authentic and the ideal of a coherent life plan still remains an ideal worth working towards, whatever concessions we feel bound to make to the importance of 'social roles'.

of his own proper issues and interests, satisfactions and ideals. Likewise (4) an agent who has developed the ability to anticipate, defuse and/or moderate any tendency to archaic panics, or to outbreaks of narcissistic rage, will increase his 'self-control', while the corresponding inability to fend off, or deal effectively with such panics or outbursts, will represent an equally clear limitation on his autonomy.

Taken in this sense, the psychology of the self can immediately be seen as clarifying and extending the language of autonomy. The everyday, auxiliary uses of the terms 'self-' and '-self' are our means of describing reflexive conduct and feelings, achievements and failings; but we can describe all these reflexive phenomena, without having any grasp of the larger patterns or syndromes that give this reflexive life its overall structure. Within a fully-fledged psychology of the self, by contrast, there will be room to draw, analyze and clarify the distinctions and relations between all these things: coherence or confusion of aims, clarity or distortion of self-perceptions, maintenance or loss of self-control, and so on and so on. Instead of a single, blanket notion of 'free will', operative solely on a *metaphysical*—or, at best, a noumenal—level of analysis, we shall arrive in this way at an *empirical* understanding of our 'autonomy', and of the manner in which that autonomy can be reinforced or threatened, broadened or restricted, as the intelligible outcome of individual experience.[5]

VI

By way of a postscript, let us glance briefly in some of the further directions along which a philosophical discussion of the present topic might proceed. (1) Firstly: let us contrast the questions about the *unity* of the 'self' that arise, respectively, for empiricist philosophers and clinical psychologists. In David Hume's arguments about personal identity, the 'self' was construed as a bearer of continuity, linking together the different 'sense-impressions' of which a given

[5] In these terms, we might even find a way of expressing—in the English language—the true interrelations and interactions between our roles and conduct as effective, autonomous *agents* (with the 'cohesive self' corresponding to the *je*) and the more incoherent experiences and sufferings to which we are exposed in our capacities as ineffectual *patients*, to whom things happen compulsively, uncontrollably, willy-nilly (with the 'fragmented self' corresponding to the *moi*).

individual is the passive recipient. So considered, it became (at best) a shadowy entity lacking specific qualities or characteristics—a mental counterpart to the material 'substratum' of John Locke's epistemology. Within psychoanalytic theory, by contrast, the characteristics attributed to any individual's 'self'—of being cohesive or fragmented, well-integrated or marked by a vertical split, etc., etc. —refer to specific active elements within that individual's feelings and conduct. It is not that the psychological 'self' *replaces* the 'man', 'person', 'spirit', 'soul' or whatever, as the immediate grammatical subject of action-verbs. (Current psychoanalytic theories happily dispense with that tautological substitution of one suppositious 'agent' for another.) Rather, the clinical terminology of the 'self' provides a means of characterizing, in significant terms, the different respects in which an agent's active, intentional and affective life may be—or may fail to be—organized and integrated. To the extent that the resulting clinical descriptions are associated with a more-or-less convincing account of the ontogeny of personality, the psychologist's ideas about the ways in which the actions and feelings of adult agents *are* integrated or fragmented have implications, also, about the ways in which those actions and feelings *came to be* integrated or fragmented. Clinical accounts of the self, that is to say, need to be supplemented for theoretical purposes by psychodynamic accounts of the developmental sequences by which individuals can achieve a 'well-integrated' self, and of the vicissitudes which can block such integration.

(1) To return to a point that we are made at the very beginning of this paper: the activities/syndromes/phenomena referred to by the use of terms like 'integration' and 'fragmentation' evidently elude classification as being exclusively *cognitive*, *affective* or *volitional*, quite as much as do the everyday varieties of 'self knowledge' and 'self understanding'. For the purposes of clinical psychology, the manner in which any individual perceives and handles his relations with other agents has aspects of all three kinds: it embraces his knowledge about those others, his feelings toward them and his active intentions in regard to them. From a clinical point of view, indeed, it would be highly artificial to treat the 'understandings' existing between different human agents as something restricted to the cognitive sphere, to which affective and volitional components happen to be annexed quite accidently. On the contrary, in all genuine dealings between real-life human beings, the 'expectations'

operative on both sides are *always expectations of*, not merely *expectations about*; and what one person 'expects of' another always involves a stance of the entire personality, undifferentiated into distinct cognitive expectations (predictive beliefs), affective expectations (confident desires) and volitional expectations (reliance in action). In the case of such human relations, correspondingly, failed expectations never involve falsified forecasts alone, aside from disappointed hopes and betrayed trusts. When we are deceived in our expectations of other people, we find that our forecasts, hopes, and trusts have been misplaced *pari passu*, and the same is true when we find ourselves failing to 'live up to' our own expectations of ourselves.

(3) In conclusion, let us touch once again on the connections that we noted in passing earlier, between epistemological considerations and ethical ones. Our discussion has turned up two reasons why it is hard to keep these considerations separate in this particular area. To begin with, any general assumption that epistemology—the theory of knowledge—can be put on a completely independent basis, divorced from all affective, volitional and/or ethical considerations, takes for granted what we are calling in question here: *viz.*, that 'cognitive' matters can be dealt with in isolation from other interpersonal experiences and transactions. To the extent that our understanding of other human beings overlaps the supposed boundaries between cognition, affect, and volition, any philosophical analysis of that understanding must follow it across those artificial frontiers, and pay proper attention to all relevant aspects of interpersonal 'knowing'.

There is also one further, more specific reason why current clinical theories of the self require us to pay special attention to certain *ethical* issues. One of the central concerns of those theories is with our ability (or inability) to perceive, clearly and realistically, the proper relationship between our own needs/wishes/hopes/fears/plans/intentions etc. and those of other agents, with whom we have to deal, and on whom we are practically and/or emotionally dependent. The clinical term 'grandiosity', for instance, covers conduct (and fantasies) in which an agent displays exaggerated expectations of others, and/or imposes inappropriate demands upon them: i.e. in which he fails to acknowledge them as equal, independent agents, with legitimate aims and interests, in their own right, on a par with his own. Similarly, the clinical term 'idealizing' refers to the converse failure, in which an agent implicitly denies his own right to independent aims and interests, and imposes upon himself, as absolute obligations, what he perceives to be the goals and wishes of some other idealized individual.

In both types of situation, the agent is said to manifest an insecure sense of the boundaries between 'self' and 'other'; and the developmental origins of this failure are presumed to lie in the very early ('pre-Oedipal') experience of the agent in question. Just as for Piaget the first stages in the infant's cognitive development involve learning to recognize—as a perceptual matter—the boundaries of his own bodily structure and sphere of influence, and the existence in the world of other, *physically autonomous* objects and agents, so likewise for Kohut the corresponding stages in personality development involve learning to recognize—as a broader matter of interpersonal expectations—the limits to one's own proper 'moral sphere of action', and the existence in the world of other, *morally autonomous* agents and objects. Bearing in mind the interdependence of the cognitive and affective/volitional elements in human relationships, indeed, we might be inclined to view as aspects of a single process, by which the young child forms a more-or-less adequate conception of the dividing-line between *self* and *other*: *viz.* the dividing-line between his own proper spheres of action (whether intellectual or practical, physical or moral) and those of his immediate family and associates.

Why do I use the phrases '*morally* autonomous' and '*moral* sphere of action'? I do so because, at this point, contemporary developments in the psychology of the self are bringing psychoanalysts very close to one of Immanuel Kant's central ethical insights.[6] For one of the most telling formulations of Kant's 'categorical imperative' principle is concerned, precisely, with the proper relationship between different co-existing agents in the world of active, practical affairs:

> So act, that you treat all other agents as ends in themselves, never as means only.

(Elsewhere, Kant speaks of moral agents as equal 'fellow-citizens', and 'fellow-legislators', within a shared 'kingdom of ends'.) So,

[6] In presenting this final comparison, between Kohut and Kant, I am greatly indebted to discussions with my colleague, Marilyn Di Salvo.

the contemporary psychology of the self contributes not just to clinical psychology, but also to moral psychology. Its results can help to clarify some crucial relations between the co-existing agents who participate in the world of moral and practical affairs. Specifically, each of these agents faces in childhood the task of coming to acknowledge his own status, as one agent among others: not just to recognize the fact of this co-existence as an intellectual matter but, more significantly, to accept it as a matter of practice, and to order his affective life around that acceptance.

No doubt, the doctrine that we should—in all circumstances, and at all times—perceive, act, and feel, in ways that are strictly realistic and appropriate, is a counsel of perfection. In actual fact, we all have 'touchy' subjects and moments of vulnerability, so that we are liable to lapse—at least temporarily—into pathological grandiosity or idealization. On these occasions, we lose our normal capacity to accept ourselves and others as 'co-equal moral citizens', and to treat our fellow-agents as ends in themselves, rather than as means only. In moments of excessive grandiosity, we may 'manipulate' our associates, so reducing them to means in the fulfilment of our goals and intentions. In moments of inappropriate idealization, we may deny our own status as ends and make ourselves the means to the fulfilment of other peoples' supposed goals and intentions. Either way, our *psychological* failure to acknowledge and accept the appropriate terms of co-existence between 'self' and 'other' regarded as autonomous agents can be viewed, alternatively, as a failure to respect the basic covenant embodied in the *moral* world. So, as the growing child comes to form a more-or-less adequate distinction between 'self 'and 'other' during his early years, he faces not one general task but three. He must achieve a more-or-less adequate grasp, firstly, of the physical (causal) boundaries between his own sphere of action and those of his fellows; secondly, of the psychological (emotional) relations between his own desires and feelings and those of his fellows; and finally—not least—of the morally just (equitable/appropriate) relations that one agent needs to respect in a well-ordered life, between the claims that his own goals, satisfactions and ideals rightly have on his own life, and the claims that the autonomous, legitimate and often different goals, satisfactions and ideals of others rightly have on theirs.

There is one last question to which we shall not have room to address ourselves here. Will it, in the long run, be helpful or even practicable for clinical psychologists to continue loading such a burden of meaning on to the deceptively simple word 'self'? All I have set out to do in this paper is indicate what they are *trying* to do: notably, when they move from the narrative language of clinical reporting—stated in terms of such familiar reflexive idioms as 'self-esteem', 'self-denial', 'self-knowledge', etc., etc.—to more theoretical formulations, in which the word 'self' is used as an independent, freestanding noun. Even at their most sophisticated (I have argued) these technical uses of the term 'self' never finally loses their affiliations back to the everyday, auxiliary uses of 'self-' and '-self'. Even at this most sophisticated level, the character of any particular agent's 'self'—whether it is cohesive or fragmented, whether it has clear or confused boundaries, whether it is vertically split, etc., etc.—remains an experiential matter, to be understood from the point of view of the agent himself; and, in this sense of the term, what the agent's 'self' is like depends on how he sees himself (his self-perception), how he judges his own capacities and propensities (his self-understanding), how he orders his goals and intentions, and how far he controls his actions (his self-command). So, the cohesiveness and autonomy of the individual's so-called 'self' is not a speculative matter for abstract psychological theories, but remains rather a practical measure of the extent to which he succeeds, on every level—intellectual, emotional and moral/cognitive, affective and volitional—in the complex, Socratic task of self-reflection: *viz.*, that of coming to 'know himself'.

12 The Self in Monodrama

ROM HARRÉ

I. General Introduction

In discussing the genesis and control of action, philosophers have been concerned very largely with the states, dispositions, processes and events referred to in action-explaining talk; comparing reasons and causes, debating whether beliefs are dispositions or states. The authors of this volume share the view that the self *is* the person and is one thing. It is both the subject of predication of the above attributes and the source of action, decision and will. Yet actual accounting talk is full of references to a multiplicity of quasi-persons, selves both internal and external to the speaker, sometimes inhabiting mysterious and unspecified realms. Self-intervention, a central activity of human beings, and perhaps even a necessary condition for self-hood, is characteristically expressed in English as the action of self upon self. Toulmin draws our attention to the cultural specificity of this way of talking, but it remains a powerful image threatening our laudable efforts to retain a concept of a human being as a unitary psychological being. It is this aspect of explicatory and justificatory talk and the status of these 'entities' I wish to explore, leaving the problem of the nature and attributes of the 'one' who is doing the talking to others.

In our hectic pursuit of fashion, we must not forget that some important insights of permanent value have been achieved in philosophy—particularly given my task in this chapter, Wittgenstein's idea that much of (some, at any rate, of) metaphysics is best conceived as philosophical grammar. I shall be arguing that, for the case of the self, there is an intermediary between grammar and metaphysics, the confusing realm of monodrama. I shall argue that we can explain the syntax of much of the talk of 'I' and 'me', 'thou' and 'we', and find perfectly good reasons for its being the way it is, by treating the talk as monodramatic performances. The same talk, treated as being within the rhetoric of psychology would include concepts referring to alarming processes such as ego-splitting; and considered within the rhetoric of metaphysics would seem to refer to such mysterious entities as the transcendental ego. Within these rhetorics the talk of 'I' and 'me' seems arbitrary and its elucidation intractable, as we are tempted vainly to attempt the empirical investigation of ego-splitting or the metaphysical grounding of a noumenal self. My endeavour chimes in with Toulmin's warning against turning a particular grammar *directly* into metaphysics and speculative psychology without looking for intermediate matters as explanations of syntax.[1]

My problem is that of preserving the self as a person in the face of a given grammar of personal pronouns in English. My solution is to treat the talk of such as 'I' and 'me' as a monodramatic presentation, a human technique that is part of our resources for the general task of the justification of action.

II. Schema for the Representation of the Genesis of Meaningful Action by a Social Agent.

Ethogenics as the successor to social psychology and microsociology is centrally concerned with the self as actor, a concept derived proximately from the analytical scheme of Burke according to which a social event is discerned as intelligible under the three-fold schema of scene/action/actor, and immediately from developments of Goffman's dramaturgical perspective.

The notion of an actor acting is complex. I propose the following as a preliminary analysis of the concept, drawing upon a general dramaturgical analogy. I want 'actor' and 'acting' to be understood throughout this paper, with an aura of the stage about them, that is the way of talking is to be seen as part of a system of dramaturgical metaphors developed for use among the folk as an explanatory social psychology.

The analysis of an actor acting, according to this system of metaphors, involves the following:

[1] References in this chapter, to the ideas of Alston, Hamlyn, Taylor and Toulmin, are directed to their contributions to this volume.

(i) An actor is an agent, that is he is involved in the genesis of his actions, and is normally seen as such by other actors.

(ii) (a) he generates his actions in accordance with a preformed plan, scenario, script, rule or habit etc., which represents the form of the action-sequence to be produced and which could be called a 'template for action', which he may himself have constructed. The meanings of his actions for others depend on their representations of his template, and a shared local theory of the modes of sociality, such as what it is to be a friend, a husband and so on.

(b) he qualifies all his actions by performing them in a manner which accords with the local stylistic conventions for the expressive manifestation of the persona appropriate to the action in the situation as he conceives it himself, and adjusts his readings of situations to the readings of others, insofar as these are available to him.

Relativized to the situation, action is then to be seen as analyzable into an instrumental and an expressive aspect. Sometimes there are separate components for the manifestation of these aspects. In general, persona or self-presentation in Goffman's sense, occurs in the expressive qualifications of actions which, with respect to practical aims, are instrumental. Of course, at a higher level of analysis, the expressive becomes instrumental with respect to the expressive task and may itself be qualified by a further level of expressive qualification.

(iii) Agency of the actor may take two forms:

(a) He actively follows a passive template of the form of his action. Such templates may be provided from the circumambient culture, more usually they are plans etc. the actor himself has constructed in accordance with his social knowledge.

(b) Sometimes the actor, having prepared a template for action, for instance a plan, allows the plan to function as a powerful particular and loosens himself to be guided by it, as for example, a well rehearsed recitation may proceed correctly from beginning to end with the elocutionist paying little attention to the evolution of the action in accordance with his knowledge of the poem.

This distinction was made by Wittgenstein (1956) who pointed out the necessity to consider the relation of agent to rule or plan in two ways. In the one activity remains with the agent, who follows the passive template. In the other, the agent makes the template active, allowing himself to be guided by it. As Wittgenstein points out, both are, of course, forms of action of agents.

The forms of self-intervention which I shall be emphasizing later in this paper, are concerned with the modifications an actor may make to the various representations which are serving as templates for his actions. These are cases which support Taylor's emphasis on the importance of second-order desires, associated with certain necessary capacities to realize them such as the power to want to be different—for example to have different wants and desires at a first level, and to make different kinds of plans. Similarly, Alston's double hierarchy of want/belief systems can also be thought to be operative, in ways which I shall detail, in the reconstruction of templates at various levels of distance from the immediate production of action. It is important to realize, and I shall return to emphasize this point later, that templates for action should be treated as constructed for occasions and that what Taylor and Alston are drawing attention to are structures and aspects of the capacity to construct and reconstruct action templates, rather than elements of action templates themselves.

To bring these matters into contact with recent discussions in the philosophy of action, I propose to argue briefly that one of our common notions of intention can be construed as the notion of templates or representations of action-sequences that are the formal causes of action. By this identification I want to locate a point of application of reflexive self-action, self-intervention in Alston's terms, and to locate it in the preparation of action rather than in the performance of an action-sequence once it is under way. That is, self-intervention is as much a modification of competence as of performance.

I shall not assume, as many philosophers have uncritically supposed, that consciousness can be brought to include awareness of the efficient causes of action as a regular thing. The recent literature on intention and motivation seems to have made the uncritical assumption that the analysis of these concepts as part of psychological explanations of action should be taken to hinge upon the possibility of their being efficient causes. It seems to me plain that intentions are implausible as efficient causes for the reasons cited by the Melden/Anscombe school of philosophers of action. However, if intentions were treated as formal causes of the structure of action sequences, that is preformed representations of that structure, then the actors' awareness of them and their capacity to manipulate and modify them would serve as a general theory of action management. It would include, for example, the explanation of such otherwise mysterious phenomena as displacement activities, where the effect of an efficient cause cannot be aborted but the shape of the produced action can be controlled by a change of intention, that is by a modification of formal cause. A full account of 'intention' would need to include the representation of the aim or upshot of the action-sequence as well; that is, of the act the action-sequence performs.

An argument in favour of such a construction requires the assembly of the agreed characteristics of one of the concepts of intention, *vis-à-vis* actions and their examination. I cite the following as agreed properties of intentions in this sense.

1. Intentions always pre-exist the manifestation of the act-action patterned sequence, as an orderly sequence of behavior and speech.

2. An intention endures throughout the performance and vanishes when it is complete.

The second clause of this property was pointed out many years ago by Kurt Lewin but has not perhaps attracted sufficient attention from philosophers.

3. Intention determines the form (and as Martin Fowler has pointed out, the conceptual boundaries) of the act-action sequence, in advance.

Of what sort of cause are these properties likely to be true? If we regard the action sequence as the realization in another substance of the structure or form realized in thought in the intention, then the most economical theory to explicate the relationship between the intention and the action is as the expression of a formal cause.

If intention is a representation of the structure of the action to come in another medium, namely that of thought, the major mystery regarding intentions can be very simply cleared up. If intentions are indeed expressions of the formal causes of actions, then they must come under the same description as the action, but as formal causes they can be ontologically distinct. On this model, efficient causes, whether stimuli or removals of impediments to action, are *both* logically and ontologically distinct from the action sequences they lead to.

The trouble with intention as a technical term in psychology, is that it comprehends both the act aimed at or achieved and the action needed to achieve it. Both aspects of meaningful behavior are *meant* by the actor. For this reason I think it better to speak of the representation in thought of act-action structures, prior to their realization in the medium of overt speech and action, as *templates*; within the template the representation of the action structure can be clearly separated from the representation of the act, though a strict Aristotelianism might require the separation of the representation of the act as 'final' cause.

Thus the templates for action *are* the intentions we form and are mostly constructed for the representation of an act-action structure. The hierarchical want-belief system, as described by Alston and the corresponding system of first and second order desires developed by Taylor are, I believe, expressions of the materials from which templates are constructed—wants being concerned with acts, and beliefs with the action-sequences for the performance of them—and in accordance with which the schema of self-intervention (or self-improvement) is to be understood. A very similar point is involved in T. Mischel's (1964) construal of Kelly's constructs as rules, and of his construct formation as rule creation. I use the term 'template for action' as a rather more general concept than rule, so as to include plans and habits under the same scheme.

According to this scheme, causal potency *in general*, remains with the person as agent, and intentions as templates for action become the formal causes of action sequences. While noting the occasional case of the vicarious acquisition of agency by a rule or plan, I follow Wittgenstein in seeing this case, not as an exception to the thesis that the person is the powerful particular in the genesis of action, but as a special case of it. In terms of this system of concepts, we can locate more precisely the locus of what I regard as the most important form of self-intervention, namely intervention in one's own plans.

Shotter (1975) has proposed the processes of self-intervention as the central focus of a radical, non-oppressive psychology—a moral science of action, aimed at enhancing autonomy, not so much in action itself as in the personal construction of selves, emphasizing that we are 'free to make ourselves as we might want to be' as much or more than we are 'free to do want we want to do'.

III. A Dramaturgical Metaphor for Self-Intervention

The structure of the process of self-intervention at the point of application I have been emphasizing (with Alston and Taylor), can be illuminated by an elaboration of the dramaturgical point of view. My use of a dramaturgical metaphor to reveal the aspects and stages of this process, derives from the concept of 'theatricality' as proposed by Evreinov.[1] Evreinov was the father of the idea of psychology as the study of the principles of monodrama, the imaginative decomposition of the person in imagined social action into a cast of characters, each representing an aspect of himself. In this and other ways Evreinov places 'theatricality' central to human social psychological functioning. There is a general tendency he believes, to try to realize ourselves in 'social space' as something always other than we currently think we are. Theatricality is a manifestation of 'the instinct of transformation, the instinct of opposing to images received from without, images arbitrarily created from within, the instinct of transmuting appearances found in nature into something else . . (Evreinov, 1927, p. 22) . . .' to imagine oneself in surroundings that are different'.

The central psychological process ethogenists have called 'rehearsal in the imagination', Evreinov treats as the composition of a historical play, alike in both anticipation and remembrance. We stage it, we appear in it, and we ourselves experience it as spectator and critic. So complementary to the self as actor, must be the self as director and author, as well as critic. In the preparation for and musings upon action, we must be capable of formulating for ourselves other worlds and other selves to play in them. However, each of these persons, director, author and critic, are also characters in another monodrama, a metamonodrama, not the play within the play, but the play that surrounds the play, and it is this monodrama that has been misconstrued by those who pursue either a metaphysics or a psychology of multiple human selves.

The pre-running of new futures available to the one who has intervened in himself, is a private showing of a multidrama, since it involves an imagined 'oneself' with imagined others. But the theatrical capacity available for checking and planning self-intervention can be used for the purposes of representing certain other

[1] I owe notice of Evreinov's theory to S. M. Lyman.

psychological processes as analogous to episodes in public life, thus creating monodramas. Accounting regresses, for example, seem to involve multiple self-like entities, if such intra personal processes as contemplation of myself are expressed in the same terms in which I might express my description of an occasion when I contemplate another.

The upshot of this is the idea that the psychology of the self is not to be pursued by introspection, but by study of the ways we express ascending orders of meta-awareness of the nature of the action, in accounting. Each order of awareness appears in the monodrama as a separate character, sometimes named by a separated personal pronoun, as if it were another self. The first monodrama is the 'I'—'me' discourse. As we shall see, psychologists have drawn our attention to the further fragmentation of both of these pronouns as more separated characters appear requiring to be named. On this view, philosophical theories of the self are nothing but fanciful expressions of the rules of grammar of personal pronouns as used in the giving and constructing of accounts according to the conventions of monodrama. I shall try to show the plausibility of this hypothesis in a later section of the paper.

IV. Some Accounting Regresses: Ontological Temptations of a Form of Speech

One needs no more than reflection on common experience to be aware that the relation of the self as person to action is represented as very variable in everyday explanatory schemata. For example, the degree of claimed awareness of the action commonly differs from type to type of action and on different occasions of the same type of action. I believe this feature of accounts reflects an actual expanding and contracting of awareness of the Burkean components of the constituted social world discerned as scene/action/actor. Even the scene of the action is an *Umwelt* endowed with meaning and attention can shift from meanings to physical properties and back again. In addition, description of each of the three components of a particular social occasion may involve different and varying degrees of *self*-consciousness.

Action comes under scrutiny as an object of awareness not only in shift of attention during performance but, as revealed in empirical studies, in the complementary cases of preparation and contemplation of the action in various forms of rehearsal and reflection upon action. This is further complicated by the fact that much of this scrutiny involves the awareness of available alternatives to the contemplated or completed action-sequence in retrospective rumination in the course of self-reproach, or more rarely, of self-congratulation. In both cases it is not the action itself that is scrutinized from a reflective standpoint, but a representation of the action, either in the memory or imagination. Sometimes this kind of contemplation and imaginative representation is coupled with an actual performance of an action-sequence. In general, then, we rarely reflect upon past or future performances without imagining alternative action-sequences than those which did, or will, occur.

This suggests the possibility of two forms of regress in the form of talk we call accounting, that is, the explanation and justification of social action. One is from act or outcome aimed at, to the action required for performance, consciousness expanding by including the means and the style, as well as the aim of the action among its contents. The second form of regress involves the inclusion of the preparative and reflective process and its contents within the content of awareness. Each *seems* to suggest a multiplicity of that which the official general theory takes to be unitary, namely the self.

Regress 1—*the 'How' regress*:

Stage A Act—Action—Style.

How did you take leave of him?
I farewelled him
How did you farewell him?
I said 'Goodbye'.
How did you say 'Goodbye'?
Regretfully.

Stage B

But we may go further and pursue the question of how speech and its stylistic qualification is achieved. Further steps may be natural queries say for an actor who is concerned to understand and enhance self-control. They may lead to awareness of the control of such matters as the length of vowels, and on to the control of breathing and its musculature.

Temptation: 'I am here controlling myself as performer'.

Regress 2—*the 'Why' regress: Acts to Actions*

Why did you . . . .
I wanted to . . . .
How did you think you would accomplish that?
I thought I would have to . . . .
But wouldn't that require you to . . . . ?
No, I hoped it could only be done by . . . . , so that I would have needed only to . . . .
How did you propose to . . . . ?
I reckoned . . . . would have done it.

The first two items define 'act', the remaining items 'actions'.

Temptation: 'I am here controlling myself as planner'.

The second regress is a double duality, one branch leading into the past, that is to the preparation of the action, and the other, which I have not exemplified, into the future, via contemplation of the consequences of the action and their consequences, and so on. Each of these regresses to past or future, depends on the consideration of alternatives and thus can ramify indefinitely as we are prepared to consider a wider and wider range of action-sequences as possible in the situation and the preparatory conditions for their coming into being.

These regresses involve successively more self-conscious scrutiny of the engagement of the self in the preparation and management of action. They have the same subject matter as ethnomethodology. At first sight they threaten the unity of the self as person since they seem to direct the self upon the self and look to be involved in the deeper philosophical problems of the self raised by the second phenomenological reduction, Hume's 'Fleeing Self' and the like.

Both microsociology and private self-reflection seem to raise another matter of interest for the discussion of the self, namely the idea of a typified and interactively defined social self, a social presentation distinct from the inner self or person. This is the subject matter of Goffman-type studies and is related to the use of the dramaturgical model. The self scrutinizes the way it manifests itself to others and from the phenomenological point of view remains within the first phenomenological reduction. The managing self hides behind a colony of public selves.

The modulation of Regress I in the course of Stage A, from action to style, stems from the distinction between the instrumental actions required to perform the act, and the style in which they are performed, expressive of the socially presented self, the persona, assembled for and by others. Since persona presentation is achieved by stylistic *qualification* of action we might be tempted to treat the account as a description of the way the true managing self can reflect upon the social or expressive self, on this reading necessarily distinct from it. In this way the accounting regresses I have exemplified are cross connected with the distinction between self and social personas. This is how the matter is presented in *accounts*. The representation of these selves as distinct is clearly revealed in empirical studies, for the multiplicity of social selves (personas) is in contrast to the unity of the individual self which expresses itself in these ways. In accounting, both a regress of further selves intervening upon each other, and an inner or managing self controlling a bouquet of personas, are conjured up. It is the status of these other beings which I shall take as through and through problematic, that is, not as a taken-for-granted reality to be explained, but as a problem to be resolved.

V. Grammatical Form as a Presentational Device for Monodrama

A monodrama is portrayed in syntax through what I shall call, following Torode (1976), 'the conjuring up of Voices and Realms', a construction deriving in part from the technique of Structuralist Poetics (Cullers, 1974). A repeated pronoun, for example, is not accepted at its face value as having identical reference, but scrutinized for its 'Voice'. The structure of the discourse is revealed by linking 'Voices', not instances of lexically identical pronouns. Thus,

'You never know, do you?'

addressed to another involves two voices—You, the Voice of abstract humanity, (Voice 1) and you (Voice 2) that of the addressee; and via this separation of Voices we can understand why the proper response is,

'No, you don't', and not, 'No, I don't',

since the 'You' who doesn't, is Voice 1. In this way the structure of the stanza comprising the two speeches becomes clear.

Realms are the characteristic territories of Voices and may be more or less filled out in the presentation of monodrama.

(A) INTERNAL CONSTITUTING OF VOICES AND REALMS: THE 'I'—'ME' SEPARATION

As might be expected, monodramatic presentations of social psychological matters involving the self are a prominent feature of accounts. A very common accounting technique involves the separation in speech of 'I' from 'me'. Typically, the account involves a scenario in which the 'I' is represented as losing control of the 'me', who then as an independent being, performs the action for which the account is being prepared. In some scenarios the 'I' is a helpless spectator of the unleashed 'me'; in others the 'I' fails to attend, or looses consciousness, or in some other way is prevented from knowing anything about what the 'me' has been doing. In the former scenario, the 'I' loses control and releases the 'beast within'. In the other, the 'I' in loosing consciousness releases the 'automaton within'.

This form of social accounting is a central topic of concern in a wide variety of philosophical and psychological investigations.

Questions raised by 'I'—'me' separations:

1. What is the philosophical status of the 'I' which is separated thus from the 'me'? Since it has certain quasi-personal properties one is tempted to treat it as a person, a self. For example,

(i) it is usually said to be conscious. Sometimes it is treated as capable of self-consciousness, which suggests a second move in the 'I'—'me' separation, a further self which contemplates the contents of the consciousness of the 'I', as the 'I' contemplates the automatisms of the 'me'.

(ii) it is also supposed generally to be directly in control of the action. Only when that control is said to have lapsed is accounting called for in this form.

But 'ego-splitting' in other monodramas may occur along another plane. This occurs, for example, in psycho-dynamic accounts in the interests of 'defence'. In the pathological cases Freud and others were concerned with, there is said to be a duality of control at the action-level, some of which is exercised by a second self, a detachment from the original 'I'. I shall return to this scenario in more detail since it is the basic plot of the monodrama called 'self-description'.

2. Are these separated selves the very same entities as are revealed in the analysis of the preparation of social action? Certainly sometimes the necessity for the presentation of a monodrama is the pretext for an overt action-sequence. But in general the separation of the planner from his plan is within the unity of a person, while the multiplication of selves in Freudian and Sartrean analyses of certain kinds of action is a further step, not so far as I can see a necessary condition for the possibility of active preparation of action by a conscious agent, and hence demanding explanation only along monodramatic lines.

3. So far I have raised some problems that derive from considering individual selves in relation to their actions in social contexts, as if we could examine each person in isolation. But it is a central ethogenic tenet that there are no such entities as individual selves capable of sustaining an existence as persons in isolation. Persons are interactively produced. This leads to a further range of problems, namely those concerned with how I as actor am related to you as actor and how you are related to me, particularly when representations of each other begin to appear in our monodramas. The 'Self' as a concept for understanding our mutual performance and as a kind of object revealed in such activity must be taken as problematic, largely because we must allow for the possibilities of the person both appearing as actor and concealing himself as actor in the intersubjective world, and of so prestructuring the possibility of action and speech that another person is forced to play a puppet-role in another's monodrama.

Example 1. Self-deception as a vicarious monodramatic rendering by someone of another's avoidance of a topic.

'*You* are deceiving *your* self' is the fundamental speech form as an accounting technique. I propose to treat self-deception as a scenario offered to another person in the form of a 'you'—'yourself' separation, making available the grammar of 'I'—'me' separation as an accounting technique.

There have been two classical investigations of the problems associated with the idea of self-deception treated as a possible psychological condition. There is the investigation of *mauvais foi* by Sartre and of 'defence' by Freud. I shall concentrate on the attempt by Fingarette (1969) to resolve the ontological problems that are generated by a literal espousal of the idea of a separation of egos, or as we might say, by the taking of the casting of the monodrama as a contribution to ontology. He proposes a reformulation of Freud and Sartre which is in keeping with the ethogenic theory of accounting in that what is at issue is a person's unreadiness to speak of certain matters, and the technique of disavowal of awareness, as well as of responsibility, by which he avoids their public (and indeed possibly private) contemplation. As Fingarette says, 'The core of self-deception is the disavowal of responsibility for, and the consequent refusal to reflect upon, some project of consciousness'. (op. cit. p. 99). One might be inclined to quarrel with Fingarette's order of consequence in that perhaps the refusal to reflect upon a project of consciousness is responsible for the availability of disavowal as a technique of avoiding responsibility.

The application of this idea to the analysis of the Freudian notion of defence works in a neat and convincing fashion in that it explains without paradox the seemingly regressive requirement of the regulation of the defence by 'the ego'. As it is put in psycho-analytic terms, the problem arises because it seems to be necessary for the ego to be dynamically unconscious, that is choosing unconsciousness as a manoeuvre for keeping some matter uninvestigated and, of course, that is itself a matter which must be prevented from being investigated, requiring a second-level manoeuvre, and so on. Secondly, there is the issue raised by Fingarette of the point of concealment, since each character in Freud's attributed psychomonodrama is aware of what is being concealed and how. But from whom is it being hid? If we ontologize the psychodrama it looks as if we require the casting of a fourth character, namely the ego of primary awareness. Various solutions have been proposed, none entirely satisfactory. Fingarette generalizes his disavowal theory so as to allow for a policy to be adopted by a person in the course of which he regularly and as a matter of that policy, disavows some interest. For Fingarette, disavowal 'amounts to a removal of some mental content from the status of being available for spelling out'. (op. cit. p. 121). Spelling out is, so far as I can see, Fingarette's conception of a social practice which we would call an aspect of accounting.

How, on this view, are we to cope with the idea of the separation of the 'I' and the 'me' and the further separation of first persons we might be tempted into? Fingarette offers us a psychodynamic explanation in terms of two rational systems clustered around nuclear dynamic complexes, the second of which is produced by techniques of defence and is, as we might say, a quasi-ego. Defence, then, is a manoeuvre entirely within the realm of speech and possible speech, and ego-splitting no more than a distribution of first person pronouns in that speech designed to achieve the sociolinguistic activity of 'disavowal'.

In this way the problem that loomed so threateningly as a problem in the ontology of persons is resolved by referring it to a mode of speech whose social role is readily available to commonsense understanding. It is primarily an imposed scenario, a 'you'—'yourself' separation in the speech of another, leading to the adoption of an 'I'—'me' separation in the speech of the one concerned.

One is tempted to suggest, though I am by no means in a position to establish, that much of what is accommodated under the concept of false consciousness in Marxist theory, could easily be explicated in terms of accounting devices. The Marxist theory of consciousness could be transmuted into a theory of accounting, and false consciousness could be an attribution to a society's accounting techniques, rather than a psychical property of its individual members considered collectively as a class. To be in a state of false consciousness is to have available only one of several possible accounting systems, where some of those which are not available to the members of a class may have certain scientific, moral, political, or other properties, more desirable than the system which is available. Thus interpreted, Marx can be seen to be preciently proposing the ethogenic idea that forms of speech are one of the influences that preempt social reality.

Example 2. Reflexive Self-work

(α) 'I made myself do it', (β) 'I talked myself into it', (γ) 'I taught myself the clarinet'.

(a) The conditions for the possibility of reflexive self-work.

Shotter (1973) has pointed out that the possibility for reflexive self-work depends upon the maintenance of a distinction between natural and acquired powers, since it requires the exercise of a power to change our powers and capacities; there must be a category of natural powers of self-intervention since the process must have a beginning somewhere. But for our purposes it is more helpful to focus on another necessary condition, that there exists the possibility of taking the contemplative attitude to the formal causes of action and even to our self-intervening operation upon them. The conditions for this as a *phenomenon* are explored by Alston, Taylor and myself, but as a monodramatic presentation the speech conjures up not Taylor's, Alston's, nor my reasonable internal architecture of the activity of self-intervention, but a pair of characters in various homely relationships, such as teacher and pupil, advocate and addressee, etc. To preserve the reasonable architecture of self-intervention against the threat of a multiplicity of selves, these forms of speech, I claim, are to be taken as explicable on monodramatic lines.

What are the monodramas conjured up in the use of such expressions? Their plots are based upon social vignettes, drawing upon commonsense understandings of commonplace multidramas. By virtue of their origin they have an explanatory function, e.g., I represent myself as using the same technique of self control as I use to control others when, for example, I say 'I made myself do something which I was reluctant to undertake': or at least, that is how I represent the matter monodramatically.

(b) Reasons for setting about reflexive self-work; the concepts for accounting in this area.

Taylor's development of the idea of first and second order desires could be construed within my conceptual scheme, as a specification of the forms and content of accounting that would be produced by one proposing to provide reasons for some reflexive self-work. Hamlyn's discussion of self-knowledge and its consequences might also serve in this respect, since a reason for undertaking reflexive self-work might be some form of self-depreciation or self-disgust arising from self-knowledge in Hamlyn's sense.

The self-justifying aspects of the resort to a monodramatic representation of the reasons for setting about reformatory self-work appear clearly when we notice that *my* failings are transformed into personal characteristics of the characters of the monodramatic presentations conjured up in 'I talked myself into it' etc.; thus my reluctance to act, or my weakness of character, is masked in part by attributing it to a separated and, in the plot, rather feeble-willed quasi-fellow, the 'me' who can be brought round by the eloquence of 'I'. Thus the 'I' as primary self-person can hog all the *Herrschaft* available in the little drama.

Thus monodrama is not just presentative of the dynamics of self-management but is also technique, a way of talking that facilitates self-mastery by separating, as into another person, situation-relative undesirable characteristics. Sometimes self-congratulation can also be emphatically expressed by separating off and claiming desirable characteristics for *all* the members of my self-colony of selves, as in the little monodrama 'Myself, I did it!'

(B) EXTERNAL CONSTITUTING OF VOICES AND REALMS: 'I'—'WE' SEPARATION; TRAPPING OTHERS IN A SELF-CONSTITUTED MONODRAMA

Example—Exclusion and Election

I take this example and its general method of analysis from Torode's study of teacher's speech, though the analysis I shall propose is somewhat more elaborate than his.

'We don't have any talking when we do compositions. I hope that is clear'. The first person plural appears here in two voices. The first voice is that of the populace of a transcendent world, authoritarian and sources of orderliness. They 'don't have' things. The second occurrence of the first person plural pronoun 'we' denotes a different set of voices, those of the members of the imminent world of the classroom—the subjects, those who 'do'.

Mr. Crimond presents himself both as a member of both realms—a status to which we shall return—and as a separated individual able to look at both from an external standpoint. In his character or voice as 'I', Mr. Crimond is

(i) the only person in the classroom who is a member of the populations of both realms:

(ii) however, he also appears in the second sentence of the stanza as 'I', in which voice he is both benevolent and aspiring for the citizens of the imminent realm, that is, he hopes for them.

At the same time he occupies the important role of the channel of mediation and interpretation between realms. His hoping is directed to the possibility of his making clear to the members of the imminent realm the authoritarian wishes of the Voices of the transcendent realm. Furthermore, as a member of the transcendent realm, he is elect, while the members of the imminent realm are mundane and unable to address the issue of order except through his mediation. However, they are shown the possibility of election. One of them, namely Mr. Crimond, is a member of both realms. But, aspiration to membership of the transcendent realm is matched by the possibility of being cast out of 'Heaven' altogether into what Torode calls 'Hell', an act in the monodrama expressed by such phrases as 'you boys . . .'. The members of the imminent realm are trapped in Mr. Crimond's monodrama; in particular, they are unable to address questions concerning the issue of order directly to the source of that order. If they do query these matters, Mr. Crimond replies in such phrases as 'We'll have to see', conjuring up an image of lofty deliberation among the immortals and of reserved judgments which may or may not be handed down. It should surprise no-one that Mr. Crimond maintains an amazing degree of discipline and order without resource to anything other than speech.

Torode also raises the question of different Voices of the 'I', particularly the 'I' of concern (that above which 'hopes') and the 'I' of action and authority, for Mr. Crimond occasionally speaks in the person of that Voice, as when he says, 'I will not have that sort of thing'.

The idea of Voices from a transcendent realm as the source of authority can also be seen, I think, to make sense of certain features of imperative speech. Only philosophers ever quote as real speech such sentences as 'I order you to get out'. Real people say such things as 'Get out!' The choice of the impersonal form of the imperative, rather than the first person performative, makes the issue of the legitimacy of the order much more difficult to address, because monodramatically the order seems to derive from the transcendent realm of authority. Alternatively, an order in real life would be expressed by, 'I wish you'd stop that', or 'I'd be grateful if you'd get this done by next week', and so on. Here, since the speaker is appearing in the person of a Voice rather close to his 'real self', a different sort of performative style seems proper to adopt, namely a style in which an apologetic tone, or something of the sort, is available as a way of side-stepping the issue of his right to give orders.

VI. Metaphysics, as Casting for Monodramatic Discourse, Reinterpreted as Grammatical Rules.

(a) MYSELF AS ACTOR: The role of the principle character 'I' is expressed as rules for the use of 'I' in monodramatic discourse. In this way the grammar of the discourse is seen as reflecting not a metaphysical theory, but a dramatic convention.

It has become more and more clear as work on the form and place of language in human life has developed that, from a social point of view, language is as much a form of action as it is an expression or vehicle of thought. Those peculiar uses of language on which the logicians of the tradition have concentrated, which are typical of discourse in the scientific mode, that is, discourse which attempts to convey information and aims at nothing else, are much restricted in real social life. Taking this thought as fundamental, we must look for the social actions performed by the distribution of personal pronouns in a discourse. What role, for example, does the 'Fleeing I' play in the presentation of myself in the course of a discourse in which I account to myself, and others, by withdrawing as commentator from the scene of the action? One obvious answer would be that such a use of the 'Fleeing I' is a way of making a claim to agenthood in principle, though repudiating it for that occasion, perhaps by introducing the helpless character 'me' on the scene. Thus the appearance of a 'Fleeing I' and a subservient 'me' ought not to be treated as an incipient ontological hypothesis, or as a tentative psychological theory, but as a social technique, a piece of ethnomethod whose logos must be revealed. These are metaphors of personhood and only the monodrama in which they play lies behind philosophical theories of the self which, from this perspective, can be seen for what they are, rather than as speculative psychology.

The most influential attempt to solve the problem of the self conceived in the ontological and speculative psychological mode, following Hume's demonstration that the regress of introspective self-awareness had no natural terminus, was to propose a category of entities whose properties were revealed not *in* experience but as the necessary conditions *for* experience. In a familiar argument, Kant created the transcendental unity of apperception as the foundation for the transcendental self. Since such a self could not be given to internal sense, he distinguished the self as transcendental from the self which is given in intuition, merely, he says, 'as I appear'. In a way that has become a familiar aspect of transcendental philosophy, the solution of the problem of the agenthood of human beings, conceived as a psychological and ontological problem, was thought to be solved by Kant's proposal that the properties of the transcendental self are derived from a yet more profound and remote identity of personhood, the noumenal self whose capacities and powers were revealed in the moral life but of whose properties—that is, occurrent properties—we could know nothing.

I suppose I am not alone in feeling a combination of admiration for the concept of the transcendental and astonishment at the chicanery of the concept of the noumenal. However, if the Kantian discourse could be reinterpreted not as an ontological theory, but as the casting of a monodrama, the *dramatis personae* for accounting within the realm of action and responsibility, the implausibility of the noumenal self declines, since we are no longer required to accept it as an existent over and above, literally, persons; we can see it instead as a dynamic property of persons, set out in the dramatic mode. That is, the noumenal self is not another thing, but a separated aspect of the structure of accounting displayed as a character in a monodrama. It may be a reflection of the technique by which, in accounting, we can take a stand on the claim of having made a pure decision—as, e.g., when at the end of an accounting session, when all else fails, we can claim, 'Well, I just wanted to', or 'Well, I just decided to do it', making a claim for an agency as pure and unconditioned as that hypothesized in the noumenal self. But when the pronoun 'I' in such a discourse is treated as referring to so strange, remote and implausible an entity as the noumenal self, this is better understood, I believe, as no more than a dramatic convention. Kant's devotion to speculative ontology deprived the stage of a great dramatist.

I reconstrue Kant's *explanation* of the moral autonomy of persons (or, if you like, his grounding of the possibility of morals) in terms of some extra-experiental *entity*, as the scenario of a genre of monodrama. The plots require two characters, N and P, each with his characteristic way of speaking. N lards his discourse with the unconditional imperative, while P, less sternly, prefaces all his decisions with, 'Well, it depends . . .'.

(b) OUR SELVES AS ACTORS: PRIVATE MULTIDRAMAS V. PUBLIC MONO-

DRAMAS. The transition from imagining oneself acting in a dramatic representation of an episode to a social interaction in real life requires not only the manifestation of imagined actions in overt gestures and speeches, but it normally requires the presence of others. These others are human beings and must themselves be supposed to be ready to represent themselves as actors playing their parts. The possibility that each person's dramatic representation of the action should allow for coordinated public action in a single project requires that certain rather stringent conditions be satisfied, conditions which raise philosophical problems but which, I shall hope to show, are not the problems traditionally associated with the problematic status of other persons.

(i) The ethogenic perspective differs most strikingly from the traditional view of interaction in that the problem of other minds drops out of the center of the discussion. Instead there is a more manageable but less worked-over problem, that of the criteria we employ in making judgments of the intelligibility and warrantability of the actions of ourselves and others. Thus, instead of demanding that an organism is a person only if it has a mind, we make the demand that an organism is a person only if it is capable either of performing intelligible and warrantable actions, or of producing an account in which otherwise problematic actions are seen to have these socially desirable properties. In general, these qualities of action are achieved by acting according to a standardized scenario, or, if that fails, being able to provide an account in which the action is seen as having a proper place in some plausible scenario. But even though I do not then have a problem of other minds, it is, nevertheless, a condition for my belief that your actions are intelligible and warrantable, that you should be recognized by me as an actor and, if my accounts are to be effective, as a composer of monodrama in equal standing. The problem is not so much the difficulty I might have in penetrating to your theatre of the imagination—your private multidramas, cast, played and criticized by you—but the problem I might have in understanding that what you are saying when you produce your accounts of your actions for me is public monodramatic performance, rather than a contribution to a causal explanation, as indeed the revelation of the dramaturgical conventions of your private multidramas could well be.

(ii) But if the others are actors, each has embedded his action in his own dramatized anticipations of the episode, which are the source of his retrospective and anticipatory accounts; and this allows for the possibility of a problematic situation arising, where the meshing of our actions in a slice of life requires some fit between the anticipations of the action. The clue to the resolution of the problem of meshing is to be found in my remarks in the previous paragraph: lack of mesh, of whatever kind, can be progressively resolved, but never entirely eliminated, by accounting and counter-accounting; in the course of this the actions of each of us are brought under the scrutiny of the others as if they were my own, and their meaning and warrantability is negotiated, which requires shared conventions for the monodramatic forms we have seen accounting takes (in our culture).

We have noted that the problem which seemed to arise for the ontology of selves when we try to understand my regressive capacity to reflect upon myself as actor could be dissolved by seeing that what was at issue was not an ontological difficulty, but a rule of grammar concerning the possible constructions that could be present in accounts involving the first person pronoun. Similarly, the issue of intersubjectivity and the constitution of myself and others, has been addressed by phenomenology, in particular by Husserl and Schutz; their views and the criticisms the latter made of the former have been influential in phenomenological sociologies. One can look upon their views as an examination of the conditions under which the matters raised in (i) and (ii) above are actualized in real life. But just as Kant treated the issue of myself as actor as an ontological issue, so Husserl and Schutz treat the issue of ourselves as actors in a similar fashion.

The differences between Schutz and Husserl resolve themselves around the issue of the standing of intersubjectivity. Is it an achievement, or is it a datum from which achievement springs? According to Schutz, Husserl proposes the impossible task of the formation by constitution of a transcendental 'we', a constituting act which, in the view of Schutz, depends upon Husserl's implausible idea that 'by virtue of appresentative transfer, your body, appearing in my primordial sphere, leads to the constitution of your full psychic life and further to the constitution of your transcendental ego for me'. Thus, the condition of sociality is thought to be a constitution for me, and of you by me, of our full psychic lives, which is clearly a condition that can never be met. The idea that personal association (*Verband*) is constituted along with the common surrounding world, requires from Husserl a constitution of the other that falls a good deal short of the transcendental. Schutz's critique, then, depends upon discerning a contradiction within Husserl's line of thought, namely between the measure of constituting a common world, comparable to that of constituting a personal association, and at the same time demanding that personal association is only possible if that association is based upon a transcendental 'we'.

On Schutz's own account, 'Inter-subjectivity is not a problem of constitution which can be solved within the transcendental sphere, but is rather a datum of the life-world. It is the fundamental ontological category of human existence in the world and therefore of all philosophical anthropology'. The possibility, according to Schutz, of reflection on the self, of the discovery that one is a self, of the capacity for performing an epoché in the phenomenological manner, all of these, as well as the possibility of all communication, depend upon inter-subjectivity as given.

So far, I have been speaking in the same mode as phenomenology, taking it 'seriously' as a contribution to the ontological foundations of psycho-sociology. I wish to claim, of course, that it is nothing of the sort, that what is at issue between Husserl and Schutz are issues about the intelligibility of speech, rather than the ontology of persons; in other words, for a community properly to be able to use personal pronouns, each must take the other to be a person who is capable of the same range of uses of those pronouns (reflected e.g. in the monodramatic technique of 'ego-splitting') that is available in forms of accounting within the grammar of the first person, and so on.

What contribution, then, have Husserl and his critics made to our understanding of the grammar of personal pronouns? I believe their contribution amounts to the argument, familiar among non-phenomenologists from the conditions Strawson advanced for the personhood of a speech-actor, that my capacity to use 'I' correctly of myself depends upon your treating me as a person. Put in more clearly grammatical terms, personal pronouns are not learned as referential atomic names, but rather as a system, for which mutuality of person recognition is a necessary condition. We can thus take Schutz's remark that intersubjectivity is a datum of the life world as one way of making that point.

However, that is not the only possible interpretation of the arcane utterances of the great phenomenologists, since we may well ask for the developmental psychological aspect of a philosophical theory of grammar. And we are fortunate in that very recent work on the mastery of the sense of the self, by psychologists, has revealed a situation that is very much as one might imagine if we give Schutz's remarks a psychological rather than an ontological interpretation. The work of Richards, Newson, Shotter and others (Richards, 1974) on the fine structure of mother-infant interaction, seems to show a characteristic structure. The mother and child form a sociolinguistic entity in which the mother plays not only the part of hands as instruments for the child, but also speaks and thinks the speech and thoughts of the dyad. For example, she speaks, for 'them', a discourse in which his gropings and grabbings are spoken of as intentional actions and she forms the requisite intentions for him in 'their' speech, in response to the signs he gives from time to time. The problem as seen by these developmental psychologists, and also from a slightly different perspective by Bruner, is not that primordially solitary persons have to create an inter-subjectivity, a 'we'; rather the problem is how children constitute themselves, as social and psychological individuals, how they detach themselves from the given 'we' to maintain a separate psycho-sociolinguistic identity.[2] Bruner (1976) has instanced the game of 'Peek-a-boo' as a very widespread and commonplace series of episodes, in the course of which the separation of identity begins.

In short, what has emerged from recent close studies of developmental social psychology seems to support the Schutzian position when it is properly psychologized: human beings from a very early age form 'we's', Goffmanian 'withs', and social life develops within a given inter-subjectivity. The development of a separated persona and its subjective capacities for self-examination, and its inter-subjective skills in realizing the results of that examination in accounts, is a long and often difficult process. For example, the discovery of individuality leads in children in their middle years to the tiresome but essential over-acting of their parts in those performances we colloquially call 'showing off'.

In summary, then, phenomenology as a philosophical anthropology can be rescued and incorporated in a general ethogenics by taking its pronouncements and subjecting them to dual reinterpretation; on the one hand into the rules of the grammar of possible

[2] cf. also Taylor's paper, this volume.

forms of speech, and on the other into psychological observations about the conditions for that speech to be possible. Only, perhaps, in the psychological interpretation, do we have something touching on ontology; but it is an ontology which is firmly within the inter-subjective world and is realized in developmental stages in the constitution of socially competent selves that we can follow in the social growth of a child.

VII. The Self in an Alien Culture

The theme of this paper is the proposition that philosophical theories of self are representations of certain of the rules of grammar of monodramatic accounts, in particular the rules concerning the distribution of personal pronouns; and, of course, that philosophical theories describe the fantasy worlds of personal interactions conjured up in that speech. I am not claiming that philosophy is merely the hypothesization of grammar, but that philosophy and grammar are both reflections of certain basic cognitive structures which function as the formal causes of social action and the *general* determinants of theories of social action as they appear in accounts.

I have argued the thesis so far only in terms of the relationship between European philosophy and the distribution of pronouns in English. In order to establish my case on firmer ground I propose a comparative analysis of Japanese grammar and Japanese theories of the self. If my thesis is to be plausible, a markedly different use of social language, particularly *vis-à-vis* persons, ought to be paralleled by, and its principles represented in theories of the self that are revealed in philosophical and other forms of reflective thought on persons. The rather cursory study I have so far been able to make of this matter suggests that the proposition is borne out in the case of the Japanese.[3]

I am informed by Morsbach (1976) and Lyman (1973) that it is characteristic of Japanese speech, particularly when accounting is involved, for pronouns to drop out and that the Japanese linguistic style is such that the temptation to regard multiple forms of personal pronouns as names of separated entities is not likely to develop.

[3] In this and other fields of philosophy serious comparative studies of the culturally distinct complexes of grammar, metaphysics and socio-psychological theories and practices have yet to be undertaken.

These scholars of Japanese language and culture are inclined to think that the reflexive hierarchies which are such a feature both of our pronoun system and our philosophy of the person, are not likely to appear in Japanese thought. There is a very strong tendency for Japanese to speak and act with a conception of an undifferentiated social individual, even though they have a firmly differentiated system of style for the self-presentation, or persona, that is manifested by that unitary person in different social milieus.

Two examples of linguistic practices which reflect the absence of reference to ego-splitting as an account technique amongst Japanese, have been pointed out to me. Morsbach cites the practice of the writing of 'triangular diaries'. The Japanese will write a diary of his or her daily life, will then pass this diary on to a second person, who then writes a complementary diary, commenting upon the first diary and including a chronicle of events as seen from the second person's point of view. Both diaries are then passed on to a third person who comments upon each and then the three diaries are returned to the original author. In this way commentary is brought to bear upon the actions and self-perceptions of an individual, but by other individuals rather than by separated parts of the self. The diaries could be looked upon, then, as a multidrama occurring in public space and carrying out some of the tasks of clarification, comment and anticipation of possible futures, that are such marked characteristics of our private monodrama. This characteristic of self-commentary amongst Japanese is also shown in the phenomenon, notice of which I owe to S. M. Lyman, namely that in a conversation between a Japanese and his friend (this is reported of *nisei*, or first generation Japanese immigrants living in the United States), self-revelation and self-criticism are undertaken in a complex and indirect manner by a careful and subtle dissection of the character and situation of 'a friend', who, unlike the corresponding character in our monodramas, is a real individual known to both of the conversants. The friend's predicaments are a revelation of the speaker's situation. Thus the speaker does not, seemingly, speak reflexively about himself, but referentially and directly about another whole person.

These phenomena seem to suggest that a marked difference exists between the structure of accounts generated in the course of Japanese social life and our own proceedings. I hope to be able to show in a subsequent study, by reference to philosophical and religious and literary sources, that the Japanese theory of the self is consonant with these grammatical and structural features of this form of speech.

VIII. The Physiological Connection

Psychological theories stand between the social aspects of human life and the physiology of man. They are subject, thus, to two constraints. So far in this paper I have been trying to develop the foundations of a psychological theory which is coordinate with and compatible with the best available conception of microsociology. The further reaches of the sociological connection, namely macrosociology and the theory and analysis of unintended consequences, have not been addressed directly in this paper. It is my view, however, that there is no difference in principle in the methods by which we would relate such considerations to psychological theory. But psychological functioning is the working of an organism. I shall take it for granted that the mechanisms by which that functioning is performed are physiological. In this way psychological theories come under a second constraint.

The philosophical problem that arises is concerned with the very possibility of consistently maintaining the point of view which has been central to the ethogenic theory as I have been developing it. That is, are the physiological constraints such that they bear upon the very possibility of a person being an actor? What is at issue, even more fundamentally, is the possibility of a human being being a person. Central to the conception of the self as actor is the idea that any of our performances can be brought under conscious scrutiny and, secondly, that we as agents, are capable of reformulating and restructuring the rules, plans, habits, etc., on which the form of our actions depends. Physiology, then, must make possible two distinct but related aspects of the thought that human beings are, for scientific purposes, to be conceived as people.

Three models have successively dominated psychological thinking, each derived from a conception of a possible physiology and from the generalization of a claimed empirical discovery about the central structural properties of the nervous system.

Model 1. It is now widely agreed that the origins of S.R. behaviourism as a psychological theory are to be found in a generalization of the idea that the nervous system, as the mechanism of psychological functioning, is based upon the reflex arc. Thus, a simple mechanistic model of the form,

S . . . | black box | . . . R

is imposed upon psychological theory so that the general form that the system takes involves the following considerations:

(i) The S.R. connections are automatic and independent.

(ii) Intermediate processing is not part of the psychological system. Whatever is in the black box is presumably physiological on this theory. A notorious example of this is to be found in the first chapter of Skinner's *Verbal Behavior* (1957). I take it that, apart from the school of radical behaviourism, this point of view has been rejected on all hands. From the point of view of our discussion in this paper, it is sufficient to point out that there is no application for the concept of the self as actor under this model, and that for a variety of reasons: not only are each of the S.R. connections deterministic and automatic, but there is no *internal* standpoint representable in such a system from which internal modifications of the S.R. connections can be made, as by a person.

Model 2. A simple improvement can be made to Model 1 in such a way as to allow, apparently, for the application of a concept of agency via a formalized concept of free choice. This simple elaboration of Model 2 can be found, for example, in A. M. Munn, *Free Will and Determinism* (1960). He proposed that the black box should be held to contain a randomizing device so that, for example, the system is such that it is capable of taking on three states, A1, A2, A3, when stimulated by S. The response which the organism emits will depend upon which state A1, A2 or A3, the system takes up, but the switching from one sub-system to another depends upon the randomizing effect of interactions at the quantum mechanical level. Schematically the model is:

S . . . | A1, *A2*, A3 | . . . R2

This conception of free action, intended to physiologically ground the possibility of the minimal concept of an agent, is quite unacceptable philosophically, since it is clear, I hope, that the concept of agent associated with the social psychological concept of the actor is not that of an entity whose future is undetermined and evolves via random transitions. The conception of agency we are trying to ground is one where the future is determined in part by reflexive action by the agent himself. The Munn conception fails since it allows no standpoint within the system from which its own functioning can be monitored and regulated.

Model 3. Happily, in contemporary system theory and control theory, we have available a cybernetic model of greater sophistication whose realization in some material medium is already a possibility. In control theory the system is envisaged as containing a representation of its environment and a representation of various responses which it might make in that environment. In the process of determining which response it is going to make, the system, by reference to certain built-in criteria, scans the alternative outcomes represented in the system as possible changes in its environment under various choices of response. A more sophisticated system yet involves an internal representation, not just of the given environment but of various possible environments, and not just one set of criteria for selecting amongst possible outcomes but various sets of criteria. Such a system represents the cybernetics of something at least approaching the structure of psychological theory of the social actor which I have been proposing in this paper. The actor as agent is conceived as one who reflects upon his activity, on its consequences and, in particular, its form, and in consequence of that reflection modifies his internal states and thus finds passage among what must be regarded as real possibilities for the future. Now this model is compatible with determinism in the physiological realization of the system, but that determinism only becomes the straight-jacket of a closed future at a very high order of functioning in the model. It is not my task in this paper to investigate the relationship between the physiological grounding and the social tasks a human being has to perform as a person. I need to show only that the concept of an agent and its elaboration into the social concept of an actor is not sabotaged by restrictions deriving from the general properties of all possible physiological systems which would be capable of simulating human action at the performance level. I think I have shown that Model 1 is objectionable for its lack of sophisticated realism, Model 2 is objectionable for its philosophical *naiveté vis à vis* the concept of free action, while Model 3 is both physiologically plausible and retains the essential features of functioning which we have recognized as central to the concept of the social actor.

Finally, I should point out that the capacity for the system to represent itself in Model 3, and at the same time to represent both actual and possible outcomes of the realization of its structure in action, allows for accounting as a natural capacity for such a mechanism; for accounting is the verbal representation in speech of the processes by which the alternatives are marshalled and chosen among, by reference to some higher order set of criteria.

Conclusion

The upshot of the argument can be summarized: the complexities of the person and his reflexive investigations and modifications of himself, need not be construed as posing the ontological and psychological problems of a multiplicity and mysteriousness of the self; they emerge as features of accounting within the conventions of monodrama, that is as grammatical requirements of the speech by which the action can be treated as justified and meaningful within those conventions, and so as intelligible and warrantable. These are among the techniques by which *I* claim and disclaim responsibility.

REFERENCES

BRUNER, J. L. and SHERWOOD, V. (1976) 'Early rule structure: the case of "Peekaboo"' in *Life Sentences*, ed. R. Harré; Wiley, pp. 55–62.

BURKE, K. (1945), *A Grammar of Motives*, Prentice-Hall, Englewood-Cliffs, N.J.

CULLERS, J. (1974) *Structuralist Poetics*, Routledge & Kegan Paul, London.

EVREINOV, N. (1927), *The Theatre in Life*, trans. Navaroff, A. I., Harrap, London.

FINGARETTE, H. (1969), *Self-Deception*, Routledge & Kegan Paul, London.

GOFFMAN, E. (1963), *Stigma*, Prentice-Hall, Englewood Cliffs, N.J.

HARRÉ, R. (1976), 'The Constructive Role of Models', in *The Use of Models in the Social Sciences*, ed. L. Collins, Tavistock, London.

HARRÉ, R., and SECORD, P. F. (1973) *The Explanation of Social Behaviour*, Blackwell, Oxford.

HUME, D. (1788) *A Treatise of Human Nature*, ed. Selby-Bigge, L.A., Clarendon Press, Oxford.

HUSSERL, E. G. A. (1950), *Cartesian Meditations*, V.

KANT, I. (1781), *The Critique of Pure Reason*, trans. Meikeljohn, J. M. Dent, London, 1950.

LYMAN, S. M. (1973), 'Japanese-American Generation Gap', *Society*, **10**, 55–63.

LYMAN, S. M. and SCOTT, M. B. (1975) *The Drama of Social Reality*, Oxford University Press, New York and London.

MISCHEL, T. (1964) 'Personal constructs, rules and the logical of clinical activity'. *Psych. Rev.*, **71**, 180–92.

MORSBACH, H. (1976) Private communication.

MUNN, A. M. (1960) *Freewill and Determinism*, McGibbon & Kee, London.

RICHARDS, M. P. M. (1974) (editor) *The Integration of a Child into a Social World*, Cambridge University Press, London and New York.

SCHUTZ, A. (1970), *Collected Papers*, III, Nijhoff, The Hague.

SCOTT, M. B. and LYMAN, S. M. (1968) 'Accounts', *Am. Soc. Rev.* 133, 46–62

SHOTTER, J. (1973) 'Acquired powers: the transformation of natural into personal powers', *J. Theory of Social Behaviour*, **3**, 141–56.

SHOTTER, J. (1975) *Images of Man in Psychological Research*, Methuen, London

SKINNER, B. F. (1957), *Verbal Behavior*, Appleton-Century-Crofts, New York.

TORODE, B. (1976), The revelation of a theory of the social world as grammar, in *Life Sentences*, ed. R. Harré, Wiley, London, pp. 87–97.

TURNER, R. (1974) *Ethnomethodology*, Penguin, Harmondsworth.

WITTGENSTEIN, L. (1956), *Remarks on the Foundations of Mathematics*, V. 45, trans. Anscombe, G. E. M., Blackwell, Oxford.

Index of Names

Index of Subjects